Patisserie & Baking Foundations

CLASSIC RECIPES

THE CHEFS OF LE CORDON BLEU

DELMAR
CENGAGE Learning™

Australia • Brazil • Japan • Korea • Mexico • Singapore • Spain • United Kingdom • United States

Le Cordon Bleu's Pâtisserie & Baking Foundations Classic Recipes By the Chefs of Le Cordon Bleu

Vice President, Editorial: Dave Garza

Director of Learning Solutions: Sandy Clark

Senior Acquisitions Editor: Jim Gish

Managing Editor: Larry Main

Product Manager: Nicole Calisi

Editorial Assistant: Sarah Timm

Vice President, Marketing: Jennifer Baker

Marketing Director: Wendy Mapstone

Senior Marketing Manager: Kristin McNary

Associate Marketing Manager: Jonathan Sheehan

Senior Production Director: Wendy Troeger

Production Manager: Mark Bernard

Senior Content Project Manager: Glenn Castle

Senior Art Director: Casey Kirchmayer

Technology Project Manager: Chris Catalina

Cover Design: Stratton Design, Mike Stratton

Interior Design: Stratton Design, Mike Stratton

Cover Photo: Jim Smith Photography

Principle Photography by Jim Smith, Jim Smith Photography

Supplemental Photography by Enrique Chavarria, and Lois Siegel, Lois Siegel Productions

For product information and technology assistance, contact us at
Cengage Learning Customer & Sales Support, 1-800-354-9706
For permission to use material from this text or product, submit all requests online at **www.cengage.com/permissions.**
Further permissions questions can be e-mailed to
permissionrequest@cengage.com

Library of Congress Control Number: 2011927695

ISBN-13: 978-1-4390-5717-9

ISBN-10: 1-4390-5717-6

Delmar
5 Maxwell Drive
Clifton Park, NY 12065-2919
USA

Cengage Learning is a leading provider of customized learning solutions with office locations around the globe, including Singapore, the United Kingdom, Australia, Mexico, Brazil, and Japan. Locate your local office at: **international.cengage.com/region**

Cengage Learning products are represented in Canada by Nelson Education, Ltd.

To learn more about Delmar, visit **www.cengage.com/delmar**

Purchase any of our products at your local college store or at our preferred online store **www.cengagebrain.com**

Notice to the Reader

Publisher does not warrant or guarantee any of the products described herein or perform any independent analysis in connection with any of the product information contained herein. Publisher does not assume, and expressly disclaims, any obligation to obtain and include information other than that provided to it by the manufacturer. The reader is expressly warned to consider and adopt all safety precautions that might be indicated by the activities described herein and to avoid all potential hazards. By following the instructions contained herein, the reader willingly assumes all risks in connection with such instructions. The publisher makes no representations or warranties of any kind, including but not limited to, the warranties of fitness for particular purpose or merchantability, nor are any such representations implied with respect to the material set forth herein, and the publisher takes no responsibility with respect to such material. The publisher shall not be liable for any special, consequential, or exemplary damages resulting, in whole or part, from the readers' use of, or reliance upon, this material.

Printed in the United States of America
1 2 3 4 5 6 7 14 13 12 11

CONTENTS

FOREWORD

I am proud to present Le Cordon Bleu's *Pâtisserie and Baking Foundations*—the companion book to Le Cordon Bleu's *Cuisine Foundations*. This book is intended to provide a useful reference guide as you explore the world of pâtisserie and also to serve you well as you embark on your own journey, both personally and professionally. At first glance you might think that this is just "another culinary textbook," but on closer examination you will realize that the focus is on technique. This is particularly important in French pâtisserie, where mastering the basic techniques and recipes gives you the elements necessary to make almost any pastry, including ones to be created by you!

Provided herein are visual step-by-step photographs to demonstrate most of these basic techniques. We took our cue from the many students and graduates around the world who were looking for a single reference that would explain and demonstrate the basic techniques used in French pâtisserie and baking—techniques that have existed and been respected for more than three centuries. With human ingenuity came technical progress in the kitchen, yet the basic techniques have remained practically unchanged. Pastry chefs over the centuries have gone from cooking in the ashes of an open fire, to baking in wood-burning ovens, to the modern age and miracle of the induction oven. These advancements have certainly influenced the evolution of pâtisserie, but the tried-and-true recipes have not only endured but improved.

The Le Cordon Bleu Foundations books were written to reset the counter and refresh everyone's history and knowledge of these techniques. Here you will find recipes that have been created throughout the history of French pâtisserie and that best exemplify the application of the classic techniques. Also, because pâtisserie has become an international art form, there are also recipes for pastries and breads from other cultures that have become as familiar to many as a croissant or chocolate éclair. When you look at the integrity of each of these international recipes, you will recognize the application of the techniques used in the French classics.

Finally, it is important to pay homage to the generations of chefs who have upheld, improved upon, and passed on their passion for cooking to each succeeding generation. From Taillevant's first cookbook, to the grandmasters of classic French pâtisserie, Antonin Carême, Jules Gouffé, and Pierre Lacam, these chefs represent the patrimony of the art of pâtisserie, and this book stands as a tribute to their dedication.

Le Cordon Bleu has served its patrimony for more than a century through its chefs who have chosen a very important calling—teaching. From the moment Le Cordon Bleu opened its kitchens in 1895 on the rue St.-Honoré in Paris, students of all nationalities and all walks of life have come to join us in continuing to respect what French culinary technique represents. It is not about the recipes, but about how you work in a kitchen, whether you are cooking for loved ones or for paying customers.

It gives me great pleasure to extend our "classroom" beyond our worldwide network of schools and programs into this book and other forms of media. I hope you enjoy Le Cordon Bleu's *Pâtisserie and Baking Foundations*, not only as a guide and reference, but as an inspiration.

Amitiés gourmandes,

André J. Cointreau

President, Le Cordon Bleu International

ACKNOWLEDGMENTS

Le Cordon Bleu would like to thank the chefs and staff of the Le Cordon Bleu schools:

Le Cordon Bleu Paris, Le Cordon Bleu London, Le Cordon Bleu Ottawa, Le Cordon Bleu Madrid, Le Cordon Bleu Amsterdam, Le Cordon Bleu Japan, Le Cordon Bleu Inc., Le Cordon Bleu Australia, Le Cordon Bleu Peru, Le Cordon Bleu Korea, Le Cordon Bleu Liban, Le Cordon Bleu Mexico, Le Cordon Bleu Thailand, Le Cordon Bleu Malaysia, Le Cordon Bleu New Zealand, Le Cordon Bleu College of Culinary Arts in Atlanta, Le Cordon Bleu College of Culinary Arts in Austin, Le Cordon Bleu College of Culinary Arts in Boston, Le Cordon Bleu College of Culinary Arts in Chicago, Le Cordon Bleu College of Culinary Arts in Dallas, Le Cordon Bleu College of Culinary Arts in Las Vegas, Le Cordon Bleu College of Culinary Arts in Los Angeles, Le Cordon Bleu College of Culinary Arts in Miami, Le Cordon Bleu College of Culinary Arts in Minneapolis/St. Paul, Le Cordon Bleu College of Culinary Arts in Orlando, Le Cordon Bleu College of Culinary Arts in Portland, Le Cordon Bleu College of Culinary Arts in Sacramento, Le Cordon Bleu College of Culinary Arts in St. Louis, California Culinary Academy, Le Cordon Bleu College of Culinary Arts in Scottsdale, and Le Cordon Bleu College of Culinary Arts in Seattle.

Special acknowledgment to Chef Patrick Martin, Chef Jean Jacques Tranchant, Chef Christian Faure, M.O.F., Chef Hervé Chabert, Chef Cyril Nebout, Chef Jean-Marc Baqué, Katharyn Shaw, Carrie Carter, Charles Gregory, Adam Lemm, and Kathy McIntyre. Student assistants: Lilian Cardoza, Minjung Kim, Sawsan Ahmed Al-Aali, Kassandra Pietropaolo, Asma Alothmen, Sausha Young, and Paula Greco.

Les Biscuits et Petits Fours
Sucré et Salé
(Sweet and Savory Biscuits and Small Cakes)

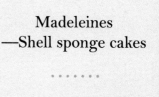

Learning Outcomes

Making a détrempe
Making a puff pastry
(*pâte feuilletée*)

Equipment

Knives:
Chef's knife (*couteau chef*)

Tools:
Sieve, plastic wrap,
parchment paper, corne,
rolling pin, brush, pastry
brush, grater, wire rack

Pans:
Baking sheets

Serving/Yield

1 ¼ pound/600 gram
portion of dough

FYI...

Allumettes are a traditional preparation made from thin strips of puff pastry (*pâte feuilletée*). Delicious as either an hors d'oeuvre when filled or spread with savory ingredients, or as a light dessert when filled or spread with sweet ingredients, the allumette is highly versatile. The name refers to the shape of the preparation, as "allumettes," the French word for matchsticks. The dish is also known as *rognures* which is French for "trimmings" or "scraps." This refers to the fact that allumettes are an excellent traditional use for extra scraps of puff pastry that are leftover from other preparations. Delicious when paired with gruyère cheese or anchovies, allumettes are an excellent bonus preparation for the sensible and thrifty chef.

ALLUMETTES
Matchsticks

Method

Make a Puff Pastry (*Pâte Feuilletée*)

1. Sift (*tamiser*) the flour onto a clean work surface and make a well in the center using a plastic scraper (*corne*). Add the salt and water to the well. Stir with your fingertips until the salt is dissolved. Add the first portion of butter (cut into pieces) and begin to incorporate the flour using your fingertips. As the flour, butter, and water begin to combine, use the *corne* to cut the ingredients together, until the mixture resembles a coarse dough. Sprinkle with additional water if the dough is too dry.

2. Once there are barely any traces of flour left, gather the dough into a ball and, using a chef's knife, score the top of it with a deep cross.

3. Loosely wrap the finished *détrempe* in plastic and transfer it to the refrigerator to rest for a minimum of 1 hour (preferably overnight).

Note

Détrempe refers to the dough before the layers of butter are added.

Buttering and Turning (*Beurrage et Tourage*)

4. Place the remaining cold butter between two sheets of parchment paper and pound it with a rolling pin until it is similar to the *détrempe* in consistency. Using the *corne*, shape the butter into a flat square about ½ in. (1 cm) thick. Set the butter aside. Place it in the refrigerator if the kitchen is warm. Lightly dust a clean work surface with flour (*fleurer*), then unwrap the *détrempe* and place it on the floured surface. Using the scored marks as a guide, roll out (*abaisser*) the corners of the *détrempe* into a cross shape. Be careful to keep the center of the cross thicker than its outer arms (this will be important when rolling out the dough and the butter). Place the square of butter in the center of the cross and fold the two side arms over it so that they overlap slightly in the center (in the process, be careful not to trap any air bubbles). Give the dough a quarter turn and fold the two remaining arms over the butter so that the butter is completely enclosed. Press the seams well to seal. Lightly tap the dough with the length of the rolling pin to even out the distribution of the butter inside. Give the dough a quarter turn and repeat the tapping process. This is called the envelope.

Quantity		Ingredient
U.S.	Metric	*Puff Pastry (Pâte Feuilletée)*
8 oz	250 g	Flour, sifted
¼ oz	5 g	Salt
3 ½ fl oz	100 ml	Cold water
3 ½ oz	100 g	Butter
3 ½ oz	100 g	Butter
		Filling
1 pc	1 pc	Egg for eggwash
4–6 each	4–6 each	Salted anchovy filets
3 ½ oz	100 g	Gruyère cheese, grated and finely chopped

Method

Turns 1 and 2

5. Roll out (*abaisser*) the dough in long, even strokes to form a rectangle that is three times the original length of the envelope or ⅜ in. (1 cm) thick. Brush off the excess flour. Fold the bottom third of the dough up; then fold the top third down over the first fold. Make sure the edges are even. Give the dough a quarter turn to the right and repeat the same rolling process. Make sure to always brush away any excess flour from the dough before and after each fold. Repeat the folding process (top third up, top third down over first fold) and give the dough a quarter turn to the right. Make two finger impressions in the top left corner of the dough.

Note

These marks are a reminder of the number of turns the dough has received; they also indicate the position of subsequent turns. Wrap the dough in plastic and transfer it to the refrigerator to rest for a minimum of 20 minutes. With 2 turns, the dough is now referred to as **pâton.**

Turns 3 and 4

6. Lightly dust the work surface with flour (*fleurer*). Remove the dough from the refrigerator and unwrap it onto the floured surface (with the 2 indents in the top left corner). Proceed to give the dough a third and fourth turn (rolling and folding in the same manner as the first and second turns). Mark the dough with 4 imprints in the top left corner before wrapping it in plastic and returning it to the refrigerator to rest for a minimum of 20 minutes.

Turns 5 and 6

7. Lightly dust the work surface with flour (*fleurer*). Remove the dough from the refrigerator and unwrap it onto the floured surface (with the 4 indents in the top left corner). Proceed to give the dough its final 2 turns, folding and rolling as in the previous turns. Wrap it in plastic and return it to the refrigerator to rest for a minimum of 20 minutes before rolling it out (the longer the dough rests, the better it will perform).

Tip

Because the **détrempe** *and the butter are at the same consistency, it is necessary to complete the turns as explained above. If you allow the dough to over-chill between turns, the butter may become too hard and crack when rolled out. Make sure you have allotted the necessary time to complete the turns.*

Assembly

1. Finely chop the anchovies and mix with ¾ of the grated cheese. Set aside.
2. After resting, roll the dough into a large rectangle (*abaisser*) about ⅛ in. (3 mm) thick. If the dough starts to retract, place it on a baking sheet and chill for 20 minutes, then start again.
3. Cut the dough in half and brush the surface with the eggwash. Sprinkle the anchovy mixture evenly over the surface. Roll the other half onto the rolling pin, and then lay it over the coated layer, sandwiching the anchovy mixture.
4. Roll (*abaisser*) the two pieces together with the rolling pin. Brush the dough with the eggwash and sprinkle the top with the remaining cheese. Chill the dough for 20 minutes.
5. Preheat the oven to 425°F (220°C).
6. Remove from the refrigerator. Using a chef's knife, cut into strips ½ in. to ¾ in. (2 cm) wide. Then cut the strips into even lengths, around 3 in. (8 cm) long. Arrange the strips on the baking sheet, leaving at least ¾ in. (2 cm) between them. Bake until golden brown and then cool on a wire rack.

Making puff pastry
(*pâte feuilletée*)
Making bite-sized puff
pastries (***bouchées***)
Making a détrempe

Equipment

Knives:
Chef's knife (*couteau chef*)

Tools:
Sieve, plastic wrap,
parchment paper, corne,
rolling pin, brush, pastry
brush, 2-in. (5-cm) and 3-in.
(8-cm) fluted round cutters,
mixing bowl

Pans:
Baking sheets, sauté pan

Serving/Yield

8 portions

Evidence of grilled snails has been found in archeological digs that are dated as far back as 3000 BC. The first evidence of snails as a food source dates back to ancient Rome, where they were reared in special gardens called *cochleariae*. In these gardens, they were fattened with milk and grain (sometimes even wine) until they were too big to fit into their shells. The Romans were so fond of snails that they brought back exotic varieties from the four corners of their empire. Under Roman reign, the Gauls of ancient France also took a liking to mollusks and ate them as a sweetened dessert.

BOUCHÉES D'ESCARGOTS
Escargot in Puff Pastry

Quantity		Ingredient
U.S.	**Metric**	**Puff Pastry (Pâte Feuilletée)**
8 oz	250 g	Flour, sifted
3 ½ fl oz	100 ml	Cold water
¼ oz	5 g	Salt
3 ½ oz	100 g	Butter
3 ½ oz	100 g	Butter
		Escargot Butter
7 oz	200 g	Butter, softened (en pommade)
1 pc	1 pc	Shallots
1 pc	1 pc	Garlic
½ bunch	½ bunch	Parsley
Dash	Dash	Pastis
Dash	Dash	Salt and pepper
		Finishing
1 pc	1 pc	Egg for eggwash
3 ½ oz	100 g	Butter
24–28 pcs	24–28 pcs	Escargots

Method

Make a Puff Pastry (Pâte Feuilletée)

1. Sift (*tamiser*) the flour onto a clean work surface and make a well (*fontaine*) in the center using a plastic scraper (*corne*). Add the salt and water to the well. Stir with your fingertips until the salt is dissolved. Add the first quantity of butter (cut into pieces) and begin to incorporate the flour using your fingertips. As the flour, butter, and water begin to combine, use the *corne* to cut the ingredients together, until it resembles a coarse dough. Sprinkle with additional water if the dough is too dry.
2. Once there are barely any traces of flour left, gather the dough into a ball and, using a chef's knife, score the top of it with a deep cross.
3. Loosely wrap the finished *détrempe* in plastic and transfer it to the refrigerator to rest for a minimum of 1 hour (preferably overnight).

Note

Détrempe refers to the dough before the layers of butter are added.

4. Place the remaining cold butter between two sheets of parchment paper and pound it with a rolling pin until it is similar to the *détrempe* in consistency. Using the *corne*, shape the butter into a flat square about ½ in. (1 cm) thick. Set the butter aside. Place it in the refrigerator if the kitchen is warm. Lightly dust a clean work surface with flour (*fleurer*), then unwrap the *détrempe* and place it on the floured surface. Using the scored marks as a guide, roll out (*abaisser*) the corners of the *détrempe* into a cross shape. Be careful to keep the center of the cross thicker than its outer arms (this will be important when rolling out the dough and the butter). Place the square of butter in the center of the cross and fold the two side arms over it so that they overlap slightly in the center (in the process be careful not to trap any air bubbles). Give the dough a quarter turn and fold the two remaining arms over the butter so that the butter is completely enclosed. Press the seams well to seal. Lightly tap the dough with the length of the rolling pin to even out the distribution of the butter inside. Give the dough a quarter turn and repeat the tapping process. This is called the envelope.

Turns 1 and 2

5. Roll out the dough (**abaisser**) in long, even strokes to form a rectangle that is 3 times the original length of the envelope or ⅜ in. (1 cm) thick. Brush off the excess flour. Fold the bottom third of the dough up. Fold the top third down over the first fold. Make sure the edges are even. Give the dough a quarter turn to the right and repeat the same rolling process. Make sure to always brush away any excess flour from the dough before and after each fold. Repeat the folding process (top third up, top third down over first fold) and give the dough a quarter turn to the right. Make two finger impressions in the top left corner of the dough.

Note

These marks are a reminder of the number of turns the dough has received; they also indicate the position of subsequent turns. Wrap the dough in plastic and transfer it to the refrigerator to rest for a minimum of 20 minutes. With 2 turns, and the butter has been incorporated into the dough it can now be referred to as **pâton.**

Turns 3 and 4

6. Lightly dust the work surface with flour (**fleurer**). Remove the dough from the refrigerator and unwrap it onto the floured surface (with the 2 indents in the top left corner). Proceed to give the dough a third and fourth turn (rolling and folding in the same manner as the first and second turns). Mark the dough with 4 imprints in the top-left corner before wrapping it in plastic and returning it to the refrigerator to rest for a minimum of 20 minutes.

Turns 5 and 6

7. Lightly dust the work surface with flour (**fleurer**). Remove the dough from the refrigerator and unwrap it onto the floured surface (with the 4 indents in the top left corner). Proceed to give the dough its final 2 turns, folding and rolling as in the previous turns. Wrap it in plastic and return it to the refrigerator to rest for a minimum of 20 minutes before rolling it out (the longer the dough rests the better it will perform).

Tip

Because the **détrempe** *and the butter are at the same consistency, it is necessary to complete the turns as explained above. If you allow the dough to over-chill between turns, the butter may become too hard and crack when rolled out. Make sure you have allotted the necessary time to complete the turns.*

8. After the final turn, allow the dough to rest for a minimum of 20 minutes before rolling it out. The longer it rests, the better it will perform.

Make an Escargot Butter

1. Mix the shallots, garlic, parsley, pastis, salt, and pepper into the softened butter (**en pommade**). Set aside.
2. Roll out the dough (**abaisser**) to a thickness of about an ⅛ in. (3 mm). Place on a baking sheet and chill for 20 minutes.
3. Preheat the oven to 400°F (200°C).
4. Slightly dampen a baking sheet with water.
5. Cut out 16 rounds using the 3-in. (8-cm) cutter and then brush 8 of the rounds with the eggwash. Using the smaller round cutter, cut out the centers from the remaining 8 rounds. Flip the rings over and lay on top of the whole disks, press gently to secure. Using a toothpick or the tip of a paring knife, pierce each small pastry (**bouchées**) at equal intervals three or four times, being sure to pierce both layers. Transfer to the damp baking sheet and brush the tops with eggwash, being careful not to let any drip down the sides.
6. Place in a hot oven and bake until they have risen and are evenly colored, about 15 to 20 minutes. Remove from the oven and allow to cool slightly. Using the tip of a paring knife, loosen the crust from the center. Cut around the edges to loosen any inner layers and discard.
7. Melt some butter in a heavy-bottomed sauté pan over medium heat. Add the escargots and toss until heated through. Then add the escargot butter and toss until the escargots are well coated and the butter has melted and is hot. Spoon the escargots into the **bouchées**. Drizzle some of the melted butter around to finish.

Learning Outcomes

Making a choux pastry
(*pâte à choux*)
Piping (*coucher*)

Equipment

Tools:
Sieve, wooden spatula,
mixing bowls, piping bag,
medium round tip,
pastry brush, fork,
wire rack

Pans:
Baking sheet, saucepan

Serving/Yield

1 ¾ pound/820 gram
portion of dough

The origin of sweet choux balls (chouquettes) can be traced back to the master Italian pastry chef Panterelli, who came to France in 1547 with the court of Catherine de Medici for her wedding to the French King, Henry II. Chef Panterelli developed a light, airy pastry that he called pâte à Panterelli. This pastry was extremely versatile and came to form the base of many mainstay French preparations, including profiteroles, croquembouche, éclairs, and beignets, just to name a few. In the 18th century, a pastry chef named Avice created a pastry known as choux buns from Panterelli's dough. The buns were called choux (French for cabbage) because they bore an uncanny resemblance to tiny heads of cabbage. The dough for those buns began to be known as pâte à choux. This is how the chouquette gained its name, by being a delicious, light snack named after a large vegetable.

CHOUQUETTES
Sweet Choux Balls

Method

Preheat the oven to 425°F (220°C).

1. Lightly grease a heavy baking sheet.
2. Sift (**tamiser**) the flour.
3. Place the butter, sugar, salt, and water into a saucepan. Bring to a boil, stirring to make sure the salt and sugar are dissolved. Once the water comes to a boil and the butter has melted, remove the pan from the heat and add all the flour at once. With a wooden spatula, stir well. Place the pan back onto the heat and continue to stir until a clean ball of dough forms and comes cleanly off the sides and bottom of the pan. Transfer the hot dough to a bowl and spread out to cool slightly.
4. Add the eggs, one at a time, beating well after each addition. After three eggs have been incorporated, check the consistency by lifting some of the dough. It should stretch before breaking. If the dough is still too stiff, beat the last egg, and add just enough until the dough forms a soft peak that falls when the spatula is lifted.
5. Transfer to a piping bag fitted with a medium round tip. Pipe (**coucher**) 1-in. (2.5-cm) rounds of dough onto the prepared baking sheet. Brush with eggwash, and even out the tops using a fork. Sprinkle with the nib sugar and bake until puffed up and evenly colored, about 25 minutes.
6. Transfer to a wire rack to cool.

Quantity		Ingredient
U.S.	**Metric**	*Choux Pastry (Pâte à Choux)*
4 ¼ oz	163 g	Flour
3 ½ oz	100 g	Butter, cut into pieces
½ oz	5 g	Sugar, granulated
¼ oz	3 g	Salt
8 fl oz	250 ml	Milk or water
4 pcs	4 pcs	Eggs
		Finishing
1 pc	1 pc	Egg (for eggwash)
As needed	As needed	Nib sugar

Learning Outcomes

Making a choux pastry
(*pâte à choux*)
Making a Chantilly cream
(*crème Chantilly*)
Piping (*coucher*)
Building shapes from
finished choux pastry

Equipment

Knives:
Serrated knife
(*couteau à scie*)

Tools:
Sieve, wooden spatula,
mixing bowls, piping bag,
medium round tip, medium
star tip, balloon whisk,
pastry brush, fork,
wire rack

Pans:
Saucepan

Serving/Yield

1 dozen pieces

The Choux à la Crème et Cygnes is an intricate and delicate pastry. The preparation is designed to resemble a swan, and the name literally translates from French to "choux swans and cream." The swans are made by piping shapes of choux pastry, with larger teardrops for the body, and delicate "S" shapes for the neck and head. This delicious pastry is truly fit for royalty, as the swan has long been a favorite meal of English monarchs. Since the time of Elizabeth II, all the swans in England have been the sole property of the British monarchy, a tradition that remains a law even today. In the past, swan meat was considered to be too fine to be eaten daily or by commoners, and was reserved for special banquets, often being presented to the monarch wearing a crown before before being cooked.

CHOUX À LA CRÈME ET CYGNES
Cream-Filled Choux Pastries and Swans

Method

1. Preheat the oven to 425°F (220°C).
2. Lightly grease a heavy baking sheet.
3. Sift (*tamiser*) the flour.
4. Place the butter, sugar, salt, and water into a saucepan. Bring to a boil, stirring to make sure the salt and sugar are totally dissolved. Once the water comes to a boil and the butter has melted, remove the pan from the heat and add all the flour at once. Stir well with a wooden spatula.
5. Place the pan back onto the heat and continue to stir until a clean ball of dough forms and comes cleanly off the sides and bottom of the pan. Transfer the hot dough to a bowl and spread out to cool slightly.
6. Add the eggs, one at a time, mixing well with the wooden spatula after each addition. After three eggs have been incorporated, check the consistency by lifting some of the dough. It should stretch before breaking. If the dough is still too stiff, beat in only as much of the last egg as is necessary to make the dough form a soft peak that falls when the spatula is lifted.
7. Transfer the mixture to a piping bag fitted with a medium round tip. Pipe (*coucher*) 1 ½-in. rounds of dough onto the prepared baking sheet, reserving a small amount. Brush with eggwash, and even out the tops using a fork. Bake until puffed up and evenly colored, about 25 minutes. Transfer to a wire rack to cool.
8. Once cooled, slice off the top third of each of the choux.

Make the Chantilly Cream (Crème Chantilly)
1. Whisk the cream and powdered sugar to medium peaks.
2. Transfer to a piping bag fitted with a medium star tip.
3. Pipe large spirals into the choux and cover with the top.
4. Dust with powdered sugar just before serving.

To Make Swans
1. Lay out (*coucher*) thick ovals of choux pastry (pâte à choux) onto the baking sheet, pulling gently away with the pastry tip to form a point.
2. Reserve some of the choux pastry (pâte à choux) and place in a small pastry bag fitted with a small round tip.
3. Lay out some question mark shapes with the pâte à choux on the prepared baking sheet. Bake until golden, about 8 minutes. Remove and cool on a wire rack.
4. Cut the large choux as above, but then cut the tops in half lengthwise. These will make the wings.
5. Make the Chantilly cream (Crème Chantilly) as directed above. Pipe the cream into the choux and place the sliced top on each side.
6. Make a shallow, angled cut in the top of the question mark pieces and gently insert the wide part of the sliced almond in. Place the opposite end of the question mark into the cream.
7. Dust with powdered sugar before serving.

Quantity		Ingredient
U.S.	Metric	*Choux Pastry (Pâte à Choux)*
4 ¼ oz	125 g	Flour
3 ½ oz	100 g	Butter, cut into pieces
½ oz	15 g	Sugar, granulated
¼ oz	5 g	Salt
8 fl oz	250 ml	Water
4 pcs	4 pcs	Eggs
1 pc	1 pc	Egg for eggwash
		Chantilly Cream (Crème Chantilly)
13 ¼ fl oz	400 ml	Heavy cream
2 oz	60 g	Powdered sugar
		Finishing
As needed	As needed	Sliced almonds
As needed	As needed	Powdered sugar for dusting

Learning Outcomes

Making a choux pastry
(*pâte à choux*)
Piping (*coucher*)
Making pastry cream
(*crème pâtissière*)
Filling choux pastry
(*coucher des choux*)
Flavoring pastry cream
and fondant
Glazing with fondant
(*glaçage*)

Equipment

Tools:
Wooden spoon,
rubber spatula, pastry bag,
12-mm plain tip,
small star tip,
6-mm plain tip, fork, whisk

Pans:
1 large russe
1 medium russe
2 small russes
baking sheet

Serving

12–16 pieces

FYI...

Conjecture surrounds the history of the éclair. In the *Oxford English Dictionary*, 1864 is cited as the earliest the word *éclair* was being used to describe this pastry. Some historians use this date to discredit claims that the inventor of the éclair was Antonin Carême; however, he still may have invented this filled puff pastry under a different name. The pastry was also known in France as *bâton de Judas*, an appellation that may or may not predate the use of *éclair*. On a less quarrelsome note, it is said that the éclair (which is French for "lightning") is named because it is so good, that it is eaten as fast as lightning!

ÉCLAIRS AU CAFÉ ET AU CHOCOLAT
Chocolate and Coffee Éclairs

Method

Choux Pastry (Pâte à Choux)

1. Preheat the oven to 425°F (220°C).
2. *Prepare a panade*: Combine the water, milk, butter, sugar, and salt in a large pan and bring to a boil over medium-high heat. Once the butter has completely melted, remove the pan from the heat and add the flour. Stir with a wooden spatula until combined; then, over medium heat, stir until the mixture doesn't stick to the spatula and it makes a thin skin on the bottom of the pan (**dessécher**). Transfer to a clean bowl and cool until warm. Beat the eggs into the panade one at a time. The dough should be stretchy and slightly sticky.
3. Transfer the mixture to a pastry bag fitted with a 12-mm plain tip.
4. On a lightly greased baking sheet, pipe out 4 ¾ in. (10 to 12 cm) long lines of pâte à choux. Brush the pâte à choux with eggwash, then run the prongs of a fork (dipped in eggwash) down the length of the éclairs to even out their shape.
5. Transfer the éclairs to the oven and immediately reduce the temperature to 400°F (205°C). Bake until golden (*20 to 25 minutes*), rotating the baking sheet as soon as they begin to color.
6. Remove the éclairs from the oven and transfer to a wire rack to cool.
7. Using a small star tip, pierce the bottoms of the éclairs with 3 holes (1 in the middle and 1 at each end).

Pastry Cream (Crème Pâtissière)

1. Pour the milk into a medium saucepan and bring it to a boil over medium-high heat. Add about one-quarter of the sugar to the milk and stir to dissolve it.
2. Meanwhile, place the egg yolks in a small mixing bowl and add the remaining sugar. Whisk the sugar into the eggs until it completely dissolves and the yolks lighten in color (**blanchir**). Add the flour or cornstarch to the yolks and stir until well combined.
3. When the milk begins to come to a boil, remove it from the stove and pour one-third of it into the egg yolks. Stir well to temper the yolks, then whisk the tempered mixture into the remaining hot milk. Place back onto the heat and cook until the crème pâtissière begins to bubble. Continue whisking (being sure to press the whisk around the corners of the pan) and allow to cook for 1 minute in order to cook the starch. The pastry cream (crème pâtissière) will become very thick.

Quantity		Ingredient
U.S.	**Metric**	*Choux Pastry (Pâte à Choux)*
4 fl oz	125 ml	Water
4 fl oz	125 ml	Milk
4 oz	125 g	Butter
½ oz	12 g	Sugar, granulated
½ tsp	2.5 g	Salt
4–5 pcs	4–5 pcs	Eggs
5 oz	150 g	Flour
1 pc	1 pc	Egg for eggwash
		Pastry Cream (Crème Pâtissière)
1 ½ pt	750 ml	Milk
6 pcs	6 pcs	Egg yolks
5 oz	150 g	Sugar, granulated
1 ½ oz	45 g	Flour
1 ½ oz	45 g	Cornstarch
To taste	To taste	Coffee extract
2 oz	60 g	Dark chocolate, finely chopped
2 oz	60 g	Unsweetened chocolate, melted
		Glazing (Glaçage)
7 oz	200 g	Coffee fondant*
7 oz	200 g	Chocolate fondant*
		*Fondant can be purchased at specialty stores.

Method

4. Separate the pastry cream (crème pâtissière) into two equal batches in separate mixing bowls and mix coffee extract into one batch and the melted unsweetened chocolate into the other using whisks. Pat the surface of the pastry cream (crème pâtissière) with a piece of cold butter held on the end of a fork (**tamponner**) to create a protective film. Let the pastry cream (crème pâtissière) cool to room temperature and refrigerate it.

Assembly (Montage)

1. Beat the pastry cream (crème pâtissière) until its texture loosens, then transfer it to a pastry bag fitted with a 6-mm plain tip. Fill half the éclairs with chocolate-flavored pastry cream (crème pâtissière) and the other half with coffee-flavored pastry cream (crème pâtissière), piping it in through the holes underneath.
2. Gently heat the coffee fondant in a medium saucepan over the lowest heat setting, stirring it gently with a wooden spatula. If the fondant stays very thick even when heated, add a few drops of warm water and stir it in. Continue to gently stir the fondant until it coats the back of a spoon in a thick, shiny layer. The ideal temperature to work with fondant is approximately 98.6°F (37°C).
3. To ice the éclairs (using coffee fondant for the coffee éclairs and chocolate fondant for the chocolate éclairs):
   Hold the éclair upside down over the pan of fondant and dip one end into it. Lower the rest of the éclair into the fondant to coat the top while simultaneously pulling the first end out. Once the éclair is covered, clean the edges of the fondant using your fingers.
4. Lay the éclairs out on a clean tray and transfer them to the refrigerator to set the fondant.
5. Reserve in the refrigerator until serving.

Learning Outcomes

Browning butter
(*beurre noisette*)
Piping (*coucher*)

Equipment

Tools:
Piping bag, medium round
tip, whisk, mixing bowls,
wire rack, plastic wrap,
wooden spoon

Pans:
Baking sheet, saucepan,
financier mold

Serving/Yield

2 ¾ pound/1.4 kilogram
portion of dough

While not as widely known as its near relative the Madeleine, this delicious golden pastry should certainly not be forgotten. Created in the late 19th century in a pastry shop on Paris's Rue St. Denis, the financier is a truly Parisian delicacy. The financier was created by the renowned Paris pastry Chef M. Lasne, and the story behind the invention of this delicious snack is intricately tied to the cake's Parisian roots. The story goes that Chef Lasne's pastry shop was located on the Rue St. Denis, which was right in the heart of Paris's financial district. His shop was next to "La Bourse de Commerce" (the Paris Stock Exchange), and all day long bankers would hurry into Chef Lasne's shop looking for a quick bite. This gave the Chef the brilliant idea to create a small, easily portable cake that would be dry to the touch, giving the bankers a simple and tasty, on-the-go snack. He named his creation for its target clientele, and thus the financier was born. It is widely believed that Chef Lasne, in a brilliant marketing strategy, chose the financier's distinctive rectangular shape and beautiful golden color to make his invention resemble something his clients would be very familiar with and adored— gold bricks. The cake was a huge hit with the bankers, and thanks to Chef Lasne's creativity and business savvy, today we can all enjoy this delicious snack, which is truly worth its weight in gold.

FINANCIERS

Quantity		Ingredient
U.S.	Metric	Financiers
4 oz	120 g	Flour
9 oz	270 g	Hazelnut powder
8 oz	250 g	Powdered sugar
10 ¼ fl oz	305 ml	Egg whites
3 ½ oz	100 g	Trimoline
11 fl oz	340 g	Butter

Method

1. Sift (*tamiser*) together the flour, hazelnut powder, and powdered sugar.
2. Add the egg whites and trimoline to the dry ingredients and mix until a smooth dough is formed.
3. In a small saucepan, melt the butter and cook until it begins to color. Once the milk solids turn a dark golden color (*beurre noisette*), remove from the heat and add to the dough. Stir it in immediately.
4. Place the dough in a large bowl, cover it with plastic wrap and leave it overnight to rest in the refrigerator.
5. Preheat the oven to 425°F (220°C). Lightly grease the molds with butter and arrange them on a baking sheet.
6. Transfer the batter to a piping bag fitted with a medium round tip.
7. Fill the financiers molds two-thirds full and bake until golden brown, about 10 minutes.
8. Unmold the financiers and place them on a wire rack to cool.

Learning Outcomes

Making Florentines
(*Florentins*)

Equipment

Tools:
Wooden spoon, silicone
baking mat, cooling rack,
mixing bowls

Pans:
Baking sheet

Serving/Yield

2 ¼ pound/ 1.1 kilogram
portion of dough

The history behind the Florentine (also known as the lace cake) is shrouded in mystery. While common sense would lead one to believe that this deliciously sweet, wafer-thin biscuit originated in the Italian city of Florence, this appears to not be the case. The name Florentine literally means "of Florence" ; however, there is little evidence to connect this sweet treat to this Renaissance city. What we do know is that the Florentine originated somewhere in Europe, at some point in the mid-17th century. From there, speculation of its exact origin varies widely. However, the most widely believed theory of origin states that the biscuit was created by the master pastry chefs of Louis XIV sometime between the years of 1682 and 1715, when the "Roi soleil" (Sun king) resided at his palace in Versailles. The story goes that the biscuit was invented as gift for the Medici of Florence (the Grand Duke of Tuscany, ruler of the Florentine city-state). This explains how the biscuit came to bear the name Florentine, created as a delicious gift from one European monarch to another.

FLORENTINS
Florentines

Quantity		Ingredient
U.S.	**Metric**	*Florentines (Florentins)*
7 oz	200 g	Butter, softened (***en pommade***)
7 oz	200 g	Brown sugar
4 oz	120 g	Flour
4 oz	120 g	Almonds, chopped
4 oz	120 g	Walnuts, chopped
4 oz	120 g	Hazelnuts, chopped
8 oz	250 g	Candied orange peel, finely diced

Method

1. Preheat the oven to 375°F (180°C).
2. Cream (***crémer***) together the softened (***en pommade***) butter and brown sugar.
3. Mix in the flour until smooth.
4. Add the chopped nuts and candied orange peel.
5. Place spoonfuls of the dough on a baking sheet lined with a silicone baking mat, 3 in./7.5 cm apart, to allow the Florentines to spread.
6. Bake until the Florentines begin to color. Remove from the oven and allow to set for 5 minutes, then carefully transfer them to a cooling rack to finish cooling.

Optional

If desired, the bottoms of the Florentines (Florentins) can be coated with chocolate.

Learning Outcomes

Making a meringue
Coloring mixtures
Piping rounds (*coucher*)
Making a ganache
Filling macarons

Equipment

Tools:
Mixing bowls, sieve,
silicone pad, rubber spatula,
whisk, pastry bag, large
round tip, small round tip,
wire rack

Pans:
Heavy baking sheet

Serving/Yield

Approximately 4 pounds/
2 kilograms of batter

The macaron (also known as the gerbet) is one of the most popular confections in the world. The macaron originated in Italy, created by monks in the 8th century. Oddly enough, the pastry is thought to have been modeled after the monks' belly buttons. The name macaron is derived from the Italian word *maccerone*, which means "to crush," and is believed to represent the crushed almonds, one of the macarons' most essential ingredients. The macaron was first introduced to France in 1533 when Catherine de Medici of Florence arrived with a large entourage, including some of the finest Italian pastry chefs, for her wedding to King Henry II of France. Since the French first sampled the macaron at this royal wedding, the popularity of the pastry has grown exponentially in France. The early macaron was a very simple almond-based biscuit similar to the modern amaretti. Since that time the French have truly made it their own. The birth of the macaron as we know it today can be traced to Pierre Desfontaines, a master pastry chef of the world-renowned Pâtisserie Ladurée of Paris. In the early 1900s, Chef Desfontaines had the brilliant idea of sandwiching a layer of ganache between two meringue biscuits. The innovation was hugely popular and the Pâtisserie Ladurée continues to produce the confection it invented to this day. The macaron remains immensely popular in France, so much so that the French town of Montmorillon created the Almond and Macaron Museum to honor this delicious treat.

Quantity		Ingredient
U.S.	Metric	*Vanilla Macarons*
8 oz	250 g	Almond powder, sifted
14 oz	400 g	Powdered sugar
8 fl oz	225 ml	Egg whites
3 ½ oz	100 g	Sugar, granulated
1 drop	1 drop	Red food coloring
		Raspberry Filling for Vanilla Macarons
10 oz	300 g	Raspberry jam
		Pistachio Macarons
Two drops	Two drops	(use vanilla recipe) Green food coloring
		Pistachio Filling
2 ½ fl oz	75 ml	Cream
¾ fl oz	25 ml	Glucose
8 oz	250 g	Almond paste
2 ¾ oz	80 g	Pistachio paste
¾ fl oz	20 ml	Kirch
		Chocolate Macarons
1 ¾ oz	50 g	Cocoa powder
14 oz	400 g	Powdered sugar
8 oz	225 g	Almond paste
8 fl oz	250 ml	Egg whites
3 ½ oz	100 g	Sugar
		Ganache
1 lb	500 g	Dark chocolate
23 fl oz	700 ml	Heavy cream
3 ½ oz	100 g	Cocoa powder
7 oz	200 g	Butter (unsalted)
1 ¾ fl oz	50 ml	Water

MACARONS: CHOCOLAT, VANILLE, ET PISTACHE
Macarons: Chocolate, Vanilla, and Pistachio

Method

Vanilla

1. Preheat the oven to 320°F (160°C).
2. Sift (*tamiser*) together the almond powder and powdered sugar.
3. Beat the egg whites (*monter les blancs*) to medium peaks. Whisk in the sugar and add 1 drop of red food coloring and beat the whites until tight and glossy.
4. Gently fold in the sifted ingredients.
5. Transfer the mixture to a piping bag fitted with a large round tip.
6. Pipe (*coucher*) small rounds onto baking sheet with a silicone pad.
7. Place in the oven and bake until the macarons can be lifted cleanly from the silicone, about 10 minutes.
8. Remove from the oven and transfer the silicone pad onto a wire rack for cooling.
9. Filling: Once the macarons are cool, fit a pastry bag with a small round tip and fill it with the raspberry jam. Pipe a small amount of jam onto a macaron half and place another macaron on top. Make sure the domed sides of the macarons are facing out. Repeat this process with the remaining macarons.

Pistachio

1. Follow the same recipe as for the vanilla macarons, substituting the green food coloring for the red food coloring.
2. Filling: Combine the cream and the glucose in a bowl, mixing well. Gradually add the pistachio paste, incorporating a small amount at a time, until smooth and well combined. Add the almond paste to this mixture, combine until smooth. Add the kirch and mix well. Fit a pastry bag with a small round tip and fill it with the almond/pistachio paste. Repeat the same steps that were completed when filling and assembling the vanilla macarons.

Method

Chocolate

1. Sift (**tamiser**) together the cocoa powder, the almond powder, and the powdered sugar. Follow the same recipe as for the vanilla macarons, omitting the red food coloring.

2. Filling (**ganache**): Bring the cream to a boil in a heavy-bottomed saucepan over medium heat. Gradually add the chocolate to the cream while beating with a whisk. Continue whisking until all of the chocolate has melted and has formed an emulsion with the cream.

3. In a separate bowl, stir the water and the cocoa powder together until no clumps remain. Add the unsalted butter to the cocoa powder and water mixture. Combine until smooth.

4. Add the chocolate and cream emulsion to the butter and cocoa mixture. Combine (**crémer**) until smooth. Fit a pastry bag with a small round tip and fill it with the ganache. Repeat the same steps that were completed when filling and assembling the vanilla and the pistachio macarons.

Learning Outcomes

Making a brown butter
(*beurre noisette*)
Beating eggs and sugar
(*blanchir*)
Preparing and baking
Madeleines

Equipment

Tools:
Zester, sieve,
whisk, rubber spatula,
pastry bag,
12-mm plain tip,
mixing bowls

Pans:
Madeleine pan,
small saucepan

Serving

Approximately 3 dozen

HISTORY

The origin of this inconspicuous little shell-shaped cake has caused more than its fair share of controversy. It is attributed by some to Cordon Bleu Chef Madeleine Paumier in 1843, and is also referred to by Carême as being a creation of the renowned pastry Chef Jean Avice. There is also much earlier evidence that the cake was the innovation of a peasant girl named Madeleine who worked for the Duke of Commercy. Despite the controversy, the Madeleine holds a special place in the hearts of the French as a fondly remembered childhood treat. This fondness is epitomized by the venerable French writer Marcel Proust, who describes a childhood memory in which eating a Madeleine is akin to a religious experience.

MADELEINES
Shell Sponge Cakes

Method

1. Preheat the oven to 465°F (240°C).
2. Melt the butter in a small saucepan over medium heat. Brush the Madeleine molds with butter and place in the refrigerator for 1 or 2 minutes to set. Apply a second layer of butter, then coat the molds with flour (**chemiser**) and set aside.

Madeleines

1. Melt the butter in a small saucepan over medium heat and cook it until it begins to brown (**beurre noisette**). Set aside.
2. Sift (**tamiser**) the flour and baking powder together onto a piece of parchment paper. Sift a second time. Combine the lemon zest and sugar in a large mixing bowl and add the eggs. Using a whisk, beat the eggs and sugar together until the mixture is pale in color and creates ribbons when the whisk is lifted (**blanchir**). Pour in the milk and stir until combined. Add the flour and carefully fold it in using a rubber spatula. Add 2 tablespoons of the batter to the melted butter and stir until homogeneous (**détendre**). Fold this mixture back into the batter. Cover the bowl in plastic wrap and let the batter rest in the refrigerator for a minimum of 1 hour.

Baking

1. Transfer the batter to a pastry bag fitted with a large plain tip. Pipe teardrop shapes that half fill the Madeleine molds. Transfer the Madeleines to the oven to bake for 6 minutes, then turn the temperature down to 390°F (200°C) and bake them until golden (*3 to 4 minutes*). When the Madeleines are golden and have formed a bump on the top, remove them from the oven and unmold them onto a wire rack. Serve the Madeleines warm or let them cool to room temperature.

Quantity		Ingredient
U.S.	**Metric**	*Pan Lining (Chemisage)*
1 oz	30 g	Butter
1 oz	30 g	Flour
		Madeleines
12 oz	360 g	Flour
5 ¾ oz	170 g	Butter
½ oz	15 g	Baking powder
⅛ oz	3 g	Lemon zest, finely grated
8 oz	250 g	Sugar, granulated
4 pcs	4 pcs	Eggs
2 fl oz	60 ml	Milk

Learning Outcomes

Making a meringue
Piping (*coucher*)
Using a nappage (*abricoter*)

Equipment

Tools:
Piping bag (4–5 mm round tip), mixing bowls, sieve, rubber spatula, whisk, wire rack, pastry brush

Pans:
Baking sheet

Serving/Yield

1 ¾ pound/900 gram portion of dough

Mirror Biscuits (miroirs) are deliciously flaky almond biscuits finished with a glaze. The name *miroir* is French for "mirror" and the biscuit gains its name from the shiny, reflective appearance of the biscuits' nappage.

MIROIRS
Mirror Biscuits

Method

1. Preheat the oven to 350°F (180°C).
2. Butter and flour a baking sheet (**chemiser**). Prepare a piping bag with a ⅛ in. (4–5 mm) round tip.

Almond Cream (Crème d'Amandes)

1. Beat the softened butter (**en pommade**) with the powdered sugar until smooth (**crémer**).
2. Add the almond powder and beat in the eggs one at a time until well combined. Flavor it with the rum.

Mirror Biscuits (Miroirs)

1. Sift (**tamiser**) together the almond powder, hazelnut powder, powdered sugar, and flour.
2. Beat the egg whites (**monter les blancs**) to medium peaks with some of the granulated sugar. Then add the remaining sugar and meringue the whites by beating them until tight and glossy.
3. Gently fold (**incorporer**) the dry ingredients into the meringue until just incorporated. Transfer the mixture to the prepared piping bag. Then pipe (**coucher**) small rings, approximately 2 in. (5 cm) in diameter onto the prepared baking sheet. Sprinkle with chopped almonds and fill the centers with the almond cream.
4. Bake until golden around the edges and the centers are lightly colored. Transfer to a wire rack to cool.
5. Gently heat the nappage until it liquefies. With a pastry brush, lightly coat the centers of the miroirs until even and shiny.

Quantity		Ingredient
U.S.	**Metric**	*Almond Cream (Crème d'Amandes)*
4 ¼ oz	125 g	Butter, softened (**en pommade**)
4 ¼ oz	125 g	Powdered sugar
4 ¼ oz	125 g	Almond powder
2 pcs	2 pcs	Eggs
¼ fl oz	10 ml	Rum
		Mirror Biscuits (Miroirs)
2 oz	60 g	Almond powder
2 oz	60 g	Hazelnut powder
2 oz	60 g	Powdered sugar
¾ oz	25 g	Flour
4 pcs	4 pcs	Egg whites
2 oz	60 g	Sugar
		Finishing
As needed	As needed	Nappage

Learning Outcomes

Cutting biscuits
with a cutter
Glazing (*dorer*)

Equipment

Tools:
Rolling pin, large round
cutter, pastry brush, mixing
bowls, whisk, wire rack,
fork

Pans:
Baking sheet

Yield

2 pound/100 gram portion
of dough

The Breton biscuit (palet breton) originated in the French region of Brittany in the early 20th century. These delicious, buttery tea biscuits gained their name from the region of France where they were created. Holding true to its coastal roots, the palet breton is also known as the "sables" Breton, which, of course, means "sand." This alternate name is derived from the grainy texture of the biscuit and the coastal region where it was created.

PALETS BRETON
Breton Biscuits

Method

1. Preheat the oven to 350°F (175°C).
2. Cream (*crémer*) together the butter and brown sugar, then mix in the vanilla and the egg yolks.
3. Sift (*tamiser*) the flour, sea salt, and baking powder together and mix into the previously incorporated ingredients. Once the dough forms and just holds together, gather it into a ball.
4. Roll out the dough (*abaisser*) onto a floured surface, about ½ in. (1 cm) thick, and cut large rounds with a round cutter. Place on a greased baking sheet.
5. Beat the egg with a little water to make the eggwash, and brush it over the tops of the palets. Allow to dry, then brush with a second coating. Using the tines of a fork, lightly score the top of the palets. Bake until golden brown, about 12 to 15 minutes, then remove from the oven and transfer to a wire rack to cool.

Quantity		Ingredient
U.S.	**Metric**	*Palets Breton*
8 oz	250 g	Butter, salted
6 ¼ oz	190 g	Brown sugar
¼ fl oz	5 ml	Vanilla extract or seeds of 1 vanilla bean
4 pcs	4 pcs	Egg yolks
13 oz	385 g	Flour
¼ oz	8 g	Baking powder
Pinch	Pinch	Sea salt
1 pc	1 pc	Egg for eggwash

PALMIERS AND SACRISTAINS

Learning Outcomes

Making a puff pastry (*pâte feuilletée*)
Making a *détrempe*

Equipment

Knives:
Chef's knife (*couteau chef*)

Tools:
Corne, rolling pin, brush, pastry brush

Pans:
Baking sheets

Serving/Yield

2 ¼ pound/1.1 kilogram portion of dough

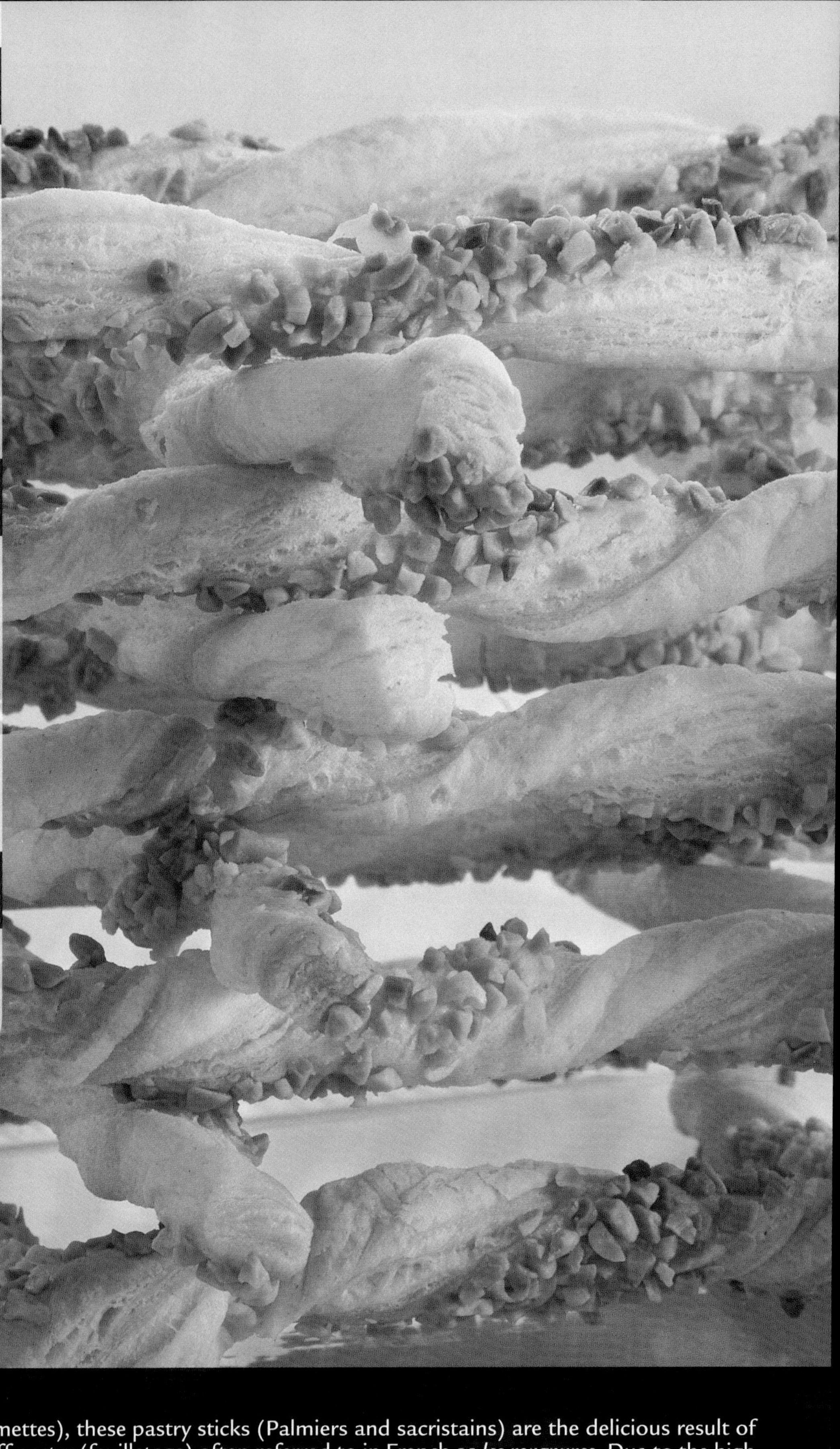

FYI...

Similar to matchsticks (allumettes), these pastry sticks (Palmiers and sacristains) are the delicious result of using up the scraps from puff pastry (feuilletage) often referred to in French as *les rongnures*. Due to the high butter content, making feuilletage can become costly for a pastry chef to produce, so every scrap is used. Both shaping techniques ensure that there are no leftovers!

PALMIERS AND SACRISTAINS
Pastry Sticks

Method

Make a Puff Pastry (*Pâte Feuilletée*)

1. Sift (*tamiser*) the flour onto a clean work surface and make a well in the center using a plastic scraper (*corne*). Add the salt and water to the well. Stir with your fingertips until the salt is dissolved. Add the butter (cut into pieces) and begin to incorporate the flour using your fingertips. As the flour, butter, and water begin to combine, use the *corne* to cut the ingredients together until it resembles a coarse dough. Sprinkle with additional water if the dough is too dry.

2. Once there are barely any traces of flour left, gather the dough into a ball and score the top of it with a deep cross using a large knife.

3. Loosely wrap the finished *détrempe* in plastic and transfer it to the refrigerator to rest for a minimum of 1 hour (preferably overnight).

Note

Détrempe refers to the dough before the layers of butter are added.

4. Place the cold butter between two sheets of parchment paper and pound it with a rolling pin until it is similar to the *détrempe* in consistency. Using the *corne*, shape the butter into a flat square about ½ in. (1 cm) thick. Set the butter aside. Place it in the refrigerator if the kitchen is warm. Lightly dust a clean work surface with flour (*fleurer*), then unwrap the *détrempe* and place it on the floured surface. Using the scored marks as a guide, roll out (*abaisser*) the corners of the *détrempe* into a cross shape. Be careful to keep the center of the cross thicker than its outer arms (this will be important when rolling out the dough and the butter). Place the square of butter in the center of the cross and fold the two side arms over it so that they overlap slightly in the center (in the process be careful not to trap any air bubbles). Give the dough a quarter turn and fold the two remaining arms over the butter so that the butter is completely enclosed. Press the seams well to seal. Lightly tap the dough with the length of the rolling pin to even out the distribution of the butter inside. Give the dough a quarter turn and repeat the tapping process. This is called the envelope.

Quantity		Ingredient
U.S.	**Metric**	*Puff Pastry (Pâte Feuilletée)*
1 lb	500 g	Flour, sifted
7 fl oz	200 ml	Cold water
¼ oz	8 g	Salt
7 oz	200 g	Butter
7 oz	200 g	Butter
1 pc	1 pc	Egg for eggwash
		Finishing
As needed	As needed	Sugar (either powdered or granulated)
As needed	As needed	Toasted chopped almonds

Method

Turns 1 and 2

5. Roll out (**abaisser**) the dough in long, even strokes to form a rectangle that is three times the original length of the envelope or ⅜ in. (1 cm) thick. Brush off the excess flour. Fold the bottom third of the dough up; fold the top third down over the first fold. Make sure the edges are even. Give the dough a quarter turn to the right and repeat the same rolling process. Make sure to always brush away any excess flour. Repeat the folding process (top third up, top third down over first fold) and give the dough a quarter turn to the right. Make two finger impressions in the top left corner of the dough.

Note

*These marks are a reminder of the number of turns the dough has received; they also indicate the position of subsequent turns. Wrap the dough in plastic and transfer it to the refrigerator to rest for a minimum of 20 minutes. With the butter incorporated into the dough, and two turns completed, it can now be referred to as **pâton**.*

Turns 3 and 4

6. Lightly dust the work surface with flour (**fleurer**). Remove the dough from the refrigerator and unwrap it onto the floured surface (with the 2 indents in the top left corner). Proceed to give the dough a third and fourth turn (rolling and folding in the same manner as the first and second turns). Mark the dough with 4 imprints in the top left corner before wrapping it in plastic and returning it to the refrigerator to rest for a minimum of 20 minutes.

Turns 5 and 6

7. Lightly dust the work surface with flour (**fleurer**). Remove the dough from the refrigerator and unwrap it onto the floured surface (with the 4 indents in the top left corner). Proceed to give the dough its final 2 turns, folding and rolling as in the previous turns. Wrap it in plastic and return it to the refrigerator to rest for a minimum of 20 minutes before rolling it out (the longer the dough rests, the better it will perform).

8. After resting, divide the dough in half.

Tip

*Because the **détrempe** and the butter are at the same consistency, it is necessary to complete the turns as explained above. If you allow the dough to over-chill between turns, the butter may become too hard and crack when rolled out. Make sure you have allotted the necessary time to complete the turns.*

Palmiers

1. Using the first half of the dough, fold it in half lengthwise to create a reference crease down the middle. Unfold the dough, brush it with the eggwash, and sprinkle it with sugar.
2. Fold each long edge in toward the center crease, leaving a small gap at the center. Brush with eggwash and sprinkle with more sugar, then fold in two on the crease. Press firmly. Let it rest in the freezer until hard (approximately 30 minutes).
3. Slice the roll of dough ½ in. (1 cm) thick and then lay the slices on a lightly greased baking sheet.

Sacristains

1. Cut the other half of the dough in two and roll it out (**abaisser**) evenly to a thickness of about ⅛ in. (3 mm). Place the dough on a baking sheet and then place it in the refrigerator to chill for approximately 15 to 20 minutes.
2. Brush the surface of the dough with eggwash, then sprinkle it with sugar and toasted chopped almonds. Run the rolling pin over the dough once or twice to ensure the sugar and nuts are well embedded. Using a large, sharp knife, cut the dough into ½ in. to ¾ in. strips.
3. Holding one end down, twist the dough with the other hand. Lift the dough by both of the ends and then transfer it to the baking sheet, pressing the ends down to secure the strips and keep them from unrolling. Place the sacristains about ¾ in. apart to allow the dough room to expand. Bake them until golden, for approximately 12 to 15 minutes. Remove from the oven and gently transfer to a wire rack to cool.

Learning Outcomes

Using a pastry bag
(*coucher*)
Eggwash (*dorer*)
Glazing (*glaçage*)
Using a gutter mold
(*goutière*)

Equipment

Tools:
Sieve, whisks, pastry brush,
fork, wire rack, mixing
bowls, rubber spatula,
pastry bag, 10-mm plain
tip, spoon, gutter mold
(*goutière*)

Pans:
4 baking sheets, saucepan

Serving/Yield

8 persons

FYI...

Before the advent of the gas oven, a baker had to be resourceful in order to make the best of the wood-fired oven. Requiring a lower heat, *petitis fours* were the perfect preparation to bake once the oven had cooled down after the larger gâteaux were done. *Petits fours* translates loosely as "little flame," simply referring to the low flame in the oven. The word *sec* in "petits fours secs" indicates a dry biscuit, perfect as an accompaniment with tea, custard desserts, ice cream, and sorbets.

Quantity		Ingredient
U.S.	**Metric**	*Bâtons de Maréchaux*
4 ½ oz	130 g	Powdered sugar
4 ½ oz	130 g	Almond powder
5 fl oz	150 ml	Egg whites
1 oz	30 g	Sugar, granulated
7 oz	200 g	Crushed almonds
10 fl oz	300 ml	Dark chocolate, melted
		Pâte à Cigarette
1 ¾ oz	50 g	Butter
3 ½ oz	100 g	Powdered sugar
2 pcs	2 pcs	Egg whites
1 ½ oz	45 g	Flour
		Palet de Dames
4 oz	125 g	Powdered sugar
4 oz	125 g	Butter
Pinch	Pinch	Salt
2 pcs	2 pcs	Eggs
5 oz	150 g	Flour
2 ¾ oz	80 g	Raisins, macerated
		Tuiles aux Amandes
1 ¼ oz	40 g	Flour
4 ¼ oz	125 g	Powdered sugar
1 pc	1 pc	Egg
2 pcs	2 pcs	Egg whites
5 oz	150 g	Sliced almonds

PETITS FOURS SECS
Assorted Light Biscuits

Method

Preheat the oven to 370°F (188°C).
2. Lightly grease a baking sheet with cold butter and reserve it in the refrigerator.

Bâtons de Maréchaux
1. Sift (**tamiser**) the powdered sugar and almond powder together (**tamiser**) into a bowl.

Note
*The combination of equal amounts of powdered sugar and almond powder is referred to as **tant pour tant.***

2. Whisk the egg whites in a large mixing bowl until soft peaks form. Gradually add the sugar and continue to whisk until the whites are stiff and glossy. Add the **tant pour tant** and fold it in until combined.
3. Transfer the mixture to a pastry bag fitted with a 10-mm plain tip. Pipe small dollops of the batter at each corner of the baking sheet and glue down a sheet of parchment paper. On the parchment, pipe short lines of batter, about 3 in. (8 cm) long in rows along the length of the baking sheet.
4. Generously sprinkle with crushed almonds. Tip the baking sheet and tap to shake off any excess almonds.
5. Bake the bâtons de maréchaux until lightly golden (*10 to 15 minutes*).
6. As soon as they are out of the oven, slip them straight off the baking sheet onto the marble.
7. When they are cold, dip the bottoms in melted chocolate and lay them flat on a parchment paper–covered baking sheet in the refrigerator to set.

Pâte à Cigarette
1. Cream the butter and sugar together. Stir in the egg whites until smooth. Add the flour. Allow to rest at least 1 hour before using. Line a baking sheet with a silicone mat. Spread 4–6 small spoonfuls of the pâte à cigarette on the mat, leaving at least 3 in. (8 cm) in between. Place in the oven and cook about 6 minutes or until they spread out and the edges begin to brown. Remove from the oven, and working very quickly, remove each cookie with a metal spatula and roll around the handle of a wooden spoon. If the cookies become too stiff, return to the oven to soften. Adjust the number of cookies you can roll for the remaining dough.

Method

Palets des Dames

1. Grease and flour a baking sheet. Reserve it in the refrigerator.
2. Sift (*tamiser*) the powdered sugar into a bowl.
3. With a whisk, cream (*crémer*) the butter in a large mixing bowl until light and fluffy. Add the powdered sugar and salt to the butter and cream them together. Add the eggs one at a time and beat until the mixture is light in color. Sift the flour and add it to the mixture. Fold it in using a rubber spatula. Let the batter rest in the refrigerator for 30 minutes.
4. Drain the rum out of the raisins.
5. Transfer the batter to a pastry bag fitted with a 10-mm plain tip. On the baking sheet, pipe rows of batter in the form of circles, ¾ in. (2 cm) in diameter. Make sure that the palets are at least 2 in. (5 cm) apart on the baking sheet, as they will spread. Place 3 raisins on each circle, pressing them in a little, and transfer the baking sheet to the oven to bake until the palets are golden around the edges (*6 to 8 minutes*).
6. Mix some water into powdered sugar to create a paste and brush it onto the palets using a pastry brush as soon as the palets come out of the oven.
7. Transfer the palets to a wire rack to cool.

Tuiles aux Amandes

1. Preheat the oven to 350°F (175°C).
2. Toast the almonds in the oven until lightly golden on the edges.
3. Sift (*tamiser*) the flour and powdered sugar together.
4. Prepare baking sheets by lining with silicone pads.
5. When the almonds are cool, add them to the flour and sugar. Mix in the egg and egg whites. Form the batter into circles with a wet fork (make sure to leave enough room for the tuiles to spread during baking). Transfer the baking sheet to the oven and bake the tuiles until golden.
6. Immediately after the tuiles are removed from the oven, lift them off the baking sheet with a metal spatula and place them in the tuile or gutter mold (*goutière*).

Learning Outcomes

Making a choux pastry
(*pâte à choux*)
Making pastry cream
(*crème pâtissière*)
Filling choux pastry
(*coucher des choux*)
Flavoring pastry cream
and fondant
Glazing with fondant
(*glaçage*)
Making rosettes with
buttercream icing

Equipment

Tools:
Wooden spoon, rubber
spatula, pastry bag,
12-mm plain tip,
small star tip, 6-mm
plain tip, fork, whisk,
small off set spatula

Pans:
1 large russe, 1 medium
russe, 2 small russes,
baking sheet

Serving

8 persons

According to Pierre Lacam in "Le Mémoriale Historique," la religieuse was created at Frascati, a 19th-century Paris restaurant that was shut down for gambling. Such immoral beginnings for a pastry so piously named! La religieuse translates as "the nun" and the pastry itself is modeled after the habit worn by nuns.

RELIGIEUSES AU CAFÉ ET CHOCOLAT
Chocolate and Coffee Cream Puffs

Method

Preheat the oven to 425°F (220°C)

Choux Pastry (Pâte à Choux)
1. *Prepare a panade*: Combine the water, milk, butter, sugar, and salt in a large pan and bring to a boil over medium-high heat. Once the butter has completely melted, remove the pan from the heat and add all the flour at once. Stir with a wooden spatula until combined; then, over medium heat, stir until the mixture forms a smooth ball and comes cleanly away from the sides of the pan (**dessécher**). Transfer to a clean bowl and allow to cool slightly. Beat the eggs into the panade one at a time. The dough should be stretchy and slightly sticky. Transfer the mixture to a pastry bag fitted with a 12-mm plain tip. Pipe 2 rows of large choux [*approximately 2 in. (5 cm) across*] and 2 rows of small choux [*about 1 in. (2.5 cm) across*] onto a very lightly greased baking sheet. Brush the choux with eggwash, then dip a fork in eggwash and lightly press to even their shape.
2. Transfer the choux to the oven and immediately reduce the temperature to 400°F (205°C). Bake until golden (*20 to 25 minutes*), rotating the baking sheet as soon as they begin to color.
3. Remove the choux from the oven and transfer to a wire rack to cool.
4. Using a small star tip, pierce a hole in the bottoms of the choux.

Pastry Cream (Crème Pâtissière)
1. Pour the milk into a medium saucepan. Split the vanilla bean in half lengthwise and scrape out the seeds. Stir the seeds into the milk and bring it to a boil over medium-high heat. Add about one-quarter of the sugar to the milk and stir to dissolve it.
2. Meanwhile, place the egg yolks in a small mixing bowl and add the remaining sugar. Whisk the sugar into the eggs until it completely dissolves and the yolks lighten in color (**blanchir**). Add the flour and cornstarch to the yolks and stir until well combined.
3. When the milk begins to come to a boil, remove it from the stove and pour one-third of it into the egg yolks. Stir well to temper the yolks, then whisk the tempered mixture into the remaining hot milk. Place back onto the heat and cook until the crème pâtissière begins to bubble. Continue whisking (being sure to press the whisk around

Quantity		Ingredient
U.S.	Metric	Choux Pastry (Pâte à Choux)
4 fl oz	125 ml	Water
4 fl oz	125 ml	Milk
4 oz	125 g	Butter
½ tsp	5 g	Salt
½ oz	12 g	Sugar, granulated
5 oz	150 g	Flour
4–5 pcs	4–5 pcs	Eggs
1 pc	1 pc	Egg, slightly beaten, for eggwash
		Pastry Cream (Crème Pâtissière)
1 ½ pt	750 mL	Milk
1 pc	1 pc	Vanilla bean
6 pcs	6 pcs	Egg yolks
5 oz	150 g	Sugar, granulated
1 ½ oz	45 g	Flour
1 ½ oz	45 g	Cornstarch
1 tsp	5 ml	Coffee extract
2 oz	50 g	Dark chocolate, melted
		Assembly (Montage)
3 ½ oz	100 g	Coffee fondant*
3 ½ oz	100 g	Chocolate fondant*
3 ½ oz	100 g	Buttercream icing (crème au beurre)
As needed	As needed	Cocoa powder
		*Available at specialty stores

Method

the corners of the pan) and allow to cook for 1 minute in order to cook the starch. The pastry cream (crème pâtissière) will become very thick. Separate the pastry cream (crème pâtissière) into 2 equal batches in separate mixing bowls and mix coffee extract into one batch and melted chocolate into the other using whisks. Pat (***tamponner***) the surface of the pastry cream (crème pâtissière) with a piece of cold butter held on the end of a fork to create a protective film. Let the pastry cream (crème pâtissière) cool to room temperature and refrigerate.

Assembly (Montage)

1. Beat the pastry cream until its texture loosens, then transfer it to a pastry bag fitted with a 6-mm plain tip. Fill half the choux with chocolate-flavored pastry cream (crème pâtissière) and the other half with coffee-flavored pastry cream (crème pâtissière), piping it in through the holes underneath. *Fondant:* Stirring gently with a wooden spatula, heat the coffee fondant in a medium saucepan over the lowest heat setting. If the fondant stays very thick even when heated, add a few drops of simple syrup and stir it in. Continue to stir the fondant until it coats the back of a spoon in a thick, shiny layer. The ideal temperature for use is 98.6°F (37°C).

2. Repeat all the same steps to prepare the chocolate fondant.

3. To ice the choux, dip the tops in the fondant corresponding to their filling; make sure to clean off any drips with your fingers. When all the choux have been iced, place the crème au beurre in a pastry bag fitted with a small star tip and pipe a small rosette on top of each large choux. For the chocolate religieuses, mix cocoa powder into the buttercream icing (crème au beurre). Stick 1 small choux on each rosette. Pipe a collar (***collerette***) around each little choux, then finish them with a small rosette on top.

Learning Outcomes

Combining two different
colored doughs to build
one product
Make a biscuit dough
(*pâte sablée*)
Kneading (*fraisage*)

Equipment

Knives:
Chef's knife (*couteau chef*)

Tools:
Sieve, rolling pin,
pastry brush, plastic scraper
(*corne*), rolling pin, wire
rack

Pans:
Baking sheet

Serving/Yield

3 ¾ pound/ 1.9 kilogram
portion of dough

HISTORY

This is one of a number of regional biscuits collectively described as "sablées" that all take advantage of the friable and buttery qualities of pâte sablée, which itself is also used as a base for tarts. The term sablée, or "sandy/sanded," refers to the texture of the dough after the butter and flour have been rubbed together between the fingers to form a sandy texture. The Sablées Hollandais are visually striking for their use of a chocolate sablée interwoven, often in checkerboard fashion, with a vanilla sablée.

Quantity		Ingredient
U.S.	Metric	*Vanilla Biscuit (Sablée)*
14 oz	400 g	Flour
¼ oz	4 g	Baking powder
¼ fl oz	5 ml	Vanilla
7 oz	200 g	Powdered sugar
½ fl oz	15 ml	Water
4 pcs	4 pcs	Egg yolks
7 oz	200 g	Butter, softened (en pommade)
		Chocolate Biscuit (Sablée)
14 oz	400 g	Flour
¼ oz	5 g	Baking powder
¼ fl oz	5 ml	Vanilla
7 oz	200 g	Powdered sugar
½ fl oz	15 ml	Water
4 pcs	4 pcs	Egg yolks
7 oz	200 g	Butter, softened
¾ oz	20 g	Cocoa powder, sifted
		Finishing
1pc	1 pc	Egg, for eggwash

SABLÉES HOLLANDAIS
Checkered Biscuits

Method

Preheat the oven to 340°F (170°C).

Make a Vanilla Biscuit Dough (Pâte Sablée) Using the Creaming (Crémer) Method

1. Sift (*tamiser*) the flour and baking powder together. Place on the work surface and make a large well (*fontaine*). In the center of the well, add the powdered sugar and push it to the sides to reform the well. Add the water, egg yolks, and vanilla to the center of the well and mix them together while gradually incorporating the sugar. Add the softened butter and work until combined.
2. Using the *corne*, gradually incorporate the flour from the sides of the well by turning and cutting it into the rest of the ingredients. Once the dough forms and just holds together, gather it into a ball and smear it away from yourself with the heel of your palm (*fraiser*). Continue this action until the dough is smooth, then wrap it in plastic and chill.

Make a Chocolate Biscuit Dough (Pâte Sablée) Using the Creaming Method (Crémer)

1. Follow the same method for vanilla pâte sablée, mixing the sifted cocoa powder in directly after the butter is added to the well.

Assembly

1. For checkerboards: Using a rolling pin, roll (*abaisser*) the vanilla dough into a thick rectangle (the thickness will depend on the size of your checkerboard), then roll out the chocolate dough to the same thickness.
2. Cut the chocolate and vanilla dough into strips, then stack alternating colors, using eggwash between the layers. Roll out (*abaisser*) the scraps of vanilla dough in a thin layer that is large enough to wrap the finished layers completely. Wrap the layered dough in plastic and chill.
3. For spirals: Roll out (*abaisser*) thinner layers of chocolate and vanilla dough. First, brush a layer of vanilla dough with eggwash, then lay a chocolate layer on top. Continue alternating the layers while smoothing out any air bubbles. Trim the edges of the dough, then roll tightly. Wrap and chill.

Method

4. Cut the dough into slices about ⅛ in. (3 mm to 5 mm) thick and arrange on a clean baking sheet. Bake until the edges just begin to color. Place on a wire rack to cool.

Note

By combining the chocolate and vanilla doughs in different ways, a variety of patterns can be achieved. For example, scraps of dough can be rolled together into a log for a marbled effect. Remember to use eggwash to hold the layers of dough together.

Learning Outcomes

Making choux pastry
(*pâte à choux*)
Piping salambos
Making pastry cream
(*crème pâtissière*)
Filling choux pastry
(*coucher des choux*)
Caramel

Equipment

Tools:
Wooden spoon, rubber
spatula,
pastry bag,
12-mm plain tip,
small star tip,
6-mm plain tip,
pastry brush, fork,
whisk, corne,
silicone mat

Pans:
1 large saucepan,
2 medium saucepans,
1 baking sheet

Serving

8 persons

FYI...

A small gâteau filled with rum-flavored pastry cream (crème pâtissière), the salambos was created in the late 1800s and was named after Reyer's Opera *Salammbô*, which was itself named after Flaubert's novel of the same name.

SALAMBOS
Caramel Coated Cream Puffs Filled with Rum Cream

Method

Preheat the oven to 425°F (220°C).

Choux Pastry (Pâte à Choux)

1. *Prepare a panade:* Combine the water, milk, butter, sugar, and salt in a large pan and bring to a boil over medium-high heat. Once the butter has completely melted, remove the pan from the heat and add the flour. Stir with a wooden spatula until combined; then, over medium heat, stir until the mixture forms a smooth ball and comes cleanly away from the edge of the pan. Transfer to a clean bowl and cool until warm. Beat the eggs into the panade one at a time using a wooden spatula. The dough should be elastic and slightly sticky, and should create a V shape when the spatula is lifted out of the bowl. Transfer the dough to a pastry bag fitted with a 12-mm plain tip and pipe (**coucher**) rows of short, fat éclair shapes called salambos onto a lightly greased baking sheet.

2. Brush the salambos with eggwash using a pastry brush, and even them out with the prongs of a fork dipped in eggwash. Transfer the baking sheet to the oven and bake until golden, rotating the tray when the choux pastry begins to color. When cooked, transfer the salambos to a wire rack to cool. When cool, pierce the bottoms with two holes, using a small star tip.

Pastry Cream (Crème Pâtissière)

1. Line a small serving tray or platter with plastic wrap. Pour the milk into a medium saucepan. Split the vanilla bean in half lengthwise and scrape out the seeds. Stir the seeds into the milk and bring it to a boil over medium-high heat. Add about one-quarter of the sugar to the milk and stir to dissolve it.

2. Meanwhile, place the egg yolks in a small mixing bowl and add the remaining sugar. Whisk the sugar into the eggs until it completely dissolves and the yolks lighten in color (**blanchir**). Add the flour and cornstarch to the yolks and stir until well combined.

3. When the milk begins to come to a boil, remove it from the stove and pour one-third of it into the egg yolks. Stir well to temper the yolks, then whisk the tempered mixture into the remaining hot milk. Place back onto the heat and cook until the pastry cream (crème pâtissière) begins to

Quantity		Ingredient
U.S.	**Metric**	*Choux Pastry (Pâte à Choux)*
4 fl oz	125 ml	Water
4 fl oz	125 ml	Milk
4 oz	125 g	Butter
½ oz	12 g	Sugar, granulated
Pinch	Pinch	Salt
5 oz	150 g	Flour
4–5 pcs	4–5 pcs	Eggs
1 pc	1 pc	Egg (for eggwash)
		Pastry Cream (Crème Pâtissière)
1 ½ pt	750 ml	Milk
1 pc	1 pc	Vanilla bean
6 pcs	6 pcs	Egg yolks
5 oz	150 g	Sugar, granulated
1 ½ oz	45 g	Flour
1 ½ oz	45 g	Cornstarch
¼ fl oz	2 ml	Rum or cognac
		Caramel
5 oz	150 g	Sugar, granulated
1 ¾ fl oz	50 mL	Water
As needed	As needed	Sliced blanched almonds

Method

bubble. Continue whisking (being sure to press the whisk around the corners of the pan) and allow to cook for 1 minute in order to cook the starch. The pastry cream (crème pâtissière) will become very thick. Immediately transfer the finished pastry cream (crème pâtissière) to the plastic-lined serving tray. Pat (**tamponner**) the surface with a piece of cold butter held on the end of a fork to create a protective film. Completely cover with a second piece of plastic wrap, pressing out any air bubbles. Let the pastry cream (crème pâtissière) cool to room temperature before refrigerating.

Assembly (Montage)

1. Transfer the cooled pastry cream (crème pâtissière) to a mixing bowl and whisk until smooth and elastic. Add the rum and stir well. Transfer the pastry cream (crème pâtissière) to a pastry bag fitted with a 6-mm plain tip, and fill the salambos through the holes in the bottom of the pastry.
2. On a silicone mat, arrange little motifs of sliced almonds.

Caramel

1. Bring the sugar and water to a boil in a medium saucepan over medium-high heat and cook this mixture until it turns a light caramel color. Stop the cooking process by briefly dipping the base of the saucepan in ice water. Dip the salambos into the caramel and place them, caramel side down, on top of the almond motifs that have been arranged on the silicon mat. Be careful not to touch the hot caramel with your fingers. Let the caramel harden before removing the salambos from the mat. Serve the salambos caramel side up.

Learning Outcomes

Making a sweet
shortcrust pastry dough
(*pâte sucrée*)
Making a Swiss meringue
Using a nappage
(*abricoter*)

Equipment

Knives:
Serrated knife (*couteau à scie*), palette knife (*spatule*)

Tools:
Round bottomed bowl, mixing bowls, sieve, plastic scraper (*corne*), pastry docker (*pique-vite*), rolling pin, balloon whisk, pastry brush, rubber spatula

Pans:
Baking sheet, bain-marie

Serving/Yield

1 ¼ pound/1.1 kilogram
portion of dough

HISTORY

Tranche noix de coco can be found in so many variations that it's next to impossible to assign the preparation a specific date or a particular pastry chef as its creator. In terms of the preparation's ingredients, the coconut (noix de coco) first shows up as a botanical curiosity in the French Academy of Sciences in 1674. While not exactly a breakthrough in terms of historical research, it is at least fair to say the fruit was being incorporated into French cuisine sometime after its introduction to France. In Southeast Asian and particularly Indian desserts, a number of preparations could have been the rough conceptual inspiration for French and other European sweets that feature coconut. Coconut barfi, an Indian delicacy, for example, has certain ingredients as well as visual similarities to rochers a la noix de coco. One also finds that a variety of Indian coconut desserts are served in slices (tranches). However, the use of meringue and chocolate in the tranche de noix de coco clearly distinguishes it from these Indian and Southeast Asian sweets.

Quantity		Ingredient
U.S.	Metric	**Sweet Shortcrust Pastry Dough (Pâte Sucrée)**
8 oz	250 g	Flour
4 ¼ oz	125 g	Butter
Pinch	Pinch	Salt
¼ fl oz	5 ml	Vanilla
3 pcs	3 pcs	Egg yolks
4 ¼ oz	125 g	Sugar, powdered
As needed	As needed	Apricot glaze (*nappage*)
		Swiss Meringue (Meringue Suisse)
5 pcs	5 pcs	Egg whites
8 oz	250 g	Sugar, granulated
7 oz	200 g	Grated coconut
½ oz	15 g	Flour
¼ fl oz	5 ml	Vanilla extract
		Finishing
10 fl oz	300 ml	Chocolate, melted

TRANCHE NOIX DE COCO
Coconut Biscuits

Method

Preheat the oven to 355°F (180°C).

Sweet Shortcrust Pastry Dough (Pâte Sucrée)

1. Sift the flour (**tamiser**) onto a clean work surface and gather it into a neat pile. Sift (**tamiser**) the powdered sugar in a separate pile in front of the flour. Sprinkle the salt over the sugar, then use a plastic scraper (**corne**) to make a large well (**fontaine**) in the center of these ingredients.

Note

In the following steps, keep one hand clean and dry (for the plastic scraper) and use the other to stir in the wet ingredients.

2. Add the butter to the center of the sugar and work it in with your fingertips until it is soft. Using the **corne**, gradually add the powdered sugar from the edge of the well while simultaneously working it into the butter with your hands. Continue to mix the butter and sugar together (**crémer**) until they are fully incorporated and creamy.
3. Add the egg yolk and water to the butter and sugar and mix it in with your fingertips. The result will be slightly lumpy. Add the vanilla extract to the mixture and work it in with your fingers until it is completely incorporated.
4. With your clean hand, use the **corne** to gradually add some flour to the creamed ingredients while simultaneously mixing with your fingertips. Continue until the mixture resembles a thick paste. Using the **corne**, cut in the remaining flour until a loose dough is formed.
5. Using the heel of your palm, firmly smear the dough away from yourself to ensure that no lumps are left (**fraiser**). Scrape up the dough and repeat until a smooth dough forms. Form the dough into a smooth ball, wrap it in plastic, and flatten it into a disk. Let it rest in the refrigerator for a minimum of 30 minutes (preferably overnight).
6. Roll the dough out (**abaisser**) into a ⅛ in. (3 mm) thick rectangle. Roll the dough onto the rolling pin and transfer to a lightly greased baking sheet. Prick the dough with a docker (**pique-vite**) and place in the oven. Bake until just beginning to color, then remove and brush with the apricot glaze (**nappage**). Allow to dry then brush another layer.
7. Reduce the oven to 260°F (130°C).

Method

Make a Swiss Meringue (Meringue Suisse)

8. Prepare a hot water bath (**bain-marie**). Place the sugar and egg whites in a round-bottom bowl and place over the simmering water. Whisk until sugar is melted and the mixture feels hot to the touch, about 120–130°F (50–55°C). Remove from the heat and continue whisking until cooled (98°F/37°C).

9. Toss the grated coconut with the flour and vanilla, then gently fold into the meringue. As soon as the coconut is incorporated, stop mixing and spread the mixture onto the pâte sucrée. Return the baking sheet to the oven and bake until the meringue feels dry to the touch, about 25 to 30 minutes. Remove from the oven and allow to cool.

10. Once completely cooled, trim the edges. Cut into 3 or 4 strips lengthwise, then cut into rectangles or triangles. Dip in melted chocolate.

Tartes
(Tarts)

Learning Outcomes

Making a sweet shortcrust
pastry dough (*pâte sucrée*)
Lining tartlet molds
(*fonçage*)
Making almond cream
(*crème d'amandes*)
To press out dough by hand
(*fraiser*)
Glazing with jelly/nappage
(*abricoter*)

Equipment

Knives:
Paring knife (*couteau d'office*)

Tools:
Corne, sieve, mixing bowls,
whisk, 4 in. (10 cm) round
cutter, plastic wrap, rolling
pin, pastry brush

Pans:
12, 3 in. (8 cm) tartlet
molds, baking sheet, wire
rack

Serving/Yield

12 small tartlets

The word *amandine* is the French culinary term for the incorporation of almonds into a preparation. Used in sweet as well as savory dishes, the almond is one of the most widely used nuts in cooking. Along with its delicious, mildly sweet flavor, the almond is also an extremely healthy food. It is generally considered to be a "super food," the group of foods that nutritionists consider most beneficial for optimum health.

AMANDINES
Almond Tarts

Method

Sweetcrust Pastry Dough (Pâte Sucrée)

1. Sift the flour (**tamiser**) onto a clean work surface and gather it into a neat pile. Sift the powdered sugar in a separate pile in front of the flour. Sprinkle the salt over the sugar, then use a plastic scraper (**corne**) to make a large well (**fontaine**) in the center of the sugar mound.

Note

In the following steps, keep one hand clean and dry (for the plastic scraper) and use the other to stir in the wet ingredients.

2. Add the butter to the center of the sugar and work it in with your fingertips until it is soft. Using the **corne**, gradually add the powdered sugar from the edge of the well while simultaneously working it into the butter with your hands. Continue to mix the butter and sugar together (**crémer**) until they are fully incorporated and creamy.

3. Add the egg yolk and water to the butter and sugar and mix it in with your fingertips. The result will be slightly lumpy. Add the vanilla extract to the mixture and work it in with your fingers until it is completely incorporated.

4. With your clean hand, use the **corne** to gradually add some flour to the creamed ingredients while simultaneously mixing with your fingertips. Continue until the mixture resembles a thick paste. Using the **corne**, cut in the remaining flour until a loose dough is formed.

5. Using the heel of your palm, firmly smear the dough away from yourself to ensure that no lumps are left (**fraiser**). Scrape up the dough and repeat until a smooth dough forms. Form the dough into a smooth ball, wrap it in plastic wrap, and flatten it into a disk. Let it rest in the refrigerator for a minimum of 30 minutes (preferably overnight).

6. Lightly grease your tartlet molds with butter.

7. Using your rolling pin, roll out (**abaisser**) the pâte sucrée to a thickness of about ⅛ in. (3 mm).

8. Using the round cutter, cut out as many rounds as possible. Lay a disk of dough into the tartlet mold, making sure it is evenly centered. Take a piece of excess dough and work it into a ball. Coat the dough ball in flour and use it to gently press the disks of dough lining each tartlet mold into the

Quantity		Ingredient
U.S.	**Metric**	**Sweet Shortcrust Pastry Dough (Pâte Sucrée)**
7 oz	200 g	Flour
3 ¼ oz	100 g	Powdered sugar
Pinch	Pinch	Salt
3 ¼ oz	100 g	Butter
2 pcs	2 pcs	Egg yolks
1 Drop	1 ml	Water
1 tsp	5 ml	Vanilla
		Almond Cream (Crème d'Amandes)
2 oz	60 g	Butter
2 oz	60 g	Sugar, granulated
1 pc	1 pc	Egg
1 pc	1 pc	Vanilla bean
2 oz	60 g	Almond powder
2 tsp	10 ml	Rum
4 ½ oz	125 g	Sliced almonds
8 oz	250 g	Apricot glaze

Method

base of the molds. With your thumbs, press the dough against the edges while turning the molds. Trim off any excess dough with the paring knife. Arrange the molds onto a baking sheet and chill until needed.

Almond Cream (*Crème d'Amandes*)

1. Cream (*crémer*) the butter and sugar together until light and fluffy. Mix the egg until well combined. Using a small knife, split the vanilla bean in half lengthwise and scrape out the seeds and whisk them into the mixture. Finish the cream by mixing in the almond powder and rum.

2. Transfer the almond cream to a piping bag fitted with a medium round tip. Cover the bottoms of the chilled tartlet molds with the almond cream until they are half full. Sprinkle with sliced almonds and then place the molds onto a baking sheet and bake until the almond cream has puffed up and is nicely colored, approximately 25 minutes. The surface should feel dry to the touch and spring back when lightly pressed.

3. Transfer the tartlets to a wire rack to cool slightly, then gently unmold and allow to finish cooling. In a small saucepan, heat your apricot glaze until just melted and, once the tartlets are cool, brush (*nappage*) them with the apricot glaze.

Learning Outcomes

Making a sweet dough
(*pâte sucrée*)
Making a flan
Lining a tart pan
(*fonçage*)
Beating eggs and sugar to
ribbon stage (*blanchir*)
Unmolding (*démouler*)

Equipment

Knives:
Palette knife (*spatule*)

Tools:
Mixing bowls, rolling pin,
wooden spatula, whisk,
serving dish or cake board

Pans:
8 in (20 cm) ring mold
saucepan

Serving/Yield

One 8 in./20 cm flan tart,
8–10 servings

The Flan tart (Flan Boulanger), also known as the flan Parisien, is the inspiration of many childhood memories in France. The flan is a good example of how to stretch the profitability of food by using leftover dough for the crust and ingredients that are typically on hand, such as eggs, sugar, and milk. In the "old days," the flan would have been baked using the residual heat of the oven left over from dinner. Modern variations substitute the sweet yeast dough (pâte levée sucrée) with a shortcrust pastry dough (pâte brisée) or a puff pastry (pâte feuilletée) to hold the sturdy baked custard with its distinctive dark crust on the surface.

FLAN BOULANGER
Flan Tart

Quantity		Ingredient
U.S.	**Metric**	*Sweet Shortcrust Dough (Pâte Sucrée)*
3 ¼ oz	100 ml	Milk
½ oz	15 g	Fresh yeast
2 oz	60 g	Sugar, granulated
8 oz	250 g	Flour
1 pc	1 pc	Egg
Pinch	Pinch	Salt
2 ½ oz	75 g	Butter, softened
		Flan (Appareil à Flan)
1 pint	500 ml	Milk
4 pcs	4 pcs	Egg yolks
5 oz	150 g	Sugar, granulated
1 tsp	5 ml	Vanilla
1 ½ oz	40 g	Cornstarch
1 ½ oz	40 g	Flour

Method

1. Gently warm the milk to body temperature being sure not to let it get too hot [*max 90°F (32°C)*]. Place the yeast in a medium-sized bowl, pour the lukewarm milk over the top and stir to dissolve the yeast. Stir in the sugar and some of the flour to create a smooth paste. Stir in the egg and salt until well combined. Add the butter, then gradually incorporate the remaining flour until a dough forms.

2. Sprinkle some flour onto your work surface (**fleurer**), remove the dough from the bowl and knead it on the floured surface until smooth and no longer sticky, adding more flour as needed. Place the dough in a clean bowl, cover, and allow to double in volume, about 1 hour.

3. Butter the ring mold and place on the baking sheet.

4. Punch the dough down, and using a rolling pin, roll it out (**abaisser**) into a circle large enough for the dough to cover the sides of the ring mold. Roll the dough gently around the rolling pin and carefully lay it over the ring mold. Lift the edges in order to tuck the dough into the corner (**fonçage**). *(See pages 200–203 in Pâtisserie and Baking Foundations.)* Set aside.

5. Preheat the oven to 355°F (180°C).

6. Make the appareil a flan: Pour the milk into a saucepan and bring to a boil over medium heat. In a bowl, whisk the egg yolks with the sugar until thick and light yellow in color (**blanchir**). Whisk in the vanilla, cornstarch, and flour into the egg mixture until smooth. Once the milk comes to a boil, remove it from the heat and add some of the warmed milk to the egg mixture to temper. Add the tempered eggs to the rest of the hot milk and place the pan back onto the heat. Whisk over the heat until it begins to boil, allowing to cook for about 1 minute. Remove from the heat and immediately transfer the custard to the lined ring mold. Smooth the top with a palette knife. Place it in the hot oven to bake until the top has puffed up and is darkly colored. Remove from the oven and allow to cool. Gently remove from the ring mold and serve.

Learning Outcomes

Making a sweet dough
(*pâte sucrée*)
Making almond cream
(*crème d'amandes*)
To press out dough by
hand (*fraiser*)
Lining a tart pan
(*fonçage*)
Pricking the dough
(*piquer*)
Score or crimp (*chiqueter*)
Glazing with jelly/
nappage (*abricoter*)

Equipment

Knives:
Paring knife (*couteau
d'office*)

Tools:
Corne, whisk, rolling pin,
sieve, plastic wrap, wooden
spatula, pastry docker
(*pique-vite/pique pâte*)

Pans:
8 in. (20 cm) tart mold with
removable bottom,
one 10 in./25 cm tart

Serving/Yield

8–10 servings

FYL...

Joseph Favre (1849-1903), chef, writer, and authority of all things culinary during the period known as La Belle Époque in France, attributes the creation of the tarte Bourdaloue to M. Fasquelle, whose pastry shop was located on rue Bourdaloue in Paris. While there are detractors who rightfully point to Bourdaloue preparations with poached fruit that predate M. Fasquelle, the recipe for the tart as we know it today supports Joseph Favre's assertion. Recipes that predate Fasquelle, as well as the street named Bourdaloue, all pay homage to the famous Jesuit priest Louis Bourdaloue (1632-1704).

Quantity		Ingredient
U.S.	**Metric**	*Sweet Shortcrust Pastry Dough (Pâte Sucrée)*
10 oz	300 g	Flour
5 oz	150 g	Powdered sugar
Pinch	Pinch	Salt
5 oz	150 g	Butter, softened (**en pommade**)
3 pcs	3 pcs	Egg yolks
½ fl oz	10 ml	Water
½ fl oz	10 ml	Vanilla
		Almond Cream (Crème d'Amandes)
2 oz	60 g	Butter
2 oz	60 g	Sugar, granulated
1 pc	1 pc	Egg
1 pc	1 pc	Vanilla
2 tsp	10 ml	Rum
2 oz	60 g	Almond powder
8 pcs	8 pcs	Poached pear halves in syrup
As needed	As needed	Sliced almonds, toasted (optional)
As needed	As needed	Apricot nappage
As needed	As needed	Powdered Sugar (optional)

TARTE BOURDALOUE
Bourdaloue Tart

Method

Make a Sweet Shortcrust Pastry Dough (Pâte Sucrée)

1. Sift the flour (**tamiser**) onto a clean work surface and gather it into a neat pile. Sift the powdered sugar in a separate pile in front of the flour. Sprinkle the salt over the sugar, then use a plastic scraper (**corne**) to make a large well (**fontaine**) in the center of the sugar mound.

Note

In the following steps, keep one hand clean and dry (for the plastic scraper) and use the other to stir in the wet ingredients.

2. Add the softened butter (**en pommade**) to the center of the sugar and work it in with your fingertips until it is soft. Using the **corne**, gradually add the powdered sugar from the edge of the well while simultaneously working it into the butter with your hands. Continue to mix the butter and sugar together (**crémer**) until they are fully incorporated and creamy.

3. Add the egg yolk and water to the butter and sugar and mix it in with your fingertips. The result will be slightly lumpy. Add the vanilla extract to the mixture and work it in with your fingers until it is completely incorporated.

4. With your clean hand, use the **corne** to gradually add some flour to the creamed ingredients while simultaneously mixing with your fingertips. Continue until the mixture resembles a thick paste. Using the **corne**, cut in the remaining flour until a loose dough is formed.

5. Using the heel of your palm, firmly smear the dough away from yourself to ensure that no lumps are left (**fraiser**). Scrape up the dough and repeat until a smooth dough forms. Form the dough into a smooth ball, wrap it in plastic wrap, and flatten it into a disk. Let it rest in the refrigerator for a minimum of 30 minutes (preferably overnight).

6. Lightly dust your work surface with flour (**fleurer**) and place the dough in the center. Roll out the pastry (**abaissser**), giving it quarter turns with each stroke of the rolling pin. Continue rolling and turning the dough until it is approximately ⅛ in. (3 mm) thick and 3 fingers wider than the tart mold. Prick the bottom of the dough (**piquer**) with the docker (**pique-vite**) or a fork. Then roll the dough onto a rolling pin and gently unroll onto the tart pan, centering it well. Lift the dough's edges and press it into the shape of the mold (**fonçage**)

Method

see pages 200–203 in Chapter 4 of *Pâtisserie and Baking Foundations*. Roll the rolling pin over the top of the tart to trim the excess dough. Gently pinch all around the top edge of the tart to create a decorative border (**chiqueter**). Place the lined tart pan in the refrigerator to rest for at least 30 minutes.

Almond Cream (*Crème d'Amandes*)

1. Cream (**crémer**) the butter and sugar together until light and fluffy. Add the egg and beat until well combined. Using a small knife, split the vanilla bean in half lengthwise and scrape out the seeds and whisk them into the mixture. Add the rum and finish by mixing in the almond powder. Reserve the crème d'amandes in a covered bowl in the refrigerator until ready to use.

Note

Vanilla bean can be replaced with 1–2 tsp of vanilla extract.

Assembly

1. Preheat the oven to 350°F (170°C).
2. Assemble the tart. Spread the almond cream evenly over the bottom of the lined tart mold. Then arrange the pears cut side down in the cream, with the wide end toward the outside. If needed, trim the pear for the middle.
3. Place in the oven and bake until the almond cream puffs up and turns a golden color, approximately 30 to 35 minutes.
4. Remove the tart from the oven and allow it to cool. Gently heat the nappage until it liquefies. With a pastry brush, lightly apply the nappage to the pears until even and shiny and sprinkle it with powdered sugar (and toasted almonds if desired) around the edges of the tart crust.

Note

It is important to wait until the tart has cooled before brushing with nappage. If the pears are still hot, the heat will melt and absorb the nappage and the pears will turn mushy.

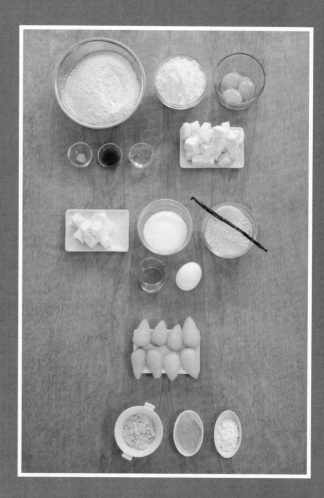

Learning Outcomes

Making a sweet shortcrust pastry dough (*pâte sucrée*)

Making almond cream (*crème d'amandes*)

To press out dough by hand (*fraiser*)

Lining a tart pan (*fonçage*)

Making an Italian meringue

Coloring meringue

Cooking sugar

Using a St. Honoré tip

Beating eggs and sugar to a ribbon stage (*blanchir*)

Crimping dough (*chiqueter*)

Equipment

Knives:
Paring knife (*couteau d'office*)

Tools:
Pastry brush, corne, mixing bowls, whisk, rubber spatula, zester, sieve, rolling pin, pastry docker (*pique-vite/pique pâte*), balloon whisk, pastry bag, St. Honoré tip, wire rack, serving dish or cake board

Pans:
Baking sheet, 8 in. tart mold, medium saucepan, small saucepan

Serving

6 persons

Cited in *Le Ménagier de Paris* (a 14th-century domestic guidebook), the general concept of the tart, or open pie in the United States, has undergone relatively few transformations through the centuries—aside from a multitude of fillings and the use of different types of pastry. While the technique for making meringue was still being developed up until the 17th century, versions of the lemon meringue pie go back to the Medieval period.

TARTE AUX CITRON MERINGUÉES
Lemon Meringue Tart

Method

1. Preheat the oven to 400°F (205°C).
2. Lightly grease an 8-in. tart mold with a removable bottom with softened butter using a pastry brush. Reserve the tart mold in the refrigerator.

Sweet Shortcrust Pastry Dough (Pâte Sucrée)

1. Sift the flour (**tamiser**) onto a clean work surface and gather it into a neat pile. Sift the powdered sugar in a separate pile in front of the flour. Sprinkle the salt and lemon zest over the sugar and, using a plastic scraper (**corne**), make a large well in the center of these ingredients.

Note

In the following steps, keep one hand clean and dry (for the plastic scraper) and use the other to stir in the wet ingredients.

2. Add the softened butter (**en pommade**) to the center of the sugar and work it with your fingertips until it is soft. Using the **corne**, gradually add the powdered sugar from the edge of the well while simultaneously working it into the butter with your hands. Continue to mix the butter and sugar (**crémer**) together until they are fully incorporated and creamy.
3. Add the egg yolks to the butter and sugar and mix it in with your fingertips. The result will be slightly lumpy. With your clean hand, use the **corne** to gradually add some flour to the creamed ingredients while simultaneously mixing with your fingertips. Continue until the mixture resembles a thick paste. Using the **corne**, cut in the remaining flour until a loose dough is formed.
4. Using the heel of your palm, firmly smear the dough away from yourself to ensure that no lumps of butter are left (**fraiser**). Scrape up the dough and repeat until a smooth dough forms. Form the dough into a smooth ball, wrap it in plastic, and flatten it into a disc. Let it rest in the refrigerator for a minimum of 30 minutes (preferably overnight).

Almond Cream (Crème D'Amandes)

1. Cream the butter and sugar (**crémer**) together until light and fluffy.
2. Beat in the egg until well combined.
3. Using a small knife, split the vanilla bean in half lengthwise, scrape out the seeds, and whisk them into the mixture.

Quantity		Ingredient
U.S.	**Metric**	**Sweet Shortcrust Pastry Dough (Pâte Sucrée)**
7 oz	200 g	Flour
3 ½ oz	100 g	Powdered sugar
Pinch	Pinch	Salt
1 pc	1 pc	Lemon, zest of
3 ½ oz	100 g	Butter, softened (**en pommade**)
3 pcs	3 pcs	Egg yolks
		Almond Cream (Crème d'Amandes)
2 oz	60 g	Butter
2 oz	60 g	Sugar, granulated
1 pc	1 pc	Egg
1 pc	1 pc	Vanilla bean
½ fl oz	10 ml	Rum
2 oz	60 g	Almond powder
		Lemon Filling (Appareil Citron)
3 pcs	3 pcs	Eggs
3 ½ oz	100 g	Sugar, granulated
2 pcs	2 pcs	Lemons, juice of
1 pc	1 pc	Lemon, zest of
3 ½ oz	100 g	Butter, diced
		Italian Meringue
4 fl oz	120 ml	Egg whites
8 oz	250 g	Sugar, granulated
2 ¾ fl oz	80 ml	Water
As needed	As needed	Sliced almonds

Method

4. Add the rum and finish by mixing in the almond powder.

5. Reserve the crème d'amandes in a covered bowl in the refrigerator until ready to use.

Lemon Filling (Appareil Citron)

1. Whisk the eggs and sugar together in a round-bottomed bowl until light in color (**blanchir**). Add the lemon juice and zest and stir them in. Place the bowl over a bain-marie and whisk until the mixture begins to thicken. Continue cooking until very hot and thick. Remove from the heat and stir in the butter until completely melted (**monter au beurre**). Transfer to a clean bowl and cover it in plastic wrap. Let the mixture cool to room temperature, then reserve it in the refrigerator until needed.

Lining the Tart Pan (Fonçage)

1. Lightly dust the marble with flour (**fleurer**) and place the dough in the center. Roll out the pastry (**abaisser**), giving it quarter turns with each stroke of the rolling pin. Continue rolling and turning until the dough is ⅛-in. (3-mm) thick and 3 fingers wider than the tart mold. Prick it (**piquer**) with the docker (**pique-vite**) or a fork, roll the dough onto the rolling pin, and gently lay it on the tart mold. Lift the dough's edges and press it into the shape of the mold (**foncer**). To form an even border around the inside edge of the mold, simultaneously apply side and top pressure to the dough (using a thumb and a finger). Repeat this process all the way around the mold, then pass the rolling pin over the top of the tart to trim the excess dough. Gently pinch all around the top edge of the tart to create a decorative border (**chiqueter**).

2. Place the lined mold in the refrigerator to rest for at least 20 minutes.

3. Add the almond cream to the cavity of the tart shell and spread it out in an even layer. Place the tart mold on a baking sheet and transfer it to the oven. As soon as it is in the oven, reduce the temperature to 370°F (185°C). Bake the tart shell until the crust turns a light golden color and the almond cream doesn't move when the tart is given a light shake and the surface is dry to the touch. If the pastry cooks too fast, reduce the oven temperature or cover the tart in foil. Rotate the tart about 10 minutes into cooking. Once cooked, remove the tart from the oven and set it on a rack to cool. Turn the oven up to 500°F (260°C).

Italian Meringue (Meringue Italienne)

1. In a large mixing bowl, whisk the egg whites until frothy using a balloon whisk. Set aside. Cook the sugar and water in a medium saucepan over medium-high heat to the soft-ball stage (**petit boulé**) [250°F (121°C)]. Meanwhile, whip the egg whites to soft peaks. As soon as the syrup reaches the soft-ball (**petit boulé**) stage, pour it into the egg whites in a thin stream, whisking constantly. Continue to whisk until the meringue is firm and has cooled to room temperature. Set aside.

Assembly (Montage)

1. Pour the chilled lemon mixture into the cooled tart shell and spread it out into an even layer. Transfer the Italian meringue to a pastry bag fitted with a large St. Honoré tip and pipe (**coucher**) a design onto the tart to completely cover the lemon cream. Dust the meringue with powdered sugar and sprinkle with sliced almonds. Transfer the tart to a baking sheet and place it in the oven just long enough for the almonds to lightly toast and the meringue to color on the edges. Remove the tart from the oven and set it on a wire rack to cool.

2. To unmold the tart, place the mold on an overturned saucepan (that is only slightly narrower than the mold) and slip the side of the mold down. Slide the tart off the metal disc onto a serving dish or cake board. Refrigerate before serving.

Learning Outcomes

Making a sweet dough
(*pâte sucrée*)
Making mousseline cream
(*crème mousseline*)
To press out dough by
hand (*fraiser*)
Lining a tart pan (*foncer*)
Pricking dough (*piquer*)
Crimping dough
(*chiqueter*)
Blind baking
(*cuisson à blanc*)
Glazing with jelly/
nappage (*abricoter*)

Equipment

Knives:
Paring knife (*couteau
d'office*)

Tools:
Pastry brush, corne, mixing
bowls, sieve, whisk, wooden
spatula, rolling pin, pastry
docker (*pique-vite / pique
pâte*), baking beads, pastry
bag, 0.4 in./10 mm plain
tip, pastry crimper, serving
dish or cake board

Pans:
Baking sheet, 8 in./20 cm
flan ring, small saucepan,
medium saucepan

Serving/Yield

8 persons

FYL...

Unlike the lemon meringue tart (Tart Citron Meringuée), this tart involves prebaking the sweet shortcrust pastry (pâte sucrée). To avoid shrinkage and movement of the pastry as it bakes, ceramic beads are placed in the cavity of the shell to weigh it down. This process is called "baking blind."

TARTES AUX FRAISES
Strawberry Tart

Quantity		Ingredient
U.S.	**Metric**	*Sweet Shortcrust Pastry Dough (Pâte Sucrée)*
7 oz	200 g	Flour
2 ½ oz	70 g	Powdered sugar
Pinch	Pinch	Salt
1 pc	1 pc	Lemon, zest of
3 ½ oz	100 g	Butter, diced (*en pommade*)
3 pcs	3 pcs	Egg yolks
		Mousseline Cream (Crème Mousseline)
8 fl oz	250 ml	Milk
1 pc	1 pc	Vanilla bean
2 oz	60 g	Sugar, granulated
2 pcs	2 pcs	Egg yolks
1 oz	30 g	Flour (or cornstarch)
½ fl oz	15 ml	Kirsch
4 oz	125 g	Butter, softened (*en pommade*)
10 oz	300 g	Strawberries, hulled, halved
1 oz	30 g	Apricot glaze (*nappage*)
¾ oz	20 g	Pistachio nuts, chopped (*concasser*)

Method

1. Preheat the oven to 400°F (205°C).
2. Using a pastry brush, lightly grease an 8-in. (20-cm) flan ring and a baking sheet with softened (*en pommade*) butter and reserve them in the refrigerator.

Sweet Shortcrust Pastry (Pâte Sucrée)

1. Sift the flour (*tamiser*) onto a clean work surface and gather it into a neat pile. Sift the powdered sugar in a separate pile in front of the flour. Sprinkle the salt and lemon zest over the powdered sugar and, using a plastic scraper (*corne*), make a large well in the center of these ingredients.

Note

In the following steps, keep one hand clean and dry (for the plastic scraper) and use the other to stir in the wet ingredients.

2. Add the softened butter (*en pommade*) to the center of the sugar and work it with your fingertips until it is soft. Using the *corne*, gradually add the powdered sugar from the edge of the well while simultaneously working it into the butter with your hands. Continue to mix the butter and sugar (*crémer*) together until they are fully incorporated and creamy.
3. Add the egg yolks to the butter and sugar and mix it in with your fingertips. The result will be slightly lumpy. With your clean hand, use the *corne* to gradually add some flour to the creamed ingredients while simultaneously mixing with your fingertips. Continue until the mixture resembles a thick paste. Using the *corne*, cut in the remaining flour until a loose dough is formed.
4. Using the heel of your palm, firmly smear the dough away from yourself to ensure that no lumps are left (*fraiser*). Scrape up the dough and repeat until a smooth dough forms. Form the dough into a smooth ball, wrap it in plastic, and flatten it into a disc. Let it rest in the refrigerator for a minimum of 30 minutes (preferably overnight).

Mousseline Cream (Crème Mousseline)

1. Line a small serving tray or platter with plastic wrap. Pour the milk into a medium saucepan. Split the vanilla bean in half lengthwise and scrape out the seeds. Stir the seeds into the milk and bring it to a boil over medium-high heat. Add about one-quarter of the sugar to the milk, and the kirsch, stirring to dissolve it.

2. Meanwhile, place the egg yolks in a small mixing bowl and add the remaining sugar. Whisk the sugar into the eggs until it completely dissolves and the yolks lighten in color (***blanchir***). Add the cornstarch or flour to the yolks and stir until well combined.

3. When the milk begins to come to a boil, remove it from the heat and pour one-third of it into the egg yolks. Stir well to temper the yolks, then whisk the tempered mixture into the remaining hot milk. Place back onto the heat and cook until the pastry cream (crème pâtissière) begins to bubble. Continue whisking (being sure to press the whisk around the corners of the pan) and allow to cook for 1 minute in order to cook the starch. The pastry cream (crème pâtissière) will become very thick. Transfer the crème to a clean bowl and allow to cool until warm. While the pastry cream (crème pâtissière) is cooling, soften the butter. Beat in the softened butter to the warm crème.

Note

The crème will now be referred to as crème mousseline.

4. Transfer the mousseline cream (crème mousseline) to the plastic-lined serving tray. Pat (***tamponner***) the surface with a piece of cold butter held on the end of a fork to create a protective film. Completely cover with a second piece of plastic wrap, pressing out any air bubbles. Let the mousseline cream (crème mousseline) cool to room temperature before refrigerating it.

Lining the Tart Pan (Fonçage)

1. Place the flan ring on the baking sheet.

2. Lightly dust the marble with flour (***fleurer***) and place the dough in the center. Roll out the pastry (***abaisser***), giving it quarter turns with each stroke of the rolling pin. Continue rolling and turning until the dough is $\frac{1}{8}$-in. (3-mm) thick and 3 fingers wider than the flan ring. Prick it (***piquer***) with the docker (***pique-vite***) or a fork, roll the dough onto the rolling pin, and gently lay it on the flan ring. Lift the dough's edges and press it into the shape of the ring (***foncer***). To form an even border around the inside edge of the ring, simultaneously apply side and top pressure to the dough (using a thumb and a finger). Repeat this process all the way around the ring, then pass the rolling pin over the top of the tart to trim the excess dough. Gently pinch all around the top edge of the tart with a pastry crimper to create a decorative border (***chiqueter***).

3. Place the lined mold in the refrigerator to rest for at least 20 minutes.

4. Cut a circle of parchment paper larger than the tart shell. Place it in the cavity and fill it with baking beads. Transfer the tart to the oven. As soon as the door is closed, reduce the temperature to 370°F (185°C). Bake the tart shell until the crust turns a light golden color, rotating it 10 minutes into baking. When the crust around the edge begins to color, remove the tart from the oven, take out the beads and paper, and return it to the oven to obtain an even color. When the entire shell is golden (***blond***), remove it from the oven and transfer it to a wire rack to cool completely. Once cooled, carefully remove the ring and place the baked tart shell on a cake board or serving plate.

Assembly (Montage)

1. Remove the mousseline cream (crème mousseline) from the refrigerator and whisk it until smooth and elastic. Whisk in the rest of the butter until completely incorporated, then transfer the mousseline cream (crème mousseline) to a pastry bag fitted with a 0.4-in./10-mm plain tip. Pipe (***coucher***) a tight spiral of mousseline cream (crème mousseline) into the tart shell to completely cover the bottom. Arrange the strawberry halves on top, pointing upward. Melt the apricot glaze over low heat in a small saucepan until it is completely liquid and apply it to the strawberries using a pastry brush. Sprinkle the tart with pistachio nuts and refrigerate it before serving.

Learning Outcomes

Making a sweet dough
(*pâte sucrée*)
Making a compote
(*compoter*)
Lining a tart pan (*foncer*)
Glazing (*napper*)
Score/crimping the dough
(*chiqueter*)
Pricking the dough (*piquer*)

Equipment

Knives:
Paring knife (*couteau d'office*), chef knife (*couteau chef*), vegetable peeler (*économe*)

Tools:
Apple corer, corne, pastry brush, rolling pin, mixing bowls, rubber spatula, pastry docker (*pique-vite/pique pâte*), wooden spatula, wire rack, serving dish or cake board

Pans:
8 in. (20 cm) tart mold, medium saucepan, small saucepan

Serving/Yield

8–10 people

FYI...

Apple tarts have provided warmth and comfort on cold winter nights from the Medieval period to the modern era. In the United States, apple pie (essentially a lidded Apple tart) is so significant that it is seen as a national symbol, representing hardiness and strong moral fiber. There are many excellent recipe variations of tarte aux pommes. This particular recipe distinguishes itself, among other ways, with the technique of scraping whole vanilla bean seeds directly from the pod into the compote.

64

TARTE AUX POMMES
Apple Tart

Method

1. Preheat the oven to 400°F (205°C).
2. Using a pastry brush dipped in softened butter, lightly grease a 10-in. (25-cm) tart mold with a removable bottom and reserve it in the refrigerator.

Make a Sweet Shortcrust Pastry Dough (Pâte Sucrée)

1. Sift the flour (*tamiser*) onto a clean work surface and gather it into a neat pile. Sift the powdered sugar in a separate pile in front of the flour. Sprinkle the salt and lemon zest over the sugar and, using a plastic scraper (*corne*), make a large well in the center of these ingredients.

Note

In the following steps, keep one hand clean and dry (for the plastic scraper) and use the other to stir in the wet ingredients.

2. Add the butter to the center of the sugar and work it with your fingertips until it is soft. Using the *corne*, gradually add the powdered sugar from the edge of the well while simultaneously working it into the butter with your hands. Continue to mix the butter and sugar together until they are fully incorporated and creamy (*crémer*).
3. Add the egg yolks to the butter and sugar and mix it in with your fingertips. The result will be slightly lumpy. With your clean hand, use the *corne* to gradually add some flour to the creamed ingredients while simultaneously mixing with your fingertips. Continue until the mixture resembles a thick paste. Using the *corne*, cut in the remaining flour until a loose dough is formed.
4. With the heel of your palm, firmly smear the dough away from yourself to ensure that no lumps of butter are left (*fraiser*). Scrape up the dough and repeat until a smooth dough forms. Form the dough into a smooth ball, wrap it in plastic, and flatten it into a disc. Let it rest in the refrigerator for a minimum of 30 minutes (preferably overnight).

Apple Compote (Compote de Pommes)

1. Cook the sugar in a large shallow pan over medium-high heat until it turns a light caramel color. Slice the vanilla bean in half lengthwise and use the tip of a knife to scrape out the seeds. Deglaze with the butter and add the apples (which were coated in lemon juice to prevent discoloring), the vanilla seeds and the whole pod. Reduce the

Quantity		Ingredient
U.S.	Metric	**Sweet Shortcrust Pastry Dough (Pâte Sucrée)**
7 oz	200 g	Flour
2 ½ oz	70 g	Powdered sugar
Pinch	Pinch	Salt
1 pc	1 pc	Lemon, zest of
3 ½ oz	100 g	Butter, diced
		Apple Compote (Compote de Pommes)
3 pcs	3 pcs	Egg yolks
3 pcs	3 pcs	Apples, peeled, cored, and sliced and rubbed with lemon juice
1 pc	1 pc	Vanilla bean
2 oz	60 g	Sugar, granulated
1 ¼ oz	40 g	Butter
3 pcs	3 pcs	Apples, peeled, cored, thinly sliced (*émincer*)
As needed	As needed	Apricot glaze (*nappage*), heated

Method

temperature and let the mixture stew (***compoter***) until the apples are cooked through, but retain some texture. Transfer the compote to a clean bowl and let it cool to room temperature before covering it in plastic wrap and transferring it to the refrigerator.

Lining the Tart Pan (Fonçage) (see pages 200–205 in Pâtisserie Foundations)

1. Lightly dust the marble with flour (***fleurer***) and place the dough in the center. Roll out the pastry (***abaisser***), giving it quarter turns as you roll. Continue rolling and turning until the dough is ⅛-in. (3-mm) thick and 3 fingers wider than the tart mold. Prick it (***piquer***) with the docker (***pique-vite***) or a fork, roll the dough onto the rolling pin, and gently lay it on the tart mold. Lift the dough's edges and press it into the shape of the mold (***foncer***). To form an even border around the inside edge of the mold, simultaneously apply side and top pressure to the dough (*using a thumb and a finger*). Repeat this process all the way around the mold, then pass the rolling pin over the top of the tart to trim the excess dough. Gently pinch all around the top edge of the tart to create a decorative border (***chiqueter***).
2. Place the lined mold in the refrigerator to rest for at least 20 minutes.

Blind Bake (Cuire à Blanc)

1. Cut a circle of parchment paper larger than the tart shell, place it in the cavity and fill it with baking beads. Transfer the tart to the oven. As soon as the door is closed, reduce the temperature to 370°F (185°C). Bake the tart shell until the dough is cooked but not colored, rotating it 10 minutes into cooking. Remove the tart from the oven, take out the beads and paper, and transfer it to a wire rack to cool.

Assembly (Montage)

1. Remove the vanilla pod, then spread the compote into an even layer over the bottom of the tart shell. Arrange the sliced apples in concentric circles over the compote.
2. Return the tart to the oven and bake it until the apples begin to color (*25 minutes*). Remove the tart from the oven and place it on a wire rack to cool. Melt the apricot glaze (***nappage***) over low heat in a small saucepan until it is completely liquid, being careful not to overheat. Apply it to the top of the cooled apples using a pastry brush.
3. To unmold the tart, place the mold on an overturned saucepan (that is only slightly narrower than the mold) and slip the side of the mold down. Slide the tart off the metal disc onto a serving dish or cake board.

Note

It is important to wait until the tart has cooled before brushing with nappage. If the apples are still hot, the heat will absorb the nappage making the apples mushy.

Learning Outcomes

Cooking rice
Cooking custard
Making a yeast crust
Making a meringue

Equipment

Tools:
Whisk, large plastic spatula,
mixing bowls, sieve

Pans:
Ring mold, heavy baking
sheet, heavy bottom sauce
pan

Serving/Yield

One 2 ½ lb / 1 ¼ kg g tart,
8–10 servings

FYI...

Different towns in the Belgian province of Liège claim to be the originators of the "true" tart au riz. Verviers, the town considered by many to be the birthplace of the tart, takes the notion of authenticity very much to heart; so much so that every two years a contest is held in which pastry chefs compete to be certified to bake and sell the official tart au riz. Judging criteria include the exactness of the tarts' dimensions as well as more subtle points such as the quality of the milk used and the overall consistency and flavor of the preparation. A fairly humble tart at first glance, the competitiveness surrounding tart au riz is an indication of the perfection achievable through simplicity.

TARTE AU RIZ
Rice Tart

Quantity		Ingredient
U.S.	**Metric**	*Yeast Crust*
2 ½ fl oz	75 ml	Milk or beer
½ oz	15 g	Fresh yeast
8 oz	250 g	Flour
		Rice Custard
½ fl oz	15 ml	Oil
2 pcs	2 pcs	Egg yolks
Pinch	Pinch	Salt
2 ½ oz	75 g	Butter, softened
2 ¾ oz	80 g	Rice
1 pint	500 ml	Milk
2 ½ oz	75 g	Sugar
2 pcs	2 pcs	Egg yolks
		French Meringue
3 pcs	3 pcs	Egg whites
1 oz	30 g	Sugar, granulated
¼ fl oz	5 ml	Vanilla (optional)

Method

1. Gently warm the milk or beer [*max 90°F (32°C)*]. Place it in a bowl and add the yeast and a pinch of sugar (from 75 g portion) in order to dissolve it. Add just enough flour (from the 8-oz/250-g portion) to make a smooth paste. Then stir in the oil, egg yolks, and salt, mixing well. Add the butter, then gradually incorporate the rest of the flour until a dough forms. Knead the dough until it becomes smooth and is no longer sticky, adding more flour as needed. Place the dough into a clean bowl, cover it with plastic wrap and let it rise until doubled in volume. This should take approximately 1 hour.

2. Rinse the rice to remove the excess starch. Place the rinsed rice in a heavy-bottomed saucepan, add the milk, and bring to a low boil over medium heat, stirring regularly. Once the milk comes to a boil, add the sugar and cook the rice until tender. Take the saucepan off of the heat and set aside. In a clean bowl, whisk the egg yolks together until blended and then temper them by adding a little of the hot milk/rice mixture from the saucepan to the mix. Stir the tempered yolks back into the hot milk/rice mixture, place the saucepan back over low heat, and continue stirring until the mixture thickens. Once the desired consistency has been achieved, remove from heat and allow to cool.

3. Preheat the oven to 350°F (175°C).

4. Lightly dust your work surface with flour (*fleurer*) and place the dough in the center. Punch down the dough and then, using your rolling pin, roll out the dough (*abaissser*), giving it quarter turns with each stroke of the rolling pin. Continue rolling and turning the dough until it is approximately ½-in. (1-cm) thick. Then lightly grease a ring mold with butter and line it with the round of dough.

5. Whisk the egg whites to soft peaks (***monter les blancs***). Then incorporate the sugar and continue whisking until the combination becomes glossy. Fold the mounted egg whites into the rice mixture and then immediately transfer the combination into the lined mold. Place the tart in the oven and bake it until the dough is golden, approximately 35 to 40 minutes. Remove the tart from the oven and allow it to cool before removing it from the ring. Then carefully transfer it to a serving plate.

Gâteaux
(Cakes)

Bûche de Noël
—Yule log

Cake Citron
—Lemon cake

Cake aux fruits
—Fruit cake

Croquembouche
—Croquembouche

Le fraisier
—Strawberry cake

Galette des rois
—Epiphany cake

Gâteau diplomate
—Diplomat cake

Gâteau Lorrain
—Lorraine cake

Gâteau marbré
—Marble cake

Gâteau Paris-Brest
—Paris-Brest cake

Gâteau St. Honoré
—Cream puff cake
with caramel and
chiboust cream

Génoise confiture
—Jam-filled sponge
cake

Millefeuille
—Napoleon

Moka
—Coffee butter cream
sponge cake

Pain de Gênes
—Genoese bread

Pavé du roy
—King's cobblestones
cake

Pithiviers
—Puff pastry filled
with almond cream

Pyramide noisettes
—pyramid cake

Roulé à l'orange
—Orange roulade

Savarin aux fruits
et à la crème
—Savarin cake with
fruit

Succès
—Hazelnut
buttercream meringue
cake

Learning Outcomes

Making ladyfinger sponge cake (*biscuit à la cuillère*)

Imbibing with syrup (*imbiber*)

Making a ganache

Making a buttercream (*crème au beurre*)

Making a Swiss meringue

Using almond paste

Making a pâte à bombe

Equipment

Knives:
N/A

Tools:
Mixing bowls, whisk, sieve, rubber and wooden spatula, sheet pan, pastry brush, piping bag, medium and small round tip, wire rack, parchment paper

Pans:
Bûche mold, bain-marie, small saucepan

Serving/Yield

Yield: One
4 pound/2.1 kilogram
log cake

The Yule log cake is a traditional Christmas dessert for many French-speaking people. The cake is decorated to look like a wooden log—a custom that stems from the European tradition of the lighting of the Yule log. This tradition traces its roots to the pagan ritual of burning a huge log in a bonfire to honor the winter solstice. As Christmas came to replace winter solstice celebrations, the Yule log was thrown on the fire on Christmas Eve in order to cook the midnight supper. The ashes from that log were saved and believed to hold medicinal powers.

BÛCHE DE NOËL
Yule Log

Quantity		Ingredient
		Chocolate Ladyfinger Sponge (Biscuit à la Cuillère au Chocolat)
U.S.	**Metric**	
3 pcs	3 pcs	Egg yolks
2 ½ oz	70 g	Sugar, granulated
3 pcs	3 pcs	Egg whites
2 ½ oz	70 g	Flour
½ oz	15 g	Cocoa powder
		Ganache
8 oz	250 g	Dark chocolate
8 fl oz	250 ml	Cream
		Coffee-Rum Syrup
2 oz	60 g	Sugar, granulated
2 fl oz	60 ml	Water
¼ oz	5 g	Instant coffee
2 fl oz	60 ml	Rum
		Chocolate Buttercream Icing (Crème au Beurre au Chocolat)
5 oz	150 g	Sugar, granulated
2 fl oz	60 ml	Water
6 pcs	6 pcs	Egg yolks
1 oz	30 g	Sugar, granulated
13 oz	360 g	Butter
1 ¾ oz	50 g	Unsweetened chocolate, melted
		Swiss Meringue
4 pcs	4 pcs	Egg whites
8 oz	250 g	Sugar, granulated
		Decoration
As needed	As needed	Almond paste
As needed	As needed	Meringue mushrooms
As needed	As needed	Powdered sugar
As needed	As needed	Cocoa

Method

Preheat the oven to 350°F (180°C).
Line a baking sheet with parchment paper (*chemiser*).

Prepare the Chocolate Ladyfinger Sponge Cake (Biscuit à la Cuillère au Chocolat)

1. Sift (*tamiser*) together the flour and cocoa. Set aside.
2. In a large bowl, whisk the egg yolks and sugar together (*blanchir*) until light in color and ribbons form when the whisk is lifted.
3. Beat the egg whites to medium peaks (*monter les blancs*). Stir some of the whites into the egg yolks, then fold in the remaining whites using a rubber spatula. Before the whites are completely incorporated, add the flour/cocoa mixture, folding until just incorporated.
4. Spread the batter onto the prepared baking sheet. Place it in the oven and bake until the cake feels dry to the touch, about 8 to 10 minutes. Remove the ladyfinger sponge (biscuit à la cuillère) from the oven and gently transfer it (not removing the parchment paper) to a wire rack to cool.

Make the Ganache

1. Chop the chocolate into small pieces and place them into a large bowl. Bring the cream to a boil and pour it immediately over the chocolate.
2. Allow the mixture to sit 1 to 2 minutes then stir it gently with a wooden spatula.

Make the Syrup

1. Place the sugar (5 oz/150 g) and water in a small saucepan and stir until combined. Bring to a boil.
2. Skim off any impurities that might come to the surface with the spoon; boil until the sugar has completely dissolved while brushing down the sides of the pan with a wet pastry brush. Remove from the heat, stir in the instant coffee and allow to cool. Once cooled, add the rum.

Make the Chocolate Buttercream Icing (Crème au Beurre au Chocolat)

1. Prepare a small bowl with cold water, a large spoon, and a clean pastry brush.
2. Prepare a large bowl with cold water and ice.
3. Place the sugar (5 oz/150 g) and water in a small saucepan and stir to combine. Bring to a boil.
4. Skim off any impurities that might come to the surface with the spoon, while brushing the sides of the pan with the wet pastry brush. This will prevent the syrup from re-crystallizing.
5. Blanch the egg yolks with the second quantity of sugar (1 oz/30 g) until light in color and a ribbon forms when the whisk is lifted.

Method

6. Cook the syrup to the soft-ball stage. Immediately remove from the heat and stop the cooking by dipping the bottom of the pan into the ice bath.

7. While whisking, gradually incorporate the hot syrup into the egg yolks, being careful not to pour onto the whisk. Once incorporated, continue whisking until the mixture (*pâte à bombe*) has cooled and is just warm to the touch. Whisk the butter in pieces into the mixture. Continue whisking until smooth and the mixture has lightened in color. Incorporate the melted unsweetened chocolate. Set aside.

Make the Swiss Meringue

1. Whisk the egg whites and sugar in a bowl set in a bain-marie. Continue whisking until the mixture is thick and feels hot to the touch. Remove from the heat and continue whisking until cooled. Transfer to a piping bag fitted with a plain round tip.

Decorative Mushrooms

1. Pipe (*coucher*) the bases of the mushrooms: Holding the bag vertically, pipe rounds onto a parchment-lined or silicone mat-lined baking sheet. Stop the pressure on the bag and gently pull upward to form a point. Pipe half of the mixture in this manner.

2. Pipe the heads of the mushrooms: Holding the bag at a slight angle to the baking sheet, pipe out rounds. Stop the pressure, then quickly move the tip in a circular motion, followed by an upward motion, to leave a flat round. Use a moistened fingertip to flatten any points.

3. Bake the meringue mushrooms at 200°F (100°C) for 1 hour.

4. Once finished, assemble the mushrooms by pressing the pointed ends of the stems into the bottoms of the caps.

Assembly

1. Remove the parchment from the ladyfinger sponge (biscuit à la cuillière) and then trim the edges.

2. Cut a piece of biscuit large enough to line the sides of the buche mold. Place the biscuit into the mold, with the top side over the edges. Brush it with the syrup. Cover the bottom with the ganache, then cut a strip of the biscuit for the middle.

3. Brush the strip with the syrup and finish filling the mold with the remaining ganache. Cut another strip of the biscuit for the bottom, imbibe with the syrup, and place on top of the ganache. Press down firmly.

4. Unmold the buche and mask with the buttercream. Using the tines of a fork, run it lengthwise to create a surface resembling the bark of a tree. Decorate with the meringue mushrooms and almond paste decorations.

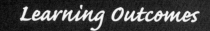

Learning Outcomes

Creaming method

Equipment

Knives:
Paring knife
(*couteau d'office*)

Tools:
Mixing bowls, grater, sieve,
wooden spatula, baking
sheet, pastry brush, wire
rack

Pans:
1 ¾ lb / 800 g cake mold

Serving/ Yield

One 1 ¾ pound/800 gram
cake, 8–10 servings

FYI...

When a preparation calls for the use of lemons, remember a few simple rules. Always choose bright yellow, fully ripened fruit without bruises or pock marks. The lemons should seem heavy for their size, have a bit of an oily residue on the skin, and have a strong, aromatic lemon scent. When incorporating the zest (ground lemon rind), wash the skin thoroughly and only shave the exterior of the skin, leaving the white interior skin (which tends to be overly bitter) intact. When squeezing the juice from the lemon, always remember to remove the seeds beforehand. These steps will ensure a delicious, tangy lemon flavor that livens up any dish.

CAKE CITRON
Lemon Cake

Quantity		Ingredient
U.S.	**Metric**	*Cake*
10 oz	300 g	Flour
½ oz	10 g	Baking powder
4 ¼ oz	125 g	Butter
6 oz	180 g	Sugar
1 pc	1 pc	Lemon zest
3 pcs	3 pcs	Eggs
As needed	As needed	Vanilla or rum
		Sugar Glaze (Glace à l'Eau)
As needed	As needed	Powdered sugar
As needed	As needed	Water or Lemon juice

Method

Preheat the oven to 340°F (170°C).

1. Butter and flour the cake mold (**chemiser**).
2. Sift (**tamiser**) together the flour and baking powder.
3. In a large bowl, cream (**crémer**) together the butter and sugar until they are well combined. Add the eggs one at a time, mixing well after each addition. Mix in the grated lemon zest and vanilla.
4. Add the flour to the egg mixture and stir it until the flour is just incorporated.
5. Fill the prepared mold and place it into the preheated oven.

Make the Glace à l'Eau

1. Mix enough water into the powdered sugar as is required to make a thin glaze. Set aside.
2. Bake the cake until a knife inserted in the center comes out clean, around 30 minutes. Remove the cake from the oven and gently unmold it onto a wire rack set over a baking sheet or tray.
3. While still hot, coat the cake with the glace à l'eau and leave it to finish cooling completely.

Learning Outcomes

Creaming method
Glazing with jelly
(*abricoter*)

Equipment

Knives:
Paring knife
(*couteau d'office*)

Tools:
Mixing bowls, parchment
paper, sieve, whisk, pastry
brush

Pans:
Two 1-pound cake molds

Serving/Yield

Two 1 pound/500 gram
fruit cakes, 6 to 8 servings
each

The fruit cake's legendary ability to stay well preserved for long periods of time is intricately tied to the history behind its creation. The heavy composition of sugar (and often alcohol) which are added to the fruits forming the base ingredient of this cake, also act as an extremely effective method of preservation. For this reason, the fruit cake has been utilized for long expeditions for centuries. The earliest form of fruit cake can be traced back to the ancient Romans, who used the cakes to feed legions of centurions on their long marches to war. The fruit cake was also a staple supply for crusading knights during their long voyages throughout the Middle Ages. Over time, as the availability of sugar increased and different varieties of fruit and alcohol became more plentiful, the fruit cakes of Europe became increasingly rich and decadent. During the Victorian period, they were deemed "sinfully rich" and were outlawed in countries throughout Europe. Thankfully, the law was soon repealed because of the enormous popularity of the cake. Today, the fruit cake is generally considered a Christmas dessert. The cake's density and remarkable longevity have led to it becoming the butt of many a comedian's joke. Johnny Carson once famously quipped: "The worst gift is fruit cake. There's only one fruit cake in the entire world and people keep sending it to each other." Despite the fun had at this cake's expense, it remains tremendously popular today, and if prepared correctly, it makes a wonderful, traditional holiday dessert.

Quantity		Ingredient
U.S.	Metric	Cake
3 ¼ oz	100 g	Raisins
3 ¼ oz	100 g	Candied fruit, chopped
1 ¾ fl oz	50 ml	Rum
7 ¾ oz	225 g	Flour
¼ oz	5 g	Baking powder
5 ¼ oz	160 g	Butter
5 ¼ oz	160 g	Powdered sugar
4 pcs	4 pcs	Eggs
As needed	As needed	Vanilla
		Finishing
As needed	As needed	Sliced almonds
As needed	As needed	Apricot nappage

CAKE AUX FRUITS
Fruit Cake

Method

Preheat the oven to 400°F (200°C).

To Make the Fruit Cake

1. Soak the raisins and candied fruit in the rum overnight. This is done well ahead of time so the fruit has a chance to soften.
2. Line the cake molds with butter and parchment paper.
3. Sift (*tamiser*) together the flour and baking powder.
4. Cream (*crémer*) the butter and sugar together until fully incorporated and the butter lightens in color. Gradually add the eggs and the vanilla.
5. Drain the fruit and raisins over a bowl to save the rum for later use, then toss them into the flour. Add the fruit/flour to the egg mixture and stir until the flour is just incorporated.
6. While being careful not to get any batter on the overhanging edges of the paper, fill the molds and push the batter into the corners. Sprinkle the tops with almonds and place the molds in the preheated oven for 4 to 5 minutes. Dip a small knife in butter or water, then make an incision down the length of the cakes.
7. Reduce the heat to 320°F (160°C) and continue baking for approximately 35 minutes, until a knife tip inserted in the middle comes out clean.

Note

The incision does not need to be too deep, as its purpose is to break the top skin. This should be done with one quick stroke.

8. Once the cakes are cooked, remove them from the oven and unmold immediately. While the cakes are still hot, pour the fruit soaking in rum saved from earlier over the tops. Allow to cool on a wire rack.
9. Once the cake has cooled, in a small saucepan heat the apricot nappage until just liquid and the brush the tops. If desired, decorate with whole candied fruit such as cherries and angelicas. Unmold and remove the parchment paper before cutting.

Learning Outcomes

Making choux pastry
(*pâte à choux*)
Making pastry cream
(*crème pâtissière*)
Making caramel
Making royal icing
Making nougatine
Piping (*coucher*)
Using a cornet

Equipment

Knives:
Chef's knife (*couteau chef*),
small palette knife (*spatule*)

Tools:
Mixing bowls, sieve, whisk,
piping bag, medium round
tip, small round tip, wire rack,
plastic and wooden spatula,
rolling pin (or nougatine
roller), fork, pastry brushes,
nougatine cutter

Pans:
Small and medium
saucepans, heavy baking
sheets, moule à manqué

Serving/Yield

One large cake composed
of approximately
150 choux balls

HISTORY

The croquembouche is one of the most spectacular and iconic preparations in all of the culinary arts. Literally translated to "crunch in mouth," this dazzling dessert has been served as a traditional wedding or baptismal cake in France for centuries. The cake consists of a conical tower of profiteroles standing on a base made of nougatine, held together by caramel and royal icing and ornately adorned with decorations, nuts, and chocolate. This type of cake is an example of a "pièce montée," a style of pâtisserie that builds grandiose towers and designs using individual candies or pastries stuck together in highly complex and beautiful ways. This method of preparation was developed by the father of haute cuisine, Antoine Carême, in the 18th century. It is not surprising that Carême was a student of architecture and once said that "architecture was the most noble of the arts and that pastry was the highest form of architecture."

Quantity		Ingredient
U.S.	Metric	Choux Pastry (Pâte à Choux)
4 fl oz	125 mL	Water
4 fl oz	125 mL	Milk
¼ oz	4 g	Salt
¼ oz	4 g	Sugar, granulated
3 ½ oz	100 g	Butter
5 ½ oz	165 g	Flour
5–6 pcs	5–6 pcs	Eggs
		Pastry Cream (Crème Pâtissière)
1 pint	500 mL	Milk
3 ½ oz	100 g	Sugar, granulated
4 pcs	4 pcs	Egg yolks
1 ½ oz	40 g	Cornstarch
dash	dash	Flavor of choice
		Caramel
1 lb	500 g	Sugar, granulated
7 fl oz	200 mL	Water
5 fl oz	150 mL	Glucose
		Nougatine
8 ½ fl oz	250 mL	Glucose
8 ½ oz	250 g	Sugar, granulated
10 oz	300 g	Almonds, sliced or chopped
		Royal Icing
2 pcs	2 pcs	Egg whites
8 ½ oz	250 g	Powdered sugar
As needed	As needed	Lemon juice
		Finishing
As needed	As needed	Sugared almonds or confetti
As needed	As needed	Pastillage leaves

CROQUEMBOUCHE
Croquembouche

Method

Preheat the oven to 425°F (220°C). Lightly grease two heavy baking sheets.

Make a Choux Pastry (Pâte à Choux)

1. Sift (**tamiser**) the flour.
2. Place the butter, sugar, salt, milk, and water into a saucepan. Bring the combination to a boil, stirring until all of the salt and sugar are dissolved and the butter is melted. Remove the pan from the heat and add all of the flour at once. Stir the mixture well with a wooden spatula. Place the pan back onto the heat and continue to stir until a clean ball of dough forms and comes cleanly off the sides and bottom of the pan. Transfer the hot dough to a bowl and spread it out to the sides of the bowl to cool slightly.
3. Add the eggs, one at a time, beating well after each addition. After three of the eggs have been incorporated, check the consistency by lifting some of the dough. It should stretch before breaking. If the dough is still too stiff, beat the last egg and add just enough of it until the dough forms a "V" shape that falls when the spatula is lifted.
4. Transfer the dough into a piping bag fitted with a medium round tip. Pipe 1-in. (2.5-cm) diameter balls onto a baking sheet. Brush with the egg wash and even out the tops using a fork. Bake until puffed up and evenly colored, about 25 minutes. Transfer to a wire rack to cool.

Make the Pastry Cream (Crème Pâtissière)

1. Pour the milk into a medium saucepan and bring to a boil over medium-high heat. Add about one-quarter of the sugar to the milk and stir it in to dissolve it.
2. Meanwhile, place the egg yolks in a small mixing bowl and add the remaining sugar. Whisk the sugar into the eggs until it completely dissolves and the yolks lighten in color (**blanchir**). Add the flour and the cornstarch to the yolks and stir until well combined. When the milk begins to come to a boil, remove it from the stove and pour one-third of it into the egg yolks. Stir well to temper the yolks, then whisk the tempered mixture into the remaining hot milk. Place back onto the heat and cook until the crème pâtissière begins to bubble. Continue whisking (being sure to press the whisk around the corners of the pan) and allow to cook

Method

for about 1 minute in order to cook the starch. The pastry cream (crème pâtissière) will become very thick at this point. Allow to cool and then place in the refrigerator to chill.

Make the Nougatine

1. Lightly oil a baking sheet and oil the outside of an 8-in. (20-cm) cake pan (*moule à manqué*).

Make the Caramel

2. Cook the sugar and glucose until it turns a medium caramel color (330°F/165°C). Remove from the heat and quickly stir in the almonds. Transfer the nougatine onto the oiled baking sheet and roll it out to a thickness of about ⅛ in. (3 mm) with a rolling pin. You will need to work quickly—the caramel will begin to harden immediately. While still soft, drape the rolled-out nougatine over the oiled cake pan and quickly press to shape around its form. Trim with a pair of scissors, and quickly lay the scraps flat on a warm baking sheet.

3. Using nougatine cutters, cut a round of nougatine, around 3 in. (7.5 cm) in diameter and set aside. With the remaining nougatine, cut out the triangles, or wolves' teeth (*dents de loups*), using a chef's knife. The nougatine should still be warm, otherwise it will break into pieces.

Make a Royal Icing

1. Sift (*tamiser*) the powdered sugar into a bowl and add the egg whites. Whisk until a thick paste forms. Continue working until the mixture softens and begins to increase in volume. If it becomes too stiff, add a little more of the egg whites to soften. Once doubled in volume, cover with a wet cloth to prevent a crust from forming.

Make a Caramel

1. Prepare a bowl of cold water with a spoon and pastry brush.
2. Prepare a large bowl of cold water with ice in it.
3. Bring the sugar, glucose, and water to a boil over high heat. When it comes a boil, skim off any foam from the surface with a spoon and brush the sides down with water. Once the sugar boils clear, leave to cook until it begins to color. When it becomes a nice, even amber color, remove it from the heat and dip the bottom of the pan in the ice bath to stop the cooking process. Place the pan on a folded towel.

Method

Assembly

1. Carefully remove the nougatine from the mold and place it on a cake board or serving platter. Transfer some of the royal icing to a pastry bag fitted with a medium star tip, and pipe (**coucher**) a border along the bottom of the nougatine base.

2. Prepare a baking sheet with a silicone baking mat. Using the tip of a paring knife, or a small pastry tip, make a hole around ⅙-in. (4–5 mm) wide in the bottom of each of the choux balls.

3. Once the pastry cream (crème pâtissière) is cold, place in a bowl and whisk until smooth. Transfer to a pastry bag fitted with a small round tip. Insert the tip into the hole of the choux balls and gently fill the choux balls with the cream.

4. Carefully dip the tops of the filled choux balls in the caramel and place caramel-side down onto the lined baking sheet. Be very careful not to touch the caramel or allow it to drip onto your fingers, as this will cause serious burns. Once the filled balls are finished, set aside for the caramel to cool.

5. Gently warm the caramel if it has begun to harden. Dip the side of a choux ball into the caramel, and then alternate between coating the choux balls in coarse sugar and almonds. Affix the balls to the edge of the base with the caramel side facing out using the sugar and almonds to form a desired pattern. Continue this process all the way around. Stagger a second row inside the first row, arranging the choux balls slightly behind the first row.

Continue in this fashion with the succeeding rows, gradually decreasing the circumference of choux ball rings, creating an inverted cone shape, with 4 choux balls forming the top.

6. Allow to cool. Once set, spread the top choux with some liquid caramel, using a small palette knife and set the round of nougatine on top. With any extra nougatine, make any desired shapes to decorate the top of the croquembouche using a brioche a têtemold to form the design. Affix the shaped nougatine to the top using caramel as the glue.

7. If using the nougatine wolves' teeth (**dents de loups**) to decorate the base of the cake, glue them in a ring around the base of the croquembouche using the caramel.

8. Fill a paper cornet with some royal icing and pipe around the edges of the nougatine triangles. Very slowly, pipe strings of royal icing between the triangles. Allow to dry.

9. If desired, make flowers using the Jordan almonds and pastillage leaves, and pulled sugar for sugar decorations (i.e., rope, leaves, ribbon, and curls).

Note

Because of the pastry cream and the caramel, the croquembouche must be served the same day it is assembled. The separate elements of the nougatine, the choux balls, and the pastry cream can be made in advance.

Learning Outcomes

Making a genoese sponge
(*génoise*)
Working with a bain-marie
Making a mousseline
cream (*crème mousseline*)
Making a pastry cream
(*crème pâtissière*)
Using a cornet
Imbibing
Ribbon stage
Piping (*coucher*)

Equipment

Knives:
Off-set palette knife
(*palette spatule coudée*)

Tools:
Mixing bowls, whisk,
rubber spatula, wire rack,
cornet, pastry brush, bain-
marie, piping bag, medium
round tip, rolling pin

Pans:
10 in. (25 cm) ring mold,
10 in. (25 cm) round
moule à manqué, medium
saucepan, small saucepan

Serving/Yield

8–12 servings

The fraisier cake is a delicious preparation that incorporates a plethora of fresh strawberries over a layer of pastry cream (crème pâtissière), and is sandwiched between two layers of Genoese biscuit (biscuit Génoise). The cake gains its name from the central ingredient, the strawberry, or "fraise" in French. The strawberry gained tremendous popularity in France in the 18th century, as the fruit was one of King Louis XIV's favorites. In fact, the French king was so fond of the berries that he is said to have organized a poetry contest on the subject!

LE FRAISIER
Strawberry Cake

Quantity		Ingredient
U.S.	**Metric**	*Genoese Sponge (Biscuit Genoise)*
4 pcs	4 pcs	Eggs
4 pcs	4 pcs	Egg yolks
5 oz	150 g	Sugar, granulated
5 oz	150 g	Flour
		Syrup
5 oz	150 g	Sugar, granulated
7 fl oz	200 ml	Water
2 fl oz	60 ml	Kirsch
		Mousseline Cream (Crème Mousseline)
1 pt	500 ml	Milk
1 pc	1 pc	Vanilla bean
5 oz	150 g	Sugar, granulated
1 ½ oz	40 g	Flour
1 ½ oz	40 g	Cornstarch
8 ¾ oz	250 g	Butter
1 ¼ fl oz	40 ml	Kirsch
		Finishing
2 lbs	1000 g	Strawberries
6 ¾ oz	200 g	Almond paste
3 ½ oz	100 g	Dark chocolate couverture

Method

Preheat the oven to 340°F (170°C).
Butter and flour (**chemiser**) a round **moule à manqué**.

Make Genoese Sponge (Génoise)

1. Sift (**tamiser**) the flour.
2. Whisk the eggs and sugar together in a heat-proof bowl. Place over a bain-marie and continue whisking until hot to the touch (60°C/140°F). When the mixture is light and doubled in volume (ribbon stage), remove it from the bain-marie and gently fold in the sifted flour.
3. When just combined, fill the moule à manqué mold one-half to three-fourths of the way full. Bake the Genoese Sponge (Biscuit Génoise) at 340°F/170°C for approximately 20 minutes.

Make a Syrup

1. Place the sugar and water in a small saucepan and heat until the mixture comes to a low boil. Leave to cook until the sugar is completely dissolved. Remove from the heat and allow to cool before adding the kirsch.

Make a Crème Mousseline

1. Make a pastry cream (crème pâtissière): Pour the milk into a medium saucepan and bring to a boil over medium-high heat. Add about one-quarter of the sugar to the milk and stir until it dissolves completely.
2. Meanwhile, place the egg yolks in a small mixing bowl and add the remaining sugar. Whisk the sugar into the eggs until it completely dissolves and the yolks lighten in color (**blanchir**).
3. Add the flour and the cornstarch to the yolks and stir until well combined. When the milk begins to come to a boil, remove it from the stove and pour one-third of it into the egg yolks. Stir well to temper the yolks, then whisk the tempered mixture into the remaining hot milk.
4. Place the milk back onto the heat and cook until the pastry cream (crème pâtissière) begins to bubble. Continue whisking (being sure to press the whisk around the corners of the pan) and allow to cook for about 1 minute in order to cook the starch. The crème pâtissière will become very thick at this point. Immediately spread the crème onto the platter lined with plastic wrap and dot with butter (**tamponner**) to prevent a skin from forming. Fold the plastic over and press out any air bubbles. Allow to cool.

5. Once cooled, place the pastry cream in a bowl and beat it until smooth. Add the kirsch. Whisk in the butter until smooth and light.

Assembly

1. Rinse and trim the strawberries. Trimming them all to the same height.
2. Line a ring mold with a strip of acetate.
3. Place the cake ring on a round cake board and trim the génoise sections to just slightly smaller than the size of the ring. Split the génoise into 2 layers horizontally like a hamburger bun cut all the way through.
4. Cut the strawberries in half, and arrange them standing with the cut side against the acetate all the way around.
5. Dice the remaining strawberries and set aside.
6. Place the top layer of the génoise cut-side up in the bottom of the lined cake ring and imbibe with the syrup.
7. Place the mousseline cream in the piping bag with a medium round tip. Pipe the mousseline in a spiral to cover the cake. Be sure to pipe in between the strawberries. Sprinkle with the diced strawberries. Place the other half of the cake on top, placing it cut-side down and press down gently. Imbibe with the syrup. Pipe another layer of the mousseline over the cake and sprinkle with the remaining diced strawberries.
8. Add a final thin layer of mousseline on top and using a palette knife, spread the cream to the top of the ring filling in any gaps.
9. Roll out (**abaisser**) the almond paste. Cut a piece of almond paste the same diameter as the cake and place on top. Refrigerate to allow the mousseline to set.
10. Finish by using a cornet fill with dark melted chocolate to decorate.

Note

*If desired, the bottom of the fraisier could be covered (**chablonner**) with a thin layer of chocolate.*

Learning Outcomes

Making puff pastry
(*pâte feuilletée*)
Making a frangipane cream
Piping
Creating a decorative
border (*chiqueter*)

Equipment

Knives:
Paring knife (*office*)

Tools:
Corne, baker's brush,
pastry brush, bowls,
rubber spatula,
rolling pin,
pastry bag,
plain 10 mm tip

Pans:
2 baking sheets

Serving

6 persons

FYI...

Called Epiphany Cake or King's cake in English, galette des rois is traditionally served on the 12th day of Christmas. As part of the festivities, a porcelain figurine is baked into the galette. Whoever gets the trinket is named either king or queen for the night—hence the name galette des rois (king).

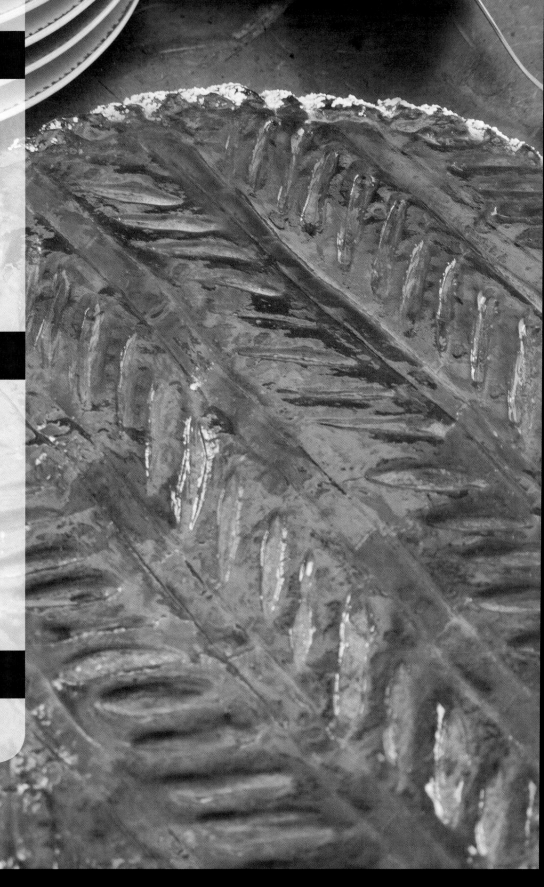

GALETTE DES ROIS
Epiphany Cake

Method

Preheat the oven to 400°F (205°C).

Puff Pastry (Pâte Feuilletée)

1. To obtain the correct amount of pâte feuilletée use the ingredients list in this recipe following the method on pages 217–222 in *Pâtisserie and Baking Foundations*.

Frangipane Cream (Crème Frangipane)

1. Prepare the almond cream (***crème d'amandes***): Cream (***crémer***) the butter and sugar together until light and fluffy. Beat in the egg until well combined. Using a small knife, split the vanilla bean in half lengthwise, scrape out the seeds, and whisk into the mixture. Add the rum and finish by mixing in the almond powder. Reserve the almond cream (crème d'amandes) in a covered bowl in the refrigerator until ready to use.
2. In a mixing bowl, whisk the pastry cream (***crème pâtissière***) (*prepared beforehand*) until it is smooth and stretchy. Add the almond cream and stir with the whisk until the two are combined. Transfer to a pastry bag fitted with a medium round tip.

Montage

1. Lightly dust a clean work surface with flour (***fleurer***). Unwrap the puff pastry onto the lightly floured work surface and roll it out (***abaisser***) (*using a rolling pin*) to a thickness of ⅛ in. (3 mm). Place the puff pastry on a parchment paper-lined baking sheet and return it to the refrigerator to rest for 10 minutes.
2. Remove the pastry from the refrigerator and lay it out flat on the work surface. Using a cake ring or ***vol-au-vent*** circle as a guide, cut 2 circles out of the puff pastry, one 8 in. (20 cm) and the other slightly larger (*refrigerate the trimmings for other uses*). Place the larger circle on the parchment paper-lined baking sheet and reserve it in the refrigerator.
3. Brush the surface of the second round with water and flip it onto a parchment paper-lined baking sheet (*wet side down*).

Note

It is important that the round be placed wet side down as the water will cause the dough to stick to the baking sheet and prevent it from warping during cooking.

Brush a 1-in. (2 ½-cm) band of egg wash around the surface of the round.

Quantity		Ingredient
U.S.	**Metric**	*Puff Pastry (Pâte Feuilletée)*
1 lb	500 g	Flour
7 ¾ fl oz	225 ml	Water
7 oz	200 g	Butter
½ oz	10 g	Salt
7 oz	200 g	Butter
1 pc	1 pc	Egg for egg wash
		Frangipane Cream (Crème Frangipane)
2 oz	60 g	Butter
2 oz	60 g	Sugar, granulated
2 oz	60 g	Almond powder
1 pc	1 pc	Egg
½ fl oz	10 ml	Rum
1 pc	1 pc	Vanilla bean
3 ½ oz	100 g	Crème pâtissière (see page 107 for recipe seen in Millefeuille)

Method

4. Pipe a tight spiral of *crème frangipane* onto the disc of pastry (*begin piping in the center and work your way outward, stopping just before the egg wash*). Transfer the baking sheet to the refrigerator for 10 minutes to let the crème frangipane harden.

5. Remove both baking sheets from the refrigerator. Lightly dust the larger round with flour and gently fold it in half. Place it on top of the disc with the frangipane spiral, taking care to line up the edges of the 2 discs. Unfold the top disc so that it completely covers the bottom one and no air is trapped inside.

   Gently press down the edges to secure the egg wash seal and, using the cake ring as a guide, cut off any irregularities from the edge of the galette. Transfer the galette to the freezer for 30 minutes before baking.

Cuisson

1. Remove the galette from the freezer, brush the surface with egg wash, and lightly score a chevron design on the top with the back of a small knife. Score the sides of the galette using the back of a paring knife (***chiqueter***).

2. Transfer the galette to the preheated oven to bake for 10 minutes, then reduce the heat to 340°F (170°C) and bake the galette for a further 20 minutes or until golden. Remove the galette from the oven and slide it onto a wire rack to cool.

3. Serve the galette des rois at room temperature on a serving dish.

Learning Outcomes

Making a custard
Making a brioche
Making a crème Anglaise
Cooking cream
"à la nappe"
Making a coulis

Equipment

Knives:
Serrated knife
(*couteau-scie*), paring knife
(*couteau d'office*)

Tools:
Mixing bowls, whisk,
wooden spatula, fine
strainer (*chinois*)

Pans:
Soufflé mold, saucepan

Serving/Yield

1 large brioche cake,
6–8 servings

The brioche, which forms the base of the gâteau diplomate, is a sweetened bread from the French region of Normandy that has been enjoyed since the 15th century. It also has the distinction of being at the center of one of the most important historical events in human history. Leading up to the French revolution of 1789, it is believed that when the French Queen Marie-Antoinette was told that the peasants had no bread and were starving, she uttered the famous words "let them eat cake." What she actually might have said was "Qu'ils mangent de la brioche," or let them eat brioche, which at the time was a much less sweet form of bread than the modern equivalent. While still not being overly sensitive to the plight of her people (although it is not known for certain if she even uttered the phrase at all), this phrasing certainly makes her a more sympathetic figure.

GÂTEAU DIPLOMATE
Diplomat Cake

Method

1. Make a loaf of brioche (see page 92).
2. Cut the brioche into cubes.

Note

For best results, prepare the brioche one day in advance.
Preheat the oven to 350°F (180°C).
Make the diplomate:

1. Butter (**chemiser**) the soufflé mold.
2. In a large bowl, whisk together the egg yolks, eggs, and sugar. Split the vanilla bean section open and scrape the seeds into the egg mixture. Whisk in the vanilla bean, and then whisk in the milk.
3. Toss the brioche with the candied fruit and raisins. Transfer the mixture to the buttered soufflé dish and press down firmly.
4. Pour the egg mixture over the tossed brioche, allowing time for it to soak in. Place in the preheated oven and bake for 30 to 35 minutes or until nicely colored and a knife inserted in the center comes out clean. Remove from the oven and set aside.

Make the Crème Anglaise

1. Place the milk into a saucepan and heat over medium heat. Add the sugar to the egg yolks, whisking immediately until the yolks lighten in color (**blanchir**).
2. Add some of the hot milk to temper and continue whisking. Add the tempered yolks back into the remaining hot milk. Stir the mixture with a wooden spatula over low heat (the mixture should be foamy on the surface). Continue cooking the crème until it thickens to the point that it coats the back of the spatula (**à la nappe**). Remove from the heat and immediately strain the mixture into a clean bowl.

Make the Raspberry Coulis

1. Blend together the raspberry pulp, powdered sugar, and lemon juice until puréed. Pour the mixture through a fine mesh strainer (**chinois**) into a clean bowl.
2. Press down on the remaining pulp with a spoon to squeeze the remaining juices through. Set aside.

Unmold the diplomate onto a serving dish and serve with the crème Anglaise and raspberry coulis.

Quantity		Ingredient
U.S.	**Metric**	**Diplomat Cake (Gâteau Diplomate)**
1 loaf	1 loaf	Brioche (see page 92)
3 pcs	3 pcs	Egg yolks
2 pcs	2 pcs	Eggs
3 ½ oz	100 g	Sugar, granulated
½ pc	½ pc	Vanilla bean
1 pt	500 ml	Milk
1 ¾ oz	50 g	Candied fruit
1 ¾ oz	50 g	Raisins
		Crème Anglaise
8 fl oz	250 ml	Milk
3 pcs	3 pcs	Egg yolks
2 oz	60 g	Sugar, granulated
		Raspberry Coulis
8 oz	250 g	Raspberry pulp
1 ½ oz	40 g	Powdered sugar
½ pc	½ pc	Lemon juice

Learning Outcomes

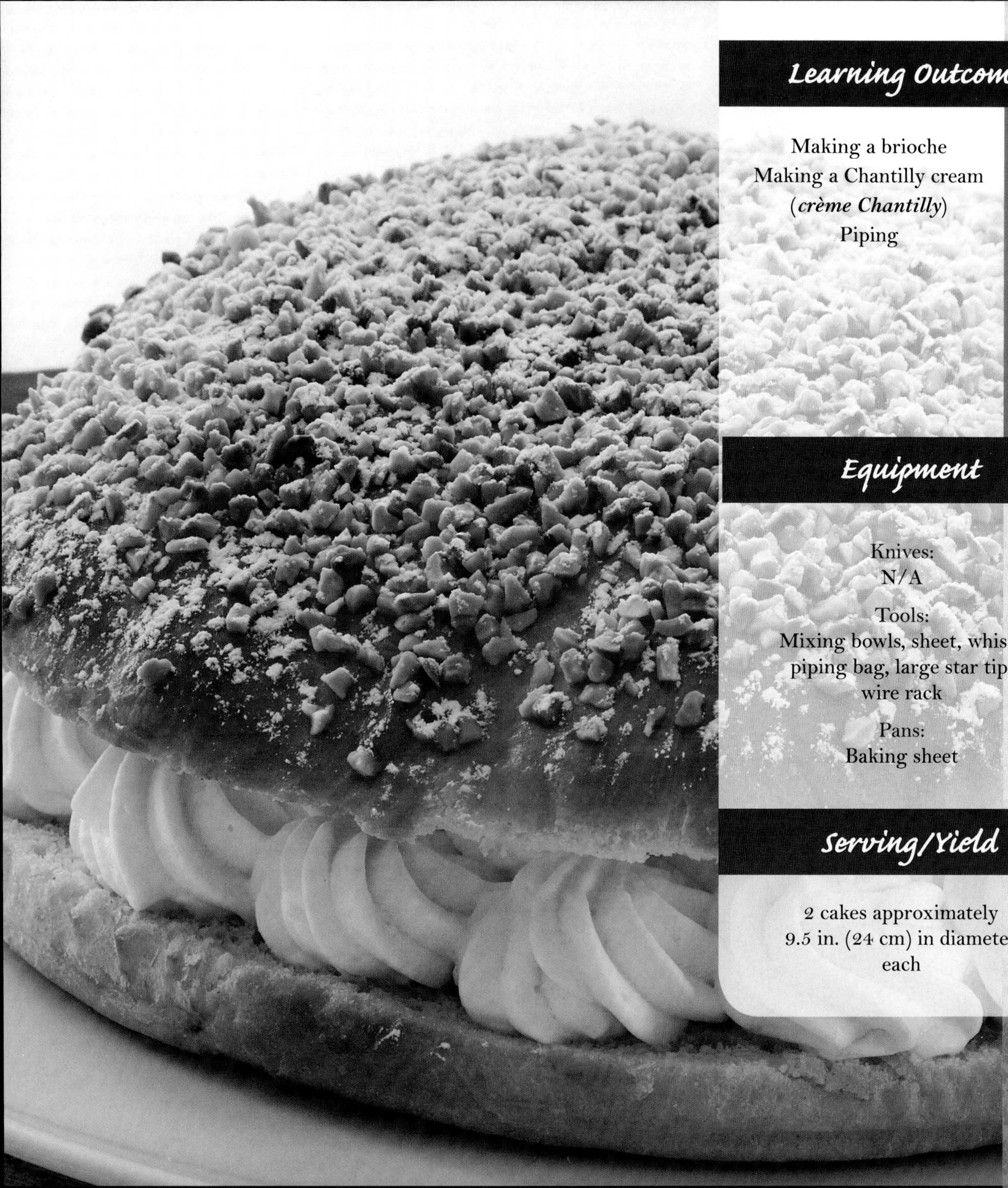

Making a brioche
Making a Chantilly cream
(*crème Chantilly*)
Piping

Equipment

Knives:
N/A

Tools:
Mixing bowls, sheet, whisk, piping bag, large star tip, wire rack

Pans:
Baking sheet

Serving/Yield

2 cakes approximately 9.5 in. (24 cm) in diameter each

HISTORY

This brioche cake gains its name from its roots as a specialty of the French region of Lorraine. The origins of this simple and hearty Franco-Germanic dessert can be traced back to the 17th century. The preparation's simplicity adds to its versatility, as many different flavors can be achieved by altering the incorporated ingredients. The dessert can be infused with fruits and liqueurs, and can be served with cream, powdered sugar, syrups, and rich icings.

Quantity		Ingredient
U.S.	Metric	*Brioche*
¾ oz	20 g	Fresh yeast
1 ¾ fl oz	50 ml	Milk (lukewarm)
2 ¼ oz	70 g	Flour
1 lb	500 g	Flour
¼ oz	5 g	Salt
2 oz	60 g	Sugar, granulated
6–7 pcs	6–7 pcs	Eggs
8 oz	250 g	Butter
		Finishing
1 pc	1 pc	Egg, for egg wash
As needed	As needed	Chopped almonds
		Chantilly Cream
13 ¼ fl oz	400 ml	Cream
2 oz	60 g	Powdered sugar
1 ¾ fl oz	50 mL	Kirsch

GÂTEAU LORRAIN
Lorraine Cake

Method

Make a Brioche Dough

1. Place the lukewarm milk in a bowl, add the yeast, and set aside. The temperature of your milk is important. If the milk is too cold and the yeast will not activate, too warm and you can kill the yeast. If the milk is cold, place it in a small saucepan over low heat until it reaches a *max 90°F (32°C)* before adding the yeast.

2. Mix the eggs and the sugar together in a bowl using a whisk. Sift (*tamiser*) the flour onto a clean, dry work surface, add the salt, and make a large well (*fontaine*) in the center using a plastic scraper (*corne*). Into the well, pour the milk and yeast mixture as well as the egg mixture. Incorporate all the ingredients in the well with your fingertips, simultaneously using the corne to add small quantities of flour from the sides. Continue until the mixture in the center of the well resembles a thick paste. Gather all the ingredients together and work them with the heel of your palm until combined.

3. With the heel of your palm, smear the dough away from yourself (*fraiser*). Note: At this point, the dough should be wet enough to stick to the work surface. If not, work in a little more milk, a spoonful at a time, until the desired consistency is reached.

4. Repeat the motion of stretching the dough out then folding it in on itself until the dough is elastic and no longer sticks.

5. Dot the dough with small pieces of softened butter and fold the dough over to enclose the butter. Knead it until the butter is incorporated. Throw the dough hard onto the work surface, fold it onto itself and repeat. Continue working the dough in this manner in order to develop the gluten.

6. Roll the dough into a ball, dust it lightly with flour, and place it in a clean bowl. Cover the bowl with a damp cloth and leave it to proof either in a warm area or in a proofer until doubled in size, about 2 hours.

7. Punch down and divide the dough in two. Form the brioche into 2 flat rounds, cover with a cloth and allow to rise a second time, about 1 hour.

8. Preheat the oven to 400°F (200°C).

9. Brush the top with egg wash and sprinkle with the chopped almonds.

Method

10. Bake until golden brown, about 35 minutes. Remove from the oven and transfer to a wire rack to cool completely.

Make the Chantilly Cream (Crème Chantilly)

11. Beat the cream with the sugar to soft peaks. Whisk in the kirsch.
12. Transfer to a piping bag fitted with a large star tip.

Assembly (Montage)

13. Split the brioche in half. Pipe the cream onto the bottom half. Gently place the top back on top of the cream.
14. Keep chilled until ready to serve.

Learning Outcomes

Marbling a cake

Equipment

Knives:
Paring knife (*couteau d'office*)

Tools:
Sieve, mixing bowls, whisk, wooden spatula, rubber spatula, cooling rack

Pan:
1 pound cake mold

Serving/Yield

1 pound loaf

The marble cake is thought to have originated in America, where recipes began to appear by around the 1870s. The cake gains its name from the beautifully distinctive swirling color patterns that resemble marble stone and have come to define this preparation. It is this color pattern that made this cake a favorite dessert of New England party hostesses, who originally achieved the swirling colors through the addition of molasses, jams, and fruits to the cake's batter. The modern incarnation of the marble cake has only increased its popularity, as the current form of producing the cake's distinctive swirling pattern requires the mixing of two distinct types of cake. This decorative style has the added bonus of providing the diner with all the flavor of two cakes for the price of one.

GÂTEAU MARBRÉ
Marble Cake

Method

Preheat the oven to 280°F (140°C).

1. Butter and flour a cake mold (*chemiser*).
2. Sift (*tamiser*) the flour and baking powder together.
3. In a large bowl, cream (*crémer*) the butter and sugar together until fully incorporated and the butter lightens in color. Add the eggs one at a time, mixing well after each addition. Using a small knife, split the vanilla bean in half lengthwise and scrape out the seeds. Whisk into the mixture. Stir in the lemon zest. Add the flour and stir until just combined and gradually mix in the milk.
4. Transfer half of the dough to a separate bowl and mix in the cocoa powder and milk.
5. Fill the mold with half of the vanilla batter, then add the chocolate batter and cover both with the remaining vanilla batter. With a paring knife, gently swirl the two batters together.
6. Place the cake in the preheated oven and bake it until a knife inserted in the center comes out clean, for approximately 35 to 40 minutes. Gently unmold and allow to cool on a wire rack.

Quantity		Ingredient
U.S.	Metric	*Vanilla Cake Batter*
4 ¼ oz	125 g	Butter
6 oz	180 g	Sugar, granulated
3 pcs	3 pcs	Eggs
10 oz	300 g	Flour
½ oz	10 g	Baking powder
3 ¼ fl oz	100 ml	Milk
1 pc	1 pc	Lemon zest
1 pc	1 pc	Vanilla
		Chocolate Cake Batter
		Half of the vanilla cake batter
10 oz	300 g	Cocoa powder
1 fl oz	30 ml	Milk

Learning Outcomes

Making choux pastry
(*pâte à choux*)
Making a pastry cream
(*crème pâtissière*)
Making a mousseline cream
(*crème mousseline praline*)
Piping (*coucher*)
Tempering

Equipment

Knives:
N/A

Tools:
Mixing bowls, whisk,
wooden spoon, rubber
spatula, piping bag, large
round tip, large channeled
tip, sieve, small platter,
wire rack, plastic
wrap

Pans:
Large saucepan, medium
saucepan

Serving/Yield

1 circular cake,
8–10 servings

HISTORY

The Paris-Brest cake is named for the 1200-km cycling race held every 4 years from Paris to the coastal city of Brest, situated in the Brittany region of France. The race began in 1891, making it the oldest French cycling race still being run today (it predates the "Tour de France" by 12 years). The cake was created by a pastry chef living in a town along the route of the race to commemorate its inaugural running. It is said that the chef shaped the cake in a circular style to resemble the wheel of a bicycle.

GÂTEAU PARIS-BREST
Paris-Brest Cake

Method

Preheat the oven to 400°F (200°C).
Butter (**chemiser**) a large baking sheet.

Make a Choux Pastry (Pâte à Choux)

1. Sift (**tamiser**) the flour.
2. Place the butter, sugar, salt, milk, and water into a large saucepan. Bring the combination to a boil, stirring until all of the salt and sugar are dissolved. Once the water comes to a boil and the butter has melted, remove the pan from the heat and add all of the flour at once. Stir the mixture well with a spatula. Place the pan back onto the heat and continue to stir until a clean ball of dough forms and comes cleanly off the sides and bottom of the pan. Transfer the hot dough to a large bowl and spread it out to cool slightly.
3. Add the eggs, one at a time, beating well after each addition. After three of the eggs have been incorporated, check the consistency by lifting some of the dough. It should stretch before breaking. If the dough is still too stiff, beat the last egg and add just enough of it until the dough forms a soft peak that falls when the spatula is lifted.
4. Transfer the dough to a piping bag fitted with a large round tip. Apply even pressure and holding the tip above the baking sheet, allow the dough to drop onto the plaque while piping (**coucher**) a large circle, approximately 7.5 in. to 8.5 in. (20–22 cm) in diameter. Pipe a second circle just inside, and then pipe a third circle on top, between the two first circles.
5. Brush with egg wash and sprinkle with sliced almonds. Place in the oven to bake until nicely browned all over (including the cracks). Remove from the oven and gently transfer to a wire rack to cool.

Make Pastry Cream (Crème Pâtissière)

1. Line a small platter with plastic wrap.
2. Pour the milk into a medium saucepan. Split the vanilla bean in half lengthwise and scrape out the seeds. Stir the seeds into the milk and bring it to a boil over medium-high heat. Add about one-quarter of the sugar and stir to dissolve it.

Quantity		Ingredient
U.S.	**Metric**	*Choux Pastry (Pâte à Choux)*
4 ¼ fl oz	125 ml	Water
4 ¼ fl oz	125 ml	Milk
¼ oz	4 g	Salt
¼ oz	4 g	Sugar, granulated
3 ⅓ oz	100 g	Butter
5 ½ oz	165 g	Flour
5–6 pcs	5–6 pcs	Eggs
As needed	As needed	Sliced almonds
		Mousseline Praline Cream (Crème Mousseline Praline)
8 fl oz	250 ml	Milk with vanilla
2 pcs	2 pcs	Egg yolks
1 ¾ oz	50 g	Sugar
¾ oz	20 g	Flour
¾ oz	20 g	Cornstarch
4 ¼ oz	125 g	Butter
2 oz	60 g	Praline paste

Method

3. Meanwhile, place the egg yolks in a small mixing bowl and add the remaining sugar. Whisk the sugar into the eggs until it completely dissolves and the yolks lighten in color (**blanchir**). Add the flour and cornstarch to the yolks and stir until well combined.

4. When the milk begins to boil, remove it from the stove and pour one-third of it into the egg yolks. Stir well to temper the yolks, then whisk the tempered mixture back into the remaining hot milk. Place back onto the heat and cook until the crème pâtissière begins to bubble. Continue whisking and allow to cook for 1 minute to cook the starch. The crème will become very thick. Immediately spread the crème onto the platter lined with plastic wrap and dot with butter (**tamponner**) to prevent a skin from forming. Fold the plastic over and press out any air bubbles. Allow to cool.

Make the Mousseline Praline Cream (Crème Mousseline Praline)

1. Once the crème has cooled, whisk until smooth. Whisk in the praline paste until well combined, then gradually incorporate the butter.

2. Beat until homogeneous. Transfer to a piping bag fitted with a large channeled tip.

3. Split the cooked pastry in half. Pipe (**coucher**) the crème mousseline praline in a circular motion to fill the center. Gently place the top back on. Dust with powdered sugar.

Learning Outcomes

Making a choux pastry
(*pâte à choux*)
Making a shortcrust
(*pâte brisée*)
Caramel
Making a crème chibouste
Using a St. Honoré tip
Making an Italian
meringue
Piping (*coucher*)

Equipment

Tools:
Corne, rolling pin, docker,
cake ring, pastry bag,
10 mm plain tip, pastry
brush, fork, whisk, wooden
spoon, rubber spatula, large
St. Honoré tip

Pans:
1 small saucepan, 1 large
saucepan, 1 medium
saucepan, 2 baking sheets

Serving

6–8 persons

This cake is named after the patron saint of bakers and is traditionally a cake made by bakers and not pastry chefs. The chibouste cream that is used in this cake was created by a pastry chef named Chibouste.

Quantity		Ingredient
U.S.	**Metric**	*Choux Pastry (Pâte à Choux)*
4 fl oz	125 ml	Water
2 oz	60 g	Butter
pinch	pinch	Salt
¼ oz	6 g	Sugar, granulated
4 oz	125 g	Flour
2 pcs	2 pcs	Eggs
		Shortcrust Pastry Dough (Pâte Brisée)
7 oz	200 g	Flour
3 ⅓ oz	100 g	Butter, diced
Pinch	Pinch	Salt
¼ fl oz	10 ml	Water
1 pc	1 pc	Egg
1 pc	1 pc	Egg, for egg wash
		Chibouste Cream (Crème Chibouste)
1 pt	500 ml	Milk
1 pc	1 pc	Vanilla bean
2 oz	60 g	Sugar, granulated
8 pcs	8 pcs	Egg yolks
1 ¼ oz	40 g	Cornstarch
6 pcs	6 pcs	Gelatin leaves
		Italian Meringue (Italienne Meringue)
8 pcs	8 pcs	Egg whites
13 ½ oz	400 g	Sugar, granulated
4 fl oz	120 ml	Water
		Caramel
3 ⅓ oz	100 g	Sugar, granulated
1 fl oz	30 ml	Water
½ pc	½ pc	Lemon

ST. HONORÉ
Cream Puff Cake with Caramel and Chiboust Cream

Method

Preheat the oven to 425°F (220°C).

Choux Pastry (Pâte à Choux)

1. To obtain the correct amount of pâte à choux use the ingredients list in this recipe following the method on pages 189–191 in *Pâtisserie and Baking Foundations*.

Shortcrust Pastry Dough (Pâte Brisée)

1. Sift (*tamiser*) the flour onto a clean work surface and make a large well (*fontaine*) in the center using a plastic scraper (*corne*).
2. Place the cold, diced butter in the center of the well. Work the butter into the flour using your fingertips while simultaneously cutting through the mixture with the plastic scraper. Continue cutting until the butter is crumbly and coated in flour.
3. Rub the mixture between the palms of your hands until it resembles fine sand (*sabler*).
4. Gather the flour–butter mixture into a neat pile and make a well in the center using the *corne*. Add the salt, water, and the egg to the center of the well. Stir these ingredients together using your fingertips until combined; then gradually incorporate the dry ingredients from the sides until the mixture in the center of the well resembles a paste.
5. Using the *corne*, incorporate the remaining dry ingredients using a cutting motion. Scoop up the mixture onto itself and continue cutting until a loose dough forms. Using the heel of your palm, firmly smear the dough away from yourself to ensure that no lumps of butter are left (*fraiser*). Scrape up the dough and repeat until the dough becomes uniform.
6. Shape the dough into a ball, wrap it in plastic, and flatten it into a disc. Let the dough rest in the refrigerator for at least 30 minutes (preferably overnight).

Base

1. Lightly dust the work surface with flour (*fleurer*). Unwrap the shortcrust pastry dough (pâte brisée) onto the floured surface and roll it out (*abaisser*) to a thickness of ³⁄₁₆ in. (5 mm), giving it a quarter of a turn with each stroke of the rolling pin. Transfer the dough to a lightly greased baking sheet, prick it with the docker (*pique vite*), and, using an 8-in. (20-cm) cake ring, cut a circle out of it. Remove

the trimmings and transfer the baking sheet to the refrigerator to let the round of dough rest. Meanwhile, transfer the pâte à choux to a pastry bag fitted with a 15-mm tip. On a lightly greased baking sheet, pipe out (*coucher*) about 10–12 balls (*choux*) 1 in. (2 ½ cm) in diameter and set aside. Remove the round of pâte brisée from the refrigerator and pipe a border around the edge of the round. Starting from the center, pipe a loose spiral of pâte à choux. Brush the choux pastry (pâte à choux) with egg wash, being careful not to let any drip and lightly flatten the tops of the choux with a fork dipped in the egg wash.

2. Bake the choux pastry (pâte à choux) and shortcrust pastry dough (pâte brisée) until they are golden (*about 12 to 15 minutes without opening the oven door*). When the choux pastry (pâte à choux) are golden, rotate the baking sheets and continue to bake until slightly dried. When cooked, remove from the oven and transfer to a wire rack. Set aside to cool.

Chibouste Cream (Crème Chibouste)

1. *Prepare a pastry cream (crème pâtissière):* Pour the milk into a medium saucepan. Split the vanilla bean in half lengthwise and scrape out the seeds. Stir the seeds into the milk and bring it to a boil over medium-high heat. Add about one-quarter of the sugar to the milk and stir to dissolve it.

2. Meanwhile, place the egg yolks in a small bowl and add the remaining sugar. Whisk the sugar into the eggs until it completely dissolves and the yolks lighten in color (*blanchir*). Add the cornstarch to the yolks and stir until well combined.

3. When the milk begins to come to a boil, remove it from the stove and pour one-third of it into the egg yolks. Stir well to temper the yolks, then whisk the tempered mixture into the remaining hot milk. Place back onto the heat and cook until the pastry cream (crème pâtissière) begins to bubble. Continue whisking (being sure to press the whisk around the corners of the pan) and allow to cook for 1 minute in order to cook the starch. The pastry cream (crème pâtissière) will become very thick. Transfer the finished pastry cream (crème pâtissière) to a clean bowl.

4. Soak the gelatin leaves in cold water until completely softened. Squeeze out any excess water, then incorporate the leaves into the hot

Method

pastry cream (crème pâtissière) using a whisk. Pat (*tamponner*) the surface of the pastry cream (crème pâtissière) with a piece of cold butter held on the end of a fork to create a protective film. Set aside to cool to room temperature.

5. *Prepare an Italian Meringue (Meringue Italienne):* Whisk the egg whites in a large mixing bowl using a balloon whisk, until frothy. Set aside. Cook the sugar and water in a medium saucepan over medium-high heat until they reach the soft-ball stage (*petit boulé*) [250°F (121°C)]. Meanwhile, whip the egg whites to soft peaks. As soon as the syrup reaches the soft-ball (*gros boulé*) stage, pour it into the egg whites in a thin stream, whisking constantly. Continue to whisk until the meringue is firm and cooled to room temperature. Set aside.

6. Whisk the pastry cream (crème pâtissière) until it is smooth and elastic. Add half the meringue Italienne and fold it in using a rubber spatula. Add the second half and fold it in until the mixture is homogeneous. Transfer half of the resulting chibouste to a pastry bag fitted with a 6-mm plain tip.

7. Using a small pastry tip, pierce the bases of the choux pastry (pâte à choux), then fill them with chibouste. Reserve them at room temperature.

Caramel

1. Bring the sugar and water to a boil in a small to medium saucepan over medium-high heat and cook this mixture until it turns a light caramel color. Stop the cooking process by briefly dipping the base of the saucepan in ice water. Dip the top of the pâte à choux in the caramel, holding them between 3 fingers and being careful not to touch the hot caramel. Place the caramel-covered side down on a silicone mat. Using the caramel as glue, stick the choux pastry (pâte à choux) to the edge of the pastry disc.

Finishing

1. Transfer the leftover chibouste to a pastry bag fitted with a large St. Honoré tip and pipe (*coucher*) the chibouste onto the center of the cake and in between the choux pastry (pâte à choux). Refrigerate the St. Honoré until ready to serve.

Learning Outcomes

Making a Genoese
Sponge (*biscuit génoise*)
Cooking with a
Bain-marie
Making a simple syrup
Imbibing with syrup
Using a cornet
Decorating with
royal icing

Equipment

Knives:
Serrated knife
(*couteau à scie*)

Tools:
Balloon whisk, rubber
spatula, sieve, whisk, mixing
bowls, wire rack

Pans:
Bain-marie, medium
saucepan, 8 inch round cake
mold, baking sheet

Serving

6 persons

Quantity		Ingredient
U.S.	Metric	*Lining the Pan (Chemisage)*
1 oz	30 g	Flour
1 oz	30 g	Butter
		Genoese Sponge (Biscuit Génoise)
¾ oz	25 g	Butter
5 oz	150 g	Flour, sifted (**tamiser**)
4 pcs	4 pcs	Eggs
2 pcs	2 pcs	Egg yolks
5 oz	150 g	Sugar, granulated
		Royal Icing (Glace Royale)
7 oz	200 g	Powdered sugar, sifted (**tamiser**)
1 pc	1 pc	Egg white
1 pc	1 pc	Lemon, juice of
		Assembly (Montage)
As needed	As needed	Almonds, blanched, sliced, toasted
As needed	As needed	Raspberry jam, with seeds
		Simple Syrup
5 oz	150 g	Sugar
5 fl oz	150 ml	Water

GÉNOISE CONFITURE
Jam-Filled Sponge Cake

Method

1. Preheat the oven to 400°F (205°C).
2. Butter an 8-in. (20-cm) cake pan/mold (**moule à manqué**) and place it in the freezer for 5 minutes to set the butter. Butter the mold a second time and coat it in flour (**chemiser**). Tap off any excess flour and reserve the mold in the refrigerator.

Making a Genoese Sponge Cake (Biscuit Génoise)

1. Melt the butter in a small saucepan over low heat and set it aside
2. Sift (**tamiser**) the flour onto a sheet of parchment paper.
3. Fill a saucepan one-quarter full of water and bring it to a simmer over medium-high heat (**bain-marie**).
4. Break the eggs into a large mixing bowl, add the sugar, and whisk together until combined. Place the bowl on the simmering bain-marie and continue whisking until the mixture lightens in color and feels hot to the touch (110°F/45°C).
5. At this point the mixture should form a ribbon when the whisk is lifted from the bowl. Remove the bowl from the bain-marie and continue to whisk until it reaches room temperature.
6. Add the flour and gently fold it into the egg mixture with a rubber spatula until the flour is just incorporated. Fold in the melted butter, then transfer the finished batter into the prepared cake mold and place it in the oven to bake.
7. Once the oven door is closed, reduce the heat to 350°F/185°C and bake the Genoese (génoise) for 18 to 20 minutes (test by inserting a knife into the center; if it comes out clean the cake is fully baked). Remove the Genoese (génoise) from the oven and let it cool in the mold for 2 to 3 minutes. Turn the cake out of the mold and finish cooling it upside down on a wire rack.

Génoise

1. To obtain the correct amount of biscuit génoise use the ingredients list in this recipe following the method on pages 180–182 in *Pâtisserie and Baking Foundations*.

Make a Simple Syrup

1. Combine the sugar and water in a small pan. Bring to a boil and cook until the sugar is dissolved. Remove from the heat and set aside to cool.

Make Royal Icing (Glace Royale)

1. Sift (**tamiser**) the powdered sugar into a large mixing bowl and make a well in the center. Whisk

Method

the egg white and lemon juice in a small mixing bowl until frothy. Pour the mixture into the well in the powdered sugar. Whisk all the ingredients until they form a smooth consistency. Cover the bowl with a moist cloth and reserve until needed.

Assembly (Montage)

1. Spread the sliced almonds out onto a baking sheet and bake them until they are lightly golden (*5 to 10 minutes*). Set aside.
2. Cut a cake board into an 8-inch circle and spread a small spoonful of raspberry jam in the center to hold the génoise in place.
3. Turn the cake over so the domed side is on top and trim it flat with a serrated knife. Turn the cake over onto the cake board. Score the cake around the side with a bread knife, marking a guide line that indicates 2 even layers. Following the guidelines, slice around the cake, slowly cutting deeper, until there are 2 even layers. Lift the top half and set aside. Using a pastry brush, wet the entire surface of the bottom layer with syrup to imbibe it (***puncher***). Place a large spoonful of raspberry jam on the bottom layer of cake and spread it out to the edges using a metal spatula. Place the second layer on top and press it down lightly. Smooth away any overflows of jam with a metal spatula. Score the top of the cake with the tip of a small knife and imbibe it (***puncher***) with syrup.
4. Place the cake on a wire rack set over a baking sheet.
5. Heat the jam in a medium saucepan over medium heat until it has the consistency of a thick syrup. Meanwhile, spoon some glace royale into a paper cone (***cornet***) and snip off the end. Pour the jam on the cake to coat it and immediately pipe a spiral of glace royale from the center to the edge of the cake. Drag a toothpick from the center outward every 45° around the cake (*forming 4 evenly spaced spokes*). Drag the icing the opposite direction between each spoke to form a web pattern.
6. Press the toasted almond slices to the sides of the cake to cover them.
7. Let the cake rest for 10 minutes in the refrigerator to set the raspberry jam.
8. Transfer the ***génoise confiture*** either to a clean cake board or serving dish and refrigerate until ready to serve.

Learning Outcomes

Making a puff pastry
(*pâte feuilletée*)
Making a pastry cream
(*crème pâtissière*)
Making a layered confection
Marbling
Blanchir
Glaçage au fondant
Icing with fondant
(*glaçage au fondant*)
Working with a cornet

Equipment

Knives:
Serrated knife (*couteau à scie*), paring knife (*office*)

Tools:
Corne, rolling pin, baker's brush, docker, pastry brush, wire rack, whisk, mixing bowls, rubber spatula, pastry bag, 10-mm plain tip, large offset spatula, cornet

Pans:
Medium russe, 2 small russes, bain-marie, baking sheet

Serving

8 persons

Invented by French pastry chef Rouget, millefeuille was met with resounding approval by the *Jurys dégustatures* (a 19th-century Parisian jury that tested innovative preparations). Characterized by its layers of puff pastry floating on crème pâtissière, this pastry is generally made into single-serving portions but can also be prepared as larger gâteaux.

If prepared correctly, one should be able to cut a millefeuille with one firm stroke of the knife without squeezing out any of the cream.

MILLEFEUILLE
Napoleon

Method

Preheat the oven to 400°F (205°C).

Puff Pastry (Pâte Feuilletée)

1. Sift (**tamiser**) the flour onto a clean work surface and make a well in the center using a plastic scraper (**corne**). Add the salt and water to the well. Stir with your fingertips until the salt is dissolved.
2. Add the butter, cut into pieces, and begin to incorporate the flour using your fingertips. As the flour, butter, and water begin to combine, use the **corne** to cut the ingredients together, until it resembles a coarse dough. Sprinkle with additional water if the dough is too dry.
3. Once there are barely any traces of flour left, gather the dough into a ball and score the top of it with a deep cross using a large knife.
4. Loosely wrap the finished **détrempe** in plastic and transfer it to the refrigerator to rest for a minimum of 1 hour (preferably overnight).

Note

Détrempe refers to the dough before the layer of butter (**beurrage**) is added.

Beurrage and Tourage

1. Place the cold butter between two sheets of parchment paper and pound it with a rolling pin until it is similar to the **détrempe** in consistency.
2. Using the **corne**, shape the butter into a flat square about ½-in. (1-cm) thick. Set the butter aside. If the kitchen is warm, place it in the refrigerator.
3. Lightly dust a clean work surface with flour (**fleurer**), then unwrap the **détrempe** and place it on the floured surface.
4. Using the scored marks as a guide, roll out (**abaisser**) the corners of the **détrempe** into a cross shape. Be careful to keep the center of the cross thicker than its outer arms (this will be important when rolling out the dough and the butter).
5. Place the square of butter in the center of the cross and fold the two side arms over it so that they overlap slightly in the center (in the process be careful not to trap any air bubbles). Give the dough a quarter turn and fold the two remaining arms over the butter so that the butter is completely enclosed. Press the seams well to seal.

Quantity		Ingredient
U.S.	Metric	Puff Pastry (Pâte Feuilletée)
1 lb	500 g	Flour
⅓ oz	10 g	Salt
7 ¾ fl oz	225 ml	Water
7 oz	200 g	Butter, room temperature
7 oz	200 g	Butter
		Sugar for dusting
		Pastry Cream (Crème Pâtissière)
½ pt	250 ml	Milk
⅓ fl oz	10 ml	Vanilla extract
1 ¾ oz	50 g	Sugar, granulated
2 pcs	2 pcs	Egg yolks
¾ oz	20 g	Cornstarch
		Assembly (Montage)
7 oz	200 g	Fondant*
¾ oz	20 g	Dark chocolate, melted
3 ⅓ oz	100 g	Blanched sliced almonds, toasted
		*Available at specialty food stores.

MILLEFEUILLE
Napoleon

Method

6. Lightly tap the dough with the length of the rolling pin to even out the distribution of the butter inside. Give the dough a quarter turn and repeat the tapping process. This is called the ***enveloppe***.

Tourage, 6 Turns (6 Tours Simples)

1. *Turns 1 and 2:* Roll out (***abaisser***) the dough in long even strokes to form a rectangle that is three times the original length of the ***enveloppe*** or ½-in. (1-cm) thick. Brush off any excess flour.

2. Fold the bottom third of the dough up; then fold the top third down over the first fold. Make sure the edges are even. Give the dough a quarter turn to the right and repeat the same rolling process. Make sure to always brush away any excess flour.

3. Repeat the folding process (top third up, top third down over first fold) and give the dough a quarter turn to the right. Make two finger impressions in the top left corner of the dough.

Note

These marks are a reminder of the number of turns that the dough has received; they also indicate the position for subsequent turns.

Wrap the dough in plastic and transfer it to the refrigerator to rest for a minimum of 20 minutes. With two turns, the dough is now referred to as the ***pâton***.

4. *Turns 3 and 4:* Lightly dust the work surface with flour (***fleurer***).

5. Remove the dough from the refrigerator and unwrap it onto the floured surface (with the 2 indents in the top left corner). Proceed to give the dough a third and fourth turn (rolling and folding in the same manner as the first and second turns). Mark the dough with 4 imprints in the top-left corner before wrapping it in plastic and returning it to the refrigerator to rest for a minimum of 20 minutes.

6. *Turns 5 and 6:* Lightly dust the work surface with flour (***fleurer***).

7. Remove the dough from the refrigerator and unwrap it onto the floured surface (with the 4 indents in the top left corner). Proceed to give the dough its final 2 turns, folding and rolling as in previous turns. Wrap it in plastic and return it to the refrigerator to rest for a minimum of

20 minutes before rolling it out (the longer the dough rests the better it will perform).

Tip

Because the détrempe and the butter are at the same consistency, it is necessary to complete the turns as explained above. If you allow the dough to over chill between turns, the butter may become too hard and crack when rolled out. Make sure you have allotted the necessary time to complete the turns.

8. Lightly dust a clean work surface with flour (***fleurer***). Unwrap the puff pastry onto the lightly floured surface and, using a rolling pin, roll it out to a thickness of ⅛ in. (3 mm) and the same dimensions as a baking sheet.

9. Transfer it to a clean baking sheet and prick it thoroughly using a docker (***pique vite***). Brush the pastry with cold water and sprinkle it with sugar.

10. Transfer it to the oven to bake until lightly golden (*20 minutes*). Reduce the oven temperature to 370°F (190°C) and bake the puff pastry 5 to 10 minutes more to dry it out. Remove the baking sheet from the oven and transfer the pastry to a wire rack to cool to room temperature. Lower the oven temperature to 350°F (175°C).

Pastry Cream (Crème Pâtissière)

1. Line a shallow tray or baking sheet with plastic wrap. Set aside.

2. Pour the milk into a medium saucepan, add the vanilla extract to the milk and bring the mixture to a boil over medium-high heat. Add about one-quarter of the sugar to the milk and stir to dissolve it.

3. Meanwhile, place the egg yolks in a small mixing bowl and add the remaining sugar. Whisk the sugar into the eggs until it completely dissolves and the yolks lighten in color (***blanchir***). Add the flour or cornstarch to the yolks and stir until well combined.

4. When the milk begins to come to a boil, remove it from the stove and pour one-third of it into the egg yolks. Stir well to temper the yolks, then whisk the tempered mixture into the remaining hot milk. Place back onto the heat and cook until the crème pâtissière begins to bubble. Continue whisking (being sure to press the whisk around the corners of the pan) and allow to cook for 1 minute in order to cook the starch. The crème pâtissière will

become very thick. Once cooked, pour the pastry cream (crème pâtissière) onto the prepared tray or baking sheet. Pat (**tamponner**) the surface with a piece of cold butter held on the end of a fork to create a protective film then cover with plastic, smoothing out any air bubbles and sealing at the edges. Let the crème pâtissière cool to room temperature then refrigerate until needed.

Toasted Almonds

1. Spread the sliced almonds out onto a baking sheet and place them in the oven to toast until lightly golden (*5 to 10 minutes*). Set aside.

Assembly (Montage)

1. Transfer the puff pastry to a clean work surface and trim the edges with a bread knife. Cut the pastry widthwise into 3 equally sized pieces. Lay 1 piece upside down on the work surface and set the others aside. Whisk the cooled pastry cream (crème pâtissière) until it is smooth and elastic, then transfer it to a pastry bag fitted with a 10-mm plain tip. Pipe parallel rows of crème pâtissière side by side lengthwise onto the puff pastry rectangle to completely cover it. Place a second piece of puff pastry upside down on top and press it down lightly using a wire rack to secure it in place. Cover it in pastry cream (crème pâtissière) using the same technique as before and place the last layer of puff pastry on top, upside down so that the smooth side is facing upward. Press it down lightly with a wire rack to secure it in place. Apply a thin layer of crème pâtissière (**masquer**) to the sides of the millefeuille using a metal spatula.

Finishing

1. Fill a paper cone (**cornet**) with melted chocolate and snip off the end. Gently heat the fondant in a medium saucepan over the lowest heat setting (stirring it gently with a wooden spatula). If the fondant stays very thick (even when heated) add a few drops of simple syrup or warm water and stir it in. Continue to gently stir the fondant until it coats the back of a spoon in a thick, shiny layer. The ideal temperature to work with fondant is approximately 98.6°F (37°C). Once the fondant has reached the correct temperature and consistency, pour the fondant onto the top of the millefeuille and spread it out to the edges using an offset metal spatula. Using the cornet, pipe thin lines of chocolate lengthwise onto the fondant, then drag a toothpick back and forth through them widthwise to create a marbled effect. Press the toasted almonds to the sides of the millefeuille. Transfer the millefeuille either to a clean cake board or serving dish and refrigerate until ready to serve.

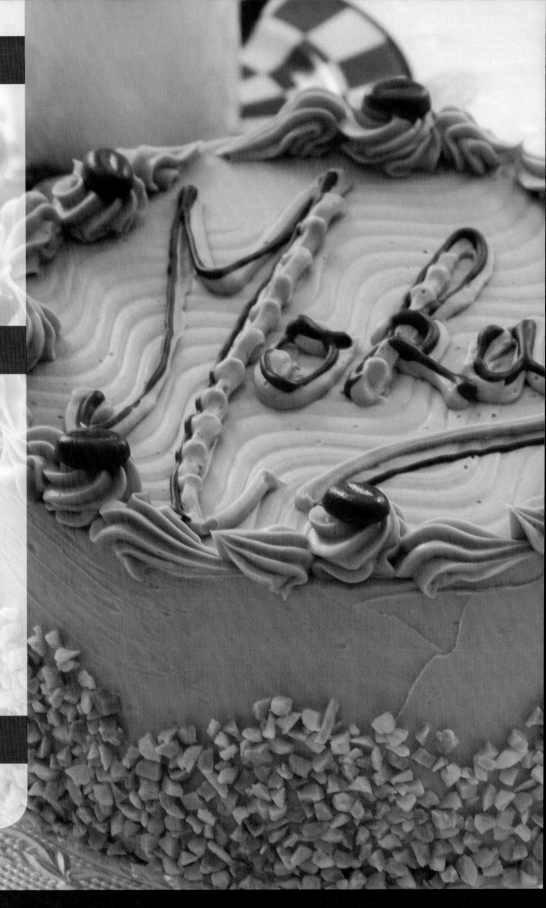

Learning Outcomes

Making a genoese sponge
(*biscuit génoise*)
Making a French
buttercream (*crème au
beurre Française*)
Masking a cake
Working with a bain-marie
Imbibing a cake
Making a pâte à bombe
Piping (*coucher*)

Equipment

Knives:
Serrated knife (*couteau-
scie*), paring knife (*couteau
d'office*)

Tools:
Pastry brush, balloon whisk,
offset spatula, mixing bowls,
corne, cornet, pastry bag,
10 mm plain tip, 24 mm star
tip, pâtisserie comb, large
offset spatula

Pans:
Bain-marie, 8 in. round cake
mold, medium saucepan,
small saucepan

Serving

8 persons

FYI...

Mocha coffee beans were first discovered by Europeans in the 17th century in the port city of Mocha (in Yemen). The popularity of the mocha bean, with its undertones of chocolate and its medium- to full-bodied taste, was fully entrenched by the mid-18th century. According to Pierre Lacam in *Le Mémorial Historique De La Pâtisserie*, gâteau mocha was invented by Guignard of the Carrefour de l'Odéon in Paris in 1857.

MOKA
Coffee Butter Cream Sponge Cake

Method

1. Preheat the oven to 400°F (205°C).
2. Butter an 8-in. cake pan (*moule à manqué*) and place it in the freezer for 5 minutes to set the butter. Butter the mold a second time and coat it in flour (*chemiser*). Tap off any excess flour and reserve the mold in the refrigerator.

Genoese Sponge (Biscuit Génoise)

1. Melt the butter in a small saucepan over low heat and set it aside.
2. Sift (*tamiser*) the flour onto a sheet of parchment paper.
3. Fill a saucepan one-quarter full of water and bring it to a simmer over medium-high heat (*bain-marie*).
4. Break the eggs and yolks into a large mixing bowl, add the sugar, and whisk them together with a balloon whisk until combined. Place the bowl on the simmering bain-marie and continue whisking until the mixture lightens in color and feels hot to the touch. At this point the mixture should form a ribbon when the whisk is lifted from the bowl. Remove the bowl from the bain-marie and continue to whisk the egg mixture until it cools to room temperature. Add the flour and gently fold it into the egg mixture with a rubber spatula (keep folding until the flour is just incorporated). Fold in the melted butter, then transfer the finished genoese sponge (biscuit génoise) into the cake mold and transfer it to the oven to bake. Reduce the oven temperature to 350°F (185°C) and bake the génoise for 15 to 18 minutes (test by inserting a knife into the center; if it comes out clean the cake is fully baked). Remove the génoise from the oven and let it cool in the mold for 2 to 3 minutes. Turn the cake out of the mold and let it cool upside down on a wire rack.

Imbibing Syrup

1. Bring the water and sugar to a boil in a small saucepan over medium-high heat until the sugar has completely dissolved. Remove the pan from the heat and pour the syrup into a clean bowl. Let it cool to room temperature, then stir in the coffee extract with a spoon. Cover and set aside.

French Buttercream Icing (Crème au Beurre Française)

1. Cook the sugar and 2 fl oz (60 mL) of water in a medium saucepan over medium-high heat until they reach the soft-ball stage (*petit boulé*)

Quantity		Ingredient
U.S.	**Metric**	
1 oz	30 g	Flour
1 oz	30 g	Butter
		Genoese Sponge (Biscuit Génoise)
¾ oz	25 g	Butter
5 oz	150 g	Flour (*tamiser*)
4 pcs	4 pcs	Eggs
2 pcs	2 pcs	Egg yolks
5 oz	150 g	Sugar, granulated
		French Buttercream Icing (Crème au Beurre Française)
6 oz	180 g	Sugar, granulated
2 fl oz	60 ml	Water
6 pcs	6 pcs	Egg yolks
12 oz	360 g	Butter
½ fl oz	2 ml	Coffee extract
		Imbibing Syrup
7 fl oz	200 g	Water
7 oz	200 g	Sugar, granulated
⅛ fl oz	2 ml	Coffee extract
		Finishing
1 ¾ oz	50 g	Chocolate couverture, melted
8 pcs	8 pcs	Chocolate-coated coffee beans
As needed	As needed	Toasted almonds, chopped

Lining the Pan (Chemisage)

Method

[250°F (121°C)]. Meanwhile, place the egg yolks in a mixing bowl. When the sugar syrup reaches the soft-ball stage (*petit boulé*), pour it onto the egg yolks in a steady stream while whisking continuously. Continue whisking until the mixture is thick and pale and creates ribbons when the whisk is lifted from the bowl. This mixture is a pâte à bombe.

2. Whisk the pâte à bombe until the mixing bowl is just warm to the touch then add all the butter. Mix vigorously with the whisk until the mixture is homogeneous and thick enough to hold its own shape. Whisk in the coffee extract and reserve at room temperature.

Tip

*To tell how well done the sugar is, dip 2 fingertips and your thumb in cold water, then rapidly scoop up a little drop of the boiling syrup before plunging your fingers straight back into the cold water. If the syrup forms a malleable ball, it is at the soft-ball stage (**petit boulé**) [250°F (121°C)]. If the sugar is too soft to form into a ball, it needs more cooking. If the sugar forms a hard ball, then it is overcooked and you need to start again.*

Montage

1. Turn the cake over so the domed side is on top. Trim it flat with a serrated knife. Then turn the cake over onto a cake board so that the flat bottom is on top. Cut the board to the same dimensions as the cake and place on a rotating cake stand. Cut two even layers with a bread knife. Remove the top half and set aside. Using a pastry brush, wet the cut surface of the bottom layer with syrup to imbibe it (*puncher*). Transfer the crème au beurre to a pastry bag fitted with a 10-mm (¼-in.) plain tip. Starting at the center, pipe (*coucher*) a tight spiral all the way to the edges of the bottom layer of cake. Place the second layer on top and press down lightly. Smooth any buttercream icing (crème au beurre) from the sides with a metal spatula. Lightly score the top of the cake with the tip of a small knife and imbibe it (*puncher*) with syrup.

2. Reserve the cake in the refrigerator. Empty the pastry bag into the bowl of buttercream icing (crème au beurre) and reserve at room temperature.

Masquage

1. Remove the cake from the refrigerator. Brush the top with syrup using a pastry brush and wait for it to soak in. Using a large metal spatula, cover the sides of the cake in buttercream icing (crème au beurre) and smooth them, scraping off any excess. Place a large dollop of crème au beurre on top and spread it out toward the edges in an even layer.

2. Smooth the top of the cake by sweeping over it using the metal spatula. Slip the spatula under the cake board and lift it up onto one hand.

3. Rotating the cake in one hand, smooth the edges and corners of the cake, removing excess crème au beurre in a continuous downward scrape of the spatula. Scrape off any excess buttercream icing (crème au beurre).

Finishing

1. Drag a pastry comb across the surface of the cake to create a textured top. Holding the cake in one hand, use the other to apply handfuls of the chopped almonds to the sides of the cake; create a scalloped or domed decoration by cupping your hand as you press in the nuts. Repeat this pattern all the way around the cake. Fill a paper cone (*cornet*) with buttercream icing (crème au beurre) and snip off the end. Use it to pipe (*coucher*) the word *Moka* onto the top of the cake.

2. Fill a second cornet with melted chocolate and snip off the end. Write over the buttercream icing (crème au beurre) with the chocolate.

3. Transfer the leftover buttercream icing (crème au beurre) to a pastry bag fitted with a 24-mm star tip. Pipe (*coucher*) 8 rosettes (*rosace*) on top of the cake and top each rosette with a coffee bean.

4. Transfer the cake either to a clean cake board or serving dish and refrigerate until ready to serve.

PAIN DE GÊNES

Learning Outcomes

Making a Genoese bread (*pain de Gênes*)

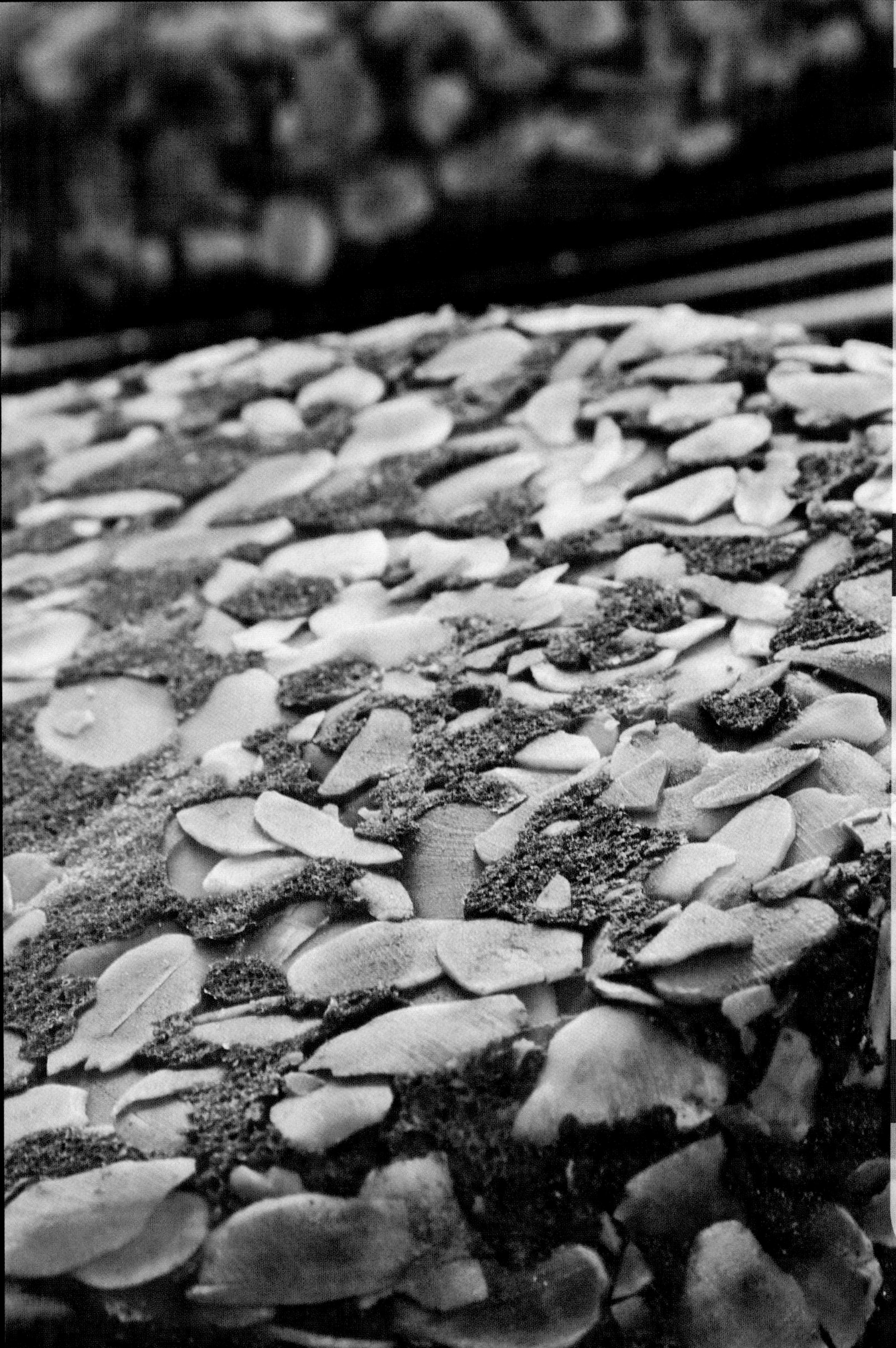

Equipment

Knives:
Paring knife (*couteau d'office*)

Tools:
Mixing bowls, wooden spatula, whisk, sieve, wire rack

Pans:
6 in. × 6 in. (15 × 15 cm) square baking pan

Serving/Yield

One 1.2 pound/600 gram cake, 8–10 servings

HISTORY

The pain de gênes is a delicious cake made with a base consisting mostly of almonds and butter. This preparation should not be confused with the similar gênoise cake, which contains large quantities of fruit and no almonds. The name of the cake literally translates to "Genoa bread," and originated in the Northern Italian port city of Genoa in the early 19th century. The cake is said to have been made to commemorate the siege of Genoa in 1800, during the French Revolutionary wars. The French troops, led by André Masséna, were forced into the fortified city of Genoa by the advance of Austrian forces into Italy. The French held the fort valiantly until their food supplies dwindled. It is said that the French troops subsisted on 50 tons of almonds, the last remaining food in the city before starvation finally forced their surrender. The siege was crucial for buying Napoleon enough time to amass his army in Italy to win the important battle of Marengo. In honor of the troops' bravery, a cake made almost entirely of the almonds, which sustained them throughout the siege, was created.

PAIN DE GÊNES
Genoese Bread

© Le Cordon Bleu International

Method

Preheat the oven to 375°F (190°C).

1. Generously butter the bottom and sides of the mold (***chemiser***). Sprinkle with the sliced almonds. Set aside.
2. Sift (***tamiser***) together the flour and cornstarch.
3. In a large bowl, soften the almond paste with a wooden spatula and gradually incorporate the beaten eggs until soft. Using a whisk, mix in the remaining eggs and beat until smooth. Stir in the rum.
4. Add some of the egg mixture to the melted butter and stir until incorporated. Stir in the remaining egg mixture. Fold in dry ingredients.
5. Fill the prepared mold. Bake until the cake is nicely colored and a knife tip inserted in the center comes out clean.
6. Allow to cool slightly, then gently unmold and finish cooling on a wire rack.

Quantity		Ingredient
U.S.	**Metric**	*Inner Lining of the Mold (Chemisage)*
As needed	As needed	Butter
As needed	As needed	Sliced almonds
		Genoese Bread (Pain de Gênes)
1 oz	30 g	Flour
Dash	Dash	Baking powder
7 oz	200 g	Almond paste
4 pcs	4 pcs	Eggs, beaten
¼ fl oz	5 ml	Rum
2 fl oz	60 ml	Butter, melted

Learning Outcomes

Making a mousse
Making meringue
Foaming method
Splitting a cake
Piping (*coucher*)
Imbibing (*imbabage*)

Equipment

Knives:
Serrated knife
(*couteau-scie*)

Tools:
Mixing bowls, whisk,
rubber spatula, pastry
brush, piping bag, medium
round tip, small food
processor, wire rack,
parchment paper

Pans:
8 in./20 cm square pan,
saucepan, bain-marie

Serving/Yield

One 2 ¼ pounds/
1.25 kilogram cake,
10–12 servings

While the pavé du roy seems simple enough from its outward appearance, this layered, alcohol-infused chocolate sponge cake will challenge the most experienced pâtissier. The pavé du roy translates literally to "the King's cobblestones," and is named for the distinctive pattern running across the top of the cake.

Quantity		Ingredient
U.S.	**Metric**	*Chocolate Mousse*
5 oz	150 g	Chocolate
2 ½ oz	75 g	Butter
4 pcs	4 pcs	Egg whites
3 pcs	3 pcs	Egg yolks
1 ¾ oz	50 g	Sugar, granulated
		Chocolate Almond Sponge (Biscuit Amande-Chocolat)
½ oz	15 g	Potato starch
½ oz	15 g	Cocoa powder
2 ¾ oz	80 g	Almond powder
3 ¼ oz	100 g	Powdered sugar
1 pc	1 pc	Egg
3 pcs	3 pcs	Egg yolks
Dash	Dash	Vanilla
		Imbibing Syrup (Imbibage)
3 ¼ oz	100 g	Sugar, granulated
4 fl oz	120 ml	Water
1 ¼ fl oz	40 ml	Cointreau liqueur
		Finishing
1 ¼ oz	40 g	Candied orange peel
1 ¼ fl oz	40 ml	Cointreau liqueur
As needed	As needed	Chocolate granules
As needed	As needed	Almond paste

PAVÉ DU ROY
Kings Cobblestones Cake

Method

Make a Chocolate Mousse

1. Melt the chocolate and butter together over a bain-marie. Once fully melted, remove from the heat and stir until smooth.
2. Beat the egg whites (**monter les blancs**) to medium peaks. Then gradually beat in the sugar until it has all been dissolved completely.
3. Whisk the egg yolks into the melted chocolate and then add some of the meringue into the mixture and stir it in well with the whisk. Gently fold in the remaining meringue using a rubber spatula, being careful not to over-mix. Set aside.

Make a Chocolate Almond Sponge (Biscuit Amande-Chocolat)

1. Preheat the oven to 320°F (160°C).
2. Butter the pan and line the bottom with parchment paper (**chemiser**).
3. Sift (**tamiser**) the potato starch and cocoa powder together and then set it aside. Mix the almond powder and flour together in a bowl. Add the egg and stir in well, then add the egg yolks one at a time, and mix in the vanilla.
4. Beat the egg whites to soft peaks (**monter les blancs**), then meringue with the sugar. Add the dry ingredients to the egg mixture and give it a few turns with the rubber spatula. Add some of the meringue and fold it in, then before completely incorporating, fold in the remaining meringue.
5. Transfer the batter to the prepared mold, pushing the batter into the corners. Bake until a knife inserted in the center comes out clean, about 20 minutes.
6. Remove the cake from the oven and allow it to cool for a few minutes. Then run the tip of a small knife around the edges and unmold it onto a wire rack. Leave the cake to cool completely.

Prepare the Imbibing Syrup (Imbibage)

1. Place the water and sugar into a small saucepan and stir to combine. Bring the water to a boil and continue boiling until the sugar is totally dissolved. Remove from the heat and allow to cool completely. Once cooled, add the Cointreau or any other orange-flavored liqueur.
2. Place the candied orange peel and the other portion of Cointreau liqueur into a small food processor and process to a purée.

Method

Assembly

1. Once cooled, if needed, trim the top to flatten. Turn the cake over and slice it into 3 layers.

2. Place a dollop of the mousse onto a cake board and place the sliced cake on top, creating a chocolate mousse base. Then gently remove the top two layers and set them aside. Imbibe the cut surface of the cake with the syrup (*imbibage*), and then spread half of the orange purée over top of the syrup (*imbibage*).

3. Cover the orange purée layer with a layer of mousse. Then top the mousse with the middle layer of cake and repeat the application of the syrup and orange purée (finishing the remaining purée) and mousse.

4. Finish by gently setting the last layer of cake. Imbibe the final layer with the syrup (*imbibage*), and then mask the cake with a thin layer of the mousse. Place it in the refrigerator to allow the mousse to set.

5. Once the cake has set, finish masking it with the mousse. Press the chocolate sprinkles onto the sides, and if desired, decorate the cake with any remaining chocolate mousse, candied orange and chocolate decorations.

Learning Outcomes

Making a détrempe
Making puff pastry
(*pâte feuilletée*)
Making an almond cream
(*crème d'amandes*)
Cutting puff pastry
Glazing (*glaçage*)

Equipment

Knives:
Paring knife
(*couteau d'office*)

Tools:
Mixing bowls, plastic
scraper (*corne*), rolling pin,
brush, whisk, wire rack,
large round dough cutters,
pastry brush, piping bag,
medium round tip

Pans:
Saucepan, baking sheet

Serving/Yield

6–8 servings

This cake, made with puff pastry and filled with almond cream (crème d'amandes), was named after the French town of Pithiviers, which is located just southwest of Paris. Similar preparations existed in various forms until Chef Antoine Carême formalized the recipe for pithiviers around 1805.

PITHIVIERS
Puff Pastry Filled with Almond Cream

Method

Make a Détrempe for Puff Pastry (Pâte Feuilletée)

1. Sift (**tamiser**) the flour onto a clean work surface and make a well in the center using a plastic scraper (**corne**). Add the salt and water to the well. Stir with your fingertips until the salt is dissolved.
2. Add the butter, cut into pieces and begin to incorporate the flour using your fingertips. As the flour, butter, and water begin to combine, use the **corne** to cut the ingredients together, until the mixture resembles a coarse dough. Sprinkle with additional water if the dough is too dry.
3. Once there are barely any traces of flour left, gather the dough into a ball and score the top of it with a deep cross using a large knife.
4. Loosely wrap the finished **détrempe** in plastic and transfer it to the refrigerator to rest for a minimum of 1 hour (preferably overnight).

Note

Détrempe *refers to the dough before the layer of butter* (**beurrage**) *is added.*

Beurrage and Tourage

1. Place the cold butter between two sheets of parchment paper and pound it with a rolling pin until it is similar to the **détrempe** in consistency.
2. Using the **corne**, shape the butter into a flat square about 1 cm/½ in. thick. Set the butter aside. Place it in the refrigerator if the kitchen is warm.
3. Lightly dust a clean work surface with flour (**fleurer**), then unwrap the **détrempe** and place it on the floured surface.
4. Using the scored marks as a guide, roll out (**abaisser**) the corners of the **détrempe** into a cross shape. Be careful to keep the center of the cross thicker than its outer arms (this will be important when rolling out the dough and the butter). Place the square of butter in the center of the cross and fold the two side arms over it so that they overlap slightly in the center (in the process be careful not to trap any air bubbles). Give the dough a quarter turn and fold the two remaining arms over the butter so that the butter is completely enclosed. Press the seams well to seal.
5. Lightly tap the dough with the length of the rolling pin to even out the distribution of the butter inside. Give the dough a quarter turn and repeat the tapping process. This is called the **enveloppe**.

Tourage, 6 Turns (6 tours simples)

1. Turns 1 and 2: Roll out (**abaisser**) the dough in long, even strokes to form a rectangle that is 3 times the

Quantity		Ingredient
U.S.	**Metric**	*Puff Pastry (Pâte Feuilletée)*
8 oz	250 g	Flour
3 ½ oz	100 g	Butter
3 ⅓ fl oz	100 ml	Water
½ tsp	4 g	Salt
3 ⅓ oz	100 g	Butter
		Almond Cream (Crème d'Amandes)
2 oz	60 g	Butter
2 oz	60 g	Powdered sugar
2 oz	60 g	Almond powder
1 pc	1 pc	Egg
1 pc	1 pc	Vanilla bean
		Finishing
1 pc	1 pc	Egg (for wash)
		Syrup
2 oz	60 g	Sugar
2 fl oz	60 ml	Water

Method

original length of the **enveloppe** or 1 cm thick. Brush off any excess flour.

2. Fold the bottom third of the dough up; then fold the top third down over the first fold. Make sure the edges are even. Give the dough a quarter turn to the right and repeat the same rolling process. Make sure to always brush away any excess flour.

3. Repeat the folding process (top third up, top third down over first fold) and give the dough a quarter turn to the right. Make two finger impressions in the top left corner of the dough.

Note

These marks are a reminder of the number of turns that the dough has received; they also indicate the position for subsequent turns.

Wrap the dough in plastic and transfer it to the refrigerator to rest for a minimum of 20 minutes. With the butter added through the first two turns, the dough is now referred to as the **pâton**.

4. Turns 3 and 4: Lightly dust the work surface with flour (**fleurer**). Remove the dough from the refrigerator and unwrap it onto the floured surface (with the 2 indents in the top left corner). Proceed to give the dough a third and fourth turn (rolling and folding in the same manner as the first and second turns). Mark the dough with 4 imprints in the top left corner before wrapping it in plastic and returning it to the refrigerator to rest for a minimum of 20 minutes.

5. Turns 5 and 6: Lightly dust the work surface with flour (**fleurer**). Remove the dough from the refrigerator and unwrap it onto the floured surface (with the 4 indents in the top left corner). Proceed to give the dough its final 2 turns, folding and rolling as in previous turns. Wrap it in plastic and return it to the refrigerator to rest for a minimum of 20 minutes before rolling it out (the longer the dough rests the better it will perform).

Tip

Because the détrempe and the butter are at the same consistency, it is necessary to complete the turns as explained above. If the dough is allowed to over-chill between turns, the butter may become too hard and crack when rolled out. Make sure you have allotted the necessary time to complete the turns

6. Lightly spritz or dampen a clean baking sheet.

7. Remove the feuilletage from the refrigerator and cut it in half. Keep one half in the refrigerator and roll out (**abaisser**) the other half out into a square about ⅛-in. (3–4 mm) thick. Transfer the rolled dough to the baking sheet, and place it in the refrigerator to rest.

Make Almond Cream (Crème d'Amandes)

1. Cream the butter and sugar together until light and fluffy (**crémer**).

2. Beat the egg until well combined. Using a small knife, split the vanilla bean in half lengthwise and scrape out the seeds. Whisk into the mixture. Add the rum and finish by mixing in the almond powder.

3. Reserve the crème d'amandes in a covered bowl in the refrigerator until ready to use.

Assembly

1. Beat the egg for the egg wash.

2. Remove the rolled out dough, and using a 5-in. (32 ¼ cm) round, slightly mark the center of the dough. Brush the surface with egg wash, then pipe (**coucher**) the frangipane (combination of two different creams) in a spiral into the circle, adding slightly more in the center. Set aside.

3. Roll out (**abaisser**) the second half of the dough into a square slightly larger than the first. Fold it in half and gently lay it over the prepared dough with the fold running down the center of the frangipane. Gently unfold the top dough, covering the frangipane while pressing out any air bubbles, moving from the edge of the filling outwards. Press evenly. Place back in the refrigerator to allow the dough to firm up, about 20 minutes.

4. Preheat the oven to 425°F (220°C).

5. Remove the baking sheet from the refrigerator. Using a sharp paring knife held vertically, cut a scalloped edge around the chilled dough. The cuts should be clean. If the dough is stretching or pulling as you are trying to cut, put it back in the fridge.

6. Brush the surface with egg wash, being careful to not let any of the egg drip down the sides, as this may inhibit the pithiviers from rising evenly. Pierce and twist the tip of the paring knife in the center of the pithiviers. Holding the paring knife by the blade, cut a spiral pattern, starting at the center and arcing outward. Brush with a second coating of egg wash, again careful not to let it drip down the sides.

7. Place in the hot oven and bake until golden brown, about 25 to 30 minutes.

8. While the pithiviers is baking, bring the sugar and water to a boil until the sugar is completely dissolved. Set aside.

9. Once the pithiviers is cooked, brush with the sugar syrup and place back in the oven to glaze, about 5 minutes.

10. Transfer to a wire rack to cool.

Learning Outcomes

Making a Joconde sponge
(*biscuit joconde*)
Making a ganache
Making meringue

Equipment

Knives:
Palette knife (*spatule*),
serrated knife (*couteau-scie*)

Tools:
Mixing bowls, whisk, sieve,
parchment paper, rubber
and wooden spatulas, cake
comb, piping bag, small
round tip, wire rack

Pans:
Saucepan, baking sheet

Serving/Yield

One 3 ¼ pound/
1.7 kilogram cake,
8–10 servings

HISTORY

Although not quite as labor intensive as building the pyramids of Egypt, the making of a pyramid noisette is nevertheless a geometrical feat that requires precision on the part of the pastry chef. The two elements that are intricately manipulated to make this preparation are biscuit joconde and ganache. Information on the history of biscuit joconde is outlined on page 366; the history of ganache, which may be made either with heavy cream as in this recipe or with butter, is largely obscure. The person generally associated with having best adapted pre-existing recipes for ganche is Chef Siraudin, who was working in Paris in the 1850s. Apart from its culinary meaning, the word *ganache* translates into English as "the lower jaw of a horse." While there may be the temptation to force a link between the two meanings—something onomatopoeic (words that sound like the action they describe) about chewing, for example—all agree there is no evidence, either etymological or historical, to support this.

PYRAMIDE NOISETTES
Pyramid Cake

Quantity		Ingredient
U.S.	**Metric**	*Joconde Sponge (Biscuit Joconde)*
1 ½ oz	40 g	Flour, sifted
4 ¾ oz	140 g	Almond powder
4 ¾ oz	140 g	Powdered sugar
4 pcs	4 pcs	Eggs
4 pcs	4 pcs	Egg whites
1 ¾ oz	50 g	Sugar
1 fl oz	30 ml	Butter, melted
		Ganache
13 ½ fl oz	400 ml	Heavy cream
13 ½ oz	400 g	Chocolate
		Finishing
5 oz	150 g	Chopped hazelnuts

Method

Preheat the oven to 460°F (240°C).
Line a large baking sheet with parchment paper.

Prepare the Joconde Sponge (Biscuit Joconde)

1. Sift the flour (***tamiser***) and set it aside. Place the almond powder, powdered sugar, and vanilla in a large bowl and mix well. Then add the eggs, one at a time, mixing well after each addition. Beat until homogenous and the mixture forms a ribbon when the whisk is lifted.
2. Mount the egg whites (***monter les blancs***) to medium peaks. Gradually whisk in the sugar and beat until tight and glossy. Stir some of the meringue into the egg mixture and mix it in well, then with a rubber spatula, fold the remaining egg whites into the flour. Just before completely incorporated, fold in the melted butter.
3. Spread the dough out onto the prepared baking sheet. Bake until light brown, about 6 to 8 minutes. Remove the biscuit from the oven and transfer the biscuit, still on the parchment paper, to a wire rack to cool.

Prepare the Ganache

1. Chop the chocolate into small pieces and place them in a bowl. Bring the heavy cream to a boil.
2. Once the cream comes to a boil, immediately pour it over the chocolate. Mix the combination gently with a wooden spatula and then allow it to cool.

Assembly

1. Remove the parchment paper from the biscuit joconde and cut it into 6 strips crosswise. Spread a thin layer of ganache over the first biscuit strip and then cover it with the second layer. Spread the second layer with ganache and then cover it with another layer of biscuit. Repeat the layering process until all of the layers have been used, then cover the top layer with a coating of ganache. Place in the refrigerator to set.
2. Trim to even out the edges. With a serrated knife, carefully cut from the top corner to the opposite corner at the bottom in order to create 2 triangles. Turn the triangles onto their sides so the layers are vertical. Match the top layer with the bottom layer and gently but firmly press them together, forming the pyramid.
3. Reheat the ganache until liquid. Place the pyramid on a wire rack. Reserving a small amount of ganache for later use, use a ladle to pour chocolate over the pyramid, evenly coating both sides. Allow the ganache to set, then (if desired) create a zigzag pattern on both sides using the teeth of a serrated knife or a cake comb. Place the reserved chocolate ganache into the piping bag and fit it with a small round tip. Pipe an attractive border along the top of the pyramid and sprinkle with toasted hazelnuts. Transfer the pyramid to a serving dish or cake board, and leave to chill until ready to serve.

Learning Outcomes

Making a Genoese sponge
cake (*biscuit Génoise*)
Making a rolled cake
(*roulade*)
Making an orange
mousseline cream
Making a syrup
candying fruit
Imbibing (*imbiber*)
Glazing (*abricoter*)

Equipment

Knives:
Palette knife (*spatule*),
paring knife
(*couteau d'office*)

Tools:
Mixing bowl, whisk, grater,
shallow pan, piping bag,
medium star tip, clean
kitchen towel

Pans:
Baking sheet, bain-marie,
small saucepan, medium
saucepan

Serving/Yield

One 4-pound/2.1-kilogram
cake, 10–12 servings

The cake that forms the base of the Orange Roulade (roulé à l'orange) is a Genoese Sponge cake (biscuit Génoise), which is a light and airy type of foam cake. The Genoese Sponge (biscuit Génoise) is thought to have originated in its current form from the Italian city of Genoa (the name literally translates to "Genoa cake") by around the year 1850. What differentiates the Génoise from other foam cakes is the use of a bain-marie in the preparation. Using the bain-marie to gradually heat the whole eggs and sugar as they're beaten together helps to leaven the batter gradually, while still maintaining the fluffy texture of the Génoise.

Quantity		Ingredient
U.S.	**Metric**	*Geneose Sponge Cake (Génoise)*
4 pcs	4 pcs	Eggs
1 pc	1 pc	Orange zest, grated
4 oz	120 g	Sugar, granulated
4 oz	120 g	Flour
¾ oz	20 g	Butter, melted
		Syrup
5 fl oz	150 ml	Water
5 oz	150 g	Sugar, granulated
3 ⅓ fl oz	100 ml	Orange juice
1 fl oz	30 ml	Cointreau (optional)
		Orange Mousseline Cream (Crème Mousseline Orange)
13 ¼ fl oz	400 ml	Orange juice
1 pc	1 pc	Orange zest, grated
4 pcs	4 pcs	Egg yolks
3 ¼ oz	100 g	Sugar, granulated
1 oz	30 g	Flour
1 oz	30 g	Cornstarch
7 oz	200 g	Butter, room temperature (en pommade)
1 pc	1 pc	Vanilla
		Decoration
1 pc	1 pc	Orange
7 oz	200 g	Sugar, granulated
7 fl oz	200 ml	Water
As needed	As needed	Almonds, toasted
As needed	As needed	Apricot nappage

ROULÉ À L'ORANGE
Orange Roulade

Method

Preheat the oven to 355°F (180°C).

Make a Genoese Sponge Cake (Génoise)
1. Prepare a bain-marie. Place the eggs, orange zest, and sugar in a large bowl and whisk together using a balloon whisk.
2. Place the mixture over the bain-marie and continue whisking until hot to the touch (60°C/140°F). Remove from the heat and continue whisking until cooled.
3. Add the flour and fold it in until just incorporated. Spread the mixture onto a lined sheet pan and bake it until golden for approximately 6 to 8 minutes. Place on a wire rack to cool.

Make the Syrup
1. Place the water, sugar, and orange juice into a small saucepan over medium-high heat.
2. Bring to a boil and continue boiling until the sugar is completely dissolved. Transfer to a clean bowl and allow to cool. Add the Cointreau.

Make the Mousseline Cream (Crème Mousseline)
1. Heat the orange juice in a medium saucepan with the grated orange zest and vanilla. Whisk the egg yolks with the sugar until light in color and a ribbon forms when the whisk is lifted.
2. Whisk in the flour and cornstarch. Once the orange juice has come to a boil, pour some into the egg mixture to temper. Stir until smooth, then remove from the heat and add to the rest of the orange juice.
3. Place the mixture back onto the heat and whisk until it thickens and comes to a boil. Allow it to boil for 1 minute while whisking, then remove from the heat.
4. Transfer the cooked cream to a platter lined with plastic. Dab the surface with a piece of butter, and then cover with a second sheet of plastic wrap, pressing out any air bubbles. Allow to cool, then chill.

Make the Decoration
1. Make a simple syrup with the sugar and water. Bring the sugar and water to a boil and cook until the sugar is dissolved, then reduce the heat to low.
2. Wash and trim the ends from the oranges, then slice them very thinly. Place the slices in the syrup and allow to gently candy until the skin becomes translucent. Do not bring to a boil.

Method

3. Remove from the heat and allow to cool in the syrup. Remove the candied slices from the syrup and drain.

Mousseline Cream (Crème Mousseline)

1. Once the cream has chilled, transfer it to a bowl and whisk until smooth.
2. Add the butter in increments, whisking well after each addition, ensuring the butter is softened (**en pommade**) at room temperature before adding.

Assembly

1. Flip the Genoese sponge cake (Génoise) over onto a clean kitchen towel and remove the parchment paper.
2. Imbibe the surface with the syrup. Spread with the mousseline cream (crème mousseline), reserving some for the final decoration. With the aid of the towel, lift up the bottom edge and roll the Genoese sponge cake (Génoise) into a log.
3. Place the log seam side down onto the serving platter. In a small saucepan, heat the nappage until just melted and brush the log. Transfer the remaining mousseline into a piping bag fitted with a medium star tip. Pipe rosettes down the center and garnish with a candied orange slice.

SAVARIN AUX FRUITS ET À LA CRÈME

Making a yeast dough
(*pâte levée*)
Imbibing a cake (*imbiber*)
Making a Chantilly cream
(*crème Chantilly*)
Glazing (*nappage*)

Equipment

Knives:
Paring knife (*office*)

Tools:
Mixing bowls, corne, whisk,
pastry brush, ladle, wire
rack, pastry bag, large star
tip

Pans:
Baking sheet, savarin mold

Serving

8 persons

HISTORY

Renowned French chefs in their own right, the Julienne brothers created the savarin aux fruits and named it in honor of Brillat Savarin, the 19th century gastronome and author of the *Physiolgie du goût*. Brillat Savarin died in 1826, approximately 20 years after tehe purported creation of the dessert.

SAVARIN AUX FRUITS ET À LA CRÈME
Savarin Cake with Fruit

Method

1. Preheat the oven to 400°F (205°C).
2. Brush a savarin mold with melted butter and reserve it in a cool area.

Savarin Dough (Pâte à Savarin)

1. Sift (**tamiser**) the flour onto a clean work surface and sprinkle it with salt and sugar. Mix the yeast into the warm water until it has completely dissolved. Make a well (**fontaine**) in the flour using a plastic scraper (**corne**) and pour the yeast mixture, eggs, and melted butter into it. Using your fingertips, gradually incorporate flour from the fountain into the center. As soon as all the flour is mixed in, work the dough by lifting it up off the marble and slapping it down onto the work surface, repeatedly. If the dough doesn't stick to the marble, it's too dry and needs more water. Continue working it until the gluten develops enough that the dough no longer sticks. Next, roll the dough into a ball, place it in a clean bowl, cover it with a humid cloth, and leave it in a warm place to proof until doubled in size. Once risen, punch down the dough and shape into a ring. Place it in the buttered savarin mold and leave it in a warm place to proof a second time until doubled in size.

Note

While preparing the dough, never add the salt directly to the yeast/water mixture; the chemical reaction will kill the yeast. A pinch of sugar can be helpful.

Imbibing Syrup (Sirop pour Imbibage)

1. Pour the water into a small saucepan and add the sugar. Bring the mixture to a boil over medium-high heat and continue to boil it until all the sugar has dissolved. Remove the pan from the stove and set aside.
2. Once the syrup has cooled to room temperature, stir in the vanilla extract and rum.

Cooking (Cuisson)

1. When the dough has risen a second time, transfer it to the oven to bake. After 20 minutes, reduce the temperature of the oven to 380°F (195°C). Bake for another 20 minutes or until golden. Once the savarin is cooked, remove it from the oven and let it rest in its mold for 5 minutes before unmolding it onto a wire rack set over a baking sheet.

Quantity		Ingredient
U.S.	Metric	*Savarin Dough (Pâte à Savarin)*
1 lb	500 g	Flour
½ oz	10 g	Salt
1 oz	30 g	Sugar, granulated
1 oz	30 g	Yeast
4 ¾ fl oz	140 ml	Water, warm
4 pcs	4 pcs	Eggs, lightly beaten, room temperature
5 fl oz	150 ml	Butter, melted, room temperature
		Imbibing Syrup (Sirop pour Imbibage)
26 fl oz	800 ml	Water
13 ½ oz	400 g	Sugar, granulated
1 drop 2 mL	2 g	Vanilla extract
1 ¾ fl oz	50 ml	Rum
		Chantilly Cream (Crème Chantilly)
7 fl oz	200 ml	Cream
1 oz	30 g	Powdered sugar
¼ fl oz	5 ml	Vanilla extract
		Finishing
5 oz	150 g	Apricot glaze, warmed
8 oz	250 g	Fresh fruit

Method

Immediately brush the savarin with syrup until it is drenched (***imbiber***) and all the syrup has been used up. Let the cake cool to room temperature.

Assembly (Montage)

1. Melt the apricot glaze in a small saucepan over medium heat until liquid. Using a pastry brush, apply it to the savarin to give it a shiny coating. Place the savarin in the refrigerator to chill.

2. Meanwhile, prepare a crème Chantilly: Using a large whisk, whip the cream in a large mixing bowl in an ice bath to soft peaks. Add the powdered sugar and the vanilla, and continue to whip the cream until stiff. Reserve the crème Chantilly in the refrigerator until needed.

3. Place the savarin on a chilled serving dish. Transfer the crème Chantilly to a pastry bag fitted with a medium star tip and fill the cavity in the center of the savarin. Arrange fresh fruit on top of the crème Chantilly and refrigerate the savarin before serving.

Learning Outcomes

Making a biscuit
dacquoise
Making a buttercream
(*crème au beurre*)
Piping (*coucher*)
Making a pâte à bombe
Using marzipan
Writing in chocolate

Equipment

Knives:
Paring knife (*office*)

Tools:
Whisk, rubber spatula,
corne, sieve, pastry bag,
10 mm plain tip, balloon
whisk, rolling pin, cornet,
mixing bowls

Pans:
Baking sheet, medium
saucepan

Serving

8 persons

FYL...

The usually expansive *Dictionnaire du Gastronome* simply indicates that the reasons for naming this preparation succès are unknown. With a general lack of information on the subject one is left to surmise: was it the success of the pastry chef who first perfected it? Or was it served at a banquet to celebrate some successful achievement? There is no question, however, that when the crème au beurre is well executed and the biscuit Dacquoise offers just the right balance of outer crispness and inner tenderness, gâteau succès fully deserves its name. One interesting side point is that gatâau succès is sometimes considered a Passover cake in Jewish baking. Unfortunately this is not an historical lead but is rather due to the fact that succès can be adapted to be made without flour—an ingredient that is prohibited at Passover.

Quantity		Ingredient
U.S.	**Metric**	*Dacquoise Sponge (Biscuit Dacquoise)*
5 oz	150 g	Almond powder
7 ¾ oz	225 g	Powdered sugar
⅓ fl oz	10 ml	Vanilla extract
2 ½ oz	75 g	Flour
6 pcs	6 pcs	Egg whites
2 ½ oz	75 g	Sugar, granulated
		Buttercream Icing (Crème au Beurre)
3 ⅓ oz	100 g	Sugar, granulated
1 fl oz	30 ml	Water
3 pcs	3 pcs	Egg yolks
7 oz	200 g	Butter
1 ¾ oz	50 g	Hazelnut praline
		Garnish (Garniture)
3 ⅓ oz	100 g	Sliced almonds
3 ⅓ oz	100 g	Almond paste
As needed	As needed	Green food dye
As needed	As needed	Whole hazelnuts
As needed	As needed	Chocolate, melted
As needed	As needed	Cocoa powder, for dusting

SUCCÈS
Hazelnut Buttercream Meringue Cake

Method

1. Preheat the oven to 380°F (195°C).
2. Lightly grease a baking sheet with cold butter and place it in the refrigerator to chill for 5 minutes. Remove the baking sheet from the refrigerator, dust it with flour (**chemiser**), and shake off the excess. Mark the baking sheet with 2 circles using a 10-in. (25-cm) cake ring and return it to the refrigerator until needed.

Dacquoise Sponge (Biscuit Dacquoise)

1. Sift together the almond powder, sugar, flour, and vanilla. Set aside.
2. *Make a meringue:* Beat the egg whites to soft peaks. Gradually incorporate the sugar until the meringue is firm and glossy and the sugar granules cannot be felt when the meringue is rubbed between 2 fingers. Fold in the sifted ingredients until just combined.
3. Transfer the mixture to a pastry bag fitted with a 10-mm plain tip. Remove the baking sheet from the refrigerator and pipe (**coucher**) two tight 10-in. spirals of dacquoise onto it using the marked circles as guides. Tap the baking sheet lightly to fill in any gaps. Dust the discs of dacquoise with powdered sugar and transfer them to the oven to bake until lightly golden (*8 to 10 minutes*).
4. Remove the baking sheet from the oven and transfer it to a wire rack to cool. Reduce the oven temperature to 350°F (175°C).

French Buttercream Icing (Crème au Beurre Française)

1. Cook the sugar and water in a medium saucepan over medium-high heat until they reach the soft-ball stage (**petit boulé**) [250°F (121°C)]. Meanwhile, place the egg yolks in a mixing bowl and stir. When the sugar syrup reaches the soft stage, pour it into the egg yolks in a steady stream while whisking continously. Continue whisking until the mixture is thick and pale and creates ribbons when the whisk is lifted from the bowl. This mixture is a pâte à bombe.
2. Whisk the pâte à bombe until the mixing bowl is just warm to the touch and add all the butter. Mix vigorously with the whisk until the mixture is homogeneous and thick enough to hold its own shape. Whisk in the praline and reserve at room temperature.

Tip

To tell how well done the sugar is, dip 2 fingertips and your thumb in the cold water, then rapidly scoop up a little drop of the boiling syrup before plunging them straight back into the cold water. If the syrup forms a malleable ball, it is at the soft-ball *stage (**petit boulé**) [250°F (121°C)]. If the sugar is too soft to form into a ball, it needs more cooking. If the sugar forms a hard ball, then it is overcooked and you need to start again.*

Assembly (Montage)

1. Using the cake ring as a guide, trim any excess off the edges of the dacquoise discs.
2. Transfer the buttercream icing (crème au beurre) to a pastry bag fitted with a 10-mm plain tip. Cut a cake board to a 10-in. (25-cm) circle and place a disc of dacquoise on top of it upside down. Starting from the center, pipe (**coucher**) a tight spiral of buttercream icing (crème au beurre) onto the dacquoise to completely cover it. Place the second disc on top, right way up and gently press on it to secure it in place. Scrape away any excess buttercream icing (crème au beurre) from the edges and place the cake in the refrigerator.

Decoration

1. Spread the sliced almonds out onto a baking sheet and place them in the oven to toast until lightly golden (*5 to 10 minutes*). Set aside.
2. Lightly dust the work surface with powdered sugar. Using a rolling pin, roll out the marzipan to a thickness of ⅛ in. (2 mm) on the sugared surface. Cut a rough rectangle out of the marzipan and set aside. Gather the rest of the marzipan into a ball and add a drop of green food coloring. Knead the marzipan until it is homogeneously colored. Roll out the marzipan again and cut out leaf shapes. Cut some small strips and wrap them around peeled hazelnuts to imitate the husks of fresh hazelnuts. Using a small, dry paintbrush, dust the finished nuts, leaves, and rectangle with cocoa powder to add detail and definition. Pour some melted chocolate into a paper cone (**cornet**) and snip off the tip. Pipe the word *Succès* onto the marzipan rectangle. Set aside.

Finishing

1. Remove the cake from the refrigerator. Holding the cake in one hand, apply buttercream icing (crème au beurre) around the outside using a metal spatula. Smooth the buttercream icing (crème au beurre) and remove any excess, being careful not to apply any to the top of the cake. Place the cake on the work surface and dust the top with powdered sugar until it is completely white. Press the toasted almonds to the side of the cake to completely cover the buttercream icing (crème au beurre) and arrange the marzipan decorations on the top. Transfer the cake either to a clean cake board or serving dish and refrigerate until ready to serve.

Entremets

Learning Outcomes

Making a crème Anglaise
Making a bavarois
Layering mousses
Making a cream Chantilly
Blanchir à la nappe
Unmolding (*démouler*)

Equipment

Knives:
Paring knife (*office*)

Tools:
Bowls, balloon whisk,
rubber spatula, wooden
spoon, chinois, charlotte
mold, ice bath, pastry bag,
large star tip

Pans:
Medium saucepan

Serving

6–8 persons

BAVAROIS RUBANÉ
Tri-colored Bavarian Cream

Method

Place a charlotte mold in the freezer to chill.

Bavarois

1. Place the milk in a medium saucepan and bring to a low boil over medium-high heat. Using a small knife, split the vanilla bean lengthwise. Scrape the seeds from both sides and add to the milk along with the bean. Whisk well.

2. Place the egg yolks in a mixing bowl, add the sugar, and immediately begin to whisk it into the yolks. Continue whisking until the sugar is completely dissolved and the mixture is pale in color (**blanchir**).

3. Once the milk is scalded, whisk about one-third of the hot milk into the yolks to temper them. Whisk until the mixture is well-combined and evenly heated.

4. Stir the tempered egg yolks into the pan of remaining hot milk and stir with a wooden spatula. Place the pan over low heat and stir in a figure 8 motion. As you stir, the foam on the surface will disappear; at the same time, the liquid will begin to thicken and become oil-like in resistance. Continue cooking until the mixture is thick enough to coat the back of a wooden spatula and when your finger leaves a clean trail (**à la nappe**). DO NOT ALLOW IT TO COME TO A BOIL. Remove the pan from the heat.

5. Bloom the gelatin in a bowl of ice water. Once it is completely softened, squeeze out the excess water and add the gelatin to the hot crème Anglaise. Stir it in until completely dissolved, then strain the hot crème Anglaise through a fine mesh sieve (**chinois**).

6. Place the chocolate couverture in a small mixing bowl and the coffee extract in another. Pour one-third of the crème Anglaise onto the chocolate, let it rest 1 minute to melt the chocolate, and stir gently with a wooden spatula until the mixture is smooth and homogeneous. Pour another one-third of the crème Anglaise onto the coffee extract and stir gently with a wooden spatula until combined. Stir the vanilla essence into the remaining crème Anglaise. Scrape the sides of all 3 bowls clean and reserve at room temperature.

7. Whip the cream in a large bowl over an ice bath, using a large whisk, until it reaches the soft peak stage. Divide the whipped cream into 3 equal portions and reserve in the refrigerator in 3 separate bowls.

Quantity		Ingredient
U.S.	**Metric**	**Bavarois**
1 pt	500 ml	Milk
½ pc	½ pc	Vanilla bean
4 pcs	4 pcs	Egg yolks
4 oz	120 g	Sugar, granulated
5 to 6 pcs	5 to 6 pcs	Gelatin leaves
1 oz	30 g	Dark chocolate, chopped
To taste	To taste	Coffee essence
To taste	To taste	Vanilla essence
13 ½ fl oz	400 ml	Whipping cream
		Chantilly Cream
3 ⅓ fl oz	100 ml	Whipping cream
½ oz	30 g	Powdered sugar
		To Serve
As needed	As needed	Chocolate couverture

Method

Assembly

1. Place the bowl of vanilla crème Anglaise in an ice bath and stir it back and forth with a wooden spatula (**vanner**) until it is cool to the touch but still liquid. Remove the bowl from the ice bath and remove 1 bowl of whipped cream from the refrigerator. Add one-third to the vanilla mixture to lighten its texture and gently stir it in with a whisk until the mixture is homogeneous. Add the rest of the whipped cream and fold it in with a rubber spatula until combined. Remove the charlotte mold from the freezer and being careful not to get any drips down the sides, pour the mixture into the bottom of the mold. Gently tap the mold on the work surface to even out the layer of bavarois and remove any air bubbles and return it to the freezer to set before going on with the next layering.

2. Meanwhile, prepare the coffee bavarois by cooling the crème Anglaise over an ice bath and adding the whipped cream to it following the same procedure as for the vanilla bavarois. Once the bottom layer has set, remove the mold from the freezer and being careful not to get any on the sides of the mold, pour in the coffee bavarois. Gently tap the mold on the work surface to even out the layer of bavarois and remove any air bubbles and return it to the freezer to set the second layer.

3. Prepare the chocolate bavarois by following the same method as for the vanilla and coffee bavarois. Remove the mold from the freezer and pour in the chocolate bavarois. Gently tap the mold on the

work surface to even out the layer and remove any air bubbles and return it to the freezer to allow the bavarois to set. The bavarois can be kept in the refrigerator once the layering is done; the use of the freezer in the process is to accelerate the setting of the different layers.

Chocolate Shavings

1. With a clean vegetable peeler, scrape a bar or piece of chocolate to make chocolate shavings. Scrape into a small bowl and set aside.

Finishing

1. *Prepare a crème Chantilly:* Whip the cream in a large mixing bowl in an ice bath using a large whisk. Whip until it reaches the soft peak stage, then add the powdered sugar and continue to whip the cream until it is stiff. Reserve the crème Chantilly in the refrigerator until needed.

To Serve

1. Attach a medium star tip to a pastry bag and half fill it with the crème Chantilly. Half fill a large mixing bowl with hot water.

2. Remove the charlotte mold from the freezer and dip it in the hot water for 2 to 3 seconds to loosen the bavarois from the mold. Unmold the bavarois (démouler) onto a chilled serving dish.

3. Once the bavarois is unmolded, pipe crème Chantilly on the top and sprinkle with chocolate shavings.

4. Serve the bavarois immediately or return it to the freezer until ready to serve.

Learning Outcomes

Making ladyfinger sponge
(*biscuits cuillère*)
Making a meringue
Making a Chantilly cream
(*crème Chantilly*)
Making a kirsch syrup
Piping (*coucher*)

Equipment

Tools:
Mixing bowls, whisk,
rubber spatula, sieve,
parchment paper, piping
bag, medium round tip, star
tip, pastry brush

Pans:
Medium charlotte mold,
baking sheets, wire rack,
saucepan

Serving/Yield

6–8 servings

HISTORY

The Charlotte Malakoff cake is a delicate, rich, and deliciously creamy dessert. It is a type of Charlotte Russe that is thought to have been created by the master French Chef Marie-Antoine Carême in the late 17th century. The cake is believed to have been created during Carême's period of service to the Russian Tsar Alexander I, which is why the cake is called Russe (French for "Russian"). The Charlotte part of the name stems from two potential sources. The first says that Charlotte is derived from the sister-in-law of Tsar Alexander, Queen Charlotte, the Queen of England, who was married to King George III. The second possible origin of the name says that Charlotte is not the name of a person at all, but rather a description of the dessert itself. Charlotte may be derived from the word "charlyt," which is an old English word meaning "dish of custard."

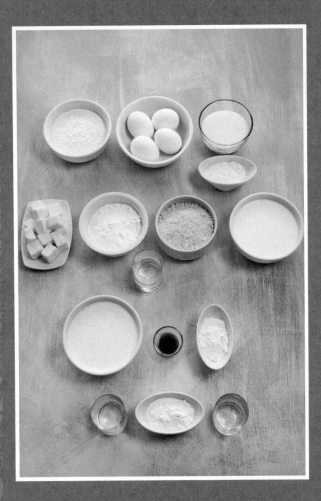

CHARLOTTE MALAKOFF

Quantity		Ingredient
U.S.	**Metric**	*Ladyfinger Sponge (Biscuits Cuillère)*
4 pcs	4 pcs	Eggs
4 oz	120 g	Sugar, granulated
4 oz	120 g	Flour
As needed	As needed	Powdered sugar for finish
		Kirsch Syrup
1 fl oz	30 ml	Water
1 oz	30 g	Sugar
1 fl oz	30 ml	Kirsch
		Malakoff
4 oz	120 g	Butter
4 oz	120 g	Powdered sugar
4 oz	120 g	Almond powder
1 fl oz	30 ml	Kirsch
8 fl oz	250 ml	Whipping cream
		Chantilly Cream
8 fl oz	250 ml	Whipping cream
1 oz	30 g	Powdered sugar
¼ fl oz	5 ml	Vanilla

Method

Preheat the oven to 375°F (190°C).

Make Ladyfinger Sponge (Biscuits Cuillère):
1. Line a baking sheet with parchment paper.
2. Separate the eggs and sift (*tamiser*) the flour.
3. Beat the egg yolks with half of the sugar until it becomes light in color (*blanchir*) and the wires of the whisk leave traces in the mixture.
4. Beat the egg whites to soft peaks (*monter les blancs*), then meringue with the remaining sugar until the whites are firm and glossy. Fold some of the meringue into the egg yolks to lighten them, and then fold in the remaining meringue. When it is just incorporated (you should still see the white of the meringue), fold in the flour.
5. Transfer the mixture to a piping bag fitted with a medium round tip. Pipe out (*coucher*) 2 small rounds. With the remaining batter, pipe out (*coucher*) fingers of the batter onto the prepared baking sheet approximately 4 in. (10 cm) in length. Be sure to leave at least 1 in. (2.5 cm) between each, allowing room for the batter to expand. Dust the batter with powdered sugar. Bake until dry to the touch, approximately 8 to 10 minutes. Remove from the oven and then gently transfer the biscuits to a wire rack to cool.

Make a Kirsch Syrup
1. Bring the water and sugar to a boil in a small saucepan until the sugar is just dissolved. Remove from the heat and allow to cool. Add the kirsch.
2. Line the charlotte mold with parchment paper (*chemiser*). Arrange the biscuit fingers around the sides with the bottoms facing in and then brush them with the kirsch syrup. Set aside.

Malakoff
1. Cream together (*crémer*) the butter and powdered sugar until light and fluffy. Whisk in the kirsch and then mix in the almond powder. Mount the cream to soft peaks. Fold a scoopful of the whipping cream into the almond powder mixture, then fold in the rest until combined.
2. Fill half of the prepared mold with the Malakoff and press a round of biscuit on top. Fill the remaining Malakoff and finish with the second round of biscuit, press well so that it is even with the top of the biscuit. Place in the refrigerator to chill until set, approximately 2 to 4 hours.

Serving
1. Make a crème Chantilly by whisking the cream and powdered sugar to medium peaks. Transfer the crème to a piping bag fitted with a small star tip.
2. Unmold the charlotte onto a serving dish. Pipe crème Chantilly between the biscuits and cover the top.

CHARLOTTE AUX POIRES, COULIS DE FRAMBOISES

Learning Outcomes

Preparing a bavarois
Making ladyfinger sponge (*biscuit à la cuillère*)
Assembly of a charlotte
Making a meringue
Piping (*coucher*)
Blanchir
Making a Crème Anglaise

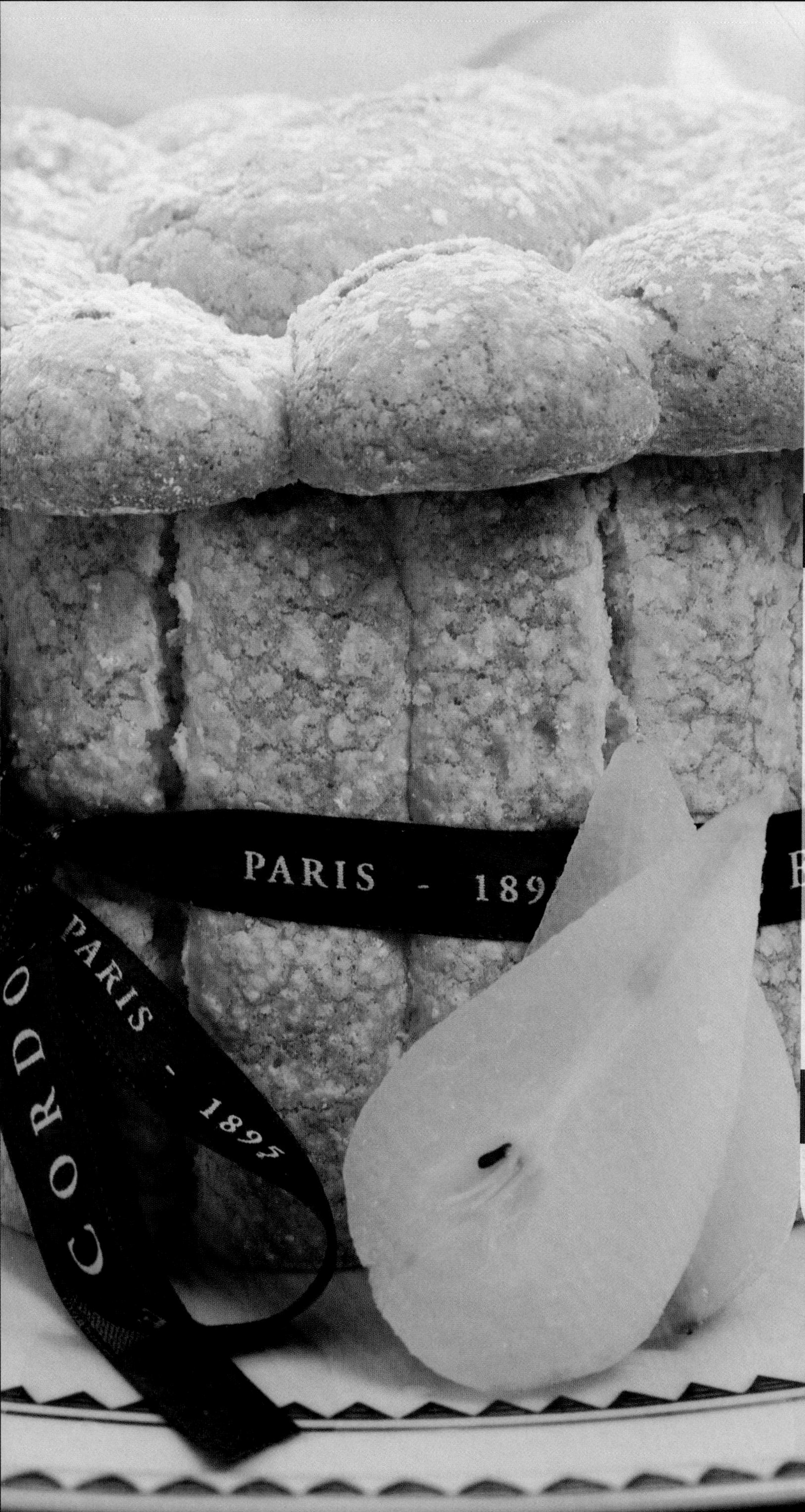

Equipment

Knives:
Paring knife (*office*), chef knife (*couteau chef*)

Tools:
Scissors, charlotte mold, balloon whisk, rubber spatula, wooden spatula, chinois, pastry bag, plain 12 mm tip, medium star tip, mixing bowls, whisk, ice bath

Pans:
1 medium saucepan, 1 small saucepan, 2 baking sheets

Serving

6 persons

Quantity		Ingredient
U.S.	*Metric*	*Ladyfinger Sponge (Biscuit à la Cuillère)*
4 oz	120 g	Flour, sifted (**tamiser**)
4 pcs	4 pcs	Egg whites
4 oz	120 g	Sugar, granulated
4 pcs	4 pcs	Egg yolks
As needed	As needed	Powdered sugar, for dusting
		Bavarois
7 fl oz	200 ml	Milk
3 pcs	3 pcs	Egg yolks
1 ¾ oz	50 g	Sugar, granulated
4 pcs	4 pcs	Gelatin leaves
7 oz	200 ml	Pear purée, room temperature
As needed	As needed	Pear liqueur, room temperature (*optional*)
7 fl oz	200 ml	Cream
		Coulis
3 ⅓ oz	100 ml	Raspberry purée
1 ¼ oz	35 g	Sugar, granulated
¼ fl oz	10 ml	Raspberry liqueur
		To Serve
3 ⅓ fl oz	100 ml	Cream
2 pcs	2 pcs	Pears, canned (*optional*)

CHARLOTTE AUX POIRES, COULIS DE FRAMBOISES
Pear Charlotte

Method

1. Preheat the oven to 380°F (195°C).
2. Place 2 large mixing bowls and whisks in the refrigerator to chill.
3. On the underside of a sheet of parchment paper, trace the contour of the open end of the charlotte mold.
4. Line a baking sheet with the parchment paper, upside down so that the pencil tracings are underneath.
5. Line a second baking sheet with a blank piece of parchment paper.
6. Cut a circle of parchment paper to line the bottom of the charlotte mold. Place it inside.

Making Ladyfinger Sponge (Biscuit à la Cuillère)

1. *Prepare the biscuit cuillère batter:* Sift (**tamiser**) the flour onto a piece of parchment paper. Separate the eggs into 2 large mixing bowls. Beat the whites (**monter les blancs**) with a balloon whisk until they are white and frothy but still fluid. Set aside. Add the sugar to the egg yolks and whisk them together until the mixture is thick and pale in color (**blanchir**). Set aside.
2. Whip the egg whites (**monter les blancs**) with the balloon whisk until they reach the soft peak stage (**bec d'oiseau**). Gradually begin to add the sugar, beating it in with the whisk. Once all the sugar has been added, continue to beat the whites until they are thick and glossy and you can no longer feel the granules when the meringue is rubbed between your fingers. Stir the flour into the egg yolks until just incorporated. Add some of the meringue to lighten the yolk mixture, then fold in the remaining meringue. The end result should be a pale, homogeneous batter with a light airy texture that is ideal for piping.
3. Transfer the batter to a pastry bag fitted with a 12-mm plain tip.
4. *Pipe (**coucher**) the biscuit cuillère:* Create a flower shape (**marguerite**) by piping teardrop shapes from the exterior of one of the circles drawn onto the parchment paper to its center, rotating the tray with each "petal." Finish the flower by piping a "chou" into its center. Next, pipe a tight spiral, beginning at the center of a traced circle, going out to the edge of the circle. Pipe straight fingers, slightly longer than the depth of the charlotte mold, onto the second baking sheet until all the batter is used up. Dust all the piped shapes with powdered sugar until they are thickly coated (**perler**) and transfer the baking sheets to the oven to bake. After 5 minutes, rotate the baking sheets and turn the oven down to 365°F (185°C). Continue to bake the biscuits until they are lightly golden and dry to the touch. Remove

the baking sheets from the oven and carefully slide the parchment paper onto a rack to cool. Dust the shapes with powdered sugar and leave them to cool.

Bavarois

1. Whip (**monter**) the cream to soft peaks in the chilled mixing bowl and whisk and reserve covered in the refrigerator.
2. Cut the pear into a small dice.

Prepare the Crème Anglaise

1. Place the milk in a medium saucepan and bring to a low boil over medium-high heat. Whisk well. Place the egg yolks in a mixing bowl, add the sugar, and immediately begin to whisk it into the yolks. Continue whisking until the sugar is dissolved and the mixture is pale in color (**blanchir**).
2. Once the milk is hot, whisk about one-third of the hot milk into the yolks to temper them. Whisk until the mixture is well combined and evenly heated.
3. Stir the tempered egg yolks into the pan of remaining hot milk and stir with a wooden spatula. Place the pan over low heat and stir in a figure 8 motion. As you stir, the foam on the surface will disappear; at the same time, the liquid will begin to thicken and become oil-like in resistance. Continue cooking until the mixture is thick enough to coat the back of a wooden spatula and your finger leaves a clean trail (**à la nappe**). Remove the pan from the heat.

Tip

Crème Anglaise should be cooked to between 167°F and 185°F (75°C and 85°C).

4. Bloom the gelatin in a bowl of ice water. Once it is completely softened, squeeze out the excess water and add the gelatin to the hot crème Anglaise. Stir it in until completely dissolved, then strain the crème Anglaise through a fine mesh sieve (**chinois**) into a large mixing bowl set in an ice bath. Stir it back and forth with a wooden spatula (**vanner**) until it is cool to the touch but still liquid. Remove the crème Anglaise from the ice bath and stir the pear purée and liqueur into it. Reserve at room temperature.

Assembly (Montage)

1. *Line the mold* (**chemiser**): Trim one end off all the ladyfingers, making sure they are all the same length

as the depth of the charlotte mold. Line the sides of the mold, making sure that the biscuits fit snugly, cut side down.

2. Give the cream a final turn of the whisk and add one-half of it to the prepared crème Anglaise. Fold it in to lighten the texture of the custard and add the second half of the whipped cream. Delicately fold it in until the mixture is homogeneous. Pour it into the mold, filling it halfway up, and then add the diced pear. Fill the mold with the bavarois to just ½ in. (1 cm) from the top of the ladyfingers and gently tap the mold on the work surface to expel any air bubbles. Cut the spiral circle of biscuit to the right size to fit in the opening of the charlotte mold and gently place it in, so that it is level with the end of the ladyfingers.
3. Transfer the charlotte to the freezer to set for 30 minutes.

Make a Coulis

1. Heat the raspberry purée and sugar together in a small saucepan over medium heat, stirring occasionally until it is thick enough to coat the back of a spoon (**à la nappe**). When the liquid has reached the desired consistency, remove the pan from the stove and stir the coulis back and forth with a wooden spatula (**vanner**) until it reaches room temperature. Add the liqueur and stir it in.

To Serve

1. Whip the cream to stiff peaks using the second chilled mixing bowl. Cover and reserve in the refrigerator.
2. When the charlotte is set, unmold it onto a chilled serving dish. Remove the parchment circle from the top.
3. Fill a pastry bag fitted with a medium star tip with the whipped cream and pipe (**coucher**) a line of teardrops into each depression between the ladyfingers. Pipe a small amount of cream onto the top of the charlotte and place the marguerite on top. Reserve the charlotte in the refrigerator until ready to serve.
4. Serve the charlotte with the coulis on the side.

Optional

Decorate the serving dish with sliced pears.

Learning Outcomes

Making a compote
(*compoter*)
Lining a charlotte mold
(*chemiser*)
Cooking à la nappe
Making a crème
Anglaise

Equipment

Knives:
Serrated knife (*couteau à scie*), paring knife (*office*), vegetable peeler (*économe*)

Tools:
Wooden spatula, mixing bowl, charlotte mold, whisk, ice bath, chinois, pastry brush, apple corer

Pans:
Large saucepan, medium saucepan

Serving

6 persons

Originally an English dessert named after Queen Charlotte (wife of George III), Charlotte aux pommes was adapted for French tastes in the 18th century. Antoine Carême, enamored with the shape of the charlotte mold, dispensed with the English use of breadcrumbs, favoring instead ladyfingers or artfully trimmed white bread for the dessert's outer layer. While this recipe is a traditional *charlotte* in that it is made with apple compote and is served hot, similar preparations may involve different fruit and can be served cold.

CHARLOTTE AUX POMMES
Traditional Bread Apple Charlotte

Method

Preheat the oven to 375°F (190°C).

Make a Compote

1. Peel and core the apples and cut them into a small dice. Place the apples and sugar together in a large saucepan over medium heat and cook them until they begin to soften. Cover the saucepan, turn the heat down to low, and cook the apples until they are completely soft and have turned a golden color. Remove the lid and cook the apples, stirring gently, until all the liquid has evaporated.

2. Transfer the compote to a clean bowl and set aside.

Assembly

1. Cut the crusts off the bread slices. Cut 2 bread slices in half diagonally. Cut each of these triangles down the center into 2 equal halves (*giving a total of 4 equally shaped triangles per bread slice*). Round off one end of all the triangles to obtain teardrop shapes. Cut the rest of the bread into 1-in. (2-½ cm) thick strips. Place the teardrop shapes in the bottom of the charlotte mold to form a flower (***marguerite***) and line the sides with the bread fingers, fitting them in snugly. If necessary, trim the shapes for a better fit.

2. Remove the bread shapes from the mold and, one by one, dip them in the clarified butter, then place them back into the mold to line it (***chemiser***).

3. Stir the apricot glaze and the vanilla extract into the compote and pour the mixture into the charlotte mold to fill it. Transfer the molds to the oven to bake for 40 to 45 minutes.

Make a Crème Anglaise

1. Place the milk in a medium saucepan and bring to a low boil over medium-high heat. Whisk well. Place the egg yolks in a mixing bowl, add the sugar, and immediately begin to whisk it into the yolks. Continue whisking until the sugar is completely dissolved and the mixture is pale in color (***blanchir***). Once the milk is scalded, whisk about one-third of the hot milk into the yolks to temper them. Whisk until the mixture is well combined and evenly heated.

2. Stir the tempered egg yolks into the pan of remaining hot milk and stir with a wooden spatula. Place the pan over low heat and stir in a figure 8

Quantity		Ingredient
U.S.	**Metric**	*Compote*
28 oz	800 g	Golden Delicious apples
1 ½ oz	40 g	Sugar, granulated
		Inner Lining of the Mold (Chemisage)
10 pcs	10 pcs	Slices of white sandwich bread
5 oz	150 g	Butter, clarified
1 ¾ oz	50 g	Apricot glaze
⅛ fl oz	2 ml	Vanilla extract
		Crème Anglaise
7 fl oz	200 ml	Milk
2 pcs	2 pcs	Egg yolks
2 oz	60 g	Sugar, granulated
½ fl oz	15 ml	Calvados
⅛ fl oz	2 ml	Vanilla extract

Method

motion. As you stir, the foam on the surface will disappear; at the same time, the liquid will begin to thicken and become oil-like in resistance. Continue cooking until the mixture is thick enough to coat the back of a wooden spatula and when your finger leaves a clean trail (*à la nappe*).

Tip

Crème Anglaise should be cooked to between 167°F and 185°F (75°C and 85°C).

3. Remove the pan from the heat and strain the sauce through a fine mesh sieve into a clean bowl set over an ice bath. Stir it back and forth with a wooden spatula (**vanner**) until it is cool to the touch. Add the calvados and vanilla and stir them in. Cover the bowl in plastic wrap and reserve it in the refrigerator.

To Serve

1. Once the charlotte is cooked and the bread is golden and crispy, trim any excess bread from the top of the mold. If the trimmings are not too dark or burned, flatten them on the surface of the charlotte. Let the charlotte rest for 5 minutes, then turn it out onto a serving dish.
2. Pour some crème Anglaise into the serving dish to coat the bottom and serve the rest on the side.

Optional

Heat some apricot glaze in a small saucepan over medium heat until it is liquid. Apply it to the unmolded charlotte using a pastry brush to add shine.

Learning Outcomes

ENTREMETS CHOCOLAT

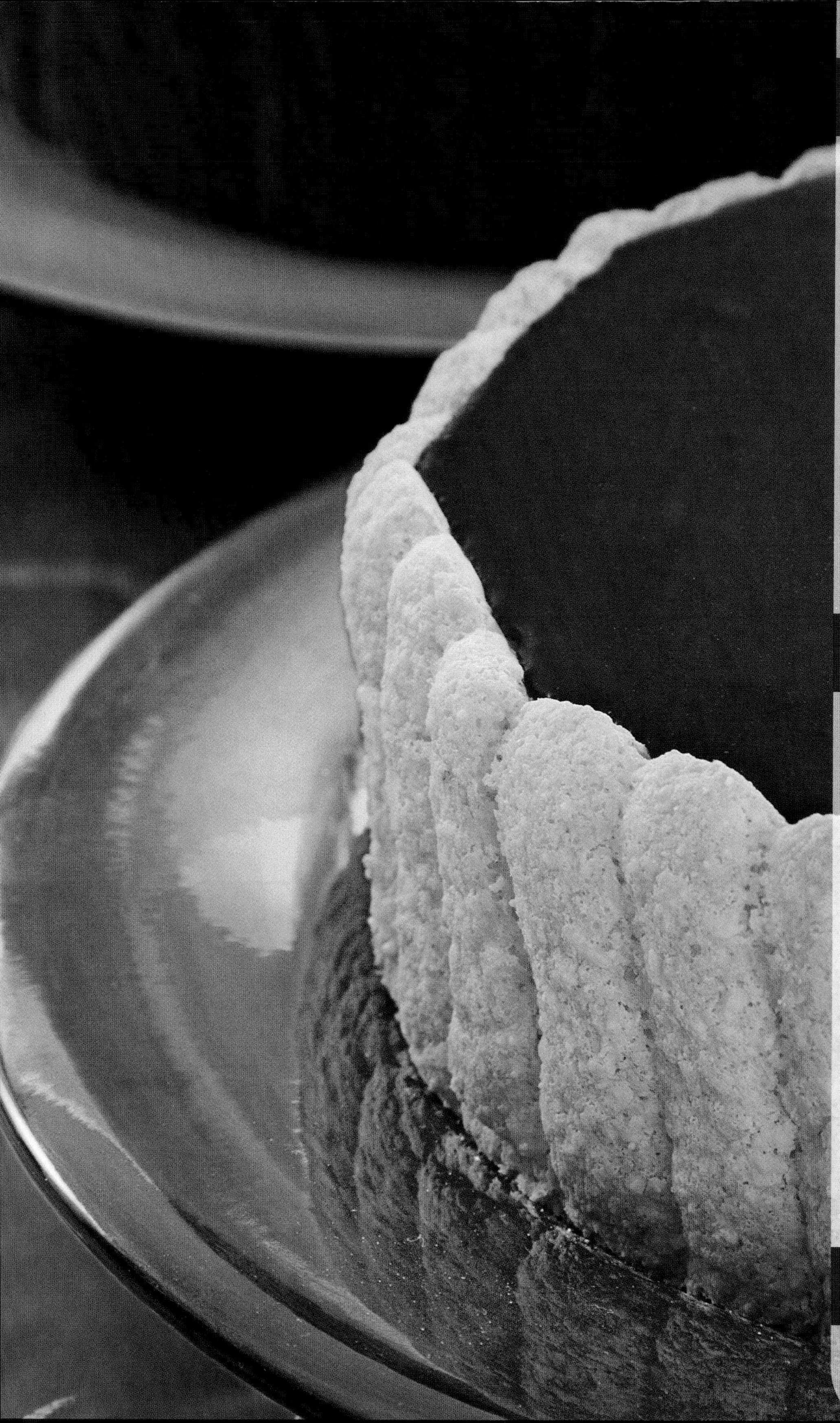

Making ladyfinger sponge (*biscuit cuillère*)
Making a meringue
Making a pâte à bombe
Making a chocolate glaze (*glaçage*)
Making a chocolate mousse
Cooking sugar
Assembling an entremets
Piping (*coucher*)

Equipment

Knives:
Serrated knife (*couteau-scie*), small offset palette knife (*palette spatule coudée petit*), paring knife (*couteau d'office*)

Tools:
Mixing bowl, whisk, sieve, piping bag, medium round tip, spoon, pastry brush, rubber spatula, parchment paper, acetate

Pans:
Saucepan, baking sheet x2, wire rack, cake board x2

Serving/Yield

Two 9 in. (23 cm) cakes

HISTORY

The ladyfingers (biscuits cuillère) that form the base of this decadent chocolate concoction originated in France in the 11th century. Like many early pastry creations, the ladyfinger's roots can be traced back to European royalty. The small, delicate cakes were developed under the royal House of Savoy, and were given to court visitors as a demonstration of the culinary tradition of the Savoy region. The cakes were also brought by dignitaries from the House Savoy when they travelled to meet other royals abroad. Through these state visits, the cakes were spread all over Europe and were commonly enjoyed by the European aristocracy from around the 15th century. This is why, in Italian, the ladyfinger is known as the "savoiardi." Today the ladyfingers are most commonly used in preparations with heavy sauces such as tiramisu and the English trifle because the dry and porous texture of the pastry makes it perfect for absorption.

ENTREMETS CHOCOLAT
Chocolate Mousse Cake

Preheat the oven to 375°F (190°C).

Make Ladyfinger Sponge (Biscuit Cuillère)

1. Line 2 baking sheets with parchment paper (**chemiser**).
2. Separate the eggs and sift (**tamiser**) the flour.
3. Beat the egg yolks with half of the sugar until it becomes light in color (**blanchir**) and the wires of the whisk leave traces in the mixture.
4. Beat the egg whites to soft peaks (**monter les blancs**), then meringue with the remaining sugar until the whites are firm and glossy. Fold some of the meringue into the egg yolks to lighten them, and then fold in the remaining meringue. When it is just incorporated (you should still see the white of the meringue), fold in the flour.
5. Transfer to a piping bag fitted with a medium round tip. Pipe out (**coucher**) 3-in. (8-cm) long fingers at a 45° angle along the length of the baking sheet. Pipe out (**coucher**) a second row. Lift the baking sheet and allow it to drop in order to close any gaps between the piped batter.
6. On a second baking sheet, pipe (**coucher**) 4 disks that are approximately the same diameter as the entremet ring.
7. Place the 2 sheets in the oven and bake the biscuits until they are lightly colored and dry to the touch, approximately 8 to 10 minutes. Remove them from the oven and slide the parchment papers onto wire racks for the biscuit to cool.
8. Line the entremets molds with acetate and place them on cake boards. Trim the strips a little taller than the sides of the entremet mold and line the sides with the top of the biscuit facing outwards. Trim the disks to fit snugly in the bottom of the molds.

Chocolate Mousse

Make a Pâte à Bombe

1. Prepare a small bowl of cold water with a spoon and a clean pastry brush. Combine the sugar and water in a saucepan and bring to a boil. Once the sugar comes to a boil, skim off any white foam that might rise to the surface and brush the sides of the pan with water. Once the syrup is clear, leave it to cook to the soft-ball stage (235°F/115°C).

Quantity		Ingredient
U.S.	**Metric**	**Ladyfinger Sponge (Biscuit Cuillère)**
8 oz	250 g	Flour
8 pcs	8 pcs	Egg whites
8 oz	250 g	Sugar, granulated
8 pcs	8 pcs	Egg yolks
		Chocolate Mousse
8 oz	250 g	Sugar
5 fl oz	150 ml	Water
10 oz (15 pcs)	300 g (15 pcs)	Egg yolks
1 lb	500 g	Chocolate
3 ½ oz	100 g	Unsweetened chocolate
1 quart	1 liter	Cream
		Chocolate Glaze (Glaçage)
8 oz	250 g	Chocolate
8 fl oz	250 ml	Cream
1 ¾ oz	50 g	Sugar, granulated
1 ¾ fl oz	50 ml	Glucose
1 ¾ oz	50 g	Butter

2. While the sugar is cooking, whisk the egg yolks in a bowl. Once the sugar comes to the soft-ball stage (235°F/115°C), remove it from the heat and dip the bottom of the pan in cold water to stop the cooking process. While whisking, add the hot syrup in a thin, steady stream to the egg yolks. Be sure to pour the syrup off to the side and not onto the wires of the whisk where it will harden. Once the sugar has been incorporated, continue whisking until cool. The yolks will thicken and become light yellow in color.

Make a Chocolate Mousse

3. Melt the 2 chocolates together then mix them into the pâte à bombe. Stir well. Beat the cream to soft peaks. Fold into the chocolate mixture. Divide the mousse between the 2 molds. Using a small offset palette knife, smooth and even out the top. Place in the refrigerator to chill and set.

Make Chocolate Glaze (Glaçage)

1. Place the chocolate into a bowl. Heat the cream, sugar, and glucose and bring them to a boil. Pour the mixture over the chocolate and allow it to sit 1 to 2 minutes, and then gently stir with a spatula until smooth. Stir in the butter and set aside.

Assembly

1. Remove the filled entremets from the refrigerator. Pour the glaçage over the cake and quickly spread it evenly with a small offset palette. Work quickly as the glaçage will begin to set. Gently tap the mold to release any air bubbles and return the entremets to the refrigerator.
2. Slice with a heated knife to serve.

Learning Outcomes

Making a joconde biscuit

Making a cigarette paste
(*pâte à cigarette*)

Making an Italian meringue

Making a fruit mousse

Glazing with nappage
(*abricoter*)

Cooking sugar

Equipment

Knives:
Off-set palette knife (*palette spatule coudée*), paring knife (*couteau d'office*)

Tools:
Silicone mat, mixing bowls, whisk, rubber spatula, wire rack, cake comb or fork, sieve, acetate

Pans:
10 in. (25 cm) ring mold, baking sheet or sheet pan, saucepan, cake board

Serving/Yield

One 10 in. (25 cm) cake,
8–12 servings

The biscuit joconde, which forms the base of the gâteau pacifique, is named for Leonardo Da Vinci's famous masterpiece, the Mona Lisa. The French refer to the Mona Lisa as "La Joconde." This is because the painting was bequeathed to Da Vinci's assistant, a man named Salai, who referred to the painting as "La Gioconda." The word *Gioconda* is thought to have a double meaning, referring to both the model for the painting, Lisa del Giocondo, as well as to the Italian word *jocund*, which means "happy," and represents the Mona Lisa's famous smile.

GÂTEAU PACIFIQUE
Lemon and Strawberry Mousse Cake

Method

Preheat oven to 375°F (190°C).
Prepare a baking sheet or sheet pan with a silicone mat.

Make the Cigarette Paste (Pâte à Cigarette)

1. Whisk together the butter and powdered sugar until fluffy. Add the egg whites and mix until smooth. Whisk in the flour and then add the green food coloring one drop at a time until the desired color has been achieved.

2. With a palette knife, spread a very thin layer of the pâte à cigarette onto the lined baking sheet or sheet pan. Using a cake comb or a fork, score a design over the surface. Set aside to dry.

Make the Biscuit Joconde

1. Sift (*tamiser*) the almond powder and powdered sugar into a bowl.

2. Sift (*tamiser*) the flour and set aside.

3. Add the eggs to the almond mixture and whisk until homogenous. Whisk in the melted butter.

4. Whisk the egg whites to medium peaks (**monter les blancs**) and meringue with the sugar. Whisk until the whites become tight and glossy. Add some to the almond mixture and stir to lighten, and then fold in the remaining whites.

5. Spread the batter (**appareil**) over the prepared baking sheet being careful not to scrape the pâte à cigarette. Bake until the biscuit is lightly colored and feels dry to the touch, approximately 8 minutes. Remove the silicone mat from the baking sheet and allow to cool on a wire rack.

6. Once cooled, flip the biscuit over and gently remove the silicone mat. Cut a long strip of the biscuit—the width being the same height as the ring mold. Using the ring mold as a guide, cut out 2 disks slightly smaller in diameter.

7. Line the inside of the ring mold with a strip of acetate, and place on a cake board.

8. Insert the strip of biscuit joconde making sure the green side is facing outward on the inside of the mold. Trim the strip to size—there should not be any overlapping or gaps. Place a disk in the bottom of the mold, trimming to size if necessary.

Make the Strawberry Mousse

1. Soak the gelatin leaves in cold water until soft.

2. Gently heat the strawberry pulp with the sugar. Once it is hot to the touch (around 100°F/40°C),

Quantity		Ingredient
U.S.	Metric	*Cigarette Paste (Pâte à Cigarette)*
1 ½ oz	40 g	Butter, room temperature
1 ½ oz	40 g	Powdered sugar
1 ½ oz	40 g	Egg whites
1 ½ oz	40 g	Flour
2 drops	2 drops	Green food coloring
		Joconde Biscuit
4 ¾ oz	140 g	Almond powder
4 ¾ oz	140 g	Powdered sugar
4 pcs	4 pcs	Eggs
1 ½ oz	40 g	Flour
1 fl oz	30 mL	Butter, melted
4 pcs	4 pcs	Egg whites
1 ½ oz	40 g	Sugar, granulated
		Strawberry Mousse
10 oz	300 g	Strawberry pulp
2 ½ oz	70 g	Sugar, granulated
5 pcs	5 pcs	Gelatin leaves
8 fl oz	250 ml	Cream
		Lemon Mousse
4 ¼ oz	125 g	Lemon juice
4 pcs	4 pcs	Gelatin leaves
		Italian Meringue
2 pcs	2 pcs	Egg whites
1 ¾ fl oz	50 ml	Water
4 ¼ oz	125 g	Sugar, granulated
7 fl oz	200 ml	Cream
		Finishing
As needed	As needed	Lemon and lime zests
As needed	As needed	Apricot glaze
As needed	As needed	Fresh fruit

GÂTEAU PACIFIQUE
Lemon and Strawberry Mousse Cake

Method

remove from the heat. Squeeze the excess water from the softened gelatin and add it to the hot strawberry pulp, stirring until the gelatin is fully melted.

3. Transfer the pulp mixture to a clean bowl. Whip the cream to soft peaks while stirring the strawberry pulp. If needed, place the bowl in an ice bath and once it begins to thicken, remove and fold in the whipped cream. Immediately spread in the bottom of the lined mold and place the second disk of biscuit on top and press down to even out the mousse.

Make the Lemon Mousse

1. Soften the gelatin in cold water. Heat the lemon juice until hot to the touch (around 100°F/40°C) and then remove from the heat. Squeeze out the excess water from the gelatin and stir into the lemon juice. Transfer to a clean bowl, stirring occasionally.

2. Place the sugar and just enough water to dissolve the sugar in a small saucepan. Bring to a boil, skimming off any white foam that comes to the surface and brushing down the sides with cold water. Once the syrup is clear, leave to cook until the soft-ball stage (235°F/115°C).

3. Meanwhile, whisk the egg whites to soft peaks (*monter les blancs*). Once the sugar is cooked, remove from the heat and whisk into the egg whites, being careful not to pour the syrup directly onto the wires of the whisk. After the syrup is incorporated, continue whisking until cooled. Fold some into the lemon mixture to incorporate, then fold in the rest.

4. Whip the cream to soft peaks, and fold into the meringue mixture. Fill the remaining half of the mold and smooth the top using a palette knife. Place in the refrigerator for 1 to 2 hours minimum, allowing it to set.

5. Once completely chilled, place the entremet on a wire rack. Gently heat the apricot glaze until liquid but not hot. Pour over the top of the entremet and quickly spread over the top evenly using a palette knife. Work quickly as the nappage will begin to set immediately when poured.

6. Decorate with fresh fruit and grated zest to finish.

Learning Outcomes

Making ladyfinger sponge (*biscuit à la cuillère*)
Making a mousse
Blanchir
Making Italian meringue
Cooking sugar
Glazing (*glaçage*)
Making whipped cream (*crème fouettée*)
Demolding (*démouler*)

Equipment

Knives:
Serrated knife (*couteau à scie*), paring knife (*office*)

Tools:
Scissors, balloon whisk, rubber spatula, mixing bowls, pastry bag, corne, 5 mm plain tip, whisk, pastry brush, metal spatula

Pans:
2 small pans, bain-marie, baking sheet, cake board

Serving

6–8 persons

This cake derives its name from its glossy top surface that shines like a mirror and should be as flat as one.

Quantity		Ingredient
U.S.	Metric	*Ladyfinger Sponge (Biscuit à la Cuillère)*
7 oz	200 g	Flour, sifted (**tamiser**)
8 pcs	8 pcs	Egg whites
5 ½ oz	160 g	Sugar, granulated
8 pcs	8 pcs	Egg yolks
2 ¾ oz	80 g	Sugar, granulated
		Mousse Base
7 oz	200 g	Black currant purée
½ oz	12 g	Sugar, granulated
½ fl oz	12 ml	Water
4 pcs	4 pcs	Gelatin leaves
		Ice water for gelatin
		Italian Meringue
3 pcs	3 pcs	Egg whites
3 ½ oz	100 g	Sugar, granulated
1 fl oz	30 ml	Water
		Mousse
7 fl oz	200 ml	Cream
		Decoration
7 oz	200 g	Glaçage miroir (**neutre**)
5 oz	150 g	White chocolate, melted, in a cornet
2 ¾ oz	80 g	Fresh black currants

MIROIR CASSIS
Black Currant Mousse Cake

Method

1. Preheat the oven to 380°F (195°C).
2. Cut a cake board into a disc just small enough to fit through a cake ring.
3. Using this disc, draw a circle onto one side of a piece of parchment paper. Turn the paper over onto a baking sheet.

Ladyfinger Sponge (Biscuit à la Cuillère)

1. *Prepare the biscuit cuillère batter:* Sift (**tamiser**) the flour onto a piece of parchment paper. Separate the eggs into 2 large mixing bowls. Beat the whites (**monter les blancs**) with a balloon whisk until they are white and frothy but still fluid and set aside. Add the sugar to the egg yolks and whisk them together until the mixture is thick and pale in color (**blanchir**). Set aside.
2. Whip the egg whites (**monter les blancs**) with the balloon whisk until they reach the soft peak stage. Gradually add the sugar, beating it in with the whisk. Once all the sugar has been added, continue to beat the whites until they are thick and glossy. Add the sifted flour to the egg yolks previously blanched with the sugar and fold it in (**incorporer**) using a rubber spatula until it is almost completely incorporated. Add one-third of the egg whites to the mixture and fold them in (**incorporer**) delicately until the mixture is streaked with thin lines of white. Fold the remaining egg whites until just incorporated. The end result should be a pale, homogeneous batter with a light, airy texture that is ideal for piping. Transfer the batter to a pastry bag fitted with a 5-mm plain tip.
3. Using the drawn circle as a size guide, pipe a tight spiral onto the parchment–lined baking sheet. Beside the disc, on the other half of the baking sheet, pipe lines at a 45° angle; ensure that the lines are touching and form a 4-in. (10-cm) band along the length of the baking sheet. Fill in the corners in order to square off the ends of the band.
4. Dust the piped batter with powdered sugar to completely coat it. Let it rest 30 seconds and dust it again (**perler**), then transfer it to the oven to bake until lightly colored (*12 to 15 minutes*). Once cooked, remove the baking sheets from the oven and slide the parchment paper off them onto a wire rack to cool. Immediately dust the biscuit with powdered sugar.

Mousse Base

1. Soak the gelatin sheets in cold water until completely softened. Meanwhile, heat the sugar, water, and black currant purée together in a small saucepan over medium heat, stirring occasionally until the sugar has melted and the liquid is hot to the touch. Remove the pan from the heat. Remove the gelatin from the cold water and squeeze out any excess liquid. Add the softened gelatin to the pan and stir it in gently until completely dissolved. Pour this mixture into the black currant purée while stirring. Continue to stir until completely combined. Reserve at room temperature.

Tip

If the marble is refrigerated, keep the bowl on a dish cloth to insulate the bottom and stop the gelatin from setting.

Method

Italian Meringue

1. Whisk the egg whites in a large mixing bowl using a balloon whisk, until frothy. Set aside. Cook the sugar and water together in a medium saucepan over medium-high heat until they reach the soft-ball stage (**petit boulé**) [250°F (121°C)]. Meanwhile, whip the egg whites until soft peaks form. As soon as the syrup reaches the soft-ball (**petit boulé**) stage, pour it into the egg whites in a thin stream, whisking constantly. Continue to whisk until the meringue is firm and cooled to room temperature.

Mousse

1. Whip the cream to soft peaks in a large mixing bowl over an ice bath. Add the jellified fruit purée to the Italian meringue and fold it in carefully using a rubber spatula. Add half the whipped cream to the bowl and fold it in until incorporated. Add the other half and fold it in gently until the mixture is homogeneous.

Assembly

1. Turn the biscuit over onto a clean piece of parchment paper and peel off the parchment paper it was baked on. Turn the biscuit over.
2. Place a cake ring on a cake board. Line the inside of the ring with a strip of acetate. Fit the cut cake board inside it. Cut 2 strips, the same thickness as a metal spatula, lengthwise from the biscuit using a serrated knife. Line the ring, with the sugared side facing outwards so that the biscuit fits snugly. Fit the biscuit disc, cooked side up into the bottom of the circle, trimming it if needed.
3. Fill the prepared cake ring with half the mousse. Using a large metal spatula, spread the mousse up the sides of the ring to completely coat them (**chemiser**). Sprinkle with some drained black currants, then cover with the remaining mousse. If desired, sprinkle the surface with additional black currants, then smooth the top of the cake flat with a metal spatula. Transfer the cake to the freezer to chill for a minimum of 30 minutes.

Finishing

1. Gently stir the **glaçage miroir** with a rubber spatula until smooth, being careful not to incorporate any air bubbles. Once the mousse is thoroughly chilled, remove it from the freezer and pour the **glaçage miroir** on top. Immediately spread it out using a metal spatula. Pour some melted white chocolate into a paper cone (**cornet**) and snip off the tip. Pipe a design onto the top of the cake. Once the glacage is set, carefully remove the ring. Place the cake on a serving dish and finish the decoration with a few black currants. Brush them with glaze using a pastry brush and place the miroir in the refrigerator to gently thaw for a minimum of 10 minutes. Before serving, remove the strip of acetate.
2. The miroir pictured here is a more modern presentation. Traditionally, it is left ungarnished so one may admire the perfect mirror finish of the cake.

Desserts

Blanc-manger

Crème brûlée

Crème renversée au caramel
—Baked caramel custard

Crêpes soufflées
—Soufflé-filled crêpes

Crêpes au sucre
—Sugar crêpes

Fondant au chocolat
—Flourless chocolate terrine

Gratin de fruits rouges
—Red fruit sabayon

Île flottante
—Floating island

Moelleux au chocolat et crème à la pistache
—Soft chocolate cake with pistachio cream

Mousse au chocolat
—Chocolate mousse

Nougat Glacé
—Iced nougat

Parfait glacé au café
—Iced coffee parfait

Petits pots de crème
—Little chocolate custard pots

Poires pochées au vin rouge
—Pears poached in red wine

Soufflée chaud aux framboises
—Warm soufflé with raspberry coulis

Soufflée glacé aux fruits rouges
—Frozen red fruit soufflé

Learning Outcomes

Making a blanc-manger
Using gelatin
Whipping egg whites
(*monter les blancs*)
Making a coulis

Equipment

Knives:
N/A

Tools:
Medium size bowl, mixing
bowls, whisk, sieve, spoon,
wooden spatula, mold

Pans:
Saucepan, small saucepan

Serving/Yield

About a 3 pound/
1.3 kilogram portion,
6–8 servings

HISTORY

Blanc-manger is a pudding-like dessert whose origins stem all the way back to the 13th century. It is believed that the dish may have been introduced to Europe by the Arab peoples of North Africa and Spain. The word *blanc-manger* stems from the old French words *blanc mangier*, which translate literally to "white dish" or "white food" (referring to the milky color of the preparation). In the Middle Ages, the blanc-manger was a savory dish that usually incorporated almond milk, ground meats, and often spices (considered a sign of wealth at the time). Early recipes for the blanc-manger have been found in almost all European countries, making it one of the most internationally popular and widespread dishes of the Middle Ages. The blanc-manger was commonly used as a popular entremet in aristocratic feasts (palette cleansing dishes served between courses) because its neutral white color meant it could be easily shaped and colored to entertain the party goers. By the 17th century, the dish had evolved into a sweeter version that was eaten as a dessert. While the modern incarnation of the blanc-manger uses gelatin as the thickening agent, this early preparation used eggs. The blanc-manger as we know it today existed by the 19th century and it remains extremely popular all across Europe.

BLANC-MANGER

Method

Make a Blanc-Manger

1. Place the milk, sugar, and almond powder in a saucepan and stir to combine. Bring to a boil, then reduce the heat to a simmer. Allow to simmer for about 10 minutes. Then remove from heat and allow to cool to room temperature.
2. Strain the mixture into a clean bowl.
3. Soften the gelatin in cold water. Squeeze out any excess water, and then gently melt in a small saucepan. Add some of the almond milk mixture to the gelatin, and then stir into the bowl of almond milk.
4. Beat the cream to soft peaks (***monter les blancs***). Gently fold it into the almond milk mixture. Transfer to the mold. Give the filled mold a couple of firm taps on the work surface to remove any air bubbles. Place in the refrigerator to set.

Raspberry Coulis

1. Mix the raspberry pulp, sugar, and raspberry liqueur together. Keep refrigerated until needed.

To Serve

Unmold the blanc-manger onto a serving platter. Decorate with fresh fruit and coarsely chopped pistachios. Serve with the raspberry coulis on the side.

Quantity		Ingredient
U.S.	Metric	Blanc-Manger
1 pint	500 ml	Milk
4 ¼ oz	125 g	Sugar, granulated
4 ¼ oz	125 g	Almond powder
½ oz	15 g	Gelatin leaves
7 fl oz	200 ml	Cream
		Raspberry Coulis
10 oz	300 g	Raspberry pulp
1 oz	30 g	Powdered sugar
1 fl oz	30 ml	Raspberry liqueur
As needed	As needed	Seasonal fruit
As needed	As needed	Pistachios

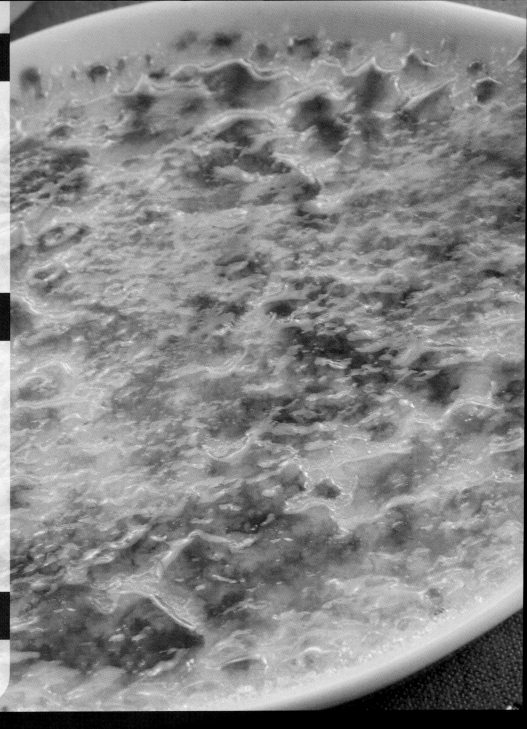

Learning Outcomes

Making a cooked custard
Caramelizing sugar

Equipment

Knives:
Paring knife (*couteau d'office*)

Tools:
10 6 oz (180 g) ramekins or
shallow crème brûlée plates,
mixing bowls, whisk, sieve,
blow torch (*optional*)

Pans:
Roasting pan, saucepan,
baking pan

Serving/Yield

10 servings

The origin of crème brûlée (burnt cream) is a hotly contested issue in annals of culinary lore. This traditional dessert made of custard topped with caramelized sugar is claimed as the invention of France, England, and Spain. The name *burnt cream* likely stems from the early mode of preparing the dish. Today, the sugar is generally caramelized using a torch or an oven grill, but the original method required the use of a burning-hot metal iron that stamped the top of the preparation and very likely burned the custard to a crisp. The British claim that the dessert was created in the early 17th century at Trinity College, Cambridge. In England they often refer to it as "Trinity burnt cream" (after the University), and the College still possesses the old branding irons that were used to burn the school crest onto the students' desserts. Despite the Brits' claims, there is little real evidence to verify exactly when the College began this practice. The Spanish, on the other hand, believe that the dish was created in the Catalonia region of Spain in the 18th century. The Spanish version, called "crema catalane," differs in that it is served cold with the caramelized sugar being the only hot ingredient. While the French would seem the obvious choice as the inventors of crème brûlée (given that the name of the dish is French), the French name was only popularized in the 19th century. Despite the late addition of the name, the French do still have the most compelling evidence for their claim as the creators of crème brûlée. The earliest known recipe for the preparation appears in a cookbook by the great French Chef François Massialot in 1691. Although it may never be concretely verified who invented it, what is known is that crème brûlée remains one of the most popular desserts in the world today.

CRÈME BRÛLÉE

Method

1. Preheat the oven to 285°F (140°C).
2. Place the milk in a saucepan. Split the vanilla bean open and scrape the seeds into the milk. Bring to a boil, then immediately remove from the heat and allow the flavors to infuse for about 15 minutes.
3. In a large mixing bowl, whisk the egg yolks with the sugar (*blanchir*) until they become thick and light yellow in color. Strain the hot milk into the egg mixture and stir in well. Then mix in the cream. Fill the ramekins halfway and arrange them on a roasting pan. Place the roasting pan into the preheated oven, and then fill the pan with boiling water until the liquid reaches about halfway up the sides of the ramekins. Cook for approximately 50 minutes, although this time may be less if using shallower dishes.
4. Remove the ramekins and allow to cool. Place in the refrigerator to chill until serving (preferably overnight).

To Serve

1. Sprinkle a thin layer of brown sugar on top of the crème brûlée.
2. Using a blowtorch, hold the flame 3–4 in. (8–10 cm) from the surface and heat until the sugar caramelizes and bubbles.

To Caramelize in the Oven

1. Set the oven to the broiler setting and allow to heat fully.
2. Sprinkle the tops of the crème brûlée with a thin layer of brown sugar. Place the ramekins on a baking sheet and then slide them onto the highest rack of the oven. Keep a close eye to avoid overcooking and remember to turn the baking sheet to ensure even caramelization of the sugar. Serve immediately.

Quantity		Ingredient
U.S.	**Metric**	
10 pcs	10 pcs	Egg yolks
5 oz	150 g	Sugar, granulated
1 pcs	1 pcs	Vanilla bean
23 fl oz	700 ml	Cream
8 fl oz	250 ml	Milk
5 ½ oz	165 g	Brown sugar

CRÈME RENVERSÉE AU CARAMEL

Making a caramel
Cooking a set cream

Equipment

Knives:
Paring knife (*office*)

Tools:
Whisk, chinois, bowls,
ladle

Pans:
Roasting pan, ramekins,
small pan, small saucepan,
medium saucepan

Serving

4 persons

FYI...

Crème renversée au caramel is a dessert preparation that is in the same family as crème brûlée, the main difference being that crème brûlée contains yolks and cream whereas crème caramel is made using whole eggs and milk. Also, in this preparation caramel is poured into the bottom of the mold before adding the appareil. The caramel becomes liquid as the appareil sets during cooking; it then acts as a sauce when the dessert is turned out of its mold onto the plate.

CRÈME RENVERSÉE AU CARAMEL
Baked Caramel Custard

Method

Preheat the oven to 340°F (170°C).

Caramel

1. Place the sugar, water, and lemon juice together in a small saucepan and cook them over medium-high heat until they reach the caramel stage. When the caramel becomes a deep amber color, remove the pan from the heat, dip the bottom of the pan in cold water to stop the cooking, and pour a thin layer of caramel into the bottom of each ramekin. Set aside.

Custard

1. Bring the milk and vanilla extract to a boil in a medium saucepan over medium-high heat.
2. Meanwhile, break the eggs into a large mixing bowl, add the sugar, and beat with a whisk until combined. As soon as the milk begins to boil, remove it from the heat and pour it into the egg mixture in a thin stream while stirring with a whisk. Strain the mixture through a fine mesh sieve (*chinois*) into a clean bowl and skim the froth off the surface. Ladle the mixture into the ramekins, filling them ½ in. from the top.
3. Transfer the ramekins to a roasting pan and fill it with hot water to two-thirds up their sides (bain-marie). Transfer the pan to the oven and cook the custards until they no longer ripple when lightly shaken (*30 minutes*) and the tip of a knife inserted in the middle comes out clean.
4. Remove the pan from the oven and let the custards cool a little before removing them. Wipe the ramekins dry with a clean cloth. Let the custards cool to room temperature before covering them in plastic wrap and reserving them in the refrigerator until needed (*minimum 2 hours*).
5. Crème caramel is best prepared the day before to allow the caramel a chance to melt into a sauce.

To Serve

1. Cut around the edge of the custard with a paring knife to loosen it from the ramekin and flip it onto a plate. Remove the ramekin.

Quantity		Ingredient
U.S.	Metric	
		Caramel
2 ½ oz	75 g	Sugar, granulated
¾ fl oz	25 ml	Water
2 to 3 drops	2 to 3 drops	Lemon juice
		Custard
8 fl oz	250 ml	Milk
¼ fl oz	2 ml	Vanilla extract
2 pcs	2 pcs	Eggs
2 ¼ oz	65 g	Sugar, granulated

Learning Outcomes

Making crêpe batter
(*pâte à crêpes*)
Making pastry cream
(*crème pâtissière*)
Cooking crêpes
Making a soufflé

Equipment

Tools:
Grater, whisk, balloon
whisk, wooden spoon,
rubber spatula,
mixing bowls

Pans:
Crêpe pan

Serving

4 persons

FYI...

The traditional thin French pancake known as the crêpe, is one of the most quintessentially French preparations there is and it is adored and revered by many. The only thing one could ask for to make it better . . . combine the light and thin delicacy with the airy delicousness of a soufflé—so they did. It is said that to eat the perfect crêpe soufflé is to feel like you are eating a cloud. Like the traditional crêpe, the crêpe soufflé can take on many different flavors—tangerine, banana, chocolate, lemon, mocha, or even something savory like broccoli and cheese. The combinations are endless. Drizzle the finished dish with a decadent crème Anglaise, chocolate or cheese sauce and some might say—you will hear angels sing.

CRÊPES SOUFFLÉES
Soufflé-Filled Crêpes

Quantity		Ingredient
U.S.	**Metric**	*Crêpe Batter (Pâte à Crêpes)*
1 ¼ oz	125 g	All-purpose flour
¾ oz	20 g	Sugar, granulated
Pinch	Pinch	Salt
2 pcs	2 pcs	Eggs
2 oz	60 g	Unsalted butter, melted
1 pc	1 pc	Vanilla bean
1 pc	1 pc	Orange, zest of, grated
8 fl oz	250 ml	Milk
		Pastry Cream (Crème Pâtissière)
8 fl oz	250 ml	Milk
¼ fl oz	5 ml	Vanilla extract
2 pcs	2 pcs	Egg yolks
2 oz	60 g	Sugar, granulated
1 oz	30 g	Flour (or cornstarch)
¾ fl oz	20 ml	Cointreau
		Finishing
2 pcs	2 pcs	Egg whites
As needed	As needed	Unsalted butter, for cooking
1 pc	1 pc	Orange, zest of, cut into a *julienne*
As needed	As needed	Powdered sugar, for dusting

Method

Make a Crêpe Batter (Pâte à Crêpes)

1. Sift (**tamiser**) the flour into a large mixing bowl and make a well (**fontaine**) in the center. Add the sugar and salt to the well and pour in the eggs. Whisk the eggs, gradually incorporating the flour from the sides. When half the flour is incorporated, add the melted butter. Continue to whisk until all the flour is incorporated and the mixture is smooth. Cut the vanilla bean in half lengthwise and scrape the seeds into the batter using a paring knife. Add the orange zest and stir. Pour in the milk in a thin stream while stirring the batter with a whisk. Cover the mixing bowl and let the batter rest for a minimum of 1 hour in the refrigerator.

Make a Pastry Cream (Crème Pâtissière)

1. Prepare a shallow tray or baking sheet by lining with plastic wrap.
2. Pour the milk into a medium saucepan, add the vanilla extract, and bring to a boil over medium-high heat. Add about one-quarter of the sugar to the milk and stir to dissolve it.
3. Meanwhile, place the egg yolks in a small mixing bowl and add the remaining sugar. Whisk the sugar into the eggs until it completely dissolves and the yolks lighten in color (**blanchir**). Add the flour or cornstarch to the yolks and stir until well combined.
4. When the milk begins to come to a boil, remove it from the stove and pour one-third of it into the egg yolks. Stir well to temper the yolks, then whisk the tempered mixture into the remaining hot milk. Place back onto the heat and cook until the crème pâtissière begins to bubble. Continue whisking (being sure to press the whisk around the corners of the pan) and allow to cook for 1 minute in order to cook the starch. The pastry cream (Crème pâtissière) will become very thick. Once cooked, pour the crème pâtissière onto the prepared tray and pat the surface with a piece of cold butter held on the end of a fork (**tamponner**) to create a protective film. Cover with plastic, pressing out any air bubbles and seal the sides. Let the crème pâtissière cool to room temperature.

Crêpes

1. Melt the butter in a small saucepan over medium heat. Set aside. Preheat a small nonstick crêpe

CRÊPES SOUFFLÉES
Soufflé-Filled Crêpes

Method

pan over medium-high heat. Using a pastry brush, brush the hot pan with melted butter. Pour a ladleful [3 fl oz (100 mL)] of crêpe batter into the center of the pan while turning it so that the batter evenly covers the bottom of the pan. Cook the crêpe until the edges begin to brown and curl away from the sides of the pan. Slip a spatula beneath the crêpe and turn it over. Cook the second side for 30 seconds to a minute, then slip the crêpe onto a clean, warm plate and cover it with a clean cloth. Repeat the cooking process, stacking the crêpes one on top of the other until the batter is used up.

Soufflé Mixture

1. Whisk the pastry cream (crème pâtissière) until it is smooth and elastic, then mix in the Cointreau. Beat the egg whites (**monter les blancs**) in a large mixing bowl with a balloon whisk to soft peaks. Using a rubber spatula, carefully fold in one-half of the egg whites into the crème pâtissière until almost completely incorporated. Add the remaining egg whites and fold them in until just incorporated.

Finishing

1. Lay the crêpes out flat and spread a layer of soufflé mixture ¼ to ½ in. (0.5 to 1 cm) thick on half of each crêpe. Gently fold the crêpes in 4 and arrange them staggered on a buttered ovenproof serving dish. Sprinkle the **julienne** of orange zest on top and place them in the oven to bake for 8 minutes, being careful not to open the door until they are cooked.
2. Remove the crêpes from the oven and sprinkle them with powdered sugar. Serve immediately.
3. There are several variations on serving crêpes soufflées. You can butter and then line a small gratin dish with crêpes, then fill and bake the soufflé mixture. You can butter and line individual ramekins with trimmed crêpes, then fill and bake the soufflé.

FYL...

The word *crêpe* comes from the Latin *crispus*, which means "wavy or curly" and describes the lacy pattern on the surface of the crêpe. Rich with eggs and butter, this preparation is equally rich in lore and symbolism: In feudal France, it was a sign of allegiance for a farmer to serve his landowner crêpes; to hold a coin while flipping a crêpe was to bring you financial luck; and on the morning after a wedding, a successful flip of the crêpe indicated the beginning of a happy marriage. To this day, serving crêpes on Shrove Tuesday is a way of celebrating family life. The Brittany region in France is known for its crêpes made from buckwheat flour.

CRÊPES AU SUCRE
Sugar Crêpes

Quantity		Ingredient
U.S.	**Metric**	*Crêpe Batter (Pâte à Crêpes)*
4 ½ oz	125 g	Flour
¾ oz	20 g	Sugar, granulated
2 pcs	2 pcs	Eggs
2 oz	60 g	Butter
1 pc	1 pc	Vanilla bean
1 pc	1 pc	Lemon, zest of
1 pc	1 pc	Orange, zest of
8 fl oz	250 ml	Milk
		To Cook
2 oz	60 g	Butter
		To Serve
3 ½ oz	100 g	Butter
1 ¾ oz	50 g	Sugar, granulated

Method

Crêpe Batter (Pâte à Crêpes)

1. Melt the butter in a small saucepan over medium heat. Set aside. Sift (**tamiser**) the flour into a large mixing bowl and make a well (**fontaine**) in the center. Add the sugar to the well and pour in the eggs. Whisk the eggs, gradually incorporating the flour from the sides. When half of the flour is incorporated, add the melted butter. Continue to whisk until all the flour is incorporated and the mixture is smooth. Cut the vanilla bean in half lengthwise and scrape out the seeds using a paring knife. Add the vanilla seeds, lemon zest, and orange zest to the batter and stir them in. Pour in the milk in a thin stream while stirring the batter with a whisk. Cover the mixing bowl with plastic film and let the batter rest for a minimum of 1 hour in the refrigerator.

Cooking Crêpes

1. Melt the butter in a small saucepan over medium heat and set aside. Preheat a nonstick 10-in. crêpe pan over medium-high heat. Using a pastry brush, brush the hot pan with melted butter. Pour a ladleful [3 fl oz (100 ml)] of crêpe batter into the center of the pan while turning it so that the batter evenly covers the bottom of the pan. Cook the crêpe until the edges begin to brown and curl away from the sides of the pan. Slip a spatula beneath the crêpe and turn it over. Cook the second side for 30 seconds to a minute, then slip the crêpe onto a clean warm plate and cover it with a clean cloth. Repeat the cooking process, stacking the crêpes one on top of the other until the batter is used up.

To Serve

1. Melt some butter in an omelette or crêpe pan. Place the crêpe to warm and sprinkle with sugar. Fold into quarters and arrange on a buttered serving dish. Keep warm until ready to serve.

FONDANT AU CHOCOLAT

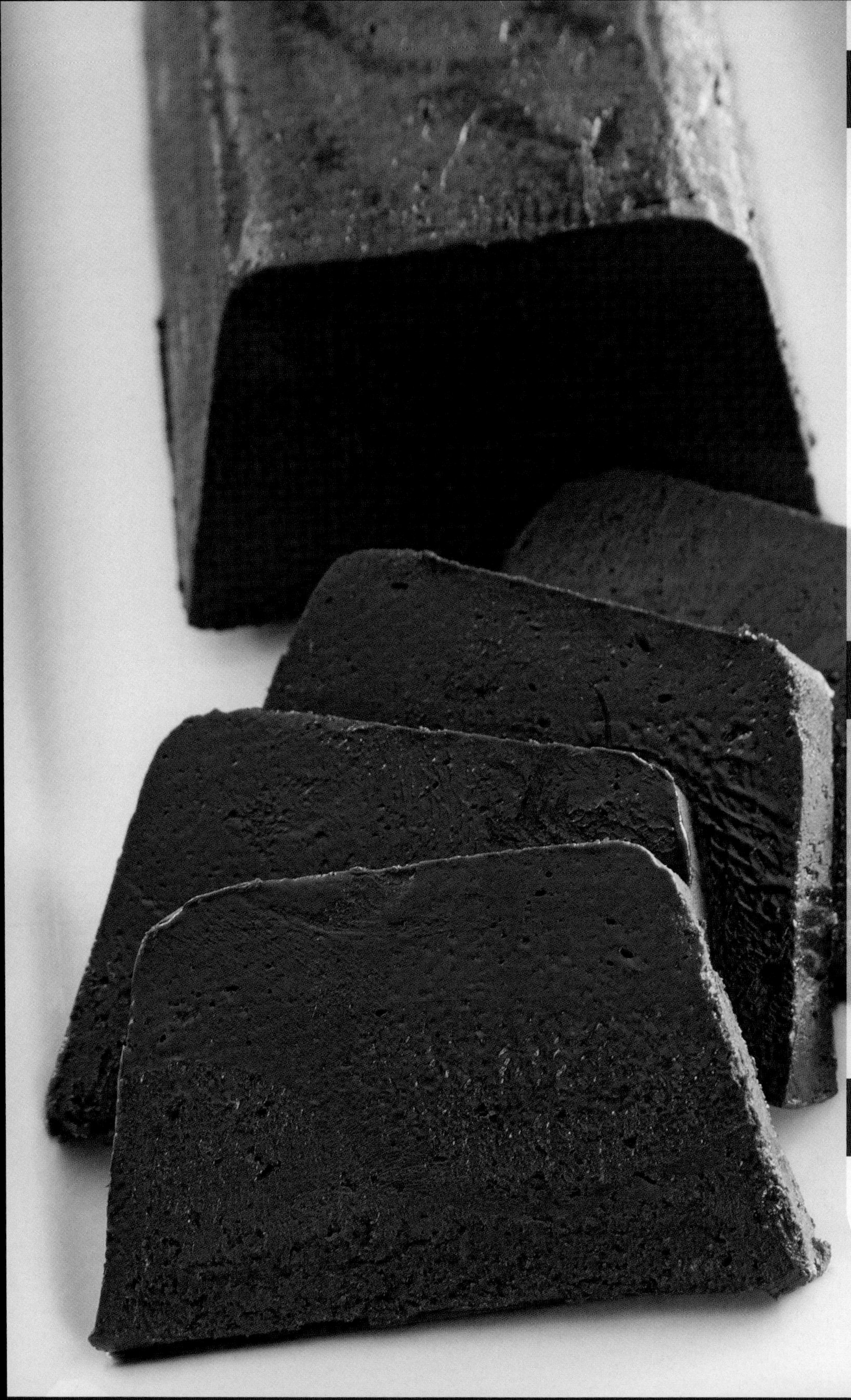

Learning Outcomes

Making a fondant
Melting chocolate
Mounting cream
Using a bain-marie

Equipment

Knives:
N/A

Tools:
Plastic wrap or parchment paper, mixing bowls, bain-marie, whisk, rubber spatula

Pans:
Terrine mold or loaf pan

Serving/Yield

1 terrine or loaf

HISTORY

Fondant au chocolat is a deliciously dense confection that can be eaten on its own or used as a filling or icing in other preparations. Originating in France in the mid-19th century, the fondant is prepared by melting the ingredients over a bain-marie, giving it a smoothness and density that would appeal to any true chocolate addict. Originally the fondant was intended to be eaten on its own as a decadent chocolate dessert, but has over time been largely relegated to a role as a secondary ingredient in other preparations.

Quantity		Ingredient
U.S.	**Metric**	
5 oz	150 g	Chocolate couverture
10 oz	300 g	Butter
6 oz	180 g	Cocoa powder
8 pcs	8 pcs	Egg yolks
8 oz	250 g	Sugar, granulated
3½ fl oz	100 ml	Espresso
1 pint	500 ml	Cream

FONDANT AU CHOCOLAT
Flourless Chocolate Terrine

Method

1. Line a terrine mold with plastic wrap or parchment paper (**chemiser**). Set aside to chill.
2. Melt the chocolate and butter together over a bain-marie. Once melted, stir until smooth. Remove from the heat and set aside.
3. Sift (**tamiser**) the cocoa powder.
4. Whisk the egg yolks with the sugar (**blanchir**) until light yellow in color and a ribbon forms when the whisk is lifted from the mixture. Fold the cocoa powder into the egg yolks, and then fold the egg yolks mixture into the melted chocolate.
5. Fold the egg yolks mixture into the melted chocolate and mix in the espresso.
6. Beat the cream to soft peaks. Fold into the chocolate mixture. Transfer to the prepared mold. Smooth the top, and then give the mold a few good taps to remove any air pockets. Cover and place in the refrigerator to chill for at least 4 hours (preferably overnight).

To Serve

1. Uncover and dip the mold in hot water for 10 seconds. Place a serving dish on top of the terrine.
2. Turn it over and gently and evenly pull the edges of the lining until the fondant unmolds. Remove the lining and discard. Dip a knife in hot water, wipe dry and slice as desired.

Note

Can be served with crème Chantilly, berry coulis, or crème Anglaise (vanilla, pistachio, or coffee).

Equipment

Knives:
Paring knife (*office*)

Tools:
Balloon whisk, large mixing
bowl, small mixing bowl,
spoon

Pans:
Small plats á gratin,
bain-marie

HISTORY

The sabayon is a light and luxurious dessert made from egg yolks, wine, and sugar. The dish originally stems from an Italian preparation known as "zabaglione" or "zabaione." The original dish is thought to have been created by the chefs of the Medici of Florence in the 16th century. From there, the dish was spread throughout Europe where it became extremely popular, and is known by several different names. In Russia, the dish was known by the colorful name, "gogul mogul," and in France by the 19th century it came to be known as "sabayon." The key to achieving the signature light and airy consistency of a sabayon is to thoroughly whisk the egg yolks to incorporate as much air as possible.

GRATIN DE FRUITS ROUGES
Red Fruit Sabayon

Quantity		Ingredient
U.S.	**Metric**	*Sabayon*
3 pcs	3 pcs	Egg yolks
2 ½ oz	75 g	Sugar, granulated
2 ½ fl oz	75 ml	White wine
		To Serve
8 oz	250 g	Berries

Method

1. Clean and cut the berries.
2. Arrange in **gratin dishes** and reserve in the refrigerator until needed.

Sabayon
1. With the aid of a balloon whisk, mix the egg yolks and sugar in a large mixing bowl (**blanchir**), then incorporate the white wine. Place the mixing bowl in a gently simmering bain-marie and beat the mixture until it becomes airy, makes ribbons when the whisk is lifted (**au ruban**), and turns light yellow in color.

Note

To incorporate maximum air into the mix and get volume, it is important to whisk the sabayon correctly from the beginning. Close attention to this technique will also prevent the egg yolks from cooking too quickly.

To Serve
1. Spoon the **sabayon** onto the berries and place under a hot salamander or broiler until the sabayon takes on a golden color.
2. Serve immediately.

Learning Outcomes

Making a French meringue
Making a crème Anglaise
Making caramel piping
Tempering eggs

Equipment

Tools:
Balloon whisk, mixing bowls, whisk, pastry bag, large plain tip, wooden spoon, ice water bath

Pans:
1 medium russe, 1 small russe, 1 large gratin dish, roasting pan, baking sheet

Serving

4 persons

FYI...

Escoffier originally named this preparation *oeufs à la neige*, referring to the way he shaped the beaten egg whites into an egg shape before poaching them in water or vanilla-infused milk. The name *île flottante* (floating island) refers to the way the egg whites float in a puddle of crème Anglaise.

Quantity		Ingredient
U.S.	Metric	French Meringue (Meringue Française)
3 ½ oz	100 g	Powdered sugar
3 ½ oz	100 g	Egg whites
3 ½ oz	100 g	Sugar, granulated
		Crème Anglaise
½ pt	250 ml	Milk
1 pc	1 pc	Vanilla bean
3 pcs	3 pcs	Egg yolks
2 oz	60 g	Sugar, granulated
		Caramel
3 ½ oz	100 g	Sugar, granulated
1 ¾ fl oz	50 ml	Water
		To Serve
¾ oz	20 g	Almonds, blanched and sliced

ÎLE FLOTTANTE
Floating Island

Method

Preheat the oven to 300°F (150°C).

Make a French Meringue (Meringue Française)

2. Sift (*tamiser*) the powdered sugar into a bowl. In a separate bowl, whip the egg whites using a balloon whisk (***monter les blancs***) until soft peaks form. Whisking continuously, add the sugar a little at a time, and continue to whisk the meringue until it is thick and glossy. Add the powdered sugar and, using a rubber spatula, fold it in until incorporated.

3. Place the silicone molds in a roasting pan. Transfer the meringue to a pastry bag fitted with a large plain tip and pipe the meringue into the molds. Fill the molds to the top and scrape the meringue flat using a plastic scraper (***corne***) or a metal spatula. Fill the roasting pan with enough water to ensure that the molds are two-thirds immersed. Cover the molds with foil, transfer the pan to the oven, and cook the meringues until set (*30 minutes*). Remove the pan from the oven and remove the foil. Let the meringues cool, then remove the molds from the roasting pan. Wrap the molds in plastic and reserve them in the refrigerator. Turn the oven up to 350°F (175°C).

Garnish (Garniture)

1. Spread the sliced almonds out onto a baking sheet and place them in the oven to toast until lightly golden (*5 to 10 minutes*). Set aside.

Crème Anglaise

1. Place the milk in a medium saucepan and bring to a low boil over medium-high heat. Using a small knife, split the vanilla bean lengthwise. Scrape the seeds from both sides and add to the milk along with the pod. Whisk well.

2. Place the egg yolks in a mixing bowl, add the sugar, and immediately begin to whisk it into the yolks. Continue whisking until the sugar is completely dissolved and the mixture is pale in color (***blanchir***).

3. Once the milk is scalded, whisk about one-third of the hot milk into the yolks to temper them. Whisk until the mixture is well combined and evenly heated.

4. Stir the tempered egg yolks into the pan of remaining hot milk and stir with a wooden spatula. Place the pan over low heat and stir in a figure 8 motion. As you stir, the foam on the surface will

disappear; at the same time, the liquid will begin to thicken and become oil-like in resistance. Continue cooking until the mixture is thick enough to coat the back of a wooden spatula and when your finger leaves a clean trail (*à la nappe*).

Tip

Crème Anglaise should be cooked to between 167°F and 185°F (75°C and 85°C).

5. Remove the pan from the heat and strain the crème Anglaise through a fine mesh sieve (**chinois**) into a clean bowl set in a bowl of ice. Stir it back and forth (**vanner**) with the spatula until cooled.

6. Cover the bowl in plastic wrap and reserve the bowl in the refrigerator until needed.

Finishing

1. Unmold the meringue domes onto individual plates and fill the bottom of each plate with crème Anglaise. Bring the sugar and water to a boil in a small saucepan over medium-high heat and cook this mixture until it turns a light caramel color. Immediately pour the caramel onto the meringue domes and sprinkle them with sliced almonds.

2. Serve immediately or refrigerate until needed.

MOELLEUX AU CHOCOLAT
ET CRÈME À LA PISTACHE

Making a crème Anglaise
Making a pistachio cream
Tempering chocolate
Making a hot dessert

Equipment

Knives:
N/A

Tools:
Four ring molds 3 in.
(7.5 cm) in diameter,
parchment paper, sieve,
whisk, wooden and rubber
spatulas, mixing bowls

Pans:
Baking sheet, saucepan,
bain-marie

Serving/Yield

Four 8 oz/250 gram
portions

FYI...

Also known as a lava cake, the moelleux chocolat is a true chocolate lover's dream. This decadent preparation combines two layers of chocolate: an outer chocolate cake surrounding an inner core of delicious, molten liquid chocolate. The word *moelleux* means "soft" and is a description of the warm, inner section of the cake. The origins of the preparation have been hotly contested and it was largely popularized in the 1980s and 1990s. Despite several chefs laying claim to its invention, the moelleux chocolat was likely derived from similar earlier preparations. The most important thing to remember when creating a moelleux chocolat is that the baking time must be short and carefully monitored to ensure the center stays liquid.

MOELLEUX AU CHOCOLAT ET CRÈME À LA PISTACHE
Soft Chocolate Cake with Pistachio Cream

Method

Make a Crème Anglaise

1. Prepare a clean bowl; set in an ice bath.
2. Heat milk and vanilla in a saucepan. Whisk the egg yolks together with the sugar (**blanchir**) until light yellow in color and a ribbon forms when the whisk is lifted from the mixture.
3. Once the milk has come to a boil, remove it from the heat and pour some into the egg yolks to temper and mix in well. Using a wooden spatula, add the tempered egg yolks into the remaining milk and then place the mixture back over low heat.
4. Stirring in a figure 8, gently cook the mixture until any foam on the surface dissipates and the liquid thickens to the consistency of a heavy oil. Do not allow the crème Anglaise to come to a boil. Cook until the cream coats the back of a spoon (**à la nappe**) and does not close up when a finger is drawn through it. Immediately strain into the prepared bowl.
5. Stir occasionally until the cream has cooled.
6. Make the pistachio cream: Dilute the pistachio paste with some of the cooled cream, then add it to the remaining cream. Keep refrigerated until needed.

Make a Chocolate Moelleux

1. Preheat the oven to 320°F (160°C).
2. Butter the ring molds and line with strips of parchment paper leaving a 1-in. (2.5-cm) cuff. Place on a heavy baking sheet.
3. Sift (**tamiser**) the flour and set aside.
4. Melt the chocolate and butter over a bain-marie. Stir the mixture until smooth, then set aside. Beat the eggs with the sugar until they have at least doubled in volume and the wires of the whisk leave a trail when lifted. Add some to the chocolate mixture and stir to lighten. Fold in the remaining egg mixture. Just before completely incorporated, add the sifted flour. Divide the mixture between the prepared ring molds and immediately place in the oven. Bake for 12 minutes.

To Serve

Spoon the pistachio cream onto plates. Once the moelleux are ready, remove them from the oven, peel off the paper liner, and transfer them to the plates. Serve immediately.

Quantity		Ingredient
U.S.	Metric	
		Crème Anglaise
8 fl oz	250 ml	Milk
1–2 drops	1–2 drops	Vanilla extract
3 pcs	3 pcs	Egg yolks
2 oz	60 g	Sugar, granulated
¾ oz	20 g	Pistachio paste
		Chocolate Moelleux
1 ¼ oz	40 g	Flour, sifted
4 ¼ oz	125 g	Bitter chocolate
4 ¼ oz	125 g	Butter
3 pcs	3 pcs	Eggs
125 g	125 g	Sugar, granulated

Learning Outcomes

Making a mousse
Melting chocolate
Beating egg whites
Folding batter

Equipment

Tools:
Bain-marie, rubber spatula,
mixing bowls, whisk,
balloon whisk

Serving

6 persons

The word *mousse* translates into English as both "foam" and as the plant "moss." This little detail causes food historians quite a lot of grief: Is the preparation named after the plant? After all, moss is light, airy, and grows in clumps that almost appear to have been formed in molds. Or is it named for its foamy or frothy texture? While the latter seems to make more sense, there is evidence to the contrary. Until the mystery is properly solved, food historians will simply have to live with this torturous uncertainty.

MOUSSE AU CHOCOLAT
Chocolate Mousse

Method

Base

1. Melt the chocolate over a simmering bain-marie. Once it has completely melted, remove the chocolate from the heat and incorporate the butter with a rubber spatula until melted. Add the egg yolks and stir until the mixture is homogeneous.
2. Beat the egg whites to soft peaks and, whisking continually, gradually add the sugar. Continue to whisk until firm and glossy.
3. Once the chocolate mixture has cooled to just above body temperature, add one-half of the meringue and fold it in using a rubber spatula. Add the second half and fold it in until combined.

Finishing

1. Whip the cream and powdered sugar to soft peaks, then fold into the mousse.
2. Transfer the mousse to molds and place in the refrigerator to set for not less than 1 hour.

To Serve

1. Dust the mousse with cocoa powder and if desired, serve with chocolate decorations.

Quantity		Ingredient
U.S.	**Metric**	*Base*
8 oz	250 g	Bittersweet chocolate
3 ½ oz	100 g	Butter
4 pcs	4 pcs	Egg yolks
6 pcs	6 pcs	Egg whites
1 ½ oz	45 g	Sugar, granulated
		Finishing
3 ½ fl oz	100 ml	Whipping cream
½ oz	15 g	Powdered sugar
		To Serve
As needed	As needed	Cocoa powder
As needed	As needed	Chocolate decorations

Learning Outcomes

Making a nougatine
Whipping cream
(*crème fouettée*)
Making an Italian meringue
Making a raspberry coulis
Cooking honey

Equipment

Knives:
Chef knife (*couteau chef*)

Tools:
Plastic wrap or parchment paper, mixing bowl, pastry brush, blender, wooden spoon, rubber spatula, sieve, candy thermometer (optional)

Pans:
Medium terrine or loaf pan, baking sheet, saucepans

Serving/Yield

One 1 ¾ pound/ 800 gram loaf

While traditional nougat is extremely dense and traditionally served at Christmas, nougat glacé is a light and airy confection that is perfect in the hot summer months. Nougat is a simple preparation that combines honey, egg whites, fruits, and nuts. This candy has existed in various forms since antiquity and was even used in religious ceremonies by the ancient Romans. The word *nougat* stems from the Provence region of France where the modern form of the confection was created and popularized in the 17th century. The French not only transformed and popularized this dessert, but more recently re-invented it from a hearty snack into true haute cuisine with the creation of nougat glacé, which can still be found as a delicate and delicious dessert in the finest French restaurants today.

NOUGAT GLACÉ
Iced Nougat

Method

Make the Nougatine

1. Prepare a container of cold water and a clean pastry brush. Lightly oil a baking sheet.
2. Place the glucose and sugar into a heavy-bottomed sauce pan. Stir well with a metal spoon and place over high heat. Once the sugar-glucose comes to a boil, allow to cook, brushing down the sides of the pan with the wet pastry brush until the sugar has completely dissolved. Leave it to cook until the solution begins to caramelize. Once the sugar-glucose solution has reached a golden-amber color, remove it from the heat and immediately stir in the almonds. Transfer the nougatine to the prepared baking sheet and allow to cool completely. Once cooled, crush the nougatine.
3. Line a terrine or loaf pan with plastic wrap or parchment paper. Set aside to chill.

Make an Italian Meringue

1. Add the honey to a small heavy-bottomed saucepan. Bring it to a boil and cook to the soft-ball stage (**petit boulé**) (235°F/115°C). While the honey is cooking, whisk the egg whites to soft peaks (**monter les blancs**). Gradually whisk the hot honey syrup into the soft peaks, being careful not to pour it onto the wires of the whisk. Once the syrup has been added, continue whisking until it has completely cooled. Set aside.
2. Beat the cream to soft peaks.
3. Fold the nougatine, nuts, candied cherries, and raisins into the Italian meringue. Fold in the whipped cream.
4. Transfer the mixture to the prepared mold (terrine or loaf pan). Smooth the top, and then give the filled mold a few good taps to remove any air pockets. Place the mold in the freezer to set for at least 4 hours (preferably overnight).

Make a Raspberry Coulis

1. Purée the raspberries and powdered sugar in a blender and then strain, pressing the pulp well. Keep chilled until needed.

To Serve

1. Dip the mold in hot water for 5 to 10 seconds. Overturn onto the serving platter and gently pull the liner until the nougat unmolds. Cut into slices using a heated knife.
2. Serve with the raspberry coulis.

Quantity		Ingredient
U.S.	**Metric**	*Nougatine*
2 ½ fl oz	80 ml	Glucose
2 ½ oz	80 g	Sugar, granulated
3 ¼ oz	100 g	Sliced almonds
¾ oz	20 g	Pistachios, finely chopped
1 ½ oz	45 g	Walnuts, finely chopped
1 oz	30 g	Candied cherries, finely chopped
1 oz	30 g	Raisins
12 fl oz	360 ml	Whipping cream
		Italian Meringue
1 oz	30 g	Sugar, granulated
2 ½ oz	75 g	Honey
1 ½ oz	45 g	Egg whites
		Raspberry Coulis
7 oz	200 g	Raspberries
¾ oz	20 g	Powdered sugar

Learning Outcomes

Making a pâte à bombe
Making a meringue
Making a whipped cream
(*crème fouettée*)
Cooking sugar
Making an iced dessert

PARFAIT GLACÉ AU CAFÉ

Equipment

Knives:
N/A

Tools:
Mixing bowls, pastry brush,
whisk, balloon whisk,
rubber spatula, piping bag,
medium star tip

Pans:
One 24 oz (750 g) mold,
saucepan

Serving/Yield

6–8 servings

HISTORY

While the modern parfait has come to mean a dessert of multi-layered ice cream served in a tall, thin glass with lots of toppings, the parfait glacé au café is true to the original parfait. This coffee infused iced dessert was created in the mid-19th century, and early parfaits were made in elaborate molds designed to impress the diner. This deliciously refreshing dessert is well encapsulated by its name, *parfait,* which is French for "perfect."

PARFAIT GLACÉ AU CAFÉ
Iced Coffee Parfait

Method

Make a Pâte à Bombe

1. Line the 24-oz (750-g) mold with plastic wrap (**chemiser**).
2. Prepare a container of cold water and a clean pastry brush.
3. Chill two bowls for later use.
4. Place the egg yolks in a bowl and set aside.
5. Add the sugar and water to a saucepan and bring to a boil, brushing down the sides of the pan with the wet pastry brush often until the sugar reaches the soft-ball stage (**petit boulé**) (235°F/115°C). Remove the boiled sugar from the heat and whisk it into the egg yolks in a thin, steady stream. Make sure to pour to the side of the bowl and not onto the wires of the whisk.
6. Once the hot syrup has been incorporated, add the instant coffee and continue whisking until the mixture (**pâte à bombe**) cools to room temperature and is thick.

Make a Whipped Cream (Crème Fouettée)

1. Place the cream [10 oz (300 mL)] into the chilled bowl and whisk it to soft peaks.
2. Fold the whipped cream into the pâte à bombe. Fill the mold with the parfait. Lightly cover with plastic wrap and place in the freezer to set for at least 4 hours (preferably overnight).
3. Remove the chilled bowl from the refrigerator and fill with cream [5 oz (150 mL)]. Whisk the cream to medium peaks. Transfer immediately to a piping bag fitted with a medium star tip.

To Serve

1. Unmold the parfait by dipping it into warm water for a few seconds. Turn over onto a chilled serving plate and gently pull on the plastic wrap lining the mold. Remove and discard the plastic.
2. Decorate by piping the whipped cream (**crème fouettée**), adding the chocolate-covered coffee beans and by dusting it with cocoa powder. Serve immediately.

Quantity		Ingredient
U.S.	Metric	
6 pcs	6 pcs	Egg yolks
8 oz	250 g	Sugar, granulated
2 ¾ fl oz	80 ml	Water
½ fl oz	15 ml	Instant coffee
10 fl oz	300 ml	Heavy cream
5 fl oz	150 ml	Heavy cream
As needed	As needed	Chocolate covered coffee beans
As needed	As needed	Cocoa powder

Learning Outcomes

Making a cooked custard
Tempering eggs

Equipment

Knives:
Paring knife (*couteau d'office*)

Tools:
Six 5 oz (150 g) ramekins, wooden spatula, whisk, mixing bowls, sieve, paper towel

Pans:
Saucepan, baking pan

Serving/Yield

Six 5 ounce/150 gram portions

The French do not have a word for custard; instead they simply refer to this delectable treat as a crème. The history of custard can be traced back to the Middle Ages when it was typically used as a filling for a tart or flan. The first flavor used for pots du crème is thought to have been vanilla. Over time, flavor variations such as chocolate and fruit began to occur. One thing is for certain: This dessert has stood the test of time and will remain a favorite far into the future.

PETITS POTS DE CRÈME
Little Chocolate Custard Pots

Method

Preheat the oven to 320°F (160°C).

Prepare a Baking Pan

1. Cover the bottom of the pan with a damp paper towel and arrange 6 ramekins spaced equally apart.
2. Place the chocolate pieces in a bowl. Pour the milk in a saucepan and bring it to a boil over medium heat. Split the vanilla bean lengthwise, scrape out the seeds and add them to the milk. Once the milk comes to a boil, immediately pour it over the chocolate. Allow the hot milk to soften the chocolate for 20 to 30 seconds, and then stir until smooth.
3. Whisk the eggs and sugar together (**blanchir**) until light in color and the wires of the whisk leave a trail when lifted. Add some of the warm chocolate milk to temper the yolks, mixing well. Then whisk in the remaining chocolate milk and strain the mixture.
4. Divide the mixture between the ramekins equally. Place the baking pan in the oven and fill with hot water until the liquid reaches halfway up the sides of the ramekins. Bake until set or until the tip of a small knife inserted in the center comes out clean, for approximately 30 minutes.
5. Carefully remove the baking pan from the oven. Remove the ramekins and allow to cool. Once cooled, place in the refrigerator to set overnight before serving.

Quantity		Ingredient
U.S.	*Metric*	
14 fl oz	420 ml	Milk
3 ¼ oz	100 g	Dark chocolate, chopped
4 pcs	4 pcs	Egg yolks
2 ¾ oz	80 g	Sugar, granulated
1 pc	1 pc	Vanilla bean

POIRES POCHÉES AU VIN ROUGE

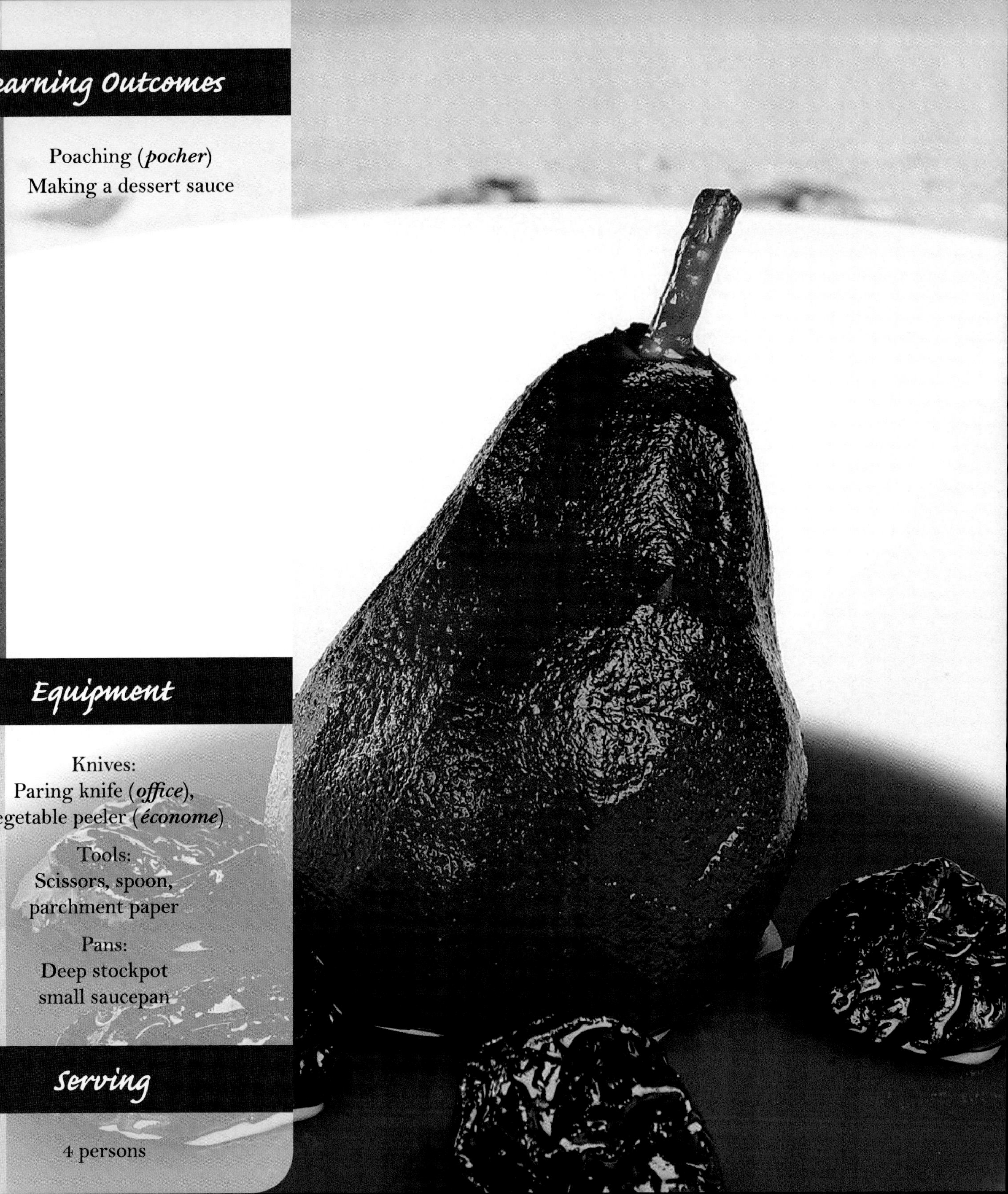

Learning Outcomes

Poaching (*pocher*)
Making a dessert sauce

Equipment

Knives:
Paring knife (*office*),
vegetable peeler (*économe*)

Tools:
Scissors, spoon,
parchment paper

Pans:
Deep stockpot
small saucepan

Serving

4 persons

Poaching is a fundamental culinary technique that has been utilized in some capacity for thousands of years. The ancient Roman cookbook *Apicius* had several recipes that utilized poaching. This included several sweet preparations, such as *Aliter Patina Versatilis,* which was a recipe for a sweet nut turnover. The technique was not heavily utilized until Taillevent published his seminal cookbook *Le Viandier* in 1490, which contained several recipes and tips on poaching, popularizing the technique in French cooking for centuries after. Today eggs are generally poached in water and vinegar, fish in white wine, poultry in stock, and fruit in red wine.

POIRES POCHÉES
AU VIN ROUGE
Pears Poached in Red Wine

Method

Poaching

1. In a deep pan or stockpot (**marmite**), bring the red wine, sugar, vanilla, and cinnamon to a boil. Cook until the sugar has completely melted. Peel the pears, keeping the stems on. Using the tip of a vegetable peeler, cut out the eye at the base of the fruits.

2. Place the pears in the wine and cover with a parchment paper lid (**cartouche**) over the contents of the pot. Add the prunes and bring the liquid to a gentle simmer over low to medium heat and cook until a knife can be easily inserted into the center of the pears.

3. Remove the pan from the stove, let the pears cool to room temperature, then refrigerate in their cooking syrup (preferably overnight).

To Serve

1. Mix 2 tablespoons of cooking syrup with the red currant jelly in a small saucepan and cook in a small pan over medium heat. Cook until the sauce is like syrup in consistency.

2. Drain the pears, and place in a chilled soup plate or shallow dish with the prunes. Trim the bottom if needed to maintain them upright. Drizzle the plate with the sauce and decorate with fresh mint.

Quantity		Ingredient
U.S.	Metric	
4 pcs	4 pcs	Pears
8 pcs	8 pcs	Prunes, pitted
		To Cook
1 pt	500 ml	Red wine
4 ¾ oz	140 g	Sugar, granulated
¼ fl oz	4 ml	Vanilla extract
2 pcs	2 pcs	Cinnamon sticks
		To Serve
2 oz	60 g	Red currant jelly
8 brs	8 brs	Fresh mint

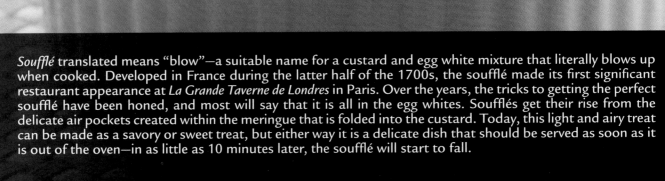

Learning Outcomes

Making a soufflé
Making a pastry cream
Making a meringue

Equipment

Tools:
Whisk, balloon whisk, large plastic spatula, mixing bowl, piping bag, large round tip

Pans:
Saucepan, 8 soufflé ramekins

Serving

8 servings

HISTORY

Soufflé translated means "blow"—a suitable name for a custard and egg white mixture that literally blows up when cooked. Developed in France during the latter half of the 1700s, the soufflé made its first significant restaurant appearance at *La Grande Taverne de Londres* in Paris. Over the years, the tricks to getting the perfect soufflé have been honed, and most will say that it is all in the egg whites. Soufflés get their rise from the delicate air pockets created within the meringue that is folded into the custard. Today, this light and airy treat can be made as a savory or sweet treat, but either way it is a delicate dish that should be served as soon as it is out of the oven—in as little as 10 minutes later, the soufflé will start to fall.

186

SOUFFLÉE CHAUD AUX FRAMBOISES
Warm Soufflé with Raspberry Coulis

Method

Preheat the oven to 400°F (200°C).

Raspberry Coulis
Grease each ramekin with butter and then coat the inside with sugar (**chemiser**).

Mix the raspberry pulp, sugar, and raspberry liqueur together. Keep refrigerated until needed.

Crème Pâtissière
1. Make a pastry cream (crème pâtissière): Pour the milk into a medium saucepan and bring to a boil over medium-high heat. Add about one-quarter of the sugar to the milk and stir until it dissolves completely.
2. Meanwhile, place the egg yolks in a small mixing bowl and add the remaining sugar. Whisk the sugar into the eggs until it completely dissolves and the yolks lighten in color (**blanchir**).
3. Add the flour to the yolks and stir until well combined. When the milk begins to come to a boil, remove it from the stove and pour one-third of it into the egg yolks. Stir well to temper the yolks, then whisk the tempered mixture into the remaining hot milk. Leave the mixture to cool slightly, but do not place in the refrigerator.

Meringue
1. In a separate bowl, add your remaining sugar and egg whites and whisk them into soft peaks (**monter les blancs**).
2. Gently fold the meringue into the now-lukewarm pastry cream, maintaining as much air in the mixture as possible.
3. Place the combined mixture into a piping bag with a large tip and gently pipe the mixture into the butter and sugar-lined ramekins. Fill them all the way to the rim.
4. Use your thumb and gently carve a thin edge around the mixture, pulling it slightly away from the edge of the ramekin. This will help ensure that the soufflé rises straight up and not to either side.
5. Place the soufflés into the preheated oven. After 2 minutes, lower the temperature to 350°F (185°C) and continue cooking until the soufflés have increased in size by a third of the height of the ramekin and are golden in color.
6. Remove from the oven. Gently squeeze a teaspoon (5 ml/¼ fl oz) of raspberry coulis into the centre of each soufflé. Coat each soufflé in a fine layer of powdered sugar and serve immediately.

Quantity		Ingredient
U.S.	Metric	
As needed	As needed	Butter
As needed	As needed	Sugar, granulated
		Raspberry Coulis
10 oz	300 g	Raspberry pulp
1 oz	30 g	Powdered sugar
½ fl oz	15 ml	Raspberry liqueur
		Pastry Cream (Crème Pâtissière)
8 fl oz	250 ml	Milk
1½ oz	45 g	Sugar, granulated
2 pcs	2 pcs	Egg yolks
1 oz	25 g	Flour
		French Meringue (Meringue Française)
¾ oz	20 g	Sugar granulated
3 pcs	3 pcs	Egg whites
As needed	As needed	Powdered sugar

SOUFFLÉE GLACÉ AUX FRUITS ROUGES

Learning Outcomes

Making a frozen soufflé
Making an Italian meringue
Whipping cream (*crème fouettée*)
Cooking sugar

Equipment

Knives:
Palette knife (*spatule*), paring knife (*couteau d'office*), scissors

Tools:
6 ramekins, mixing bowls, spoon, pastry brush, whisk, rubber spatula, parchment paper, scotch tape, piping bag and piping tip

Pans:
Small saucepan

Serving/Yield

6 portions

HISTORY

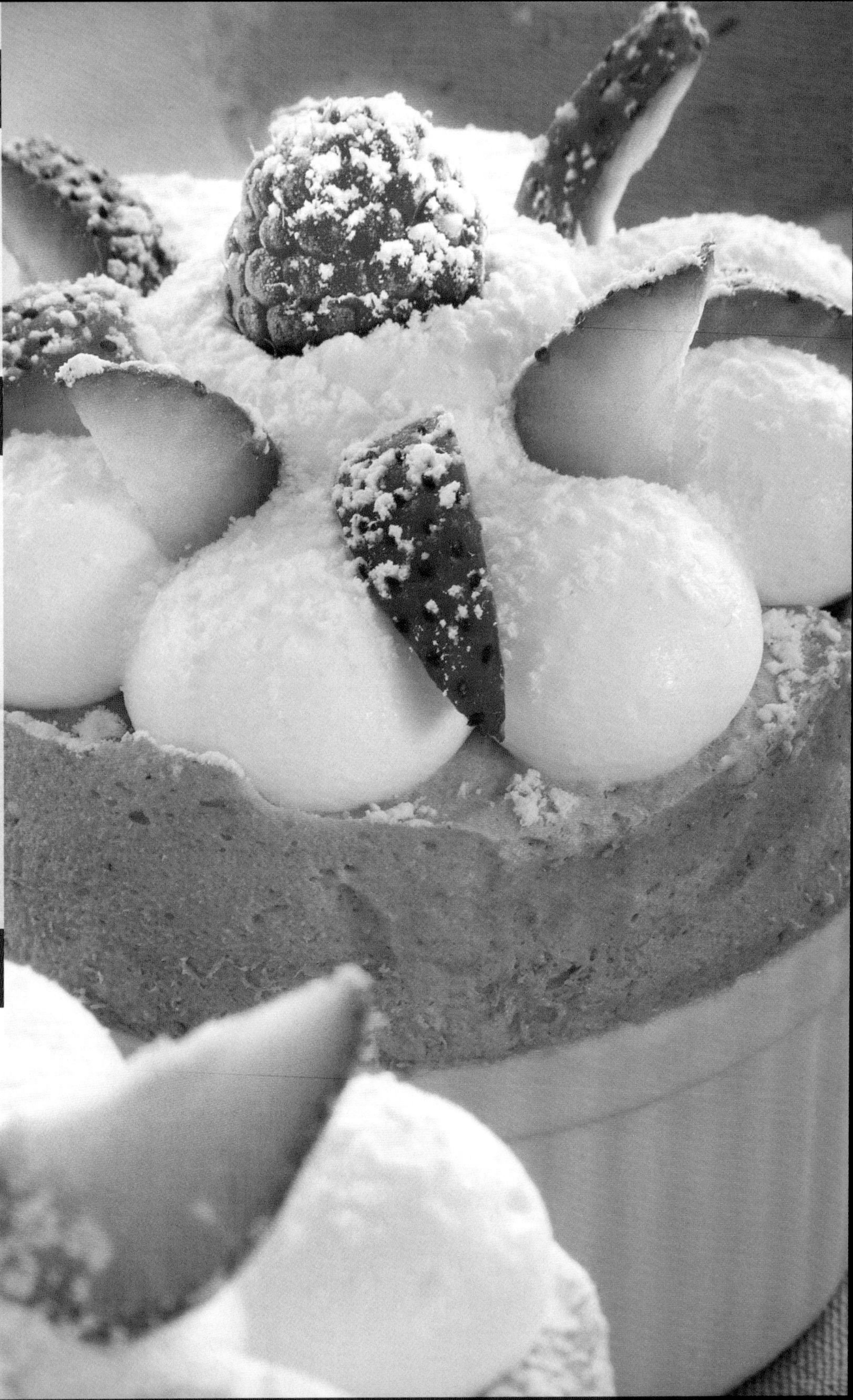

The soufflé has been a staple of French haute cuisine for centuries. The traditional soufflé, which translates to "puffed up," refers to the delicate pastry ballooning up over the pan when baked. The soufflé glacé is not actually baked at all and is called a soufflé because the preparation uses a tight collar of parchment paper, allowing the chef to overfill a ramekin. When the dish is frozen and the parchment is removed, the dessert has the appearance of being "puffed up" over the top of the ramekin.

SOUFFLÉ GLACÉ AUX FRUITS ROUGES
Frozen Red Fruit Soufflé

Method

Prepare the Ramekins

1. Cut strips of parchment leaving a cuff of about 2 in. (5 cm). Wrap each of the ramekins with a strip of parchment paper, using scotch tape to secure (**chemiser**).

Make an Italian Meringue

1. Prepare a small bowl of cold water, a spoon, and a pastry brush.
2. Place the sugar and water in a small saucepan over high heat and bring to a boil. When the sugar comes to a boil, skim off any white foam that develops from the surface and brush the sides down with cold water. Once the sugar is clear, leave it to cook until the soft-ball stage (**petit boulé**) (235°F/115°C).
3. While the sugar is cooking, begin whisking the egg whites (**monter les blancs**).
4. When the sugar is ready, remove it from the heat and (while still whisking) add the hot syrup in a thin, steady stream, being careful to pour to the sides and not onto the wires of the whisk. Once the syrup has been incorporated, continue whisking until cooled.

Assembly

1. Place the fruit puree in a separate bowl and fold in the Italian meringue.
2. Whip the second portion of cream to soft peaks with the powdered sugar, and then fold it into the meringue mixture.
3. Fill the prepared ramekins with the mixture to the edges of the paper lining. Tap the ramekins to remove any air bubbles and smooth the tops with a palette knife.
4. Place in the freezer for at least 2 hours.

To Serve

1. Remove the ramekins from the freezer and peel off the paper cuffs. Whip the remaining cream with the powdered sugar to soft peaks.
2. Transfer cream mixture to a piping bag and pipe it onto the tops of the frozen soufflés. Decorate with fresh fruit and mint.

Quantity		Ingredient
U.S.	Metric	
4 fl oz	120 ml	Egg whites
8 oz	250 g	Sugar, granulated
2 fl oz	60 ml	Water
10 oz	300 g	Raspberry or strawberry puree
13 ¼ fl oz	400 ml	Cream
7 fl oz	200 ml	Cream
1 oz	30 g	Powdered sugar
As needed	As needed	Fresh fruit
As needed	As needed	Fresh mint

Pain et Viennoiseries
(Breads and Pastries)

© Le Gordon Bleu International

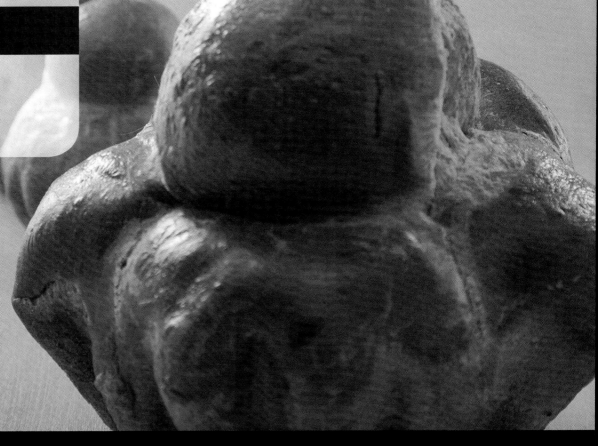

Learning Outcomes

Making a brioche dough
Kneading
Shaping brioche

Equipment

Knives:
Chef knife (*couteau chef*)

Tools:
Mixing bowl, corne, whisk

Pans:
Small saucepan,
baking sheet

Serving

6 Small brioches
1 Large brioche
1 Braided brioche

"Let them eat cake" is often quoted as an example of Marie Antoinette's arrogance at the plight of hungry Parisians during the French Revolution (1789-1799). In fact, it was not "cake" that she said but "brioche." This puts the last queen of France in a slightly better light; a simple brioche with no filling was then considered simply bread enriched with butter and eggs. This doesn't mean she wasn't being a little snarky when she said it, but it should nevertheless give historians pause to reflect.

BRIOCHE
Brioche Bread

Method

Preheat the oven to 400°F (205°C).

Brioche Dough (Pâte à Brioche)

1. Heat the milk in a small saucepan over low heat until it is warm to the touch. Remove it from the heat, mix in the yeast, and set aside.

2. Mix the eggs and the sugar together in a bowl using a whisk. Sift (**tamiser**) the flour onto a clean, dry work surface, add the salt, and make a large well (**fontaine**) in the center using a plastic scraper (**corne**). Into the well, pour the milk and yeast mixture as well as the egg mixture. Incorporate all the ingredients in the well with your fingertips, simultaneously using the **corne** to add small quantities of flour from the sides. Continue until the mixture in the center of the well resembles a thick paste. Gather all the ingredients together and work them with the heel of your palm until combined.

3. With the heel of your palm, smear the dough away from yourself (**fraiser**). **Note**: *At this point, the dough should be wet enough to stick to the work surface. If not, work in a little more milk, a spoonful at a time, until the desired consistency is reached.*

4. Repeat the motion of stretching the dough out then folding it in on itself until the dough is elastic and no longer sticks.

5. Dot the dough with small pieces of softened butter and fold the dough over to enclose the butter. Knead it until the butter is incorporated. Throw the dough hard onto the work surface, fold it onto itself and repeat. Continue working the dough in this manner in order to develop the gluten.

6. Roll the dough into a ball, dust it lightly with flour, and place it in a clean bowl. Cover the bowl with a damp cloth and leave it to proof either in a warm area or in a proofer until doubled in size.

7. Transfer the risen dough to a lightly floured work surface and press out all the air bubbles. Roll the dough back into a ball, lightly dust it with flour, and return it to the bowl to rise a second time. Let it rise overnight in the refrigerator or, for faster results, in a warm place or proofer.

8. Butter the brioche molds and divide the risen dough into 3 equal parts (see pages 241–252 in *Pâtisserie and Baking Foundations*).

Small Brioches (Petites Brioches à Tête)

1. Lightly dust the work surface with flour (**fleurer**). Place one of the pieces of dough on the floured work surface and lightly press down with the flat of your hands, shaping the dough into a rectangle. Fold the upper one-third of the rectangle down over itself and

Quantity		Ingredient
U.S.	Metric	
4 ¼ fl oz	125 ml	Milk
½ oz	15 g	Fresh yeast
4 pcs	4 pcs	Eggs
1 oz	30 g	Sugar, granulated
1 lb	500 g	Flour, sifted
¼ oz	10 g	Salt
8 oz	250 g	Butter, room temperature
1 pc	1 pc	Egg for egg wash

apply pressure with the heel of your palm to seal the seam. Turn the dough around and repeat the procedure of folding down the top one-third and sealing the seam with the heel of your palm.

2. Roll the dough out into an even cylinder, about 2-in. (5-cm) thick, and bend it in half so that the two ends touch. Score the midpoint with a knife and straighten out the cylinder. Cut it in half at the scored midpoint and proceed to cut each section into equally sized pieces [1 ¾ oz (50 g) each].

3. One by one, dip the pieces in flour and roll them into balls; using the palm of your hand, roll the dough in a circular motion until the ball is smooth and tight. Once all the dough has been shaped into balls, roll them back and forth into oblong shapes. Dip the side of your hand in flour, and place it on the oblong, one-third of the way down. With a light sawing motion, use the floured side of your hand to roll the oblongs into bowling pin shapes. When doing so, guide the long end of the dough with your free hand to keep it from flopping. Continue this process until a defined "neck" is created. Repeat with all the oblongs.

4. Dip your thumb, index finger, and middle finger in flour and pick up a piece of dough by the "neck." Lower the dough, fat end first, into a buttered mold and press your fingers down through the dough to the bottom of the mold (*still holding the "neck"*). Let go and gently remove your fingers. The result should be a small ball of dough nestled in a larger one. Dip your index finger in flour and press it deeply into the seam, between the "head" and "body." Carefully remove your finger and repeat this motion, working your way around the head.

5. Repeat with the remaining brioches.

6. Set the brioches aside to rise in a warm place or in a proofer until they double in size.

Large Brioche (Grande Brioche à Tête)

1. Lightly dust the work surface with flour (*fleurer*). Place one of the pieces of dough on the floured work surface, cut off one-quarter, and set it aside.

2. Using your hands, flatten the remaining dough into a circle. Fold an edge of the circle into the center and seal it by pressing it with the heel of your palm. Repeat this motion, turning the dough a little every time, until you obtain a small, compact "round." Turn the dough over and cup your hands around it. Roll the dough around the work surface in a circular motion with your cupped hands until it forms a smooth, tight ball.

3. Create a deep depression in the center of the ball using your fingers or the end of a rolling pin and place the dough in a large brioche mold.

4. Roll the small piece of reserved dough into a ball. Cup your hand around the dough and roll it around in a circular motion until the ball is smooth and tight. Roll one end of the ball back and forth to create a pear shape. Dip your fingers in flour and pick up the pear (*holding it upside down*). Insert the upside-down pear into the hole in the center of the brioche, pressing down deeply until your fingers touch the bottom of the mold. Carefully remove your fingers and dip your index finger in flour. Press it deeply into the gap between the "head" and the "body," working your way around to seal the seam. Set the brioche aside to rise in a warm place or in a proofer until it doubles in size.

Braided Brioche (Brioche Tressée)

1. Lightly dust the work surface with flour (*fleurer*). Place one of the pieces of dough on the floured work surface and divide it into 3 equal parts. Lightly press down one of the pieces of the dough with the flat of your hand to form a rectangle. Fold the upper one-third of the rectangle down over itself and apply pressure with the heel of your palm to seal the seam. Turn the dough around and repeat the procedure of folding down the top one-third and sealing the seam with the heel of your palm.

2. Roll the dough out into an even cylinder, about 1-in. (2.5-cm) thick. Repeat with the 2 remaining pieces of dough.

3. Place the 3 cylinders side by side and, if necessary, trim them to the same length. Attach them all at one end.

4. *Braid the brioche:* Lift the central strand of dough over the right hand one. Next, lift the strand that is now at the center over the left one. Again, lift the strand that is now at the center over the right one and continue this process, alternating right and left until you reach the end of the strands of brioche.

5. Tuck the ends under the braid and transfer it to a clean baking sheet. Set the brioche aside to rise in a warm place or in a proofer until it doubles in size (see pages 241–252 in *Pâtisserie and Baking Foundations*).

Finishing

1. Brush the brioches with egg wash, place them on the baking sheet, and transfer them to the preheated oven to bake. Once the brioches begin to turn golden, reduce the heat to 375°F (190°C) and continue to bake the brioches until they turn a deep shade of gold.

2. When the brioches are cooked, remove them from the oven and turn the brioches à tête upside down in their molds to cool.

Learning Outcomes

Making a laminated
enriched dough
Making pastry cream
(*crème pâtissière*)

Equipment

Knives:
Pastry scraper (*corne*) [or
paring knife (*couteau d'office*)]

Tools:
Mixing bowls, wooden spatula,
rolling pin, pastry brush,
parchment paper

Pans:
Baking sheet, wire rack

Serving/Yield

3¼ pounds/1.7 kilogram
portion of dough or
8 moulins or oreillons

The Danish is a rich pastry that can be prepared using a number of different fillings, but is most commonly filled with cheese or fruit. While the roots of the Danish seem obvious, there is more to the story of their creation than meets the eye. While the Danish did originate in Denmark, ironically it was not actually created by Danes. In 1850, the Confectioners, Bakers and Chocolate Makers Association of Denmark went on a prolonged strike. The bakeries and pastry shop owners decided to hire foreign workers to fill in for the Danish bakers and mostly ended up hiring Austrian bakers from Vienna. The Viennese bakers began making the popular preparations from their homeland, including one called "plundergebäck." When the Danish bakers returned to work, they continued baking the Viennese specialties, adding their own spins to the Austrian bakers' recipes. It was the adapted version of the "plundergebäck" pastry that would become to be known globally as "Danish. Oddly enough, within Denmark, *Danish* is actually called *wienerbrød*, which translates to "Viennese bread."

Quantity		Ingredient
U.S.	**Metric**	*Danish Dough*
2 fl oz	60 ml	Water, warm
1 oz	30 g	Fresh yeast
2 oz	60 g	Sugar, granulated
22 oz	675 g	Bread flour
8 fl oz	240 ml	Milk
3 pcs	3 pcs	Eggs
½ oz	15 g	Orange zest
¼ oz	5 g	Lemon zest
¼ fl oz	5 ml	Vanilla
1 dash	1 g	Cardamom
¼ oz	5 g	Salt
11 ¾ oz	350 g	Butter
		Pastry Cream
8 fl oz	250 ml	Milk
1 pc	1 pc	Vanilla bean
2 pcs	2 pcs	Egg yolks
2 oz	60 g	Sugar, granulated
1 oz	30 g	Flour
		Fruit
8 pcs	8 pcs	Prunes, canned (for Moullins)
16 pcs	16 pcs	Apricot halves, canned (for Oreillons)
		Finish
1 pc	1 pc	Egg, for egg wash

MOULINS ET OREILLONS
Danishes and Pinwheels

Method

Make the Danish Dough

1. Add the warm water [*max 90°F (32°C)*] and yeast to a bowl and stir until the yeast is dissolved and the mixture is smooth. Add half of the sugar and 1–2 spoonfuls of the flour to form a thin paste. Set aside to develop for about 15 minutes.

2. In a separate bowl, whisk together the milk, remaining sugar, eggs, orange zest and lemon zest, vanilla, and cardamom until combined.

3. Place the remaining flour in a large bowl and make a large well (**fontaine**) in the center. Add the salt and then pour in the egg mixture as well as the sponge portion of dough. Mix the wet ingredients with your fingertips to dissolve the salt, then gradually incorporate the flour. Continue mixing until the flour is incorporated and a soft dough has formed. Scrape down the sides, cover and set aside to proof until doubled in volume, approximately 1½ to 2 hours.

4. Place the butter between 2 pieces of parchment paper and beat it with a rolling pin. Once the butter is flattened, stop and fold it onto itself, repeating the process several times until the butter is malleable but still firm. Set aside in a cool place.

5. Once the dough has risen, punch it down and turn it out onto a floured work surface. Allow the dough to rest for 10 to 15 minutes. Then roll it out into a long rectangle about ¼ in. (3–4 mm) thick.

6. Roll the butter out (**abaisser**) into a rectangle that is about the same width as the dough, but only about two-thirds of the length. Place the butter onto the upper two-thirds of the dough, leaving a slight border of dough around the butter. Fold the unbuttered third of the dough up to cover the bottom half of the butter. Press down well. Fold the top portion of dough down over the first fold and press the edges to seal the butter within an envelope of dough. Turn the dough packet to the left so the seam is on your right.

7. Roll the dough out (**abaisser**) into a long rectangle about ¼ in. (½ cm) thick. Fold the dough in half, then reopen. Fold the bottom up to meet the middle crease that was created from folding it in half moments ago. Then, fold the top down to the crease, leaving a slight space between the two. Then fold the top half down over the bottom half. Turn the dough so the seam is on your right and roll it out (**abaisser**) into a long rectangle as before. Fold the dough into thirds, brushing off any excess flour. Wrap the dough in plastic and place it in the refrigerator to rest for about 20 minutes.

8. Remove the dough from the refrigerator and place it so the seam is facing your right. Roll out (*abaisser*) the dough into a long rectangle. Fold the bottom up one-third, then fold the top down, making sure that the edges are even and there isn't a gap inside the folds. Press to even and turn to the left so the seam is on your right.

9. Place the Danish dough in the refrigerator to rest before using, preferably overnight.

Make the Moulins

Preheat the oven to 400°F (205°C).

1. Roll out the dough (*abaisser*) into a rectangle shape, so that it measures approximately 8-in. (20-cm) high by 32 in. (81 cm) in width. The rectangle should be ¼-in. (½-cm) thick.

2. Fold the top of the rectangle down to the bottom and then unfold, leaving a mark in the dough. Measure and score the length of the dough into 4 equal strips (creating 4 strips, each about 8 in. wide), scoring the dough with a knife from top to bottom, marking 4 rectangular strips with a crease through the center from your first fold.

3. Using a small knife, cut the scored dough into 4 in. (10 cm) by 4 in. (10 cm) squares.

4. Each square of dough now needs to be cut into triangular flags while leaving them attached at the centre of the square. Take one square of dough and make 4 incisions, each starting at different corners and going almost to the center of each square. Leave ½ in. (1.2 cm) uncut at the center. Your square should look like 4 triangles joined at the center.

5. Using a pastry brush, add egg wash to the center of each square.

6. Gently hold down one corner of a triangle and take the other corner of your triangle and fold it into the middle of the square where the 4 points of the triangles meet. Repeat for the remaining 3 triangles.

7. Add egg wash to the center of your moulin and place a piece of prune on top. Repeat for the remaining squares.

8. Set aside to proof for 10 to 15 minutes.

9. Bake until golden, approximately 12 to 15 minutes and place on wire rack to cool.

Make the Oreillons

Preheat the oven to 400°F (205°C).

Make the Pastry Cream

1. Line a small serving tray or platter with plastic wrap.

2. Pour the milk into a medium saucepan. Split the vanilla bean in half lengthwise and scrape out the seeds. Stir the seeds into the milk and bring it to a boil over medium-high heat. Add about one-quarter of the sugar to the milk and stir to dissolve it.

3. Meanwhile, place the egg yolks in a small mixing bowl and add the remaining sugar. Whisk the sugar into the eggs until it completely dissolves and the yolks lighten in color (*blancher*). Add the flour to the yolks and stir until well combined.

4. When the milk begins to come to a boil, remove it from the stove and pour one-third of it into the egg yolks. Stir well to temper the yolks, then whisk the tempered mixture into the remaining hot milk. Place back onto the heat and cook until the pastry cream (*crème pâtissière*) begins to bubble. Continue whisking (being sure to press the whisk around the corners of the pan) and allow to cook for 1 minute in order to cook the starch. The pastry cream will become very thick. Immediately transfer the finished pastry cream to the plastic-lined tray. Pat the surface with a piece of cold butter (*tamponner*) held on the end of a fork to create a protective film. Completely cover with a second piece of plastic wrap, pressing out any air bubbles. Let the pastry cream cool to room temperature before refrigerating.

Make the Oreillons

1. Roll out the dough (*abaisser*) into a rectangle shape, so that it measures approximately 8-in. (20-cm) tall by 32-in. (81-cm) wide. The rectangle should be ¼-in. thick.

2. Fold the top of the rectangle down to the bottom and then unfold, leaving a mark in the dough. Measure and score the length of the dough into 4 equal strips (creating 4 strips, each about 8 in. wide), scoring the dough with a knife from top to bottom, marking 4 rectangular strips with a crease through the center from your first fold.

3. Using a small knife, cut the scored dough into 4 in. (10 cm) by 4 in. (10 cm) squares.

4. Using a pastry brush, apply egg wash to the center of each square.

5. Gently holding opposite corners of a square, fold the points into the center.

6. Place a dollop of pastry cream into each of the 2 unfolded and exposed portions of the square. Place a piece of apricot on top of each pastry cream dollop. Repeat for the remaining squares.

To Finish

1. Using a pastry brush, apply egg wash to the tops of the oreillons. Set aside to proof for 10 to 15 minutes.

2. Bake until golden, approximately 12 to 15 minutes, and place on wire rack to cool.

Learning Outcomes

Making a basic mixed flour
dough
Using a starter (*levain*)
Kneading
Shaping boules

Equipment

Knives:
Razor blade

Tools:
Mixing bowls, clean kitchen
towel

Pans:
Baking sheet (as needed),
wire rack

Serving/Yield

About 2 pounds/900 grams
of dough, making 2 small
round loaves

FYI...

Pain de Campagne is traditionally formed into boules, although the dough lends itself well to many other shapes and sizes. The recipe here calls for the addition of whole wheat or rye flour, but some bakers will often use a mixture of both. Different bakers will have their own mix that they prefer. When asked to envisage French bread, one immediately conjures images of the long, elegant baguette. However, for true French culinary purists, the real French bread has always been la pain de campagne. The name translates literally to "country bread" and stems from the bread's long tradition of being baked in country mills throughout France. The pain de campagne is a much heartier bread than its baguette counterpart. The use of whole wheat flour and baking the bread as a thick, round loaf allow the bread to stay fresh for much longer than the skinny baguette. While the 20th century has seen baguette dominance in France, over the past few decades the pain de campagne has experienced a major resurgence in popularity. Food critics link the resurgence of healthier whole-wheat breads to a decline in the quality of mass-produced baguettes, combined with people's desire for a more healthy diet.

PAIN DE CAMPAGNE
Country Bread

Method

1. Make a levain (see pages 338–339 in *Pâtisserie and Baking Foundations*).
2. In a large bowl, dissolve the yeast in the warm water [*max 90°F (32°C)*]. Add the starter (**levain**) and mix until combined. Add the salt and then add the flours. Work until a smooth dough forms. Add more water if too dry.
3. Turn the dough onto a floured work surface and knead until smooth and no longer sticky. Place it in a lightly oiled bowl, cover, and allow the dough to rise until it doubles in volume, approximately 2 hours. Punch the dough down and allow it to rest for 10 minutes.
4. Turn dough out onto a work surface and divide it in half. Flatten one of the pieces of dough into a circle. Fold the outer edge into the center and press it down with the heel of your hand, turn the dough and repeat the process several times. Turn the dough over, cup your hands around the ball and move it in a circular motion. Repeat the same procedure for the second piece of dough. Place on a clean baking sheet, cover and, allow to proof until doubled in size, about 1 hour.
5. Preheat the oven to 475°F (245°C).
6. Before baking, dust the tops of the bread with flour and score the top using a razor blade.
7. Place in the hot oven and allow to bake until golden in color, approximately 30 to 40 minutes. Transfer to a wire rack to cool.

Quantity		Ingredient
U.S.	Metric	
7 fl oz	200 ml	Water, warm [*max 90°F (32°C)*]
½ oz	10 g	Baker's yeast
8 oz	250 g	Levain
10 oz	300 g	Bread flour
2 oz	50 g	Whole wheat or rye flour, or a mixture of the two/ Or Campagne flour
1 ½ tsp	10 g	Salt
As needed	As needed	Bread flour for dusting (fleurer)

Learning Outcomes

Making a sponge
Kneading
Shaping dough
Making whole wheat bread

Equipment

Knives:
N/A

Tools:
Mixing bowls, wooden
spatula, pastry brush,
clean kitchen towel

Pans:
3 small 1 lb loaf pans, wire
rack

Serving/Yield

Approximately 3 ½
pounds/1.5 kilograms of
dough, making 3 1 lb loaves

Pain complet, or the English "whole wheat bread," refers to breads that are partly or wholly created using whole wheat flour. Whole wheat flours are unrefined, which means they use all parts of the wheat grain. These parts include the endosperm, bran, and germ of the wheat grain as opposed to just the endosperm used in refined white flour. This makes these breads much more nutritious, as many of the vitamins as well as the fiber and proteins are lost during the refining process. This flour does have some issues—the other grain elements add oils, making the dough denser and more difficult to make rise. Whole wheat breads are also prone to spoiling sooner than white breads. This is why whole flours are often cut with refined flour, making them lighter and easier to raise during baking.

PAIN COMPLET
Whole Wheat Bread

Method

1. Make the sponge section of dough: Place the warm water [*max 90°F (32°C)*] into a bowl and crumble the yeast into it. Stir until dissolved. Stir in the brown sugar, salt, and oil, then gradually stir in the first portion of flour to create a soft, sticky dough. Cover and set aside to develop, about 20 minutes.

2. Place all but 3 ¼ oz (100 g) of the second quantity of flour on the work surface and make a well (**fontaine**) in the center. Place the sponge in the center, and using your fingertips, gradually incorporate the flour. Begin kneading the dough, adding the reserved flour as required. Continue to knead the flour until smooth and no longer sticky and the dough bounces back when poked, about 10 to 15 minutes. Place in a lightly oiled bowl and cover. Set aside to proof until doubled in volume, approximately 2 hours.

3. Lightly brush 3 small loaf pans with oil.

4. Once the dough has doubled in volume, punch it down and turn it out onto a lightly floured surface. Divide the dough into three pieces. Flatten one of the dough sections into a rectangle and lay it horizontally. Make a furrow down the center with your fingertips, then fold the top edge down and press it into the furrow, seal using the heel of your hand. Fold the bottom up and repeat. Fold the two sides in to make a loaf the same length as the loaf pan. Place the shaped loaf into the pan, seam side down. Repeat the same process for the other 2 loaves. Lightly cover with a kitchen towel and set aside to proof until doubled in volume, about 60 to 90 minutes.

5. Preheat the oven to 350°F (170°C).

6. Place the 3 loaves in the center of rack of the hot oven, making sure the pans are not touching. Bake until fragrant, golden in color, and dry and firm to the touch, about 30 minutes.

7. Once out of the oven, remove from their pans and allow to cool on a wire rack.

Quantity		Ingredient
U.S.	**Metric**	
15 fl oz	450 ml	Water, lukewarm [*max 90°F (32°C)*]
1 oz	30 g	Yeast
2 oz	60 g	Brown sugar
¾ oz	20 g	Salt
2 ¾ fl oz	85 ml	Oil
11 ¼ oz	340 g	Whole wheat flour
16 oz	480 g	Whole wheat flour
As needed	As needed	Whole wheat flour for dusting (fleurer)
As needed	As needed	Oil for loaf pans

Learning Outcomes

Making a détrempe
Kneading
Beurrage
Turning (*tourage*)
Working with croissant
dough

Equipment

Knives:
Paring knife *(couteau d'office)*, slicing knife *(couteau à trancher)*, serrated knife *(couteau-scie)*

Tools:
Rolling pin, baker's brush, whisk, wooden spoon, rubber spatula, mixing bowls, pastry brush, corne

Pans:
Small saucepan, medium saucepan, baking sheet

Yield/Serving

8 to 10 portions of each

...FYI

Pâte à croissant is the base dough for the iconic croissant pastry. However, this delicious, flaky, and buttery viennoiserie can also be infused with a host of different flavorings. Whether a croissant is stuffed with chocolate, praline, almond paste, preserves, fruits, cheeses, meats, or raisins—they are all delicious. To truly enjoy a decadent pain au chocolat or any croissant in the traditional French fashion, head to your favorite Boulangerie and eat one for breakfast, fresh out of the oven with a large cup of rich café au lait. Now that's a good way to start a day!

PAINS AUX CROISSANTS, PAIN AUX RAISINS, ET PAIN AU CHOCOLAT
Croissants, Raisin Croissants and Chocolate Croissants

Method

Détrempe

1. In a small bowl, combine the warm water [*max 90°F (32°C)*] and the yeast.
2. Sift (*tamiser*) the flour onto a clean work surface and make a well (*fontaine*) in the center. Add the sugar and salt into the well, then stir in the melted butter, the dissolved yeast, and half of the milk. Stir the ingredients with your fingers, slowly incorporating the flour from the sides of the well. When the mixture becomes thick, add the rest of the milk and continue to mix.
3. Once all the liquid has been absorbed into the flour, gather the ingredients together and work them with a plastic scraper (*corne*) until combined into a dough. Lightly knead the dough and gather the dough into a ball. Score the top with a deep cross using a large knife and loosely wrap the finished *détrempe* in plastic before placing it in the refrigerator to rest for a minimum of 20 minutes (*preferably overnight*).

Note

Détrempe *refers to the dough before the layer of butter (*beurrage*) is added.*

4. Although the procedure for incorporating the butter is the same as feuilletage, croissant dough is made from yeast-leavened dough that is much more elastic than that of feuilletage.

Beurrage and Tourage

1. Place the cold butter between two sheets of parchment paper and pound it with a rolling pin until it is similar to the *détrempe* in consistency.
2. Using the *corne*, shape the butter into a flat square about ¾-in. (2-cm) thick and about the same size as the ball of *détrempe*. If the kitchen is hot, reserve the butter in the refrigerator, or set it aside on a cool surface.
3. Lightly dust a clean work surface with flour (*fleurer*). Unwrap the *détrempe* and place it on the floured surface.
4. Using the scored marks as a guide, roll out (*abaisser*) the corners of the *détrempe* into a cross shape. The center of the cross should be slightly thicker than the rolled-out arms.
5. Place the square of butter in the center of the cross and fold the 2 side arms over it so that they overlap slightly in the center (*in the process, be careful not to trap any air bubbles*). Give the dough a quarter turn and fold the 2 remaining arms over the butter so that no butter is visible. Press the seams well to seal.
6. Lightly tap the dough with the length of the rolling pin to even out the distribution of the butter inside. Give the dough a quarter turn and repeat the process. This is called the *enveloppe*.

Quantity		Ingredient
U.S.	**Metric**	
1 lb	500 g	Flour
6 fl oz	180 ml	Water
½ oz	15 g	Fresh yeast
2 oz	60 g	Sugar
¼ oz	5 g	Salt
5 fl oz	150 ml	Milk
1 ¾ fl oz	50 ml	Butter, melted, cooled
8 oz	250 g	Butter
1 ½ pt	750 ml	Milk
6 pcs	6 pcs	Egg yolks
5 oz	150 g	Sugar, granulated
2 ½ oz	75 g	Flour (or cornstarch)
¼ fl oz	5 ml	Vanilla extract
7 oz	200 g	Raisins
15 pcs	15 pcs	Chocolate Sticks
1 pc	1 pc	Egg for egg wash
As needed	As needed	Flour for dusting (fleurer)

Method

Turning (Tourage), 3 Turns (3 tours simples)

1. *First turn:* Roll out (*abaisser*) the dough in long even strokes forming a rectangle that is twice the original length of the **enveloppe** or ½-in. (1-cm) thick. Brush off any excess flour. Fold the bottom third of the dough up; then fold the top third down over the first fold. Make sure the edges are even. Give the dough a quarter turn to the right so the seam is on the left and make one finger impression in the top left corner of the dough.

Note

These marks are a reminder of the number of turns that the dough has received; they also indicate the position for subsequent turns.

2. Wrap the dough in plastic and transfer it to the refrigerator to rest for 15 to 20 minutes.
3. *Second turn:* Lightly dust the work surface with flour (**fleurer**). Remove the dough from the refrigerator and unwrap it onto the floured surface (*with the indent in the top left corner*). Repeat the folding process (*bottom third up, top third down over first fold*) and give the dough a quarter turn to the right. Make two finger impressions in the top left corner of the dough before wrapping it in plastic and returning it to the refrigerator to rest for 15 to 20 minutes.
4. *Third turn:* Lightly dust the work surface with flour (**fleurer**). Remove the dough from the refrigerator and unwrap it onto the floured surface (*with the 2 indents in the top left corner*). Proceed to give the dough a third turn (*rolling and folding in the same manner as the first and second turns*). Mark the dough with 3 imprints in the top left corner before wrapping it in plastic and returning it to the refrigerator to rest for 15 to 20 minutes. When the dough has finished resting, cut it into 3 equal parts, wrap each separately, and refrigerate until needed.

Croissants

1. Lightly dust the work surface with flour (**fleurer**). Remove one section of dough from the refrigerator and unwrap it onto the floured surface.
2. With a rolling pin, roll the dough out (*abaisser*) to a rectangle about 8-in. (20-cm) wide by 8-in. (20-cm) long (*the dough should be ³⁄₁₆ in./5 mm thick*). Cut the dough into triangles with a 4-in. (10-cm) base using a large knife. Gently stretch the triangles lengthwise, and place on the work surface. Roll the triangles up from the large end to the point. If the croissant is rolled correctly, it should have 5 segments from one end to the other. Transfer the finished croissants to a parchment paper-lined baking sheet, making sure that the tip of the triangle is underneath the rolled croissant. Leave the croissants to proof in a warm area or a proofer until they double in size.

Pains aux Raisins

1. Prepare a pastry cream (crème pâtissière): see 257–260 in *Pâtissière and Baking Foundations*.
2. *Montage:* Lightly dust the work surface with flour (**fleurer**). Remove a section of dough from the refrigerator and unwrap it onto the floured surface. Using a rolling pin, roll out the dough (**abaisser**) to a rectangle about 8-in. (20-cm) wide by 18-in. [0.5-m (46-cm)] long (*the dough should be ³⁄₁₆ in./5 mm thick*). Trim the edges of the dough to obtain straight sides. Transfer it to a sheet of parchment paper and brush a 1 ½-in. (3-cm) wide line of egg wash onto the edge closest to you. Beat the pastry cream (crème pâtissière) with a whisk until it becomes smooth. Avoiding the egg-washed section, spread the crème pâtissière thinly onto the rectangle of croissant dough using a small offset spatula. Sprinkle the raisins onto the pastry cream (crème pâtissière) and roll the rectangle toward yourself using the parchment paper as a tool to ensure even shaping. Seal it closed using the egg washed edge. Place the roll in the freezer for 30 minutes to harden the dough and ensure a neat cut. Cut the roll into 10 equal slices. Leave the *pains aux raisin* to proof in a warm area or a proofer until they double in size.

Chocolat Croissants
(Pains au Chocolat)

1. Lightly dust the work surface with flour (**fleurer**). Remove part of the dough from the refrigerator and unwrap it onto the floured surface.
2. Using a rolling pin, roll out the dough (**abaisser**) to a rectangle about 6-in. (15-cm) wide by 18-in. (0.5-mm) long (*the dough should be ³⁄₁₆ in./5 mm thick*). Square off the edges using a knife. Cut the dough into vertical strips that are 0.5 in. (1 cm) wider than the length of the chocolate sticks. Place a chocolate stick near the top of each strip. Loosely roll the strip over the chocolate stick. Place another chocolate stick under the seam and roll over again. Making sure that the seam is hidden underneath, place the *pains au chocolat* on a baking sheet lined with parchment paper.
3. Leave the *pains au chocolat* to proof in a warm area or a proofer until they double in size.

Cooking (for any of the above)

Preheat the oven to 425°F (220°C).

1. When the pastries have doubled in size, brush them with egg wash and transfer them to the oven to bake until golden, 20 to 30 minutes depending on their size.
2. Transfer to a wire rack to cool.

Learning Outcomes

Making a spiced bread
(*pain d'épices*)

Equipment

Knives:
Paring knife (*couteau
d'office*)

Tools:
Wooden spatula, pastry
brush, corne

Pans:
Saucepan, two 1 lb loaf
pans

Yield/Serving

2 × one pound loaves

While spiced breads have existed since antiquity, the pain d'épices of today generally refers to the honey- and spice-infused, whole wheat breads of France. It is believed that the Chinese developed the first recipe for a spiced honey bread called *mi-king* in the 10th century. These cake-like breads were introduced to Europe through the Mongol armies of the East, who shared the recipe with Turks and Arabs, who in turn shared it with crusading European knights.

By the Middle Ages, France had emerged as the producer of some of the finest pain d'épices in the world. These cakes were taken very seriously, and even had separate guilds from regular bakers who were dedicated exclusively to the production of pain d'épices. The town of Reims in the Champagne-Ardenne region was the first to establish such a guild, known as the "Corporation of Spiced-bread Makers" in 1571. In order to join this guild, one needed to be a master spiced bread maker, capable of producing a masterpiece of spiced bread dough weighing at least 200 pounds, from which he had to bake three 20 pound loaves of perfect bread. Similar guilds soon formed in Paris and Dijon; the latter would go on to become the best known spiced bread-making city in France, an honor it continues to hold today.

Quantity		Ingredient
U.S.	Metric	
10 fl oz	300 ml	Honey
2 ½ oz	75 g	Sugar, granulated
4 fl oz	120 ml	Milk
6 oz	180 g	Eggs
3 ½ oz	100 g	Butter, softened (*en pommade*)
12 oz	360 g	Flour
5 oz	150 g	Rye flour
½ oz	15 g	Baking powder
¼ oz	5 g	Salt
½ oz	10 g	Cinnamon powder
Dash	2.5 g	Clove powder
¼ oz	5 g	Ginger powder
1 ¼ oz	35 g	Nutmeg powder
½ oz	10 g	Vanilla powder
1 pc	1 pc	Orange zest (optional)

PAIN D'ÉPICES
Spice Bread

Method

Preheat the oven to 350°F (175°C).

1. Grease 2 medium loaf pans (**chemiser**) and set aside.
2. Place the honey, sugar, and milk in a saucepan over medium heat. While stirring, heat until the sugar has dissolved and mixture is well combined. Remove from the heat and set aside at room temperature.
3. Cut the softened butter (**en pommade**) into pieces.
4. Sift (**tamiser**) together the spices, salt, and baking powder with the 2 flours into a large bowl. Make a large well (**fontaine**) in the center. Add the sweetened milk, the butter, and the eggs in the center and mix well. Gradually begin to incorporate the flour until a thick batter forms.
5. Divide the batter between the loaf pans and smooth it flat. Place in the preheated oven and bake until a knife inserted in the center comes out clean, about 25 to 30 minutes.
6. Remove from the oven and unmold onto a wire rack to cool.

Learning Outcomes

Making a basic bread
dough
Sponge method
Kneading
Shaping a loaf

Equipment

Knife:
N/A

Tools:
Mixing bowls, clean kitchen
towel, wire rack

Pans:
1 lb loaf pan

Serving/Yield

1 pound/500 gram loaf

FYI...

A highly versatile dough, pain de mie is traditionally baked in loaves, then sliced and used in sandwiches or for toast. It can be baked in a covered pan, forming a perfectly flat top, making each slice a perfect square. These are referred to as Pullman loaves and are preferred by caterers for the making of canapés. The dough can also be shaped into rolls or rounds.

PAIN DE MIE
White Loaf Bread

Quantity		Ingredient
U.S.	**Metric**	
¾ oz	20 g	Yeast
8 fl oz	250 ml	Milk, lukewarm [*max 90°F (32°C)*]
¾ oz	20 g	Sugar, granulated
1 lb	500 g	Flour
½ oz	15 g	Salt
1 ¾ oz	50 g	Butter, softened (**en pommade**)
As needed	As needed	Oil for the loaf pan
As needed	As needed	Flour for dusting (fleurer)

Method

1. Dissolve the yeast and sugar in the warmed milk [*max 90°F (32°C)*] in a large bowl. Add some flour to make a paste and set aside to proof for 10 to 15 minutes. Stir in the salt, sugar, and softened butter (**en pommade**), then gradually add the remaining flour until a dough forms.
2. Turn the dough onto a floured (**fleurer**) work surface and begin kneading it, adding flour as needed to prevent sticking. If the dough becomes too dry, sprinkle it with a little water. Continue kneading the dough until it is smooth and no longer sticks. Place it in a lightly oiled bowl, cover, and set aside to proof until doubled in volume, about 2 hours.
3. Lightly oil the loaf pan.
4. Punch the dough down and turn it out onto a clean work surface. Flatten it into a long oval, approximately the length of the loaf pan. Using your fingertips, make a furrow down the center. Fold the top edge down and press it firmly into the furrow using the heel of your hand, then do the same with the bottom edge. Fold the two ends in and press well. Roll the dough over and roll back and forth to tighten the seams. Place it in the oiled pan and allow it to proof until doubled in size, approximately 60 to 90 minutes.
5. Preheat the oven to 435°F (225°C).
6. Place the pan in the oven and bake until the bread is nicely browned, about 35 to 40 minutes. Gently unmold and cool on a wire rack.

Learning Outcomes

Making a rye bread
Using a fermented dough
(*pâte fermentée*)
Kneading and shaping a
long loaf

Equipment

Knives:
Razor blade

Tools:
Mixing bowls,
clean kitchen towel

Pans:
Baking sheet, wire rack

Serving/Yield

About 2 pounds /
1 kilogram of dough for
1 large loaf or 2 small loaves

Rye bread is traditionally served with oysters, spread with salted butter. Rye flour absorbs more water than regular flour and the dough is a bit heavier to work with.

209

PAIN DE SEIGLE
Rye Bread

Quantity		Ingredient
U.S.	**Metric**	
12 ½ oz	375 g	Rye flour
10–12 fl oz	300–350 ml	Water, warmed (max 90°F/32°C)
½ oz	10 g	Yeast
½ oz	15 g	Salt
12 ½ oz	375 g	Fermented dough (**Pâte fermentée**)
As needed	As needed	Oil
As needed	As needed	Flour for dusting (fleurer)

Method

1. Make the fermented dough (**pâte fermentée**) (see *Pâtisserie and Baking Foundations* pages 338–339).
2. Place the flour on a clean work surface and make a well (**fontaine**) in the center. Add the yeast and water and stir to dissolve. Add the salt, then add the fermented dough (**pâte fermentée**). Gradually incorporate the flour. Knead the dough until smooth and no longer sticky, adding additional white flour as needed.
3. Place in a lightly oiled bowl and cover with a cloth. Set aside to proof until doubled in volume, about 2 hours.
4. Punch the dough down and turn it out onto a floured work surface. Flatten it into a long oval. Fold the dough's top third down and then press the seam with the heels of your palm.
5. Fold down again to meet the bottom edge and press with the heels of your palms. Roll the dough so the seam is at the bottom and then roll it back and forth to tighten. Place the dough on the baking sheet and cover. Set aside to rise for about one hour.
6. Preheat the oven to 435°F (220°C).
7. Using a razor blade or exacto knife, make diagonal slashes along the top of the loaf. Place in the oven to bake until golden in color, approximately 25 to 30 minutes.
8. Cool on a wire rack.

Learning Outcomes

Making a basic yeast dough

Equipment

Knives:
N/A

Tools:
Mixing bowl, clean kitchen towel

Pans:
Baking pans, baking sheet (as needed)

Yield/Serving

1 lb 13.5 oz/900 grams of dough, about 12–14 pieces

The nib sugar (also known as pearl sugar) that serves as a delicious finishing element of the pain au sucre is a tasty ingredient common to Nordic pastry making. Nib sugar is made from compressed sugar that is broken down into dense, rounded chunks. This makes this type of sugar excellent for sprinkling over the top of preparations, as its density gives it a much higher melting point than ordinary sugar. This type of sugar originated in Scandinavia, where it is known as *perlesukker* or *pärlsocker*.

PAIN AU SUCRE

Quantity		Ingredient
U.S.	**Metric**	
1 oz	30 g	Yeast
8 fl oz	250 ml	Milk, lukewarm [*max 90°F (32°C)*]
1 ¾ oz	50 g	Sugar, granulated
1 lb	500 g	Flour
½ oz	10 g	Salt
3 ¼ oz	100 g	Butter, softened (**en pommade**)
As needed	As needed	Nib sugar
1–2	1–2	Eggs (for egg wash)
As needed	As needed	Flour for dusting (fleurer)

Method

1. Dissolve the yeast in the lukewarm milk [*max 90°F (32°C)*] in a large bowl. Add the sugar and some flour to make a paste and set aside to proof for 10 to 15 minutes. Stir in the salt, then add the softened butter (**en pommade**) in pieces. Mix well, then gradually add enough flour until a soft dough forms. Turn the dough onto a floured work surface (**fleurer**) and begin to knead the dough, adding flour as needed to prevent sticking. If too dry, sprinkle a little water.
2. Continue kneading the dough until smooth and it no longer sticks. Place in a lightly oiled bowl, cover, and set aside to proof until doubled in volume, about 1 to 1 ½ hours.
3. Punch the dough down, and turn it out onto a clean work surface. Divide the dough into 2 oz (60 g) balls. Roll lightly to elongate. Arrange on a lightly greased baking sheet and set aside to proof, about 1 hour.
4. Preheat the oven to 410°F (210°C).
5. Brush the tops with some beaten egg, then, if desired, take a pair of pointed scissors and snip the dough along the length of the top. Sprinkle with nib sugar. Bake about 15 to 20 minutes or until golden.
6. This dough can be formed into different shapes such as rounds, small braids, or in a loaf pan.

Les Glaces et Les Sorbets

(Ice Creams and Sorbets)

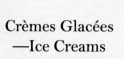
Crèmes Glacées
—Ice Creams

Granité au Vin Rouge
—Red Wine Granité

Les Sorbets
—Sorbets

Vacherin
—Frozen cake

Learning Outcomes

Making a crème Anglaise
Tempering egg yolks
Making an ice cream

Equipment

Knives:
Serrated knife
(*couteau-scie*), paring knife
(*couteau d'office*)

Tools:
Wooden spatula, mixing
bowls, whisk, chinois, ice
cream churner, ice bath

Pans:
Medium saucepans

Yield

Vanilla ice cream yield
5 quart (0.5 liter)
Coffee ice cream yield
1 quart (1 liter)
Chocolate ice cream yield
1 quart (1 liter)

FYI....

The origins of ice desserts can be traced back to many of the most prominent historical figures of the ancient world. While many people had presumably eaten frozen treats prior to him, Alexander the Great is the first documented person to eat a mixture of snow, fruit, wine, and honey in 336 BCE. In his 77 AD work the *Naturalis Historia*, the great historian, Pliny the Elder, makes mention of the eccentric Roman emperor Nero ordering his troops to collect large quantities of snow for the making sweet frozen preparations. Upon returning from his 1292 voyages in China, Venetian explorer Marco Polo was a crucial figure in the development of European ice cream making methods. During his travels, Polo was introduced to the Chinese method of using salt and saltpeper mixed with snow to lower its freezing point. The snow/salt mixture is then packed around a contained substance allowing it to be super cooled. Since that time, European frozen preparations evolved dramatically. From the frozen beverages brought to France with the court of Catherine De'Medici, to a frozen molded dessert created by Francesco Procopio, people throughout history have always enjoyed the refreshing flavor of a cold treat on a hot day.

CRÈMES GLACÉES
Ice Creams

Method

Vanilla Ice Cream

1. *Prepare a crème Anglaise.*
2. Place the milk and heavy cream in a medium saucepan and bring to a low boil over medium-high heat. Using a small knife, split the vanilla bean lengthwise. Scrape the seeds from both sides and add to the milk along with the bean. Whisk well.
3. Place the egg yolks in a mixing bowl, add the sugar, and immediately begin to whisk it into the yolks. Continue whisking until the sugar is completely dissolved and the mixture is pale in color (**blanchir**).
4. Once the milk is hot, whisk about one-third of the hot milk into the yolks to temper them. Whisk until the mixture is well combined and evenly heated.
5. Stir the tempered egg yolks into the pan of remaining hot milk and stir with a wooden spatula. Place the pan over low heat and stir in a figure 8 motion. As you stir, the foam on the surface will disappear; at the same time, the liquid will begin to thicken and become oil-like in resistance. Continue cooking until the mixture is thick enough to coat the back of a wooden spatula and when your finger leaves a clean trail (**à la nappe**). DO NOT ALLOW IT TO COME TO A BOIL.

Tip

Crème Anglaise should be cooked to between 167°F and 185°F (75°C and 85°C).

6. Remove the pan from the heat and strain the crème Anglaise through a fine mesh sieve (**chinois**) into a clean bowl set in a bowl of ice. Stir it back and forth (**vanner**) with the spatula until cooled.
7. Cover the bowl in plastic wrap and reserve in the refrigerator for 24 hours to develop the flavors.
8. Pour the cold custard into a running ice cream churner and let it run until the ice cream is set.
9. Once churned, reserve the ice cream in an airtight container in the freezer.

Coffee Ice Cream

1. *Prepare a crème Anglaise* as described above, with the addition of the instant coffee to the milk and replacing vanilla bean with extract.
2. Once the crème Anglaise is cooked, remove the pan from the heat and strain the crème Anglaise through a fine mesh sieve (**chinois**) into a clean bowl set in a bowl of ice. Stir it back and forth (**vanner**) with the spatula until cooled.

Quantity		Ingredient
U.S.	**Metric**	*Vanilla Ice Cream*
8 fl oz	250 ml	Milk
4 fl oz	125 ml	Cream
3 pcs	3 pcs	Egg yolks
3 ½ oz	100 g	Sugar, granulated
1 pc	1 pc	Vanilla bean
		Coffee Ice Cream
8 fl oz	250 ml	Milk
8 fl oz	250 ml	Cream
¼ fl oz	5 ml	Vanilla extract
4 pcs	4 pcs	Egg yolks
4 oz	125 g	Sugar, granulated
½ fl oz	15 ml	Instant coffee
		Chocolate Ice Cream
1 pt	500 ml	Milk
5 oz	150 g	Dark chocolate
3 ½ oz	100 g	Sugar, granulated
6 pcs	6 pcs	Egg yolks

Method

3. Cover the bowl in plastic wrap and reserve in the refrigerator for 24 hours to develop the flavors.
4. Pour the cold custard into a running ice cream churner and let it run until the ice cream is set.
5. Once churned, reserve the ice cream in an airtight container in the freezer.

Chocolate Ice Cream

1. Finely chop the chocolate (**hacher**) and place it in a large mixing bowl.
2. *Prepare a crème Anglaise:*
3. Once the crème Anglaise is cooked, remove the pan from the heat and pour it into the mixing bowl containing the chocolate. Let it sit for 1 to 2 minutes to melt the chocolate, then stir gently with a wooden spatula until the chocolate has melted. Strain the mixture through a fine mesh sieve into a mixing bowl set on an ice bath. Stir the custard back and forth with a wooden spatula (**vanner**) until it is cold. Cover the bowl in plastic wrap and place the bowl in the refrigerator for 24 hours to develop the flavors. Pour the cold custard into a running ice cream churner and let it run until the ice cream is set.
4. Once churned, reserve the ice cream in an airtight container in the freezer.

Learning Outcomes

Making a granité

Equipment

Knives:
Paring knife *(couteau d'office)*

Tools:
Juicer, zester, fork

Pans:
Large saucepan,
shallow pan

Serving/Yield

1 ¼ pound/1.2 kilogram
portion

HISTORY

The granité originated in Sicily where it is known as a "granite." It dates back to ancient times and is the precursor to the sorbet. The name is based on the verb "granire," which means to make grainy, or granular. The sugar that is added, as well as the sugar in the juice, slows the crystallization of the water, allowing it to be broken up during the freezing process and maintain this texture. Today, granité can be made from fruit juice, almond milk, coffee, and wine. This preparation is often used as a palate cleanser between courses.

GRANITÉ AU VIN ROUGE
Red Wine Granité

Method

1. Pour the red wine into a large saucepan over medium heat.
2. Add the sugar, orange zest, and orange juice. Once the wine mixture comes to a boil, remove it from the heat and allow to cool.
3. Once cooled, if desired, stir in the crème de cassis.
4. Pour the liquid into a shallow pan and place in the freezer.
5. Once the wine begins to freeze (it should take about 2 hours), break it up, scraping and stirring it with a fork. Continue to do so every 30 to 45 minutes until there is no more liquid.
6. Transfer the granité into a covered storage container.

Quantity		Ingredient
U.S.	*Metric*	
24 fl oz	750 ml	Red wine
7 oz	200 g	Sugar
1 pc	1 pc	Orange zest and juice
7 fl oz	200 ml	Crème de cassis (optional)

Learning Outcomes

Making a sorbet
Making a simple syrup

Equipment

Tools:
Wooden spatula, whisk, ice
bath, ice cream churner,
mixing bowls

Pans:
Small and medium
saucepans

Yield

Strawberry sorbet
(Sorbet à la fraise)
3/4 pt (400 g)
Lemon Sorbet (sorbet au
citron) 1 pt (500 g)

Quantity		Ingredient
U.S.	*Metric*	*Sorbet à la Fraise*
2 ½ fl oz	75 ml	Water
2 ½ oz	75 g	Sugar, granulated
½ pc	½ pc	Lemon juice
8 fl oz	250 ml	Strawberry purée
		Sorbet au Citron
7 ½ fl oz	225 ml	Water
7 ½ oz	225 g	Sugar, granulated
3 ½ fl oz	100 ml	Lemon juice
10 fl oz	300 ml	Water
1 pc	1 pc	Egg white

LES SORBETS
Sorbets

Method

Strawberry Sorbet (Sorbet à la Fraise)

1. Bring the water and sugar to a boil in a small saucepan over medium-high heat and remove the pan from the stove once the sugar has completely dissolved. Pour the contents of the pan into a large mixing bowl set on an ice bath. Mix it back and forth using a wooden spatula (**vanner**), and once it is cold, add the lemon juice and strawberry purée. Stir the liquids together and continue stirring until the mixture is cold.
2. Pour the mixture into a running ice cream churner and let it run until the sorbet is set.
3. Once churned, reserve the sorbet in an airtight container in the freezer.

Lemon Sorbet (Sorbet au Citron)

1. Bring the water and sugar to a boil in a small saucepan over medium-high heat and remove the pan from the stove once the sugar has completely dissolved. Pour the contents of the pan into a large mixing bowl set on an ice bath. Mix it back and forth using a wooden spatula (**vanner**), and once it is cold, add the lemon juice and the extra water. Stir the liquids together and continue stirring until the mixture is cold.
2. Pour the mixture into a running ice cream churner and let it run until the sorbet is set. When the sorbet resembles a thick slush, remove 2 tablespoons and mix it with the egg white in a small mixing bowl. Mix the two together with a whisk until combined and pour the mixture back into the churner. Once churned, reserve the sorbet in an airtight container in the freezer.

Note

In this sorbet recipe, the egg whites serve as a natural stabilizer while at the same time adding texture to the preparation.

*Generally, the basic syrup for sorbet has a density of 28 degrees (**Baumé**) and is characterized by equal amounts of water and sugar. The different densities of syrup can be measured using a hydrometer (**pèse sirop**).*

Learning Outcomes

Making a frozen cake
Making a French meringue
Making a sorbet
Making an ice cream
Making a Chantilly cream

VACHERIN

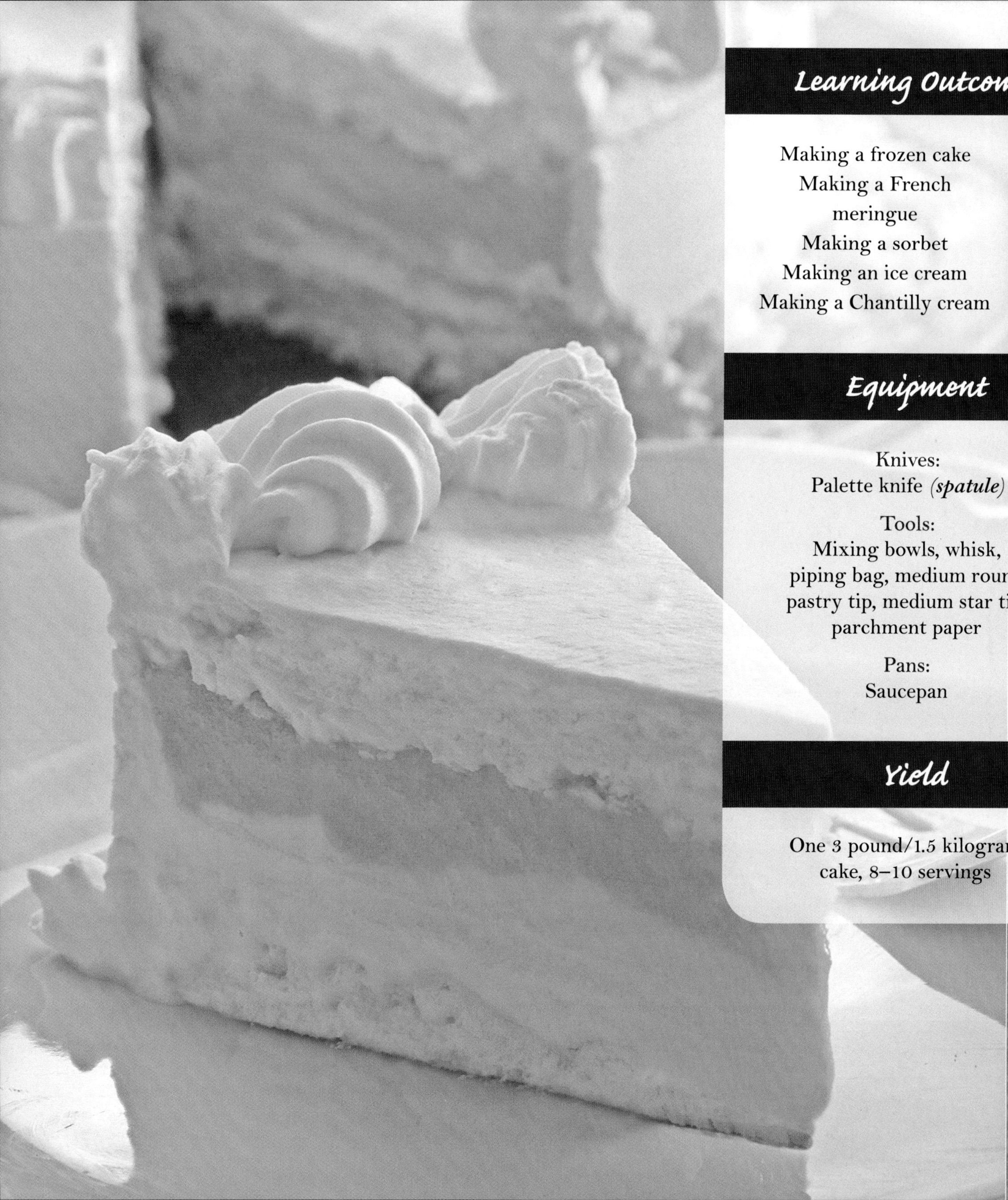

Equipment

Knives:
Palette knife *(spatule)*

Tools:
Mixing bowls, whisk, piping bag, medium round pastry tip, medium star tip, parchment paper

Pans:
Saucepan

Yield

One 3 pound/1.5 kilogram cake, 8–10 servings

FYI...

This delicious, traditional French dessert is composed of several meringue rings layered between rich ice cream, refreshing sorbet, and masked in a layer of crème Chantilly. This preparation is said to have been named for its circular shape and light coloring, which bear an uncanny resemblance to Vacherin Mont D'Or cheese, arguably one of the finest Swiss cheeses ever produced. This preparation is highly versatile and can be served frozen with ice cream and sorbet layers, or nonfrozen with layers of crème Chantilly and any kind of fruit desired. The only constant is the meringue layers, leaving a great deal of leeway for the imaginative chef to get creative.

Quantity		Ingredient
U.S.	**Metric**	*Meringue*
4 pcs	4 pcs	Egg whites
7 ½ oz	225 g	Sugar, granulated
		Ice Cream
1 lb	500 g	Vanilla ice cream
		Sorbet
1 lb	500 g	Lemon Sorbet
		Chantilly Cream
7 fl oz	200 ml	Whipping cream
1 ½ oz	40 g	Sugar, granulated
As needed	As needed	Powdered sugar

VACHERIN
Frozen Cake

Method

Preheat the oven to 300°F (150°C).

Line a baking sheet with parchment paper, then draw two 9-in. (23-cm) circles.

Make a Meringue

1. Beat the egg whites (**monter les blancs**) to soft peaks, gradually whisking in the sugar until smooth and glossy. Transfer the meringue to a piping bag fitted with a medium round tip. Starting from the center of each circle, pipe the meringue in a close spiral. Tap the pan to fill any gaps. Place in the oven for 1 hour, then turn off the oven and leave until cooled.

Make a Vanilla Ice Cream (see page 217)

2. Place the milk and heavy cream in a medium saucepan and bring to a low boil over medium-high heat. Using a small knife, split the vanilla bean lengthwise. Scrape the seeds from both sides and add to the milk along with the pod. Whisk well.

3. Place the egg yolks in a mixing bowl, add the sugar, and immediately begin to whisk it into the yolks. Continue whisking until the sugar is completely dissolved and the mixture is pale in color (**blanchir**).

4. Once the milk is hot, whisk about one-third of the hot milk into the yolks to temper them. Whisk until the mixture is well combined and evenly heated.

5. Stir the tempered egg yolks into the pan of remaining hot milk and stir with a wooden spatula. Place the pan over low heat and stir in a figure 8 motion. As you stir, the foam on the surface will disappear; at the same time, the liquid will begin to thicken and become oil-like in resistance. Continue cooking until the mixture is thick enough to coat the back of a wooden spatula and when your finger leaves a clean trail (**à la nappe**). DO NOT ALLOW IT TO COME TO A BOIL.

Tip

Crème Anglaise should be cooked to between 167°F and 185°F (75°C and 85°C).

6. Remove the pan from the heat and strain the crème Anglaise through a fine mesh sieve (**chinois**) into a clean bowl set in a bowl of ice. Stir it back and forth (**vanner**) with the spatula until cooled.

7. Cover the bowl in plastic wrap and reserve in the refrigerator for 24 hours to develop the flavors.

8. Pour the cold custard into a running ice cream churner and let it run until the ice cream is set.

9. Once churned, reserve the ice cream in an airtight container in the freezer.

Make a Sorbet (Sorbet au Citron) (see page 222)

1. Bring the water and sugar to a boil in a small saucepan over medium-high heat and remove the pan from the stove once the sugar has completely dissolved. Pour the contents of the pan into a large mixing bowl set on an ice bath. Mix it back and forth using a wooden spatula (**vanner**), and once it is cold, add the lemon juice and the extra water. Stir the liquids together and continue stirring until the mixture is cold.
2. Pour the mixture into a running ice cream churner and let it run until the sorbet is set.
3. Once churned, reserve the sorbet in an airtight container in the freezer.

Make a Chantilly Cream

Whisk the cream and powdered sugar to medium peaks.

Assembly

1. Soften the vanilla ice-cream until spreadable. Place one of the meringue circles on a freezer proof platter. Spread evenly with the vanilla ice cream, then place in the freezer to set, about 15 to 20 minutes. Soften the sorbet until spreadable and spread it on top of the vanilla ice cream. Cover with the second disk of meringue and press down gently. Place back in the freezer to set.
2. Whisk the cream and sugar to soft peaks to make the Chantilly cream.
3. Remove the vacherin from the freezer and mask the sides and top with the Chantilly cream.
4. Transfer the remaining cream to a piping bag fitted with a medium star tip and pipe rosettes along the base and on top of the vacherin.
5. Place back in the freezer until ready to serve.

Recettes Regionale
(Regional Recipes)

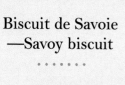
Biscuit de Savoie
—Savoy biscuit

Bugnes
—Fried dough

Clafoutis Limousin
—Cherry flan

Bourdelots
—Apple pastries

Far Breton
—Breton wheat

Gâteau Forêt Noire
—Black forest cake

Fougasse

Gâteau Basque
—Cream-filled
butter cake

Kouglhof

Kouign Amann

Nougat de Montelimar
—Montelimar Nougat

Tarte au sucre
—Sugar tart

Tarte tatin
—Reversed apple tart

Learning Outcomes

Making a Savoy biscuit
Separated egg method
Making a meringue

Equipment

Knives:
N/A

Tools:
Mixing bowls, whisk,
rubber spatula, sieve

Pans:
Large brioche mold,
wire rack

Serving/Yield

Serves 4–6

HISTORY

The biscuit de Savoie is a tasty, light, and fluffy sponge cake. The cake originated in the French region of Savoy (the name translates literally to "Savoy biscuit") in the 18th century. It is important to bear in mind that the recipe for Savory biscuit (biscuit de Savoie) contains no leavening agents. This means that the batter must be thoroughly beaten in order to infuse the cake with air, creating the light and airy texture that defines this cake.

BISCUIT DE SAVOIE
Savoy Biscuit

Method

1. Preheat the oven to 350°F (180°C).
2. Butter and flour (**chemiser**) a large brioche mold.
3. Sift (**tamiser**) the flour and cornstarch together into a bowl and set aside.
4. Make a meringue in a separate bowl. Beat the egg whites (**monter les blancs**) to soft peaks. Add the sugar and beat until stiff and glossy.
5. Using your spatula, fold some of the meringue into the reserved egg yolks until incorporated. Fold this mixture into remaining meringue. Fold the dry ingredients into the meringue mixture.
6. Fill the prepared brioche mold. Bake until the biscuit springs back when touched and the tip of a knife inserted in the center comes out clean.
7. Remove the biscuit from the oven and allow it to cool slightly before gently unmolding onto a wire rack. Serve dusted with powdered sugar.

Quantity		Ingredient
U.S.	Metric	Chemiser
As needed	As needed	Butter
As needed	As needed	Flour
		Savoy Biscuit
2 oz	60 g	Flour
2 oz	60 g	Cornstarch
5 ¾ oz	170 g	Sugar, granulated
4 pcs	4 pcs	Eggs, separated
As needed	As needed	Powdered sugar, for dusting

Learning Outcomes

Making a rich yeast dough
Kneading
Deep-frying
Shaping dough

Equipment

Knives:
Paring knife *(couteau d'office)*

Tools:
Mixing bowls, wooden spatula, rolling pin, deep fryer

Pans:
N/A

Serving/Yield

12–16 pieces, approximately 60 g/2 oz each

The bugne is a traditional deep-fried treat from the French region of Lyon. The preparation's name stems from the old French word for lump, *buigne*, which is also where the bugne's close relative the *beignet* derives its name. The bugne probably originated in the Middle Ages. The first mention of the word we see in the historic record is in 1538, in a list of "spécialités Lyonnaises" being assembled for a banquet honoring the great French Renaissance writer Rabelais. This tasty snack has always been closely associated with the festivals of Carnival and Mardi Gras, the wild celebrations preceding the period of Lent for the Catholic people. It is thought that people traditionally enjoyed these high fat content pastries as a way to indulge before the 40-day period of fasting began, a tradition that continues to this day.

BUGNES
Fried Dough

Method

1. Pour the warm water or milk into a large clean bowl and dissolve the yeast into it. Add 3 ¼ oz (100 g) of the flour, the sugar, and salt to the milk mixture and stir until a paste forms.
2. Add the eggs, rum, orange/lemon zest, butter, and all of the remaining flour and mix until a smooth dough forms.
3. Lightly dust your clean work surface with flour (*fleurer*). Turn the dough out onto the floured area and knead it until it becomes smooth and no longer sticky. Place the dough in a clean bowl and cover it with a clean kitchen towel. Set aside in a warm place to proof until doubled in volume, around 2 hours.
4. Prepare a deep fryer and heat the oil to 325°F (160°C).
5. Punch the dough down and then, using your rolling pin, roll it out (*abaisser*) into a rectangle about ⅛-in. (½-cm) thick. Cut into diamond shapes and separate. Make a 1-in. (2-cm) incision in the center of each section of dough. Take one of the long ends of the diamond and push it through the incision and pull it through to form a knot.
6. Fry the bugnes in hot oil until golden, approximately 2 to 3 minutes. Transfer to a platter lined with paper towels then dust with powdered sugar.

Quantity		Ingredient
U.S.	**Metric**	
4 fl oz	120 ml	Water or milk, lukewarm [*max 90°F (32°C)*]
¾ oz	20 g	Baker's yeast
1 lb	500 g	Flour
1 ¼ oz	40 g	Sugar, granulated
¼ oz	8 g	Salt
3 pcs	3 pcs	Eggs
4 ¼ oz	125 g	Butter
¼ fl oz	10 ml	Rum
pinch	pinch	Orange or lemon zest
As needed	As needed	Flour for dusting
As needed	As needed	Oil for frying (canola or vegetable)
As needed	As needed	Powdered sugar for dusting

CLAFOUTIS LIMOUSIN

Learning Outcomes

Making a flan
Baking fruit

Equipment

Knives:
Paring knife
(couteau d'office)

Tools:
Mixing bowls, wooden spatula, whisk, sieve

Pans:
Ovenproof baking dish

Servings/Yield

8 servings

HISTORY

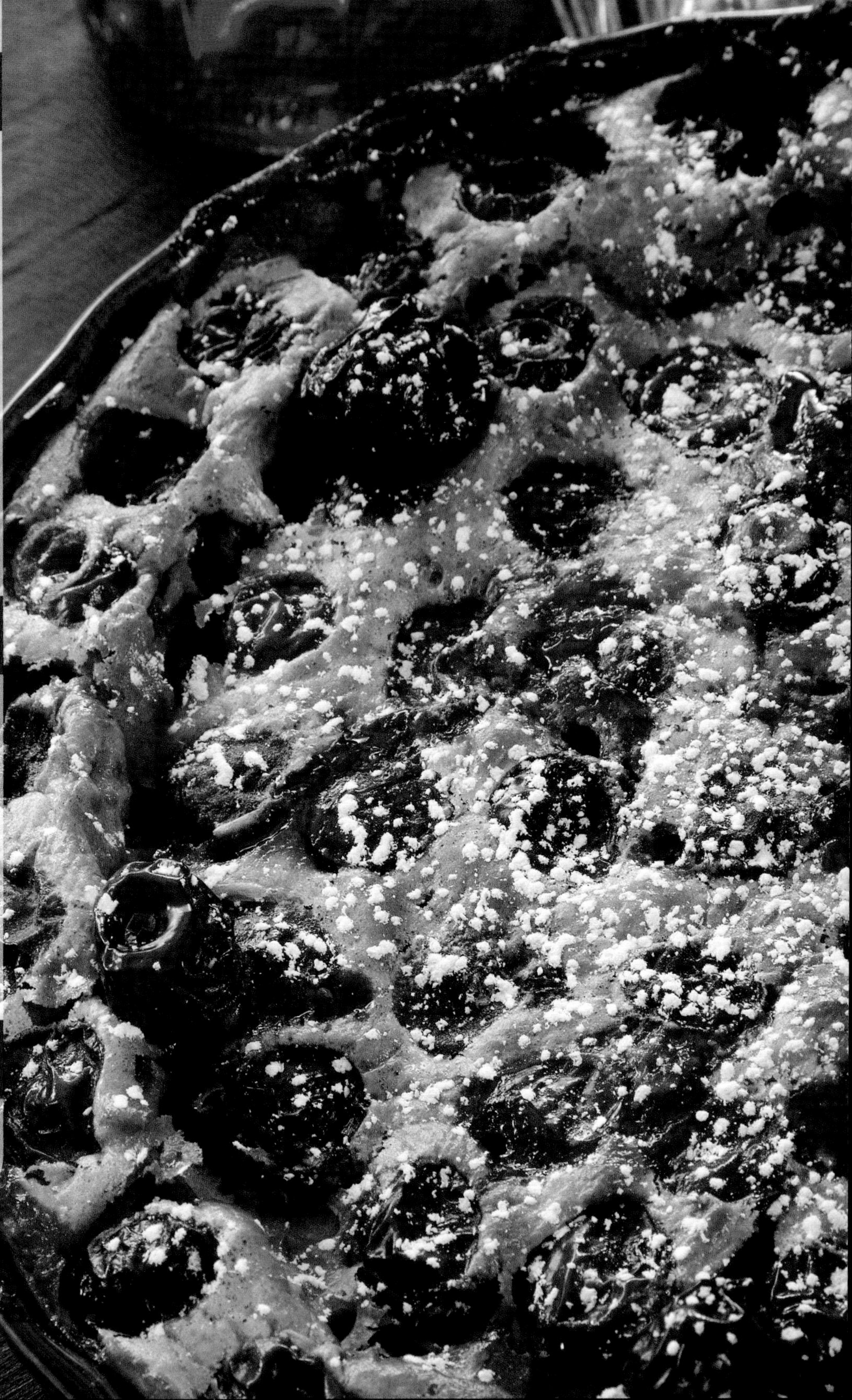

The clafoutis Limousin is a delicious flan dessert from the Limousin region of France. The name *clafoutis* is an old Occitan word meaning "to fill up." This refers to the ample amount of cherries that "fill up" the center of this rich and dense preparation. It is interesting to note that while other fruits can be used to make this dish, you only refer to it as "clafoutis" when cherries form the main ingredient. When any other fruit is used, the preparation should be referred to as a "flaugnarde." Always remember that clafoutis made in the traditional Limousin way always utilizes black cherries with the pits still intact, which is said to release a much richer cherry flavor during baking.

CLAFOUTIS LIMOUSIN
Cherry Flan

Method

1. Preheat the oven to 350°F (180°C).
2. Mix the flour and sugar together in a clean bowl. Add the eggs one by one, mixing well after each addition. Using a small knife, split the vanilla bean in half lengthwise and scrape out the seeds and add to the eggs. Once the vanilla bean has been incorporated, add the milk and salt and stir until well combined. Strain the mixture into a clean bowl to remove any lumps out of the mixture and set aside.
3. Butter a baking dish and coat it with sugar (*chemiser*). Remove and discard all of the stems from the cherries. Spread all of the de-stemmed cherries evenly over the bottom of the baking dish. Pour the egg mixture over the top, coating the cherries completely.
4. Place the clafoutis in the oven and bake it until it becomes puffy and nicely colored, or until a knife inserted comes out clean, about 35 to 45 minutes.
5. Serve immediately.

Quantity		Ingredient
U.S.	**Metric**	
2 oz	60 g	Flour
5 ¾ oz	125 g	Sugar, granulated
3 pcs	3 pcs	Eggs
10 fl oz	300 ml	Milk
1 pc	1 pc	Vanilla
Pinch	Pinch	Salt
24 oz	750 g	Black cherries

Learning Outcomes

Baking fruit
Baking en croute
Making a puff pastry
(*pâte feuilletée*)
Making an almond cream
(*crème d'amandes*)
Making caramel
Glazing

Equipment

Knives:
Paring knife *(couteau d'office)*, vegetable peeler *(économe)*

Tools:
Mixing bowls, corer, rolling pin, pastry brush, whisk, wooden spatula

Pans:
Baking sheet, saucepan, baking dish

Serving/Yield

6 servings

FYI...

The bourdelot is a rich and comforting preparation that wraps a baked apple, filled with crème d'amandes, in a light and flaky pâte feuilletée. The origins of this dessert stem from the French region of Normandy, an area that has had a longstanding tradition of gastronomy. The region is widely known for its apple and cattle production, which is why Norman cheeses are widely acknowledged as some of the finest in the world. The region is also famous for its apple orchards and has many traditional, apple-based culinary preparations (such as the bourdelots), as well as delicious ciders and apple brandies. The preparation can also be made using a center of pears instead of apples. Those are referred to as douillons rather than bourdelots.

BOURDELOTS
Apple Pastries

Preheat the oven to 350°F (180°C).

1. Peel and core the apples. Rub the outsides of the apples with the cut side of the lemon and squeeze some juice into the centers to prevent browning.

2. Arrange the apples in a buttered baking dish and sprinkle with the sugar. Dot with the butter and drizzle with the water. Place in the hot oven, basting at least once, and bake until the apples are cooked but still firm, about 20 to 25 minutes. Remove from the oven and allow them to cool completely.

Make the Crème d'Amandes

1. Cream together the softened butter (*en pommade*) and sugar (*crémer*) until fluffy. Add the eggs one at a time, mixing well after each addition. Split the vanilla bean lengthwise and scrape out the pulp. Reserve the empty pod for other uses. Add the vanilla and rum to the butter and egg mixture, stirring in well. Whisk in the almond powder until smooth. Transfer to a piping bag fitted with a medium round tip.

2. Preheat the oven to 425°F (215°C).

3. Lightly dust a clean work surface with flour (*fleurer*). Roll out the puff pastry (*pâte feuilletée*) (*abaisser*) on the floured surface (see page 320 in *Pâtisserie and Baking Foundations* for recipe and step by step instructions) to a thickness of ⅛ in. (3 mm). Cut into 6 squares approximately 6 in. X 6 in. (16 cm X 16 cm) depending on the size of your apples. Place a cooled apple in the center and fill the center with almond cream. Brush the dough with egg wash, then bring the corners up to the top of the apple, pinching the seams together. Shape the dough to the form of the apple. Repeat the process with the remaining apples and place on a baking sheet.

4. Brush the exterior of the bourdelots with the egg wash, and use the scraps of dough to decorate (if desired). Brush a second time with the egg wash, then place in the oven to bake until the pastry is nicely colored, about 15 minutes.

Make a Caramel Sauce

1. Place the sugar in a saucepan and add enough water to wet. Bring to a boil over high heat and cook until it begins to caramelize. Once it is a dark golden brown, remove from the heat and add the cream. Stir until the caramel has dissolved. Add more cream if desired.

2. Place a bourdelot on a plate and drizzle with the caramel sauce.

Quantity		Ingredient
U.S.	**Metric**	
6 pcs	6 pcs	Apples, such as Golden Delicious
1 pc	1 pc	Lemon
2 oz	60 g	Sugar, granulated
2 oz	60 g	Butter
2 fl oz	60 ml	Water
		Almond Cream (Crème d'Amandes)
3 ½ oz	100 g	Butter, softened (*en pommade*)
½ fl oz	10 ml	Rum
3 ½ oz	100 g	Sugar, granulated
2 pcs	2 pcs	Eggs
1 pc	1 pc	Vanilla bean
3 ½ oz	100 g	Almond powder
13 oz	400 g	Puff Pastry (Pâte feuilletée) (see page 320 in *Pâtisserie and Baking Foundations*)
1 pc	1 pc	Egg
7 oz	200 g	Sugar, granulated
As needed	As needed	Water
3 ½ fl oz	100 ml	Cream

Learning Outcomes

Making a flan

Equipment

Knives:
Paring knife
(*couteau d'office*)

Tools:
Mixing bowls, whisk

Pans:
10 in. (25 cm) shallow
gratin dish

Serving/Yield

6–8 persons

Far Breton is a traditional French flan that remains one of the most popular desserts in France today. Oddly enough, in its original form, this preparation was never intended to be eaten as a dessert. The roots of far Breton stem back to the French region of Brittany in the 18th century. The name literally translates to "Breton wheat," and the preparation was originally created as a savory wheat-based accompaniment to meat dishes. Over time, the far Breton evolved into a dessert with the addition of sugar, milk, and fruit, creating the dish we know today.

FAR BRETON
Breton Wheat

Method

1. Place the flour in a large bowl and make a well (**fontaine**) in the center. Add the sugar and salt to the well, then add the eggs and mix together, gradually incorporating the ingredients from the well into the flour.
2. Once the flour mixture has formed a thick dough, gradually whisk in the milk until a smooth batter forms. Stir in the oil.
3. Butter a baking dish (**chemiser**) and arrange the prunes so they are covering the bottom of the dish. Pour the batter over the prunes. Bake until the mixture puffs up and is golden in color, about 45 minutes. A knife inserted should come out clean.
4. Remove from the oven and serve.

Quantity		Ingredient
U.S.	**Metric**	
6 oz	180 g	Cake flour
6 oz	180 g	Sugar, granulated
¼ oz	8 g	Salt
3 pcs	3 pcs	Eggs
24 fl oz	750 ml	Milk
¾ fl oz	22 ml	Oil
7 ½ oz	225 g	Dried prunes

Learning Outcomes

Making a chocolate génoise
Montage
Making a Chantilly cream
(*crème Chantilly*)
Making rosettes
Masking a cake

Equipment

Knives:
Vegetable peeler (*économe*),
serrated knife
(*couteau-scie*), chef knife
(*couteau chef*), paring knife
(*couteau d'office*)

Tools:
Cake board, rotating cake
stand, pastry brush, balloon
whisk, rubber spatula,
tamis, corne, pastry bag,
10-mm round tip, 24-mm
star tip, scissors, mixing
bowls, ice bath

Pans:
Small saucepan, bain-marie

Serving

8 persons

FYI...

The black forest cake (Schwarzwalder Kirschtorte) is named after the Schwarzwald (literally, "Black Forest") in Germany. Joseph Keller, of Café Agner in Bad Godesberg, is thought to be the creator of this cake, although this is not certain. Although little is known about the history of the cake until the mid-1930s, it is now one of the most famous of German cakes. In its original version, it uses sour cherries and large amounts of kirsch. However, in its modern American version, the sour cherries have been replaced by maraschino cherries and the kirsch is, more often than not, nonexistent.

GÂTEAU FORÊT NOIRE
Black Forest Cake

Method

1. Preheat the oven to 400°F (205°C).
2. Butter an 8-in. cake pan (**moule à manqué**) and place it in the freezer for 5 minutes to set the butter. Butter the mold a second time and coat it in flour (**chemiser**). Tap off any excess flour and reserve the mold in the refrigerator.

Géneois Sponge (Génoise)

1. Melt the butter in a small saucepan over low heat and set it aside.
2. Sift (**tamiser**) the flour and cocoa powder onto a sheet of parchment paper.
3. Fill a saucepan one-quarter full of water and bring it to a simmer over medium-high heat (**bain-marie**).
4. Break the eggs and yolks into a large mixing bowl, add the sugar, and whisk them together with a balloon whisk until combined. Place the bowl on the simmering bain-marie and continue whisking until the mixture lightens in color and feels hot to the touch. At this point the mixture should form a ribbon when the whisk is lifted from the bowl. Remove the bowl from the bain-marie and continue to whisk the egg mixture until it cools to room temperature. Add the flour and gently fold it into the egg mixture with a rubber spatula (keep folding until the flour is just incorporated). Fold in the melted butter, then transfer the finished génoise into the cake mold and place it in the oven to bake. Reduce the oven temperature to 350°F (185°C) and bake the génoise for 15 to 18 minutes (test by inserting a knife into the center; if it comes out clean the cake is fully baked). Remove the génoise from the oven and let it cool in the mold for 2 to 3 minutes. Turn the cake out of the mold and let it cool upside down on a wire rack.

Chantilly Cream (Crème Chantilly)

1. Whip the cream in a large mixing bowl in an ice bath using a large whisk until it reaches the soft peak stage. Add the powdered sugar and vanilla, and continue to whip the cream until it is stiff. Reserve the crème Chantilly in the refrigerator until needed.

Imbibing Syrup

1. Bring the water and sugar to a boil together in a small saucepan over medium-high heat until the sugar has completely dissolved. Remove the pan from the heat and pour the syrup into a clean

U.S.	Metric	Ingredient
		Chemisage
1 oz	30 g	Flour
1 oz	30 g	Butter
		Géneois Sponge (Génoise)
¾ oz	25 g	Butter
4 oz	120 g	Flour, sifted (**tamiser**)
1 oz	30 g	Cocoa powder (**tamiser**)
4 pcs	4 pcs	Eggs
2 pcs	2 pcs	Egg yolks
5 oz	150 g	Sugar, granulated
		Chantilly Cream (Crème Chantilly)
19 fl oz	600 ml	Cream, cold
2 oz	60 g	Powdered sugar
¼ fl oz	5 ml	Vanilla extract
		Imbibing Syrup
7 oz	200 g	Sugar, granulated
7 fl oz	200 ml	Water
1 fl oz	30 ml	Kirsch
		Assembly (Montage)
10 oz	300 g	Bittersweet chocolate, tempered
4 ½ oz	130 g	**Griotte** cherries

Method

bowl. Let it cool to room temperature, then stir in the kirsch with a spoon. Cover and set aside.

Assembly

1. Turn the cake over so the domed side is on top. Trim it flat with a serrated knife. Turn the cake onto a cake board cut to the same dimensions as the cake and place on a rotating cake stand. Score the cake around the sides with a bread knife to create 3 even layers. Cut off the top layer, slicing around the cake, slowly cutting deeper until the layer comes off. Set aside. Repeat the cutting process with the middle layer and set it aside. Using a pastry brush, wet the entire surface of the bottom layer with syrup to imbibe it (*puncher*). Remove the crème Chantilly from the refrigerator and whisk it until it reaches the stiff peak stage (*serrer*). Transfer the crème Chantilly to a pastry bag fitted with a 10-mm plain tip. Starting from the center, pipe (*coucher*) a tight spiral all the way to the edges of the bottom layer of cake. Evenly scatter one-third of the cherries onto the crème Chantilly and pipe (*coucher*) a few lines of crème Chantilly over them to help the next layer hold in place. Place the middle layer on top and press it down lightly. Smooth any crème Chantilly that seeps out with a metal spatula. Repeat the imbibing (*puncher*), piping (*coucher*), and cherry scattering, followed by piping a few lines over the cherries. Place the last layer of cake on top and press down lightly. Smooth any crème Chantilly with a metal spatula. Lightly score the top of the cake with the tip of a small knife and imbibe it (*puncher*) with syrup.

2. Reserve the cake in the refrigerator. Empty the pastry bag into the bowl of crème Chantilly and reserve in the refrigerator.

Tip

If you need to refill the pastry bag at any time, empty it completely into the bowl of crème Chantilly, re-whip it until stiff, and refill the pastry bag.

Chocolate Shavings

1. Using a clean vegetable peeler or a sharp knife, scrape a bar or piece of chocolate for chocolate shavings.

Masking (Masquage)

1. Remove the cake from the refrigerator. Brush the top with syrup and wait for it to soak in. Whip the crème Chantilly to stiffen it (*serrer*). Using a large metal spatula, cover the sides of the cake in crème Chantilly and smooth out, scraping off any excess. Place a large dollop of crème Chantilly on top and spread it out toward the edges in an even layer. Smooth the top of the cake by sweeping over it using the metal spatula. Slip the spatula under the cake board and lift it up onto one hand. Rotating the cake in one hand, smooth the edges and corners of the cake, removing excess crème Chantilly in a continuous downward scrape of the spatula. Scrape off any excess crème Chantilly.

Finishing

1. Transfer the leftover crème Chantilly to a pastry bag fitted with a 24-mm star tip. Pipe (*coucher*) 8 rosettes (*rosace*) on top of the cake. Lightly press chocolate shavings to the sides of the cake and scatter them on the top between the rosettes. Sprinkle the cake with powdered sugar and top each rosette with a cherry.

2. Transfer the cake either to a clean cake board or to a serving dish and refrigerate until ready to serve.

Learning Outcomes

Making a levain
Shaping bread
Seasoning bread

Equipment

Knives:
Paring knife (*couteau d'office*), chef's knife (*couteau chef*)

Tools:
Mixing bowls, sieve, cutting board, pastry brush, cloth, rolling pin

Pans:
Sauté pan, saucepan, baking sheet

Serving/Yield

One loaf of fougasse

The fougasse and its distinctive leaf shape are closely associated with the Provence region in the South of France. There are many different regional variations, such as fouace or the Italian focaccia. The fougasse was originally the first piece of dough baked in the wood burning ovens of a bakery and was used to gauge the heat of the oven. It was then served as a morning snack for the apprentice bakers.

Quantity		Ingredient
U.S.	**Metric**	
10 fl oz	300 ml	Water, lukewarm [*max 90°F (32°C)*]
½ oz	15 g	Baker's yeast
1 lb	500 g	Flour
¼ oz	5 g	Salt
1 fl oz	30 ml	Olive oil
2 oz	60 g	Black olives, pitted and sliced in half
2 fl oz	60 ml	Olive oil
As needed	As needed	Sea salt
As needed	As needed	Thyme, fresh or dried

FOUGASSE

Method

1. In a large bowl, dissolve the baker's yeast with the warm water [*max 90°F (32°C)*] and 4 oz (120 g) of the flour. Cover the bowl with a cloth and set it aside in a warm place to proof until doubled in volume. This will be your starter dough (*levain*).
2. Once your *levain* is ready, place the remaining flour onto your work surface and make a well (*fontaine*) in the center. Add the salt, 1 ¾ fl oz (50 ml) of water, 1 fl oz (30 ml) of olive oil, and the olives.
3. Add your *levain* and mix it in until all the elements are incorporated while gradually kneading in the remaining flour. Shape the dough into a ball, and using a knife, score it with a deep 'X.' Set aside in a warm place to proof until doubled in volume.
4. Preheat the oven to 445°F (230°C).
5. Roll the dough out (*abaisser*) into a large oval approximately 1 ½ in. (4 cm) thick. Transfer it to a lightly oiled baking sheet. Using a sharp knife, cut slits in the dough, being sure to cut all the way through. Gently pull the dough to separate the cuts.
6. Brush the dough with 2 fl oz (60 ml) of olive oil, and then sprinkle with some thyme and sea salt.
7. Bake until golden, about 35 minutes.

Learning Outcomes

Making a pastry cream
(*crème pâtissière*)
Filling a cake before
baking
Scoring a cake surface

Equipment

Tools:
Sieve, whisk, corne,
colander, pastry bag,
medium round pastry tip,
mixing bowls, pastry brush

Pans:
Medium saucepan,
8 inch cake pan

Serving

6 persons

Originating from the town of Cambo-les-Bains in the Aquitaine region of France, gâteau Basque was first sold under the Basque name Biskotxak. The anecdotal history of the gâteau is that a baker by the name of Marianne Hirigoyen had been handed down the recipe by her mother in the 1830s. With the growing fame of Cambo-les-Bains as a spa town, well-to-do people from all over France started coming into Marianne's shop to sample the unique delicacy of Biskotxak.

Quantity		Ingredient
U.S.	**Metric**	*Pastry Cream (Crème Pâtissière)*
8 fl oz	250 ml	Milk
¼ fl oz	5 ml	Vanilla extract
2 pcs	2 pcs	Egg yolks
2 oz	60 g	Sugar, granulated
1 oz	30 g	Flour (or cornstarch)
1 oz	30 g	Almond powder
¾ fl oz	20 ml	Rum or Izzara
½ oz	14 g	Butter
		Garnish (Garniture)
5 oz	150 g	Cherries in syrup, drained
1 oz	30 g	Flour
1 oz	30 g	Sugar, granulated
		Custard (Appareil)
8 oz	250 g	Flour
¼ oz	6 g	Baking powder
¼ oz	4 g	Salt
5 oz	150 g	Butter, softened (**pommade**)
5 oz	150 g	Sugar, granulated
3 pcs	3 pcs	Eggs
¼ fl oz	5 ml	Vanilla extract
1 pc	1 pc	Lemon, zest of
1 pc	1 pc	Egg for egg wash

GÂTEAU BASQUE
Cream-Filled Butter Cake

Method

1. Preheat the oven to 370°F (185°C).
2. Butter the inside of an 8-in. round cake mold (**moule à manqué**) and reserve it in the refrigerator.
3. Place the cherries in a colander over a mixing bowl to drain.

Pastry Cream (Crème Pâtissière)

1. Combine the milk and the vanilla extract in a medium saucepan and bring the mixture to a boil over medium-high heat. Add about one-quarter of the sugar to the milk and stir to dissolve it.
2. Place the egg yolks in a small mixing bowl and add the remaining sugar. Whisk the sugar into the eggs until it completely dissolves and the yolks lighten in color (**blanchir**). Add the flour or cornstarch to the yolks and stir until well combined.
3. When the milk begins to come to a boil, remove it from the stove and pour one-third of it into the egg yolks. Stir well to temper the yolks, then whisk the tempered mixture into the remaining hot milk. Place back onto the heat and cook until the crème pâtissière begins to bubble. Add the almond powder, and continue whisking (being sure to press the whisk around the corners of the pan) and allow to cook for 1 minute in order to cook the starch. The crème pâtissière will become very thick. Transfer the finished pastry cream (crème pâtissière) to a clean bowl. Pat (**tamponner**) the surface with a piece of cold butter held on the end of a fork to create a protective film and let the pastry cream (crème pâtissière) cool to room temperature.
4. Prepare a shallow tray or baking sheet by lining with plastic wrap. Once cooked, pour the crème pâtissière onto the prepared sheet. Pat (**tamponner**) the surface with a piece of cold butter to create a protective film, then cover with plastic wrap, pressing out any air bubbles, and seal the edges. Set aside to cool to room temperature.

Cake Batter (Pâte à Gâteau)

1. Sift the flour, baking powder, and salt together. Cream (**crémer**) the butter and sugar together until fluffy. Add the eggs one at a time, mixing well after each addition. Add the vanilla and lemon zest and stir well. Stir in the flour until incorporated and a thick batter is formed. Transfer to a pastry bag fitted with a large round tip.

Method

Assembly

1. Remove the cake mold from the refrigerator and lightly dust with flour. Starting at the center of the prepared mold, pipe a tight spiral of the batter outward. When you reach the sides of the pan, continue piping around the circumference of the pan to the top so that the sides are evenly covered. Lightly tap the pan to fill in any gaps. Whisk the crème pâtissière until it is smooth and stretchy, then mix in the rum. Toss the drained cherries in the flour and sugar, then mix into the creme. The coating will help absorb any excess juice. Add the pastry cream to the center of the cake mold. Spread the pastry cream (crème pâtissière) into an even layer. Pipe the remaining cake batter in a spiral over the crème. Smooth any gaps with a palette knife. Drag a finger around the inside of the rim of the cake mold to create a shallow channel. Smooth the surface of the cake using a palette knife dipped in hot water. Let the cake rest in the refrigerator for 30 minutes before baking.

Cooking

1. Remove the cake from the refrigerator and brush the surface with egg wash. Using a fork, lightly score the surface with a decorative pattern. Place the cake in the oven to bake until golden, then turn the oven down to 340°F (170°C) and bake the cake for a further 25 minutes. Remove the cake from the oven and, leaving it in the mold, let it rest on a wire rack for 10 minutes. Turn the cake out of its mold and let it rest on the wire rack until cool.

Optional

Decorate with a marzipan rose.

Learning Outcomes

Making a kouglhof

Equipment

Knives:
N/A

Tools:
Mixing bowls, wooden spatula, kitchen towel, pastry brush, rolling pin, wire rack

Pans:
Kouglhof mold, saucepan

Serving/Yield

One large or two small cakes

The kouglhof (which can also be spelled kougelhpf, kugelhopf, kuglhof, or the German gugelhupf) is a delicious Germanic brioche from the Alsace region of France. Alsace is the eastern-most region of France and the Alsatian peoples' roots are largely mixed between German and French. A local legend regarding the creation of the kouglhof says that the dessert was created in the Alsace town of Ribeaupré by the biblical three wise men on their pilgrimage to Bethlehem. The wise men were said to have created the dessert as a way of thanking a pastry shop owner who provided shelter for them in his shop. The wise men shaped the cake to resemble their turbans as a reminder of their visit. This distinctive turban shape remains a defining feature of this preparation to this day.

KOUGLHOF

Method

1. Warm the milk to around body temperature [*max 90°F (32°C)*] in a saucepan over a low heat. Once warmed, pour the milk into a large bowl and dissolve the yeast into it. Then add about 3 oz (100 g) of the flour, as well as the sugar, salt, and eggs. Mix until well incorporated. Add the remaining flour until a soft dough forms. Turn the dough out onto the work surface and knead until smooth and no longer sticky. Place in a clean bowl, cover, and allow to proof until doubled in volume.
2. Generously butter a kouglhof mold and sprinkle it with sliced almonds (**chemiser**).
3. Punch the dough down, then add the butter and work the dough until homogeneous. Add the raisins and knead until evenly distributed.
4. Roll the dough out (**abaisser**) into a rectangle and then roll it lengthwise into a log. Place the log in the prepared mold, pressing the ends together. Set aside to proof for 1 hour.
5. Preheat the oven to 375°F (190°C).
6. Place the kouglhof in the oven to bake until golden brown and dry to the touch, approximately 40 minutes.
7. Remove from the oven and gently unmold. Allow to cool on a wire rack, and then dust with powdered sugar before serving.

Quantity		Ingredient
U.S.	**Metric**	
3 ¼ fl oz	100 ml	Milk
1 oz	30 g	Baker's yeast
13 ¼ oz	400 g	Flour
2 ½ oz	75 g	Sugar, granulated
¼ oz	8 g	Salt
3 pcs	3 pcs	Eggs
5 oz	150 g	Butter
3 ¼ oz	100 g	Raisins
As needed	As needed	Butter (to grease mold)
1 ¾ oz	50 g	Sliced almonds
As needed	As needed	Powdered sugar for dusting

Learning Outcomes

Making a yeast dough
(*pâte levée*)
Glazing

Equipment

Knives:
Paring knife *(couteau d'office)*

Tools:
Mixing bowls, rolling pin, wooden spatula, pastry brush

Pans:
Baking sheet

Serving/Yield

4–6 servings

Kouign amann is a delicious, buttery treat with an odd-sounding name. The cake originated in the small town of Douarnenez in the French region of Brittany in 1865. The name sounds strange because it stems from the Breton language. In Breton, the word *kouign* means "bread" and the word *amann* means "butter." The cake is said to have been created by accident by a Douarnenez baker who was attempting to make a new form of bread dough. The story goes that as his bread failed to turn out as desired, he began layering the dough with ample quantities of butter and sugar. His error turned out to be a delicious one, and the French region of Finistère where the town is located remains famous for its kouign amann to this day.

KOUIGN AMANN

Method

Make a Sponge

1. Dissolve the yeast in the warm water [*max 90°F (32°C)*]. Stir in the 1 ¾ oz (50 g) portion of flour, and then set it aside in a warm place to proof until doubled in volume to make your starter dough.

2. Mix the salt in with the 6 ¾ oz (200 g) portion of flour in a large bowl. Add the starter dough to the flour and work it in with the tips of the fingers, adding just enough water to form a supple dough. Knead until smooth.

3. Set aside in a warm place to rise. When doubled in volume, turn out onto a floured surface (*fleurer*) and roll out (*abaisser*) into a large round. Distribute the butter evenly over the dough, then sprinkle it with the sugar. Fold the dough into thirds and roll out (*abaisser*) again. Fold into thirds again and then roll out (*abaisser*) for a third time. Set the dough aside to rest for 15 minutes. Roll it out into a large circle, then fold it into thirds and allow it to rest for another 15 minutes. Roll out (*abaisser*) the dough one last time and then fold it into thirds.

4. Preheat the oven to 460°F (240°C).

5. Roll the dough out (*abaisser*) to a round that is 8.5 in. (22 cm) in diameter. Score the top with a criss-cross pattern using a paring knife, then brush with the egg wash. Place the dough on a baking sheet and set it in the preheated oven, allowing it to bake for 20 minutes. As melted butter seeps up through the dough, brush it evenly over the kouign amann. Remove it from the oven when golden brown, then sprinkle with sugar to finish.

U.S.	Metric	Ingredient
½ oz	12 g	Fresh yeast
1 fl oz	30 ml	Lukewarm water [*max 90°F (32°C)*]
1 ¾ oz	50 g	Flour
6 ¾ oz	200 g	Flour
1 pinch	1 pinch	Salt
4 oz	125 g	Butter
2 oz	60 g	Sugar, granulated
1 pc	1 pc	Egg (for egg wash)
As needed	As needed	Sugar

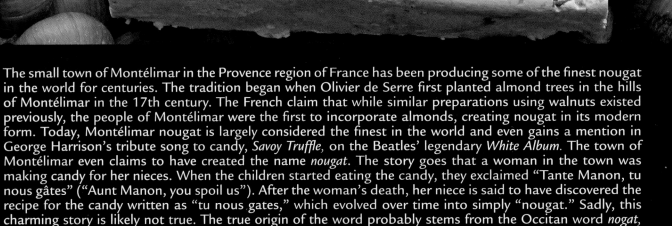

Learning Outcomes

Making a nougat
Cooking honey
Cooking sugar
Making a meringue

Equipment

Knives:
Serrated knife *(couteau-scie)*

Tools:
Mixing bowls, whisk,
caramel ruler (optional),
candy thermometer, wooden
spatula, rolling pin, wafer
paper (optional)

Pans:
Saucepans, baking sheet,
bain-marie

Serving/Yield

Approximately 5 dozen
1 oz/30 g pieces

HISTORY

The small town of Montélimar in the Provence region of France has been producing some of the finest nougat in the world for centuries. The tradition began when Olivier de Serre first planted almond trees in the hills of Montélimar in the 17th century. The French claim that while similar preparations using walnuts existed previously, the people of Montélimar were the first to incorporate almonds, creating nougat in its modern form. Today, Montélimar nougat is largely considered the finest in the world and even gains a mention in George Harrison's tribute song to candy, *Savoy Truffle*, on the Beatles' legendary *White Album*. The town of Montélimar even claims to have created the name *nougat*. The story goes that a woman in the town was making candy for her nieces. When the children started eating the candy, they exclaimed "Tante Manon, tu nous gâtes" ("Aunt Manon, you spoil us"). After the woman's death, her niece is said to have discovered the recipe for the candy written as "tu nous gates," which evolved over time into simply "nougat." Sadly, this charming story is likely not true. The true origin of the word probably stems from the Occitan word *nogat*, which means "nut."

NOUGAT DE MONTELIMAR
Montelimar Nougat

Method

1. Line a baking sheet with a piece of parchment paper (*chemiser*) and generously dust it with powdered sugar.
2. Place the honey in a heavy saucepan over medium-high heat and bring it to a boil. Keep an eye on it, as honey can foam up and overflow the pan when heated. Cook the honey to 275°F (135°C) using a candy thermometer to gauge the temperature. At the same time, place the remaining sugar, glucose, and water in another saucepan and bring it to a boil. Skim and brush down the sides of the pan, then cook the mixture to 295°F (145°C).
3. While the honey and sugar are cooking, in a large bowl, whisk the egg whites (*monter les blancs*) to soft peaks. Add 1 ¼ oz (35 g) of the sugar to the whites, and whisk together until the sugar has been totally dissolved. Whisk in the honey in a thin, steady stream. Once it is incorporated, continue mixing, then add the cooked sugar in a thin, steady stream. Check the consistency by lifting the whisk out of the meringue—if the point of the meringue falls (*bec d'aigle*), it needs to be cooked longer. Place the bowl over a bain-marie and cook until the point of the meringue remains stiff when the whisk is lifted. Remove from the heat and gently fold in the nuts.
4. Transfer the nougat to the prepared baking sheet. Dust it with more powdered sugar and pat the nougat flat, to about ¾-in. (2-cm) thick, while shaping it into a square or rectangle. Allow to cool completely, then cut into desired sizes, using a serrated knife.

Optional

*If using wafer paper, arrange the wafer paper on a baking sheet and frame it with caramel rulers. Spread the warm nougat on top and flatten. Cover with a second sheet of wafer paper and flatten with a rolling pin (**abaisser**), using the caramel rulers as a guide. Allow to cool.*

Quantity		Ingredient
U.S.	**Metric**	
16 fl oz	500 ml	Honey
1.8 lb	830 g	Sugar, granulated
6 ½ fl oz	185 ml	Glucose
9 fl oz	250 ml	Water
3 ½ oz	100 g	Egg whites
13 ¼ oz	400 g	Whole almonds, toasted
4 ¼ oz	130 g	Shelled pistachios, toasted
4 ¼ oz	130 g	Whole hazelnuts, toasted
3 ¼ oz	100 g	Candied cherries
As needed	As needed	Powdered sugar
		Wafer paper (Optional)

Learning Outcomes

Making a yeast dough
(*pâte levée*)
Making a sugar tart

Equipment

Tools:
Sieve, mixing bowls, whisk,
rolling pin, corne, pastry
brush

Pans:
Baking sheet, 8 inch deep
tart pan, small saucepan

Serving

6–8 persons

© Le Cordon Bleu International

FYI...
Using yeast-raised dough, this style of sugar pie appears to have originated in the northern part of France (Flanders, in particular) where the production of sugar from sugar beets has been of economic importance for centuries.

TARTE AU SUCRE
Sugar Tart

Method

1. Preheat the oven to 350°F (175°C).
2. Lightly grease a high-sided 8 in. (20 cm) tart mold with softened butter and reserve it in the refrigerator.

Yeast Dough (Pâte Levée)

1. Add the yeast and sugar to the warm water and stir them in until completely dissolved. Let the mixture rest until it is covered in a thin layer of foam. Meanwhile, sift (*tamiser*) the flour onto a clean, dry work surface and make a well (*fontaine*) in the center. Pour the yeast mixture into the well and stir it using your fingertips while gradually adding flour from the sides using a plastic scraper (*corne*). When the center of the well resembles a thick paste, gather the flour on top and begin to work it into the yeast mixture with your hands. Once the ingredients are combined, make a well in the center. Whisk the egg and salt together in a small bowl and pour them into the well. Stir them with your fingertips, gradually adding the mixture from the sides of the well until all the egg is absorbed. Gather the mixture into a pile and knead it until it forms a dough. Continue to knead it until smooth and add the butter. Knead the dough until the butter is completely incorporated. Stretch and fold the dough repeatedly until it is elastic enough to form a thin skin (*diaphragm*) when stretched between the hands (*10 to 15 minutes*). Work the dough into a ball and place it in a lightly oiled mixing bowl. Cover the bowl with a damp cloth and leave it in a warm area to rise until doubled in size (*pousser*).

Custard (Appareil)

1. Whisk the sugar and egg in a large mixing bowl until light in color (*blanchir*). Add the milk while stirring continuously. Pour 2 tablespoons of the sugar/egg/milk mixture into the melted butter and stir until combined. Recombine all the ingredients.

Cooking

1. Lightly dust a clean work surface with flour (*fleurer*). Once the dough has doubled in size, turn it out onto the lightly floured surface and knead it for 10 to 15 minutes. Roll the dough out (*abaisser*) into a circle 2 in. (5 cm) wider than the tart mold. Place the dough in the tart mold and fold the edges in to create a raised border, pressing the seam

Quantity		Ingredient
U.S.	**Metric**	**Yeast Dough (Pâte Levée)**
8 oz	250 g	Flour
½ oz	10 g	Fresh yeast
1 oz	30 g	Sugar, granulated
2 ¾ fl oz	80 ml	Water, warm
1 pc	1 pc	Egg
¼ oz	5 g	Salt
3 ½ oz	100 g	Butter, softened (**pommade**)
1 pc	1 pc	Egg for egg wash
		Custard (Appareil)
3 ½ oz	100 g	Sugar, granulated
1 pc	1 pc	Egg
1 ¾ fl oz	50 ml	Milk
1 ¾ fl oz	50 ml	Butter, melted and cooled
As needed	As needed	Flour for dusting

Method

down to secure it. Proof the dough a second time in the tart shell before cooking (*15 to 20 minutes*). Brush the surface of the dough with egg wash and transfer it to the oven to bake until lightly golden (*20 to 25 minutes*). Remove the tart base from the oven and press down the center using your knuckles or the back of a large spoon. Brush the edge with egg wash a second time and fill the depression with the custard mixture (***appareil***). Return the tart to the oven to bake for 10 to 15 minutes.

Finishing

1. Transfer the cooked tart to a wire rack to rest for 5 to 10 minutes. Unmold it and serve it warm or at room temperature.
2. Before serving, the tart can be brushed with simple syrup to give it shine and the center can be further decorated with a sprinkle of sugar.

Learning Outcomes

Making a puff pastry
(*pâte feuilletée*)
Making caramel
Making an upside down
tart
Baking fruit

Equipment

Knives:
Paring knife
(*couteau d'office*), vegetable
peeler (*économe*)

Tools:
Rolling pin, wooden spatula,
mixing bowls, spoon

Pans:
Tatin mold or heavy-
bottomed 9 in. (23 cm)
sauté pan

Serving/Yield

One 9 in./23 cm tart,
8–10 servings

In the early 1900s, the Tatin sisters, Stéphanie and Caroline, ran a hunting lodge and restaurant in the French region of Solonge. The story goes that in a hurry, one of the sisters accidentally baked an apple tart with the pastry base facing up and the apple garnish facing down. To cover her mistake, the sister flipped (*renversée*) the tart once it was baked. The mistake created a preparation with a crispy golden crust and apples that were caramelized to perfection, and the tart was an instant hit with the hungry hunters. One problem with this story is the question of how one would accidentally assemble a tart upside down. A less-quaint hypothesis is that the sisters, who had a far-reaching reputation as exemplary hostesses, did an exceptional job of preparing and possibly altering a pre-existing regional tart and merited the honor of having their family name applied to it.

Method

Make a Puff Pastry (*Pâte Feuilletée*) (see page 320 in *Pâtisserie and Baking Foundations*)

1. Preheat the oven to 350°F (175°C).
2. Peel and core the apples, then cut them in quarters. Cut the lemon in half and rub the apples thoroughly with the cut sides of the lemon to prevent them from browning.
3. Place the tatin mold over medium-high heat and add the butter. Once the butter has melted, add the sugar and stir it in well. Using a paring knife, split the vanilla bean in half lengthwise and scrape out the seeds. Stirring regularly, cook the sugar until it begins to caramelize. Once the sugar has turned a golden brown, begin to arrange the apples around the outer edge of the mold. Turn the apples over and arrange them standing vertically with their cored sides in the caramel and all facing the same direction. The apples should be packed fairly tightly. Make a second circle of apples within the outer circle. You may need to cut the apples in to wedges to fill the center. Cook until the caramel darkens and bubbles and the apples begin to soften, approximately 20 minutes. Baste the apples with the cooking juices.

Note

You can sprinkle the apples with a combination of sugar (¼ oz or 5g) and pectin (¼ oz or 5 g) to help prevent the apples from softening too much. This would be done after the sugar has been cooked to golden brown stage and apples are arranged in the tarte mold.

4. Roll the puff pastry (*pâte feuilletée*) out until it is slightly larger than the pan and about ⅛-in. (3-mm) thick. Remove the pan from the heat. Then roll (*abaisser*) the dough onto the rolling pin and quickly lay it over the apples. Working quickly (the dough will begin to soften from the heat of the apples), tuck the edges of the dough inside the edges of the pan using the back of a spoon.
5. Place the tart in the oven and bake it until the pastry is nicely browned and a knife can be easily inserted into an apple. Remove the tart from the oven and allow it to cool slightly. Place the serving dish over the pan and quickly flip the pan over. Then gently lift the mold.

Note

The tart can be left to cool in the mold. To unmold, gently heat to melt the caramel before unmolding. The cooled tart can be brushed with an apricot glaze if desired.

Quantity		Ingredient
U.S.	*Metric*	
5 pcs	5 pcs	Apples (firm)
1 pc	1 pc	Lemon
2 ½ oz	70 g	Butter
7 oz	200 g	Sugar, granulated
1 pc	1 pc	Vanilla bean
8 oz	250 g	Puff pastry (pâte feuilletée)

Autre Préparations
(Other Preparations)

Learning Outcomes

Making a fritter batter
(*pâte à beignets*
or *pâte à frire*)
Sweet marinades
Sweet sauces

Equipment

Knives:
Vegetable peeler (*économe*),
apple corer, paring knife
(*office*)

Tools:
Sieve, mixing bowls, rubber
spatula, whisk, skimmer
(*écumoire*),
sugar dredger

Pans:
Small saucepan,
shallow pan

Serving

4 persons

FYI…

Since the Middle Ages, cooks have been coating both sweet and savory ingredients in batter and cooking them in hot oil. *Beignets*, also known as fritters in English, have evolved from region to region with some recipes calling for a choux paste and others, such as *beignets de pommes*, calling for beer-based dough. In terms of sweet fillings, apples are one of the oldest and best-loved filling ingredients for *beignets*.

BEIGNETS AUX POMMES, SAUCE ABRICOT
Apple Fritters with Apricot Sauce

Method

Heat the oil in the deep fryer to 360°F (180°C).

Fritter Batter (*Pâte à Beignet*)

1. Melt the butter in a small saucepan over low heat and set aside.
2. Sift the flour, place it in a large mixing bowl, and make a well (**fontaine**) in the center. Add the eggs, salt, and sugar into the well and stir them into the flour with a wooden spatula. [*It is normal for the mixture to be lumpy at this stage.*]
3. Pour in one-half the beer and stir it in with a whisk until the mixture resembles a smooth paste. Add the remaining beer and stir until incorporated. Pour a little of the batter into the melted butter and mix them together until smooth. Pour this back into the batter and stir it in with the whisk.

Note

If the dough is difficult to stir with a spatula, add a bit of water.

4. Scrape the sides of the bowl clean with a rubber spatula or plastic scraper (**corne**) and cover the bowl in plastic wrap. Let the batter rest in the refrigerator for 15 to 20 minutes (*minimum*). The dough can be reserved for longer if necessary.

Marinade

1. Peel and core the apples and slice them into ½-in. (1-cm) thick slices (**rouelles**). Arrange the rouelles in a single layer in a shallow pan. Dredge with powdered sugar; then drizzle with Calvados. Reserve in the refrigerator for 15 minutes (*minimum*).

Sauce Abricot

1. Thin out the apricot jam with enough marinade to make the sauce just thick enough to coat the back of a spoon (*à la nappe*).

To Finish

1. Drain the apple **rouelles** on a paper towel to absorb excess moisture.
2. Whisk the egg whites to soft peaks, then fold into the beignet batter until just incorporated.
3. One by one, dip the **rouelles** in the **pâte à beignets** to cover them completely, then place them in the deep fryer. Turn them over halfway through the cooking process (*when they are just beginning to color*). Remove the **beignets** from the oil when they are golden and drain them on a paper towel.

To Serve

1. Arrange the **beignets** on a serving platter, dust them with powdered sugar, and serve the sauce on the side.

Quantity		Ingredient
U.S.	Metric	
4 pcs	4 pcs	Golden Delicious apples
		Fritter Batter (Pâte à Beignet)
8 oz	250 g	All-purpose flour
2 pcs	2 pcs	Eggs
½ oz	10 g	Sugar, granulated
¼ oz	5 g	Salt
¾ fl oz	25 ml	Unsalted butter, melted
5 fl oz	150 ml	Beer, lukewarm
3 pcs	3 pcs	Egg whites
As needed	As needed	Water (optional)
		Marinade
2 oz	60 g	Powdered sugar
1 fl oz	30 ml	Calvados or domestic apple brandy
1 pc	1 pc	Lemon, juice of
		To finish
5 fl oz	150 ml	Apricot jam
As needed	As needed	Oil for deep-frying
As needed	As needed	Powdered sugar for dusting

Learning Outcomes

Making a détrempe
Making a puff pastry
(*pâte feuilletée*)
Coring fruit
Making an apple compote
Making a pastry pocket
(*chausson*)
Decorating puff pastry
(*pâte feuilletée*)
Crimping pastry edges
(*Chiqueter*)

Equipment

Knives:
Vegetable peeler (*économe*),
paring knife (*couteau
d'office*), chef knife
(*couteau chef*)

Tools:
Rolling pin, corne, baker's
brush, mixing bowls,
wooden spoon, wooden
spatula, 4-in. cookie cutter,
pastry brush

Pans:
Medium saucepan, small
saucepans, baking sheet

Serving

12 persons

In 1580, a plague swept through the French town of Saint-Calais. Those too poor to flee were left in the town to starve. According to the legend, an aristocratic lady baked an enormous apple-filled pastry that she served to the remaining townspeople—presumably saving them all from starvation. To commemorate the benevolence of this unnamed lady, the people of Saint-Calais still conduct a yearly march through town on her behalf. On this day, the bakers and pastry chefs of the town distribute chaussons aux pommes (single-serving sizes, of course!) to the cheering crowd.

CHAUSSONS AUX POMMES
Apple Turnovers

Quantity		Ingredient
U.S.	**Metric**	**Puff Pastry (Pâte Feuilletée)**
1 lb	500 g	Flour
7 ¾ fl oz	225 ml	Water
7 oz	200 g	Butter, room temperature (pommade)
½ oz	10 g	Salt
7 oz	200 g	Butter
1 pc	1 pc	Egg for egg wash
		Compote
3 pcs	3 pcs	Golden Delicious apples
½ pc	½ pc	Lemon, juice of
2 oz	60 g	Sugar, granulated
1 ½ oz	40 g	Butter
As needed	As needed	Vanilla (*optional*)
		Syrup
1 ¾ oz	50 g	Sugar, granulated
1 ¾ fl oz	50 ml	Water
As needed	As needed	Powdered sugar for dusting

Method

1. Preheat the oven to 400°F (205°C).

Puff Pastry (Pâte Feuilletée)

Note

To obtain the correct amount of pâte feuilletée, use the ingredients list in this recipe following the method in Les Bases on pages 320–321 of Pâtisserie and Baking Foundations.

Compote

1. Peel and core the apples. Cut the flesh into a small dice and toss with the lemon juice. Cook the sugar over medium-high heat in a medium saucepan until it caramelizes. Remove the pan from the stove and add the butter to deglaze. Stir with a wooden spatula until the caramel is soft. Add the diced apples and return the pan to low heat. Cook the apples gently, stirring them occasionally until they are cooked but retain some texture. Drain out any excess liquid and set the compote aside to cool to room temperature.

Assembly

1. Lightly dust the work surface with flour (**fleurer**). Place the puff pastry on the work surface and roll it out (**abaisser**) with a rolling pin to a thickness of ³⁄₁₆ in. (5 mm). Transfer the dough to a refrigerator to relax for 5 minutes. Remove the dough from the refrigerator and cut it into circles with a 4-in. (10-cm) cookie cutter. Roll each circle of dough into an oval with a couple of strokes of the rolling pin. Neatly arrange the ovals on a clean baking sheet, brush off any excess flour using a baker's brush, and leave the ovals to rest for 5 minutes in the refrigerator. Remove the baking sheet from the refrigerator and fold the ovals in half to create a guideline crease along the widest point of the oval. Brush the edge of one-half of each oval with egg wash. Place a tablespoon of compote in the center of the each egg-washed half and fold the other half over it, gently pressing out any air bubbles. Carefully press down the rim of each chausson to secure the seal. Score the edges with the back of a paring knife (**chiqueter**). The goal is to seal the seam while creating a decorative pattern.
2. Let the chaussons rest in the refrigerator for 10 minutes, then brush them in egg wash and lightly score the tops with a paring knife. Make a small hole (**cheminée**) in the top of each chausson

Method

to allow steam to escape during baking. Transfer the chaussons to the oven and bake until golden (*rotating the baking sheet as soon as the pastry begins to color*).

Finishing

1. *Prepare a syrup:* Pour the water into a small saucepan and add the sugar. Bring the mixture to a boil over medium-high heat and continue to boil it until all the sugar has dissolved. Remove the pan from the stove and set aside to cool.

2. When the chaussons aux pommes are a deep golden color, remove them from the oven and transfer them to a wire rack to cool. While they are still warm, brush them with the syrup using a pastry brush.

3. Once the chaussons are cool, dust them with powdered sugar and transfer them to a serving dish.

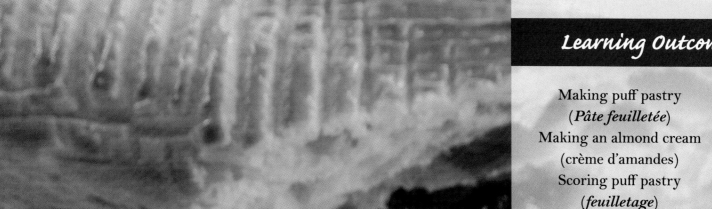

Learning Outcomes

Making puff pastry
(*Pâte feuilletée*)
Making an almond cream
(crème d'amandes)
Scoring puff pastry
(*feuilletage*)
Glazing

Equipment

Knives:
Paring knife
(*couteau d'office*), chef knife
(*couteau chef*)

Tools:
Mixing bowls, corne,
rolling pin, whisk,
pastry brush

Pans:
Saucepan, baking sheet,
wire rack

Serving/Yield

6–8 servings

The jalousie is a delicious fruit pastry similar to a strudel or a turnover. It is made by layering a fruit paste in between two sections of puff pastry and scoring lines across the surface to allow the steam to escape during baking. The name *jalousie* literally translates to "jealousy," but this delicious pastry was not named because of people feeling jealous when you serve it. A jalousie is also a form of window shutter made from angled slates that block out light. The pastry is named for these shutters because the slits scored over the surface make the preparation closely resemble them. It is important to note that because puff pastry is very light, it can become soggy during baking due to the water contained in most fruit preserves. This can be remedied by cooking the fruit paste beforehand to thicken the mixture and evaporate some of the moisture.

Quantity		Ingredient
U.S.	**Metric**	**Puff Pastry (Pâte Feuilletée)**
8 oz	250 g	Flour
3 ½ oz	100 g	Butter
3 ½ fl oz	100 ml	Water
½ tsp	4 g	Salt
		Almond Cream (Crème d'Amandes)
2 oz	60 g	Butter
2 oz	60 g	Sugar, granulated
2 oz	60 g	Almond powder
1 oz	30 g	Flour
1 pc	1 pc	Eggs
1 pc	1 pc	Vanilla bean
7 oz	200 g	Raspberry or other fruit jam
		Finish
1 pc	1 pc	Egg (for egg wash)
2 oz	60 g	Sugar, granulated
2 fl oz	60 ml	Water

JALOUSIE
Fruit Turnover

Method

Détrempe (for the Puff Pastry)

1. Sift (**tamiser**) the flour onto a clean work surface and make a well (**fontaine**) in the center using a plastic scraper (**corne**). Add the salt and water to the well. Stir with your fingertips until the salt is dissolved.
2. Add the butter (cut into pieces) and begin to incorporate the flour using your fingertips. As the flour, butter, and water begin to combine, use the **corne** to cut the ingredients together, until the mixture resembles a coarse dough. Sprinkle with additional water if the dough is too dry.
3. Once there are barely any traces of flour left, gather the dough into a ball and score the top of it with a deep cross using a large knife.
4. Loosely wrap the finished **détrempe** in plastic and transfer it to the refrigerator to rest for a minimum of 1 hour (preferably overnight).

Note

Détrempe refers to the dough before the layer of butter (**beurrage**) is added.

Beurrage and Tourage

1. Place the cold butter between two sheets of parchment paper and pound it with a rolling pin until it is similar to the **détrempe** in consistency.
2. Using the **corne**, shape the butter into a flat square about ½-in. (1-cm) thick. Set the butter aside. Place it in the refrigerator if the kitchen is warm.
3. Lightly dust a clean work surface with flour (**fleurer**), then unwrap the **détrempe** and place it on the floured surface.
4. Using the scored marks as a guide, roll out (**abaisser**) the corners of the détrempe into a cross shape. Be careful to keep the center of the cross thicker than its outer arms (this will be important when rolling out the dough and the butter).
5. Place the square of butter in the center of the cross and fold the two side arms over it so that they overlap slightly in the center (in the process be careful not to trap any air bubbles). Give the dough a quarter turn and fold the two remaining arms over the butter so that the butter is completely enclosed. Press the seams well to seal.
6. Lightly tap the dough with the length of the rolling pin to even out the distribution of the butter inside. Give the dough a quarter turn and repeat the tapping process. This is called the enveloppe.

Tourage, 6 Turns (6 Tours Simples)

1. Turns 1 and 2: Roll out (**abaisser**) the dough in long, even strokes to form a rectangle that is 3 times the original length of the enveloppe or ⅜-in. (1-cm) thick. Brush off any excess flour.
2. Fold the bottom third of the dough up; then fold the top third down over the first fold. Make sure the edges are even. Give the dough a quarter turn to the right and repeat the same rolling process. Make sure to always brush away any excess flour.
3. Repeat the folding process (top third up, top third down over first fold) and give the dough a quarter turn to the right. Make 2 finger impressions in the top left corner of the dough. Note: These marks are a reminder of the number of turns that the dough has received; they also indicate the position for subsequent turns. Wrap the dough in plastic and transfer it to the refrigerator to rest for a minimum of 20 minutes. With the butter incorporated into the dough and 2 turns completed, it can now be referred to as **pâton.**
4. Turns 3 and 4: Lightly dust the work surface with flour (**fleurer**).
5. Remove the dough from the refrigerator and unwrap it onto the floured surface (with the 2 indents in the top left corner). Proceed to give the dough a third and fourth turn (rolling and folding in the same manner as the first and second turns). Mark the dough with 4 imprints in the top-left corner before wrapping it in plastic and returning it to the refrigerator to rest for a minimum of 20 minutes.
6. Turns 5 and 6: Lightly dust the work surface with flour (**fleurer**).
7. Remove the dough from the refrigerator and unwrap it onto the floured surface (with the 4 indents in the top left corner). Proceed to give the dough its final 2 turns, folding and rolling as in previous turns. Wrap it in plastic and return it to the refrigerator to rest for a minimum of 20 minutes before rolling it out (the longer the dough rests, the better it will perform).

Tip

*Because the **détrempe** and the butter are at the same consistency, it is necessary to complete the turns as explained above. If you allow the dough to over-chill between turns, the butter may become too hard and crack when rolled out. Make sure you have allotted the necessary time to complete the turns.*

Almond Cream (Crème d'Amandes)

1. Cream (**crémer**) the butter and sugar together until light and fluffy.
2. Beat in the egg until well combined. Using a small knife, split the vanilla bean in half lengthwise and scrape out the seeds. Whisk into the mixture. Add the rum and finish by mixing in the almond powder and flour.
3. Reserve the almond cream (crème d'amandes) in a covered bowl in the refrigerator until ready to use.

Assembly

Preheat the oven to 425°F (220°C).

1. Lightly sprits or dampen a clean baking sheet. Cut the puff pastry (pâte feuilletée) in half and place one-half back in the refrigerator.
2. Dust the marble with flour (**fleurer**) and place the dough on top. Roll out (**abaisser**) the dough into a large rectangle, rolling in both directions to a thickness about ⅛ in. (3–4 mm). Transfer the rolled dough to the baking sheet and place in the refrigerator to rest. Roll out the second half of the pâte feuilletée in the same manner and place in the refrigerator to rest.
3. Bring out the first piece of dough. Beat the egg and brush the edges of the dough with it.
4. Transfer the almond cream (crème d'amandes) to a piping bag fitted with a medium round tip and pipe vertical lines of the crème, leaving about a 3-in. (7-½ cm) border of dough.
5. Whisk the raspberry jam until smooth and gently spread on top of the almond cream (crème d'amandes). Brush the exposed dough with additional egg wash and set aside.
6. Remove the second piece of dough from the refrigerator. Fold in half and lay on top of the almond cream (crème d'amandes) and raspberry jam. Lift up the top fold and carefully lay on top to finish covering the filling.
7. Gently smooth the top outwards to remove any air bubbles then firmly press around the filling to seal the two pieces of dough.
8. Place back in the refrigerator to set, about 15 to 20 minutes.
9. Once the dough is firm, with a sharp knife, trim the uneven edges of the dough leaving a border approximately 1-in. (2 ½ cm) wide. Save the scraps (**rognures**) for another use. Brush with the egg wash, being careful not to let it drip down the sides, which could prevent your jalousie from rising evenly.
10. With the tip of a small knife, score the top of the pastry decoratively being careful not to pierce the top. Brush with a second coating of the egg wash, again being careful not to let any drip down the sides.
11. Place in the hot oven and bake until golden brown, about 25 to 30 minutes.
12. While the jalousie is baking, bring the sugar and water to a boil until the sugar is dissolved. Set aside.
13. Once the jalousie is cooked, brush it with the sugar syrup and place it back in the oven to glaze, about 5 minutes.
14. Transfer to a wire rack to cool.

Learning Outcomes

Making a panade
Making a choux pastry
(*pâte à choux*)
Glazing
Piping (*coucher*)

Equipment

Knives:
Chef's knife (*couteau chef*)

Tools:
Wooden spatula, mixing
bowls, grater, cutting board,
piping bag, medium round
tip

Pans:
Saucepan, baking sheet,
wire rack

Serving/Yield

1¾ pound/830 gram
portion of dough

One of the few savory preparations made from choux pastry (*pâte à choux*), the gougère is a light snack that is most often filled with cheese. The origins of this pastry can be traced back to the Burgundy region of France. The most commonly used filling is a finely shredded gruyère cheese; however, other firm white cheeses can be easily substituted. It should be noted that because of the labor involved in preparing choux pastry, it is wise to make a large portion of dough and freeze the excess for later use.

GOUGÈRES
Cheese Pastry

Method

Make a Choux Pastry (Pâte à Choux) (see page 312 in Pâtisserie and Baking Foundations)

Preheat the oven to 425°F (220°C).

Prepare a Panade

1. Combine the water, butter, and salt in a large pan and bring to a boil over a medium-high heat. Once the butter has completely melted, remove the pan from the heat and add the flour. Stir with a wooden spatula until combined, then over medium heat, stir until the mixture doesn't stick to the pan and it forms a thin skin on the bottom of the pan (**dessêcher**). Transfer to a clean bowl and allow to cool slightly.

2. Beat 5 eggs together and gradually incorporate them into the panade, mixing well after each addition until the dough is stretchy and slightly sticky. The dough should form a limp point when the spatula is pulled from the dough. If the dough is still too stiff, beat the last egg and add enough until the dough reaches the required consistency.

3. Stir in 3 ¼ oz (100 g) of the grated cheese and transfer the dough to a piping bag fitted with a medium round tip. Pipe (**coucher**) approximately 1 ¼-in. (2 ½-cm) balls onto a lightly greased baking sheet leaving about 1 ½ in. (3 ½ cm) of space in between each ball. Brush with the egg wash being careful not to let it run down the sides. Sprinkle with remaining cheese. Bake until the gougères are puffed up and golden, about 10 to 15 minutes.

4. Transfer to a wire rack to cool.

U.S.	Metric	Ingredient
		Panade
8 fl oz	250 ml	Water
3 ¼ oz	100 g	Butter
¼ oz	6 g	Salt
6 oz	175 g	Flour
5–6 pcs	5–6 pcs	Eggs
3 ¼ oz	100 g	Gruyère cheese, grated
1 ¾ oz	50 g	Gruyère cheese, grated and finely chopped

Quantity — *Ingredient*

Learning Outcomes

Making a riz au lait
Making a crème Anglaise
Making a whipped cream
Making a bavarois
Pocher
Making rosettes (*rosace*)

Equipment

Knives:
Paring knife
(*couteau d'office*)

Tools:
Wooden spoon, whisk,
balloon whisk, rubber
spatula, mixing bowls

Pans:
2 large pans, 1 small pan

Serving

8 persons

RIZ À L'IMPÉRATRICE
Bavarian Cream Rice Pudding

Method

1. Preheat the oven to 350°F (175°C).
2. Place a jelly mold in the refrigerator to chill.

Rice Pudding (Riz au Lait)

1. Wash the rice in cold water, then drain and place in a saucepan. Cover with cold water. Bring to a boil over high heat and blanch (**blanchir**) the rice for 2 minutes. Rinse the rice in cold water and drain it through a fine mesh sieve.
2. Bring the milk to a boil in a pan over medium-high heat and immediately remove the pan from the heat.
3. Slice the vanilla bean in half lengthwise and scrape the seeds directly into the milk. Add the rice to the milk, return to the heat, and cook for approximately 20 minutes.
4. When the rice is cooked, place it in a bowl over an ice bath and remove it once it cools to room temperature.

Note

Do not let the rice cool to the point that it starts to solidify.

Crème Anglaise Custard (Crème Anglaise Collée)

1. To obtain the correct amount of crème Anglaise, use the ingredients list in this recipe following the method on pages 261–262 in *Pâtisserie and Baking Foundations*.

Tip

Crème Anglaise should be cooked to between 167°F and 185°F (75°C and 85°C).

2. Once the crème Anglaise is cooked, add the gelatin and stir to make sure that it has melted completely. Remove the pan from the heat and strain the sauce through a fine mesh sieve into a clean bowl set over an ice bath. Stir it back and forth with a wooden spatula (**vanner**) until it is cool to the touch.

Finishing

1. Whip the cream to the consistency of soft peaks in a large mixing bowl over an ice bath.
2. Mix the candied fruit (**fruits confits**) with the cooked rice, then, using a rubber spatula, add the crème Anglaise collée, little by little. Finish by incorporating the whipped cream.

Note

At this stage in the recipe, it is important to have all the elements at the right texture: If the gelatin has overset the crème Anglaise, place the bowl containing the crème over a bain-marie to help return it to the desired consistency.

Quantity		Ingredient
U.S.	**Metric**	*Rice Pudding (Riz au lait)*
3 ½ oz	100 g	Rice
10 fl oz	300 ml	Milk
½ pc	½ pc	Vanilla bean
		Crème Anglaise Custard (Crème Anglaise Collée)
7 fl oz	200 ml	Milk
4 pcs	4 pcs	Egg yolks
3 ½ oz	100 g	Sugar, granulated
½ pc	½ pc	Vanilla bean
5 pcs	5 pcs	Gelatin leaves
		Finishing
8 fl oz	250 ml	Whipped cream
4 ¼ oz	125 g	Candied fruit (*fruits confits*)
		Decoration
3 ½ fl oz	100 ml	Whipped cream
1 ¾ oz	50 g	Candied fruit (*fruits confits*)
8 fl oz	250 ml	Red currant jelly

Method

3. Fill the jelly mold with the rice mixture and gently tap the mold on the work surface to eliminate air bubbles. Smooth the top, cover in plastic wrap, and let the rice mixture set in the refrigerator overnight.

To Serve

1. Using a large whisk, whip the cream in a large bowl over an ice bath until it reaches the soft peak stage. Transfer it to a pastry bag fitted with a large star tip.

2. Fill a large recipient with hot water and carefully dip the mold into the hot water to loosen its sides. Turn the jelly mold over onto a chilled serving dish and holding it securely to the plate, give it a good shake or two. Remove the mold. Decorate the riz à l'impératrice by piping out whipped-cream rosettes (**rosace**) and decorating with the candied fruits.

3. Melt the red currant jelly in a small saucepan over low heat and pour it into the bottom of the serving dish. Refrigerate before serving.

Confiseries
(Confectionaries)

. . . .

Guimauves
—Marshmallows

. . . .

Pâtes de Fruit
—Fruit Pastilles

. . . .

Learning Outcomes

Making marshmallows
Cooking sugar
Mounting egg whites
(*monter les blancs*)

Equipment

Knives:
Palette knife (*spatule coudée*), chef knife (*couteau chef*) or scissors (*ciseaux*)

Tools:
Mixing bowls, spoon, pastry brush, whisk, sieve

Pans:
Saucepan

Serving/Yield

24–30 pieces

The marshmallow plant (*Althaea officinalis*) has been utilized for its medicinal properties since the time of the ancient Egyptians. These were some of the oldest confections known to man, and they consisted of mallow root sap that was boiled with nuts and honey. These early preparations bore virtually no resemblance to the puffy, white confections we know today. For most of its history, the marshmallow was utilized for medicinal purposes and was infused with sweeteners to make the mallow sap more palatable. By around 1850, the French were the first to develop the pâte à guimauve, which used mallow root sap as a binding agent and incorporated sugar, egg whites, corn syrup, and water all boiled together and closely resembled the modern marshmallow. In fact, today's guimauves differ very little from these early recipes. The only major change has been the use of gelatin as an alternative binding agent to mallow sap. Today, the marshmallow is utilized in a wide variety of dessert preparations as well as being a favorite accompaniment to a steaming mug of hot cocoa!

GUIMAUVES
Marshmallows

Method

1. Line a sheet pan with parchment paper (**chemiser**).
2. Mix the powdered sugar and cornstarch together and sprinkle some of it onto the parchment paper.
3. Soften the gelatin in a bowl of cold water.
4. Prepare a small bowl of cold water, a spoon, and a clean pastry brush. Bring the sugar, glucose, and water to a boil over high heat, brushing down the sides of the pan and skimming off any white foam from the surface. Once the sugar is clear, place a candy thermometer in the boiling syrup and leave undisturbed to cook until it reaches 266°F (130°C).
5. When the sugar reaches 257°F (125°C), place the egg whites in a large bowl with a pinch of cream of tartar and begin whisking to soft peaks (**monter les blancs**). (If you are coloring your marshmallows, you should add the food coloring to the egg whites now.) Add the sugar and whisk until stiff.
6. Once the sugar has reached 266°F (130°C), remove it from the heat and add the softened gelatin, after squeezing out any excess water. Then whisk into the mounted egg whites in a thin, steady stream being careful not to pour the hot syrup onto the wires of the whisk. Once all the syrup has been incorporated, add some of the flavoring and continue whisking until the marshmallow batter thickens. Add the remaining flavoring and food coloring (if desired).

Note

If you are flavoring the marshmallow, you can lightly color it to reflect its flavor. Add just enough to make a pastel shade.

7. Pour onto the prepared sheet pan and spread evenly. Sprinkle with the remaining powdered sugar mixture and allow to cool completely. Cut into squares with a knife or use a pair of scissors to cut into bite-sized pieces.

Quantity		Ingredient
U.S.	Metric	
7 oz	200 g	Powdered sugar
7 oz	200 g	Corn starch
¾ oz	25 g	Gelatin
1 lb	500 g	Sugar, granulated
1 ¾ fl oz	50 ml	Glucose
5 fl oz	150 ml	Water
5 ¾ fl oz	175 ml	Egg whites
1 ¾ fl oz	50 ml	Sugar, granulated
1 pinch	1 pinch	Cream of tartar
20 drops	20 drops	Flavoring such as vanilla, citrus, rose water
As needed	As needed	Food coloring (optional)

Learning Outcomes

Making a fruit paste
Using pectin
Cooking fruit

Equipment

Knives:
Chef knife *(couteau chef)*

Tools:
Mixing bowls, whisk,
parchment paper or plastic
wrap

Pans:
Saucepan, sheet pan

Serving/Yield

Approximately 90
1 ounce pieces

Pâtes de fruit are delicious confections made from real fruit puree reductions that are heated and allowed to solidify and then rolled in granulated sugar. The contrast between the citric acids of the fruit and the sweetness of the sugar forms an intense flavor. The density of the pâtes de fruit comes from the use of pectin as a binding agent. Pectin is a polysaccharide compound that is extracted from the cell walls of fruits. First discovered by Henri Braconnot in 1825, pectin is the main reason that fruits stay firm. When a fruit ripens, the pectin in the cells begins to break down and the fruit starts to soften, eventually turning to mush as the pectin breaks down completely. This makes pectin one of the most important natural binding agents, as well as being highly regarded for its medicinal properties in aiding digestion.

PÂTES DE FRUIT
Fruit Pastilles

Method

Strawberry or Raspberry

1. Prepare a small sheet pan by lining it with parchment paper or plastic wrap (*chemiser*).
2. Mix the pectin and 3 ½ oz (100 g) of the granulated sugar together. Dissolve the citric acid in a small amount of water.
3. Place the fruit pulp in a heavy-bottomed saucepan and bring it to a boil over medium heat, stirring often. Once a boil is reached, add the pectin/sugar mixture and stir until totally dissolved. Add the remaining sugar, glucose, and citric acid. Stir it in well and allow to gently simmer. Place a candy thermometer into the mixture and cook to 222°F (106°C) for the strawberry pulp, and 224°F (107°C) for the raspberry pulp.
4. Once the mixture reaches the correct temperature, remove it from the heat and pour it into the prepared sheet pan. Allow to cool and set at room temperature.
5. Once set, cut the pâtes de fruit into 1-in. (2 ½-cm) squares and roll them in granulated sugar.

Apricot

1. Prepare a small sheet pan by lining it with parchment paper or plastic wrap (*chemiser*).
2. Mix the pectin and the 4 ½ oz (130 g) portion of granulated sugar together. Dissolve the citric acid in a small amount of water.
3. Place the apricot pulp in a heavy-bottomed saucepan and bring it to a boil over medium heat, stirring often. Once a boil is reached, add the pectin/sugar mixture and stir until totally dissolved. Add the remaining sugar, glucose, and citric acid. Stir it in well and allow to gently simmer. Place a candy thermometer into the pulp mixture and cook it to 222°F (106°C).
4. Once the mixture reaches the correct temperature, allow the pulp to boil for 1 minute, then remove it from the heat and pour it into the prepared sheet pan. Allow to cool and set at room temperature.
5. Once set, cut the pâtes de fruit into 1-in. (2 ½-cm) squares and roll them in granulated sugar.

Lemon

1. Prepare a small sheet pan by lining with parchment or plastic wrap (*chemiser*).
2. Mix the pectin and the 5 oz (150 g) portion of granulated sugar together. Dissolve the citric acid in a small amount of water.

Quantity		Ingredient
U.S.	Metric	**Strawberry or Raspberry**
2 lbs	1 kg	Strawberry or raspberry pulp
1 ¼ oz	40 g	Pectin
39 oz	1.2 kg	Sugar, granulated
13 ¼ fl oz	400 ml	Glucose
¾ oz	25 g	Citric acid
As needed	As needed	Granulated sugar
		Apricot
2 lbs	1 kg	Apricot pulp
4 ¼ oz	130 g	Sugar, granulated
2 lbs	1 kg	Sugar, granulated
9 fl oz	270 ml	Glucose
¼ oz	5 g	Citric acid
As needed	As needed	Sugar, granulated
		Lemon
23 fl oz	700 ml	Water
26 fl oz	800 ml	Lemon juice
2 ½ oz	75 g	Pectin
36 oz	1.1 kg	Sugar, granulated
1 lb	500 g	Glucose
1 ¼ fl oz	35 ml	Citric acid
As needed	As needed	Sugar, granulated

Method

3. Place the lemon juice and water in a heavy-bottomed saucepan and bring it to a boil over medium heat, stirring often. Once a boil is reached, add the pectin/sugar mixture and stir until totally dissolved. Add the remaining sugar, glucose, and citric acid. Stir it in well and allow to gently simmer. Place a candy thermometer into the lemon juice mixture and cook it to 222°F (106°C).

4. Once the mixture reaches the correct temperature, allow the juice to boil for 1 minute, then remove it from the heat and pour it into the prepared sheet pan. Allow to cool and set at room temperature.

5. Once set, cut the pâtes de fruit into 1-in. (2 ½-cm) squares and roll them in granulated sugar.

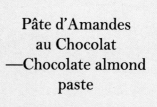

Pâte d'Amandes
au Chocolat
—Chocolate almond
paste

. . . .

Truffes et Muscadines
—Truffles and
Muscadine Chocolates

. . . .

Recipes Chocolat (Chocolates)

PÂTE D'AMANDES AU CHOCOLAT

Flavoring almond paste
Tempering chocolate
Dipping in hot chocolate
Kneading
Piping (*coucher*)

Equipment

Knives:
Chef knife (*couteau chef*)

Tools:
Rolling pin, mixing bowl,
rubber spatula, dipping
forks, cornet

Pans:
Baking sheet (or parchment
paper), bain-marie,
wire rack

Serving/Yield

About 48–60 pieces
depending on the size

FYI...

This simple and delicious preparation is made by dipping delicious almond paste (pâte d'amandes) into melted chocolate. You might be surprised and excited to discover that chocolate, which has been traditionally viewed as an unhealthy indulgence, is now starting to be considered a heart healthy snack. It has been revealed that chocolate contains a highly beneficial component known as flavinoids, which act as antioxidants and assist in lowering blood pressure and cholesterol levels in the human bloodstream. However, before you consider going out and starting a new all chocolate health diet, you should know that this only applies to dark chocolate, and only when eaten in moderation.

PÂTE D'AMANDES AU CHOCOLAT
Chocolate Almond Paste

Method

Pistachio

1. Lightly dust your work surface with powdered sugar. Knead the almond paste until malleable. Flatten and make an indentation in the middle and add the pistachio paste. Fold the almond paste over the pistachio paste and knead it until the pistachio paste has been evenly incorporated. If desired, add a few drops of green food coloring. Wrap in plastic and set aside.

Coffee

1. Lightly dust the work surface with powdered sugar. Knead the almond paste until malleable. Flatten and make an indentation in the middle and add the coffee extract. The coffee extract can be very strong, so add just a little at the start and add more as desired. Fold the almond paste over the coffee extract and knead until the coffee is evenly incorporated. Wrap in plastic and set aside.
2. Clean the work surface if needed and dust with powdered sugar. Flatten the pistachio almond paste and roll out (*abaisser*) into a square, about ¼-in./½-cm thick. Trim the uneven edges. Cut into small squares, diamonds, or triangles. Arrange on a parchment-lined rack or baking sheet. Do the same for the coffee almond paste. Set aside to dry, preferably overnight.
3. Temper the dark chocolate (see pages 276–280 in *Pâtisserie and Baking Foundations*).
4. To coat the bottoms only, place a piece of almond paste on the dipping fork and dip to the level of the surface of the almond paste. Lift and carefully tap the excess and lay onto a clean, parchment-lined rack or baking sheet.
5. Using a paper cornet, pipe (*coucher*) a little of the chocolate in the center of each almond paste and decorate with a pistachio or chocolate coffee bean accordingly.
6. To partially coat, hold the almond paste by the corner and carefully dip halfway into the chocolate, being careful not to touch the chocolate with your dipping hand to avoid being burned. Lift and gently shake off any excess, then lay on the parchment-lined rack or baking sheet. Before the chocolate sets, top with a shelled pistachio for the pistachio almond paste, or a chocolate coffee bean for the coffee almond paste.
7. To coat completely, toss pieces one at a time into the chocolate. Lift out with the dipping fork, tap off any excess, then transfer to the paper-lined rack or baking sheet. Before the chocolate sets, decorate with the shelled pistachios or chocolate coffee bean.
8. Set aside until set.

Quantity		Ingredient
U.S.	Metric	*Pistachio*
8 oz	250 g	Almond paste (55%)
½ oz	15 g	Pistachio paste
2 drops	2 drops	Green food coloring (for a more intense color)
		Coffee
8 oz	250 g	Almond paste
¼ to ½ fl oz	10–15 ml	Coffee extract
As needed	As needed	Powdered sugar (for dusting)
14 oz	400 g	Dark confectioner's chocolate
		Decoration
As needed	As needed	Whole shelled pistachios
As needed	As needed	Chocolate coffee beans

Learning Outcomes

Making a ganache
Tempering chocolate
Dipping and rolling
Piping (*coucher*)

Equipment

Knives:
N/A

Tools:
Mixing bowls, wooden
spatula, piping bag, medium
round tip, parchment paper

Pans:
Small saucepan, baking
sheet or sheet pan

Serving/Yield

40 to 60 pieces depending
on the size of each

HISTORY

The chocolate truffle is a delicate French bonbon made by coating a ball of creamy ganache in a thin layer of cocoa powder. The truffle was named for its uncanny resemblance to the much-sought-after and highly prized culinary fungus, the tuber melanosporum, or black truffle. The chocolate truffle is said to have been created by one of the fathers of haute cuisine, the great chef Auguste Escoffier, in the early 1920s. The story goes that an apprentice of Escoffier's was preparing a pastry cream (crème pâtissière) when he accidentally poured the hot cream over a bowl of chocolate. Escoffier found that he could work the cream and chocolate mixture into a ball. He then rolled the ball in cocoa powder to seal it and was impressed by the rich chocolate flavor of the resulting bonbon.

Method

Line a sheet pan with parchment paper (*chemiser*).

Truffles

1. Sift (*tamiser*) the cocoa powder into a shallow recipient.
2. Place the chocolate into a small bowl. Bring the cream to a boil over medium-high heat. When it just begins to boil, pour the cream over the chocolate and allow it to sit for 2 to 3 minutes. Gently stir the chocolate and cream together until smooth. Stir in the rum and set aside to cool.
3. Once firm but still malleable, transfer the chocolate mixture to a piping bag and pipe (*coucher*) small rounds onto the lined baking sheet. Place in the refrigerator to set.
4. Once set, remove the chocolate rounds from the fridge and roll them into balls.
5. Temper the dark chocolate (see pages 276–280 in *Pâtisserie and Baking Foundations*).
6. Drop the balls into the chocolate a few at a time. Lift them out, tap off the excess chocolate, and then transfer them to the cocoa powder. Use a fork to roll the balls immediately before the chocolate is able to set. Allow the balls to set in the cocoa, then tap off the excess and arrange on the prepared parchment paper-lined tray.

Muscadines

1. Sift (*tamiser*) the powdered sugar into a shallow recipient.
2. Place the chocolate in a bowl. Bring the cream to a boil over medium-high heat. When it just begins to boil, pour the cream over the chocolate and allow it to sit for 2 to 3 minutes. Gently stir the chocolate and cream together until smooth. Stir the Grand Marnier into the chocolate mixture. Place the praline paste in a small bowl and add some chocolate. Stir until smooth. Add to the rest of the warm chocolate mixture and mix in well. Set aside to cool and set.
3. Once firm but still malleable, transfer the chocolate to a piping bag and pipe long lines along the edge of the baking sheet. Place in the refrigerator to set.
4. Once the chocolate lines have set cut them into 1-½ in. (4-cm) long pieces.
5. Temper the milk chocolate (see pages 276–280 *Pâtisserie and Baking Foundations*).
6. Drop the pieces into the chocolate a few at a time. Lift out the pieces, tap off the excess chocolate, and then transfer them to the powdered sugar. Using a fork, roll the muscadines lengthwise immediately before the chocolate is able to set. Allow to set in the powdered sugar. Tap off any excess sugar and arrange on the prepared parchment paper-lined tray.

Quantity		Ingredient
U.S.	**Metric**	*Truffles*
8 oz	250 g	Dark chocolate, chopped or in pieces
7 fl oz	200 ml	Cream
1 fl oz	30 ml	Rum or other flavoring
3 ¼ oz	100 g	Dark chocolate
3 ¼ oz	100 g	Cocoa powder
		Muscadine
7 ½ oz	225 g	Milk chocolate
3 ¼ fl oz	100 ml	Cream
1 fl oz	30 ml	Grand Marnier
1 oz	30 g	Praline paste
3 ½ oz	100 g	Milk chocolate
As needed	As needed	Powdered sugar

Pâtisserie Étrangère
(Foreign Pastries)

Angel food cake

Banana bread

Basic muffin

Battenberg cake

Biscotti

Bread and butter pudding

Brownies

Carrot cake

Challah

Chiffon cake

Chocolate chip cookies

Cinnamon rolls

Devil's food cake

Dobos torte

Flourless chocolate cake

Focaccia

Fruit cobbler

Fudge

Gingerbread

Hot cross buns

Pie dough

Old fashioned pie filling

New York style cheesecake

Panna cotta

Peanut butter cookies

Pecan pie

Pita bread

Rice pudding

Sacher torte

Scones

Tarte Linzer

Trifle

Learning Outcomes

Making a meringue
Making a foam-based cake

Equipment

Knives:
N/A

Tools:
Mixing bowls, balloon whisk, sieve, rubber spatula

Pans:
10 in. (25 cm) tube pan, wire rack

Serving/Yield

1 cake

Angel food cake gained its heavenly name because of its white color and light, airy texture, making it the "food of angels." Although no one knows exactly who invented it, the cake's origins can be traced to the United States from around the 1870s. The cake was most likely invented by the Pennsylvania Dutch, who were the first to introduce the tube pan, which is an essential requirement for baking this cake, to America. While similar cakes existed under several other names, such as angel cake and silver cake, the angel food cake as we know it today became popularized after the recipe was published by Fannie Merritt Farmer in the *Boston Cooking School Cook Book* in 1896. Interestingly enough, the cake was able to gain popularity because of an important culinary innovation of the mid-1800s: the handheld rotary beater. The angel food cake requires a large concentration of egg whites and, previous to the invention of the handheld beater, it could take several hours of whipping whites by hand to achieve the airy consistency required for the cake. The combination of the ingenuity of the Pennsylvania Dutch and the innovation of the rotary beater allowed for the creation of this heavenly cake, which is sinfully delicious.

ANGEL FOOD CAKE

Method

Preheat the oven to 350°F (180°C).

1. Sift (*tamiser*) the flour and half of the sugar.
2. Make a meringue: Whisk the egg whites with the salt and cream of tartar to soft peaks (*monter les blancs*). Then gradually whisk in the remaining sugar. Whisk the egg whites until glossy and tight and you can no longer feel any granules when rubbed between your fingers.
3. Fold the dry ingredients into the meringue along with the vanilla and almond extract until they are just blended.
4. Transfer the mixture to the 10 in. (25 cm) tube pan and place it in the oven to bake for approximately 35 minutes, or until the cake becomes golden brown and a wooden skewer inserted between the edge and the tube comes out dry.
5. Remove from the oven and carefully invert the pan onto a wire rack. Allow to cool completely before unmolding. Optional: Dust with powdered sugar.

Quantity		Ingredient
U.S.	Metric	
5 oz	150 g	Cake flour
5 oz	150 g	Sugar, granulated
10 fl oz	300 ml	Egg whites
⅛ oz	2 g	Cream of tartar
Dash	Dash	Salt
¼ fl oz	5 ml	Vanilla extract
⅛ oz	2 g	Almond extract
5 oz	150 g	Sugar
As needed	As needed	Powdered sugar for dusting

Learning Outcomes

Muffin/quick bread method

Equipment

Knives:
Paring knife *(couteau d'office)*

Tools:
Mixing bowls, wooden or rubber spatula, whisk

Pans:
Bread loaf pan, wire rack

Serving/Yield

1 loaf

HISTORY

Banana bread has very likely existed in various forms since ancient times. The ancient Greeks infused breads with various fruits and had been aware of the existence of bananas since Alexander the Great returned from India in the 4th century BC. Given this long lineage, it is surprising that banana bread as know it today is a relatively recent creation. The origins of the modern form of banana bread are believed to have stemmed from the poverty-stricken American women of the Great Depression of the 1930s. It is believed that these resourceful women began incorporating bananas on the verge of spoiling to their breads as a way of earning some extra money. Thankfully for us, these enterprising women in dire situations created something truly delicious, and today, banana bread remains one of the most beloved baked goods in the world.

BANANA BREAD

Method

Preheat the oven to 325°F (165°C).

1. Butter and flour (**chemiser**) a bread loaf pan.
2. Sift (**tamiser**) together the sugar, flour, baking powder, baking soda, and salt.
3. In a mixing bowl, mash or puree the bananas. Mix in the eggs and oil until well combined.
4. Make a well (**fontaine**) in the center of the dry ingredients and pour the banana mixture into the well. Give the mixture a few good stirs and then add the coarsely chopped walnuts. Stir the mixture until the dry ingredients are just combined. There should still be streaks of flour visible in the batter.
5. Pour the batter into the prepared loaf pan. Bake it in the center rack of the oven until a paring knife inserted in the center comes out clean, for approximately 50 minutes.
6. Remove the bread from the oven and allow it to cool slightly. Then gently unmold the loaf and place it on a wire rack to finish cooling.

Quantity		Ingredient
U.S.	Metric	
5 oz	150 g	Sugar, granulated
12 oz	360 g	Pastry flour
½ oz	15 g	Baking powder
⅛ oz	2 ½ g	Baking soda
¼ oz	5 g	Salt
12 oz	360 g	Ripe bananas
5 fl oz	150 ml	Eggs, beaten
4 fl oz	120 ml	Oil
3 oz	90 g	Walnuts, chopped

Learning Outcomes

Muffin method

Equipment

Knives:
N/A

Tools:
Mixing bowls, whisk,
wooden spatula, toothpicks

Pans:
Muffin pans

Serving/Yield

2 ½ pounds/1.3 kilograms
of muffin batter, makes
about 12 muffins

The quantities of the basic muffin recipe can be adjusted according to taste. For a more cakelike texture, the oil can be substituted with butter and the amount of sugar can be increased as well.

Muffins can be flavored in a variety of ways; including chocolate chips and fruits such as fresh or frozen blueberries, bananas, apples, or raisins. Following the proportions of the recipe above, you can flavor your muffins by adding about 1 cup any desired ingredient. To avoid over-mixing, add the extra ingredients to the muffin batter after the dry and the wet ingredients have had only a few good strokes of the mixing spoon. The batter should be just mixed by the time any ingredients are incorporated.

The flour can also be cut with other flours such as whole wheat, corn, or oat bran to change the consistency of your muffins.

BASIC MUFFIN

Method

Preheat the oven to 350°F (175°C).
1. Lightly grease a muffin pan.
2. Sift (**tamiser**) the flour, sugar, baking powder, baking soda, and salt together in a bowl. Mix until combined.
3. In another bowl, whisk together the egg, milk, vanilla, and oil.
4. Pour the liquid mixture into the dry ingredients and stir until just combined. You should still see traces of the flour.
5. Scoop the mixture into the prepared muffin pans, about two-thirds full, and bake until a toothpick inserted into the center of a muffin comes out clean, about 20 to 25 minutes.

Quantity		Ingredient
U.S.	**Metric**	
1 lb	500 g	Flour
4 oz	120 g	Sugar, granulated
¼ oz	5 g	Baking powder
¼ oz	5 g	Baking soda
Dash	Dash	Salt
1 pc	1 pc	Egg
1 pint	500 ml	Milk
4 fl oz	120 ml	Oil
¼ fl oz	5 ml	Vanilla extract

Learning Outcomes

Making a bi-colored cake
Using marzipan

Equipment

Knives:
Serrated knife *(couteau-scie)*, small palette knife *(petit spatule)*

Tools:
Mixing bowl, sieve, whisk, rolling pin

Pans:
8 x 8 in. square cake pan

Serving/Yield

6–8 servings

HISTORY

Although the exact origin is uncertain, it is widely believed that the Battenberg cake was created in 1884 for the royal wedding of Princess Victoria of England to the German Prince Louis von Battenberg. The 4 squares of this exquisitely delicate, checkerboard cake are said to have represented the four princes of Germany. It is interesting to note that although the current British Royal family is descended from the Battenberg line, the name *Battenberg* remains virtually unknown in England. This is due to the wave of anti-German sentiment that swept Britain at the onset of World War I. This sentiment became so virulent that the Royal family was forced to change its name from the German House of Saxe-Coburg and Gotha to the House of Windsor. The Prince Louis von Battenberg also felt the anti-German pressure and changed his name to *Mountbatten* (*berg* being German for "mountain"). Under the name Mountbatten, he achieved fame as commander of the British navy in World War I. Despite the anonymity of the name, the beautifully decorated and delicious Battenberg cake remains extremely popular in England to this day.

BATTENBERG CAKE

Method

Preheat the oven to 350°F (180°C).

1. Lightly coat the cake pan with butter and flour (*chemiser*).
2. Sift together the flour, baking powder, and salt (*tamiser*). Set the sifted ingredients aside.
3. Cream (*crémer*) together the butter and sugar, then add the eggs one at a time, mixing well after each addition. Mix in the vanilla, then add the flour and mix it all together until it is well combined. Add milk to the mixture to form a thick batter.
4. Divide batter into 2 halves. Color 1 half with the pink food coloring and the other half with yellow food coloring. Place a strip of foil in the center of the pan and pour the batters in each half.
5. Bake until the cake springs back when touched and a knife tip inserted in the center comes out clean, about 25 minutes. Remove from the oven, allow to cool for a few minutes, and then carefully unmold onto a wire rack. Carefully separate the 2 cakes and set aside to cool.
6. Trim the tops of the cakes flat with a serrated knife. Stack the 2 parts of the cake and trim the long sides so that each layer is twice as wide as it is tall. Place the pink layer onto the work surface and spread with a thin layer of apricot jam.
7. Turn the yellow layer over and place on top. The cooked sides of the cake will be on the top and on the bottom. Cut in half lengthwise. Lay 1 half down with the cut side facing upwards so that you have a yellow strip on the left and spread with a thin layer of apricot jam. Turn the other half around and place cut side down, so that you are laying a pink strip on top of the yellow strip. Press the sides to even.
8. Roll out the marzipan in a rectangle that is the width of the length of the cake and long enough to cover the 4 sides. Coat the outside of the cake with a thin layer of apricot jam, then place in the center of the marzipan. Bring 1 side up and gently lay over the top of the cake. Press the side gently to remove any air bubbles and trim the edge of the marzipan so it covers three-quarters of the top. Bring the other side up and repeat. Allow the marzipan to overlap by about ¼ in. (0.5 cm) and press to seal. Gently turn the cake so the seam is on the bottom.
9. Trim the ends in order to show the four squares of cake.

Quantity		Ingredient
U.S.	Metric	
5 oz	150 g	Flour
1 pinch	1 pinch	Baking powder
1 pinch	1 pinch	Salt
5 oz	150 g	Butter
5 oz	150 g	Sugar, granulated
3 pcs	3 pcs	Eggs
¼ fl oz	5 ml	Vanilla extract
1 fl oz	30 ml	Milk
3 drops	3 drops	Pink food coloring
3 drops	3 drops	Yellow food coloring
		Finishing
1 lb	500 g	Marzipan
7 oz	200 g	Apricot jam

Learning Outcomes

Making biscotti

Equipment

Knives:
Serrated knife *(couteau-scie)*

Tools:
Parchment paper, whisk,
wire rack

Pans:
Baking sheet

Serving/Yield

About 2 pounds/
1 kilogram portion
of dough

HISTORY

Biscotti are the famous Italian hard biscuits that are often infused with nuts, especially almonds. The word *biscotti* stems from the Latin words *bis*, which means "twice" and *coctus*, which means "cooked." This name perfectly describes biscotti—the twice-baked method of preparation is one of the defining features of these biscuits and is what makes them so hard. Baking these biscuits twice eliminates virtually all the moisture in them and also has the effect of preserving them for a very long time. Historically, this has made the biscotti very popular with people travelling long distances, particularly soldiers and sailors. The Roman army referred to these biscuits as "Parthian bread" and the great Roman historian Pliny the Elder once made the claim that they could "last for centuries." Modern biscotti are most often eaten accompanying coffee, tea, or wine, as the dryness of the biscuit makes them difficult to swallow without an accompanying beverage.

BISCOTTI

Method

Preheat the oven to 350°F (180°C).

1. Line a baking sheet with parchment paper.
2. Mix flour, sugar, baking powder, and salt together. Then make a well (**fontaine**) in the center of the mixture.
3. Whisk together the eggs and vanilla, then pour the mixture into the well.
4. Gradually stir and incorporate the flour and then the almonds.
5. Form the dough into a log and place it onto the prepared baking sheet and flatten.

Note

If the dough is too soft, chill it in the refrigerator until it becomes firm.

6. Bake the biscotti for approximately 25 minutes or until they are golden brown and dry to the touch. Remove the biscotti from the oven and slide the parchment onto a wire rack, allowing them to cool until warm.
7. Reduce the oven's temperature to 325°F (162°C).
8. Transfer the dough to a cutting board. Using a serrated knife, cut the dough into thick slices. Then arrange the slices on a clean baking sheet. Place them back in the oven and bake them for approximately 15 to 20 minutes, until the biscotti are completely dry. Store in an airtight container.

Quantity		Ingredient
U.S.	Metric	
14 ¼ oz	425 g	Flour
4 ¼ oz	225 g	Sugar, granulated
¼ oz	6 g	Baking powder
Pinch	Pinch	Salt
3 pcs	3 pcs	Eggs
¼ fl oz	5 ml	Vanilla
5 oz	150 g	Whole raw almonds

Learning Outcomes

Making a bread pudding
Making a custard
Baking in a bain-marie

Equipment

Knives:
N/A

Tools:
Mixing bowls, whisk,
bain-marie, sieve

Pans:
Saucepan, ovenproof dish

Serving/Yield

4 servings

HISTORY

The story of bread and butter pudding is one of truly humble beginnings. Like many early desserts that incorporated bread, the pudding was initially used as a way for people in a time of meager resources to use up stale bread. In the 13th century, bread pudding was referred to as "poor man's pudding." Like many desserts that were created out of necessity rather than taste, the bread and butter pudding has evolved over time into a rich and decadent traditional English favorite. The addition of ingredients such as sugar, custard, currants, and butter have transformed this meager, money-saving dish into a deliciously waist-expanding, traditional favorite.

BREAD AND BUTTER PUDDING

Method

Preheat the oven to 300°F (150°C).

1. Heat the milk to 140°F (60°C). Whisk together the eggs, sugar, and salt. Whisk in the hot milk and then strain the mixture.
2. Spread the butter on the bread slices. Then layer the bread with the sultanas in an ovenproof dish. Slowly pour the milk mixture over the bread slices.
3. Place in a bain-marie and bake gently for 30 minutes. Dust with powdered sugar and continue baking another 30 minutes or until set.

Quantity		Ingredient
U.S.	**Metric**	
1 pint	500 ml	Milk
3 pcs	3 pcs	Eggs
2 oz	60 g	Sugar, granulated
Pinch	Pinch	Salt
8 slices	8 slices	White bread
3 ¼ oz	100 g	Butter, softened
2 oz	60 g	Sultana raisins
3 ¼ oz	100 g	Powdered sugar for dusting

Learning Outcomes

Making chocolate brownies

Equipment

Knives:
Paring knife *(couteau d'office)*

Tools:
Mixing bowls, bain-marie, rubber spatula, wire rack

Pans:
Two 9 in. x 9 in. *(23 x 23 cm)* square pans

Serving/Yield

About 32 individual servings

HISTORY

The brownie is a chewy and chocolaty hybrid, combining all of the richness of a cake and the portability of a cookie. There are several competing theories about the origins of the brownie, with many attributing the creation to a fortuitous accident involving a botched cake recipe. The real story is likely that the brownie evolved from other similar chocolate confections of the early 1900s. What is known is that the brownie was created in America around the turn of the 20th century. The first published brownie recipe that is similar to modern recipes appeared in the 1906 version of the *Boston Cooking School Cook Book* by Fannie Merritt Farmer. Even the origins of the name *brownie* have been disputed. Some say that the dessert was created by a person name "Brownie," while others attribute the name to a similar Scottish preparation called a *broonie*. While other origins might be more interesting, the name is most likely derived from the chocolate-brown color of the brownie.

BROWNIES

Method

Preheat the oven to 375°F (190°C).

1. Butter and flour (*chemiser*) two 9 in. x 9 in. (23 x 23 cm) square pans.

2. Sift (*tamiser*) the flour with the salt.

3. Cut or break the chocolate into small pieces. Place them in a heatproof bowl and add the butter, also cut into small pieces. Place the bowl over a bain-marie and allow the butter and chocolate to gently melt together, stirring occasionally with a wooden spatula.

4. Once both the chocolate and the butter have melted, remove the bowl from the heat and stir until smooth. Allow to cool slightly.

5. Add the sugar and mix in well. Add the eggs, one at a time, mixing well after each addition. Mix in the vanilla, then add the flour and stir until a smooth but thick batter forms.

6. Divide the batter between the 2 pans, smoothing out the top and pushing it into the corners. Place the pans in the preheated oven to bake until the surface feels dry and the tip of a small knife inserted in the center comes out barely clean, about 35 to 40 minutes.

7. Remove from the oven and allow to cool on a wire rack before gently unmolding.

Quantity		Ingredient
U.S.	Metric	
8 oz	250 g	Unsweetened chocolate
8 oz	250 g	Butter
15 ¾ oz	475 g	Sugar, granulated
5 pcs	5 pcs	Eggs
½ fl oz	10 ml	Vanilla extract
8 oz	250 g	Flour
¼ oz	6 g	Salt

Learning Outcomes

Making an oil-based cake
Baking with vegetables
Making marzipan
decorations

Equipment

Knives:
Serrated knife *(couteau-scie)*, palette knife *(spatule)*

Tools:
Parchment paper, grater, mixing bowls, whisk, plastic spatula, sieve, piping bag, small star tip

Pans:
One 10 in. (25 cm) round cake pan, small pan

Serving/Yield

One 10 in. (25 cm) cake

The roots of carrot cake can be traced back to the carrot puddings made by the people of medieval Europe. At that time, sweeteners were rare and extremely costly, so carrots were often used as an alternative because they are one of the sweetest vegetables. As sweeteners became more easily accessible and cheaper, the popularity of carrot-based preparations declined sharply. The carrot cake's place in history as a dessert of necessity seemed to be reinforced when it made a huge revival during World War II. As food rationing came into effect, the British Ministry of Food launched a major campaign to popularize the carrot as a dessert sweetener (carrots being one of the only abundant food sources available in England at the time) throughout the war. Fortunately, carrot cake soared in popularity during the 1960s and 1970s as health consciousness increased and people embraced the carrot cake as a healthy dessert. This notion was generally misguided, however, as the ample sugar and rich icings called for in most recipes make the carrot cake no healthier than any other form of cake. Thanks to this erroneous idea, the carrot cake remains one of the most delicious and popular cakes today.

CARROT CAKE

Method

Preheat the oven to 325°F (160°C).

Make a Carrot Cake

1. Lightly grease a pan with butter, then line the bottom with parchment paper and coat it with flour (**chemiser**).
2. Sift (**tamiser**) the flour, salt, cinnamon, baking soda, and baking powder together in a large bowl.
3. Whisk together the sugar and oil. Add the eggs one at a time, mixing the combination well after each additional egg is added.
4. Take a small pan and lightly toast the walnuts until slightly browned. Once toasted allow the walnuts to cool and then chop coarsely. Set the walnuts aside.
5. Peel the carrots and grate (**râpper**) them finely. Set the grated carrots aside.
6. Mix the sifted ingredients into the egg mixture. Then add the grated carrots and toasted walnuts and fold them in well with a large plastic spatula.
7. Pour the batter into the prepared pan and bake until a knife tip inserted in the center comes out clean, about 35 to 40 minutes. Allow to cool slightly before unmolding onto a wire rack to finish cooling.

Cream Cheese Icing

1. Sift the powdered sugar to remove any lumps. Place the cream cheese and butter into a bowl and blend them together. Then slowly add the powdered sugar to the mixture and continue to blend the ingredients together until the mixture is smooth and fluffy.

Make Marzipan Carrots

1. Separate ⅓ of the marzipan. Knead enough of the orange food coloring into the larger section of marzipan for it to assume the desired carrot color. Then knead enough of the green food coloring into the second section of marzipan to create the desired green carrot stalk color. Shape the marzipan into carrot shapes and stalk shapes. Then add any desired decorative details to the marzipan carrots using a toothpick.

Assembly

1. Once completely cooled, if needed, trim the top of the carrot cake to flatten. Turn over onto a cake board or serving plate and slice the cake into two

Quantity		Ingredient
U.S.	**Metric**	*Cake*
9 ¼ oz	280 g	Bread flour
⅛ oz	3 g	Salt
¾ oz	25 g	Cinnamon
⅛ oz	3 g	Baking soda
Dash	Dash	Baking powder
14 oz	420 g	Sugar, granulated
6 fl oz	180 ml	Vegetable oil
4 pcs	4 pcs	Eggs
1 lb	500 g	Carrots, peeled and grated
2 ½ oz	75 g	Walnuts, toasted
		Icing
8 oz	250 g	Cream cheese
8 oz	250 g	Powdered sugar
4 oz	120 g	Butter
		Marzipan Decoration (Optional)
6 oz	180 g	Marzipan
As needed	As needed	Green food coloring
As needed	As needed	Orange food coloring

Method

layers. Remove the top layer and set aside. Spread a layer of the cream cheese frosting on the bottom layer, then cover with the top layer. Cover the sides and top of the cake with a thin layer of the frosting. Place in the refrigerator for 15 to 20 minutes to set. This is called the crumb coat.

2. Once set, spread a layer of frosting on the sides and the top and smooth. Transfer the remaining frosting to a piping bag fitted with a small star tip. Pipe rosettes on the top of the cake and along the bottom.

3. Finish by decorating with the marzipan carrots.

Learning Outcomes

Sponge method
Braiding dough

Equipment

Knives:
Dough cutter or chef's
knife *(couteau chef)*

Tools:
Medium and large mixing
bowls, pastry brush, wooden
spatula, parchment paper,
wire rack

Pans:
Heavy baking sheets

Serving/Yield

Three 1 lb (454 g) loaves

Challah is a delicious, braided, egg-based bread that is traditionally used in Jewish religious ceremonies. In Hebrew, there are two words for bread: *lechem* and *challah*. The first type of bread is the common form, which is eaten daily, whereas the second is supposed to be eaten only on the Sabbath and on Holy days. In Jewish households, it is tradition to bake two loaves of challah that represent the loaves of bread (manna) that fell from God to preserve the Israelites as they wandered the desert for 40 years after their exodus from Egypt. Another aspect of the ceremonial uses of the challah is the tradition of separating a section of the dough to be burned. This practice stems from the ancient Judean tradition of removing a section of challah for the high priests of the Temple of Jerusalem. When the temple was destroyed by the Romans in 70 AD, the section of challah began to be burned as a sacrifice to commemorate it. In the modern age, the challah has lost much of its religious significance outside of Jewish Orthodox sects. The Jews who fled Eastern Europe during WWII brought the challah with them to America. The bread is now enjoyed daily by Jews and Gentiles alike and remains one of the most popular deli breads used for sandwich making.

CHALLAH

Method

Make the Sponge Portion of Dough

1. Add the yeast and lukewarm water [*max 90°F (32°C)*] into a medium-sized mixing bowl and stir until the yeast dissolves. Stir in the honey and the 4 oz (120 g) portion of bread flour. Stir until a smooth mixture forms and then set aside to develop.

2. In a separate large bowl, mix together 8 oz (250 g) of bread flour with the oil, egg yolks, honey, and enough of the water to form a smooth mixture. Add the sponge portion of dough and mix it in well.

3. Add the remaining quantity of flour with the salt and the remaining water. Work the dough until it becomes smooth, about 10 minutes. Place it into a lightly oiled bowl, cover and allow the dough to ferment in a warm place (80°F/27°C) until it has doubled in volume, approximately 90 minutes.

4. Punch the dough down, divide it in 2 and allow it to rest.

5. Shape each piece into a log and cut into 3 or 4 equal sections. Flatten down each piece with the heel of your hand. Lift the top edge of the dough and fold it down to the center, pressing to seal. Then lift the bottom edge of the dough, bringing it up to the center and pinching to seal. Place both hands flat in the center of the log and roll back and forth while moving your hands outward, all the way to the ends.

6. Repeat this several times until you have an evenly shaped strand. Cover and set aside to rest for about 20 to 30 minutes. This will allow the gluten to relax so you can finish rolling out the strands.

7. Roll the dough using the same technique until each strand is about 1 in. (2 cm) in diameter and approximately the same length. If using 3 strands, pinch the 3 pieces of dough together, tucking in the end.

8. Braid the dough by bringing the outer strand over the middle strand, alternating the right and left strands. Once you reach the end, pinch the dough together and tuck underneath.

Note

For a 4-strand braid, refer to pages 239–240 in Pâtisserie and Baking Foundations.

9. Place the finished braid on a parchment paper-lined baking sheet.

Preheat the oven to 400°F (200°C).

10. Beat the egg in a small bowl. Lightly brush the surface of the challah, and then sprinkle it with poppy seeds. Place the dough in the preheated oven and bake it until golden, about 35 to 40 minutes.

11. Transfer to a wire rack and allow to cool.

Quantity		Ingredient
U.S.	Metric	
4 fl oz	120 mL	Water, lukewarm [*max 90°F (32°C)*]
3 oz	90 g	Yeast
½ fl oz	15 ml	Honey
4 oz	120 g	Bread flour
8 oz	250 g	Bread flour
6 fl oz	180 ml	Oil
5 pcs	5 pcs	Egg yolks
2 fl oz	60 ml	Honey
16 fl oz	480 ml	Water
2 lbs	1 kg	Bread flour
½ oz	15 g	Salt
1 pc	1 pc	Egg (for egg wash)
As needed	As needed	Poppy seeds

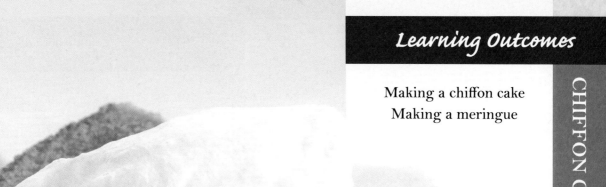

Learning Outcomes

Making a chiffon cake
Making a meringue

Equipment

Knives:
N/A

Tools:
Mixing bowls, sieve, plastic
spatula, whisk, wire rack

Pans:
10 in. (25 cm) tube pan

Serving/Yield

1 cake

Although most recipes covered in this book were created long ago by master chefs, the chiffon cake was created relatively recently by a skilled amateur. The cake was invented in 1927 by the aptly named Harry Baker, an American insurance salesman and avid baker from Los Angeles. For years, Mr. Baker guarded his secret recipe and sold his cakes as a caterer in Hollywood. Then, in the early 1940s, Mr. Baker sold his cake recipe to the General Mills Corporation for a hefty sum. By 1948, Generals Mills began selling the chiffon cake under its Betty Crocker line, promoting it heavily and proclaiming it to be the "first new cake in a hundred years." The biggest innovation of the chiffon cake (and the secret that Mr. Baker guarded so closely) was the use of vegetable oil instead of butter for the first time in a cake recipe. The oil allows the cake to rise and be light and fluffy, while still retaining the moistness that can often be lacking in similar non oil-based cakes, such as the angel food cake.

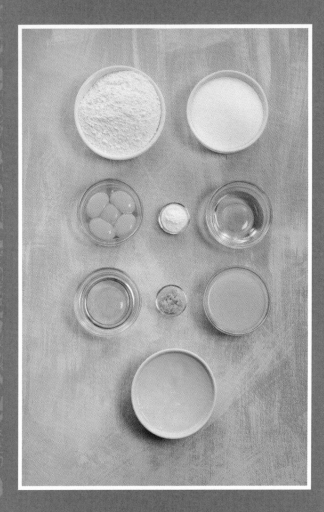

Quantity		Ingredient
U.S.	Metric	
10 oz	300 g	Cake flour
10 oz	300 g	Sugar, granulated
½ oz	15 g	Baking powder
4 ¼ fl oz	125 ml	Vegetable oil
3 fl oz	90 ml	Egg yolks
2 fl oz	60 ml	Water
1 pc	1 pc	Lemon zest
4 ¼ fl oz	125 ml	Lemon juice
8 fl oz	250 ml	Egg whites

CHIFFON CAKE

Method

Preheat the oven to 325°F (170°C).

1. Sift (*tamiser*) together the cake flour, baking powder, and half of the sugar into a large bowl.
2. Place the vegetable oil, egg yolks, water, lemon juice, and lemon zest in a bowl and then whisk until well combined.

Make a Meringue

3. Beat the egg whites to firm peaks (*monter les blancs*), then gradually whisk in the sugar. Continue whisking until glossy and tight and you no longer feel any sugar granules when rubbing meringue between your fingers.
4. Form a well (*fontaine*) in the sifted ingredients and pour in the egg yolk mixture. Then stir the combination until a batter forms, being careful not to over-stir (you should still see traces of flour). Then fold the egg white mixture into the batter using a large plastic spatula.
5. Pour the cake mixture into the 10 in. (25 cm) tube pan and bake until a skewer inserted in the center comes out clean, about 50 minutes. Remove from the oven and invert the cake onto a wire rack and allow to cool completely.

Learning Outcomes

Creaming method

Equipment

Knives:
N/A

Tools:
Mixing bowl, sieve, wooden spatula, spoon or scoop, wire rack

Pans:
Baking sheets

Serving/Yield

About 2 dozen 2 oz/ 50 g cookies

HISTORY

The iconic chocolate chip cookie is one of the most popular, most delicious, and simplest cookies in the world. It is somewhat surprising how recently it was created. The cookie was invented in 1930 by Ruth Graves Wakefield, the owner of the Tollhouse Inn in Whitman, Massachusetts. The story goes that Mrs. Wakefield was beginning a batch of chocolate cookies. After preparing the dough, she realized that she had run out of baker's chocolate. She began breaking up a semi-sweet bar of Nestlé chocolate into the dough, thinking it would melt evenly into the cookies upon baking. Instead of melting, the chocolate only softened and the result was an amazingly chewy and delicious new preparation. This new cookie soon became immensely popular in her restaurant, prompting Mrs. Wakefield to approach the Nestlé Corporation with her new use for its chocolate. She sold the company her recipe, which they began putting on all bags of chocolate chips in exchange for her own free lifetime supply. Enjoyed on its own or with a tall glass of milk, the chocolate chip cookie remains a delicious favorite all over the world.

CHOCOLATE CHIP COOKIES

Method

Preheat the oven to 350°F (175°C).

1. Sift (*tamiser*) together the flour, salt, and baking soda.
2. Cream (*crémer*) together the butter and sugars until well combined. Add the eggs one at a time, mixing well after each addition. Add the vanilla.
3. Stir in the flour and mix until homogenous. Stir in the chocolate chips and nuts.
4. Using a spoon or a scoop, arrange 2 oz (50 g) balls of dough 2 in. (5 cm) apart on a lightly greased baking sheet.
5. Bake for 8 to 10 minutes or until the cookies begin to brown at the edges. Remove from the oven and transfer the hot cookies to a wire rack to cool.

Quantity		Ingredient
U.S.	Metric	
10 oz	300 g	Flour
¼ oz	5 g	Baking soda
¼ oz	5 g	Salt
6 oz	180 g	Butter
5 oz	150 g	Sugar, granulated
5 oz	150 g	Brown sugar
3 fl oz	90 ml	Eggs
¼ fl oz	5 mL	Vanilla, extract
10 oz	300 g	Chocolate chips
4 oz	120 g	Walnuts or pecans

Learning Outcomes

Making a sweet yeast dough
Shaping a roll
Sponge method
Glazing

Equipment

Knives:
Chef's knife *(couteau chef)*

Tools:
Mixing bowls, mixing spoon, pastry brush, kitchen towel

Pans:
9 in. (23 cm) round pan or large muffin pan

Serving/Yield

Approximately 6 rolls

The delicious flavor of cinnamon has been sought after and utilized in the culinary arts for centuries. In the Middle Ages, cinnamon was extremely rare in Europe and only the highest aristocracy could afford it. It was likely during this period that the first combination of bread and cinnamon took place, as fritters of dough were often infused with exotic spices. The roots of the cinnamon roll as we know it today are thought to stem from Sweden. There, the cinnamon roll is known as *kanelbulle*, which literally translates to "cinnamon bun," and the Swedes have even dedicated October 4 as their "National Cinnamon Bun Day." Along with Sweden, America also has a long tradition of enjoying cinnamon rolls. The American version is the one more commonly known globally, and contains heavier icings and is much sweeter than the Swedish original. This version likely originated from Scandinavian immigrants in Philadelphia in the 1800s.

CINNAMON ROLLS

Method

Make the Sponge Portion of Dough

1. Sift (**tamiser**) the flour and sugar and set aside.
2. Add the yeast and lukewarm water [*max 90°F (32°C)*] to a large bowl and stir until the yeast dissolves and the mixture is smooth. Add the sugar and the 3 oz (100 g) portion of pastry flour, stirring until smooth. Cover with a kitchen towel and set aside to develop, approximately 20 to 30 minutes.
3. Cream the butter and sugar together (**crémer**). Add the egg and mix in well. Add the sponge portion of dough, milk, and salt, stirring until smooth. Add the flour and mix until combined, about 5 minutes. Cover and allow to ferment until doubled in volume, approximately 1 ½ to 2 hours.
4. Once the dough has risen, punch it down and turn it out onto a clean work surface, allowing it to rest for about 20 minutes. Butter a round baking pan or large muffin pan.
5. Roll the dough (**abaisser**) into a large rectangle, about ¼ in. (½ cm) thick. Spread the butter over it and sprinkle it with cinnamon and sugar. Roll the dough tightly and pinch the seam shut. Cut the roll into 6 X 1 in. (2 cm) thick slices. Arrange the slices on their sides and set aside to proof until doubled in size.

Preheat the oven to 400°F (200°F).

6. Bake the cinnamon rolls until they become golden, approximately 20 to 30 minutes.
7. Brush with apricot glaze or drizzle with melted fondant to finish.

Quantity		Ingredient
U.S.	Metric	
3 ½ oz	100 g	Pastry flour
2 oz	60 g	Sugar, granulated
· 2 fl oz	60 ml	Water, lukewarm [*max 90°F (32°C)*]
1 oz	30 g	Yeast
⅓ oz	10 g	Cinnamon
2 oz	60 g	Butter, softened (en pommade)
1 pc	1 pc	Egg
¼ oz	5 g	Sugar
6 ¾ fl oz	200 ml	Milk
20 oz	600 g	Bread flour
⅛ oz	3 g	Salt
As needed	As needed	Apricot glaze
As needed	As needed	Fondant, melted

Equipment

Knives:
Serrated knife *(couteau-scie)*, palette knife *(spatule)*

Tools:
Mixing bowls, sieve, whisk, pastry brush, wooden or rubber spatula, pastry bag, small star tip

Pans:
10 in. (25 cm) round cake pan

Serving/Yield

One 10 in. (25 cm) cake

The devil's food cake is a light and airy chocolate cake with a rich and decadent chocolate ganache frosting. The cake likely gained its demonic sounding name from the perceived "sinfulness" of indulging in its rich chocolate flavor. It also seems that the cake was appropriately named to serve as the counterpart of its close relative, the angel food cake. The angel food cake predates the devil's food cake, and while both cakes have a light and airy consistency, the angel cake is white in color and vanilla flavored, whereas the devil's cake is dark in color and chocolate flavored. The first written mention of the devil's food cake appears in the 1906 publication by Sarah Tyson Rorer entitled *Mrs. Rorer's New Cook Book*. Early recipes often used the names *devil's food cake* and *red velvet cake* interchangeably to describe this cake. This is because of the reddish hue the cake adopts during the baking process as the cocoa and baking powders interact chemically. Whatever name you choose to call it, the devil's food cake remains a devilishly delicious indulgence.

DEVIL'S FOOD CAKE

Method

Preheat the oven to 350°F (180°C).

1. Sift (*tamiser*) together the flour, cocoa powder, baking soda, and salt.
2. Cream (*crémer*) together the butter, sugar, and brown sugar. Add the eggs one at a time, mixing well after each addition. Add the vanilla and the buttermilk. Mix until smooth and then, lastly, whisk in the hot water. Pour the batter into the prepared cake pan and place in the center rack of the preheated oven. Bake until the tip of a paring knife inserted in the center comes out clean, approximately 30 minutes.
3. Remove from the oven and allow to cool a few minutes before gently unmolding onto a wire rack to finish cooling.

Ganache

1. Break the dark chocolate into pieces and place them in a bowl. Heat the cream and sugar in a saucepan. When the cream comes to a boil and the sugar has melted, pour it over the chocolate. Allow to sit for a few minutes, then gently stir until smooth using a wooden or rubber spatula. Add the butter and continue stirring until incorporated. Place in the refrigerator until it is thick enough to spread, approximately 20 to 30 minutes.

Assembly

1. If the cake has domed too much while baking, slice the top off horizontally evening the surface.
2. Place the cake upside down on a cake board or serving platter. Split the cake in 2 and then gently lift off the top half and set aside.
3. Spread the bottom half with about one-third of the ganache. Cover with the top layer of cake. Coat the sides and top with a thin layer of ganache and place in the refrigerator to set, for about 15 to 20 minutes.
4. Remove from the refrigerator and cover the sides with a thicker layer of ganache, finishing with the top. Smooth with a palette knife.
5. Transfer the remaining ganache to a piping bag fitted with a small star tip. Pipe a decorative edge along the top and base of the cake. Keep chilled until ready to serve.

Quantity		Ingredient
U.S.	Metric	
10 oz	300 g	Cake flour, sifted
1 ¾ oz	50 g	Cocoa powder
¼ oz	5 g	Baking soda
Pinch	Pinch	Salt
4 oz	120 g	Butter
7 ½ oz	225 g	Sugar, granulated
7 oz	200 g	Brown sugar
2 pcs	2 pcs	Eggs
½ fl oz	10 ml	Vanilla, extract
4 fl oz	120 ml	Buttermilk
4 fl oz	120 ml	Hot water
		Ganache
23 oz	600 g	Dark chocolate
1 pint	500 ml	Cream
2 oz	60 g	Butter, room temperature
2 oz	60 g	Sugar

Learning Outcomes

Separated egg sponge
Multi-layered cake
Cooked sugar

Equipment

Knives:
Palette knife *(spatule)*,
paring knife *(couteau d'office)* or scissors

Tools:
Mixing bowls, whisk,
rubber spatula, parchment
paper, pastry brush, piping
bag, medium round tip

Pans:
Heavy saucepan, baking
sheets, wire rack

Serving/Yield

One 10 in. (25 cm) cake

HISTORY

The dobos sponge cake is a delicious and delicately layered cake covered with an ornate caramel topping. The cake was created by the famed Hungarian chef József Dobos in 1884. The cake was unveiled at the National General Exhibition of Budapest in 1885 where it was presented to the Emperor and Empress of the Austro-Hungarian Empire, Franz Joseph I and Elizabeth of Bavaria. József Dobos was the proprietor of a specialty food shop in Budapest that was renown throughout Europe. Dobos was also a brilliant inventor and he was able to design a special form of packaging that allowed him to ship orders for his cakes all over Europe. Many attempted to reproduce his popular cake without luck and, after a lifetime of carefully guarding his recipe, he made the decision to bequeath it free of charge to the Budapest Pastry and Honey-bread Makers Guild in 1906. Chef Dobos is still considered a national hero in Hungary, which has held special celebrations honoring the creation of his wonderful cake.

| Quantity | | Ingredient |
U.S.	Metric	
6 oz	180 g	Almond paste
4 oz	120 g	Sugar, granulated
6 fl oz	180 ml	Egg yolks
6 oz	180 g	Cake flour
9 fl oz	270 ml	Egg whites
¼ oz	3 g	Salt
3 oz	90 g	Sugar
		Chocolate Butter Cream
6 oz	180 g	Sugar, granulated
2 fl oz	60 ml	Water
6 pcs	6 pcs	Egg yolks
12 oz	360 g	Butter, at room temperature
2 oz	60 g	Chocolate, melted
		Caramel Coating (329°F/155°C)
9 oz	270 g	Sugar
1 oz	30 g	Butter
As needed	As needed	Almonds (sliced and roasted)

DOBOS TORTE

Method

Preheat the oven to 425°F (220°C).

1. Draw 7 x 10 in. (25 cm) circles on parchment paper-lined baking sheets.
2. Mix the almond paste and sugar together. Gradually incorporate the egg yolks, one at a time, mixing well after each addition. Once incorporated, whisk in the flour.
3. Mount the egg whites (***monter les blancs***) with a pinch of salt and whisk until soft peaks form. Whisk in the sugar until the whites become tight and glossy and you can no longer feel the granules of sugar in the meringue. Gently fold into the almond mixture. Divide the batter evenly between the circles on the prepared baking sheets. Spread the batter evenly, being careful not to overwork it. Bake until lightly colored and dry to the touch, about 7 minutes. Remove and allow to cool on a wire rack. Once cooled, stack with parchment between each layer.

Make Chocolate Butter Cream

1. Prepare a small bowl of cold water with a spoon and clean pastry brush.
2. Place the sugar and water in a small saucepan and bring to a boil. When the sugar begins to boil, skim off any white foam that might rise to the surface and then brush down the sides of the pan with a wet brush. Once the syrup is clear, leave undisturbed to cook to the softball stage (***petit boule***) [235°F/115°C]. While the sugar is cooking, whisk the egg yolks in a bowl. Once the sugar has reached the softball stage, remove the pan from the heat and dip the bottom of the pan in cold water to stop the cooking process.
3. While whisking, incorporate the sugar in a thin, steady stream into the egg yolks, being careful to pour to the sides and not to pour onto the wires of the whisk. Once the sugar has been whisked in, continue whisking until the mixture has cooled to room temperature. Gradually incorporate the butter, whisking well after each addition. Continue whisking until smooth and light in color. Add melted chocolate and mix well.

Caramel Coating

1. Place a disk of the dobos sponge onto a baking sheet.
2. Prepare a small bowl of cold water with a spoon and clean pastry brush.

Method

3. Place the sugar and water into a small saucepan and bring to a boil. When the sugar begins to boil, skim off any white foam that might rise to the surface and brush down the sides of the pan with a wet brush. Once the syrup is clear, continue cooking until it becomes a light caramel color. Remove from the heat and then immediately add the butter, stirring until smooth. While still hot, spread the mixture evenly over the dobos sponge. Allow to set, but while still warm, trim the edges with a paring knife or scissors and cut the coated sponge into 8 to 10 wedges using an oiled knife. Set aside to finish cooling completely.

Assembly

1. If needed, trim the disks using a 10 in. (25 cm) ring mold and a paring knife.
2. Place a disk of sponge on a cake board and spread with a thin, even layer of butter cream. Top with a second disk and continue until all the layers have been assembled.
3. Mask the entire cake with butter cream and place in the refrigerator to set for about 15 to 20 minutes.
4. Mask the cake with a second layer of butter cream and press the toasted sliced almonds around the sides.
5. Lightly score the top of the cake with the back of a knife into wedges corresponding to the number of caramelized sponge.
6. Transfer the remaining butter cream to a piping bag fitted with a medium round tip and pipe a rosette in the center of each wedge.
7. Arrange the caramelized sponge by lining up with the marks and allow to rest on top of the rosette.

FLOURLESS CHOCOLATE CAKE

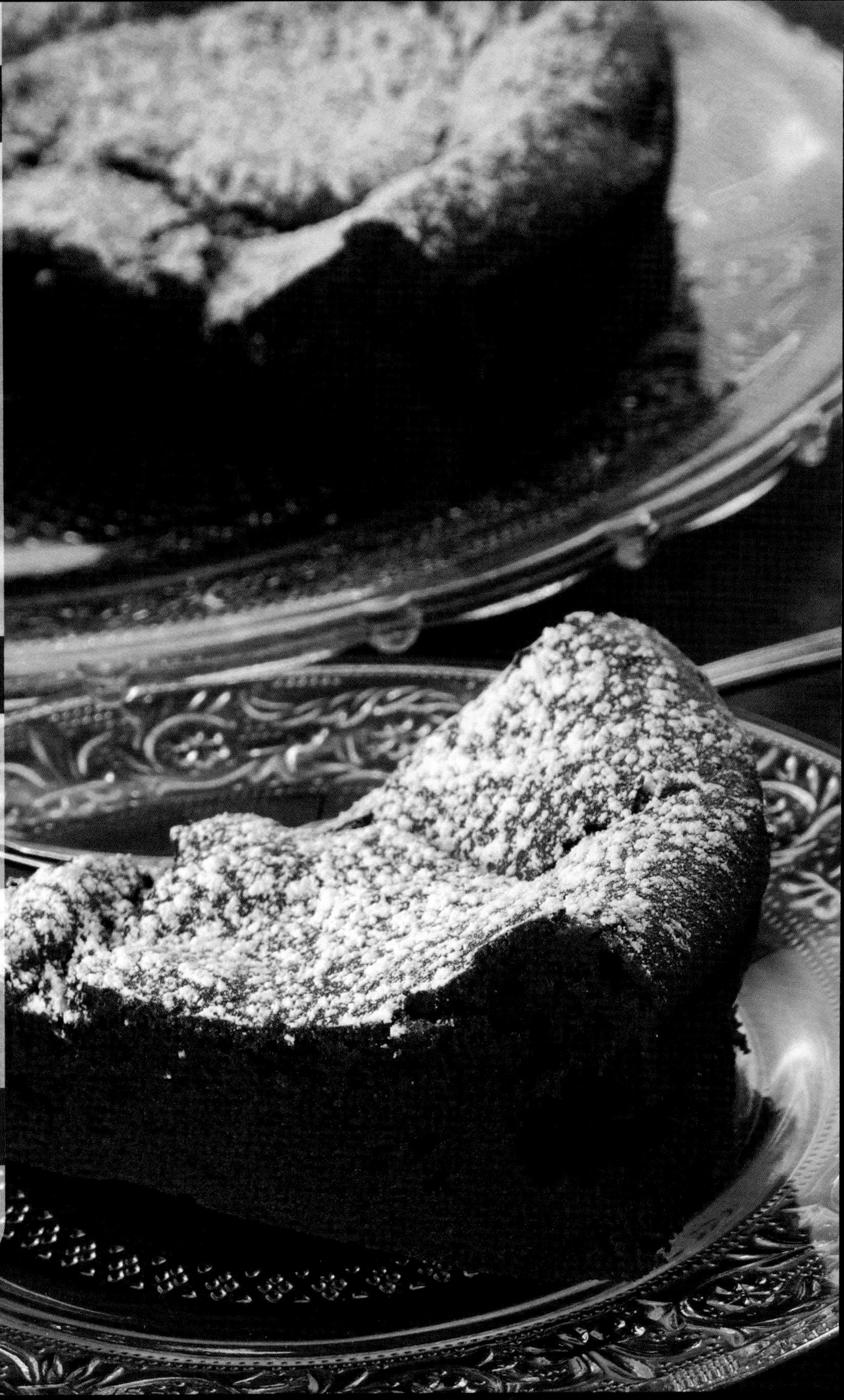

Learning Outcomes

Melting chocolate over a bain-marie
Making a meringue

Equipment

Knives:
N/A

Tools:
Mixing bowls, plastic spatula, whisk, bain-marie, parchment paper

Pans:
10 in. (25 cm) springform pan

Serving/Yield

8–12 servings

HISTORY

The flourless chocolate cake is a rich and decadent chocolate addict's dream. The lack of flour means this cake is composed mostly of butter, eggs, and chocolate, making it extremely dense and giving it a highly rich flavor. Although it is enjoyed by all chocolate lovers, this preparation's lack of flour makes it a particular favorite for people suffering from gluten allergies.

FLOURLESS CHOCOLATE CAKE

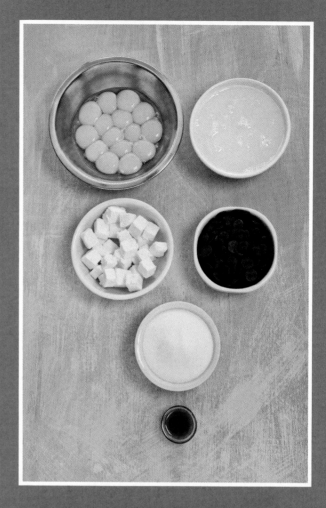

Method

Preheat the oven to 300°F (150°C).

1. Butter a 10 in. (25 cm) springform pan and line the bottom with parchment paper (**chemiser**).

2. Melt the butter and chocolate over a bain-marie, stirring the mixture until smooth. Once a smooth liquid has formed, remove the chocolate mixture from the heat and set it aside.

3. Beat the egg yolks with half of the sugar until it becomes light in color (**blanchir**), then stir in the vanilla.

4. Beat the egg whites to soft peaks (**monter les blancs**). Gradually beat in the sugar and continue mixing until the whites are smooth and glossy.

5. Add sugar to the egg yolks and fold it in until combined. Fold the egg whites into the yolk mixture.

6. Pour the batter into the prepared springform pan and bake the cake for 20 to 25 minutes, or until the batter has puffed up and the center jiggles slightly when the pan is shaken.

Quantity		Ingredient
U.S.	Metric	
6 oz	180 g	Butter
11 ¾ oz	350 g	Dark chocolate
8 oz	250 g	Sugar, granulated
15 pcs	15 pcs	Egg yolks
½ fl oz	10 mL	Vanilla
15 pcs	15 pcs	Egg whites

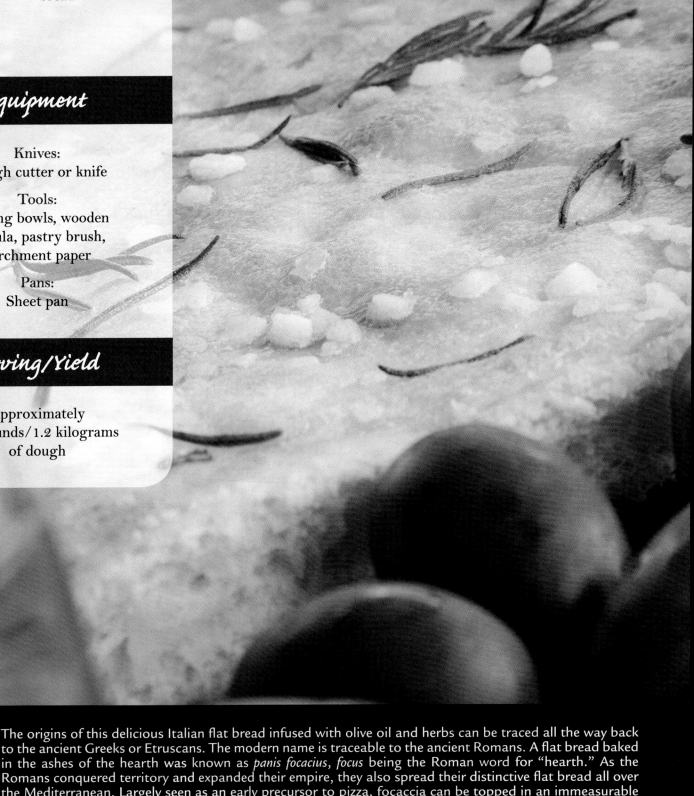

Learning Outcomes

Straight dough with sponge
Making a seasoned flat
bread

Equipment

Knives:
Dough cutter or knife

Tools:
Mixing bowls, wooden
spatula, pastry brush,
parchment paper

Pans:
Sheet pan

Serving/Yield

Approximately
2.5 pounds/1.2 kilograms
of dough

The origins of this delicious Italian flat bread infused with olive oil and herbs can be traced all the way back to the ancient Greeks or Etruscans. The modern name is traceable to the ancient Romans. A flat bread baked in the ashes of the hearth was known as *panis focacius*, *focus* being the Roman word for "hearth." As the Romans conquered territory and expanded their empire, they also spread their distinctive flat bread all over the Mediterranean. Largely seen as an early precursor to pizza, focaccia can be topped in an immeasurable number of ways and the preparation varies greatly based on regional traditions.

FOCACCIA

Method

Make the Sponge Portion of Dough

1. Sift (*tamiser*) the flour. Set aside.
2. Add the yeast and warm water to a bowl and stir until the yeast dissolves and the mixture is smooth. Add enough flour to make a smooth paste and then set aside to develop for 20 to 30 minutes.
3. Place the remaining flour into a large bowl and make a well in the center (*fontaine*). Add the salt, the second quantity of yeast, the sponge portion of dough, the oil, and the remaining water to the flour well. Mix until combined. The dough will be fairly soft at this point.
4. Cover the dough with a kitchen towel and set to ferment in a proofer until doubled in volume, approximately 30 to 40 minutes. Once the dough has risen, punch it down and then turn it out onto a clean work surface. Divide it into 2 to 3 equal pieces, cover it, and allow it to rest.
5. Oil a sheet pan and line it with parchment paper.
6. Roll the dough out (*abaisser*) to a thickness of about ½ in. (1 cm) and place it on the prepared sheet pan. Set aside and allow to rest until doubled in volume.

Preheat the oven to 350°F (180°C).

7. Make dimples in the dough, then brush it with olive oil. Sprinkle with sea salt and fresh rosemary.
8. Place the dough into the preheated oven and bake until golden, approximately 25 minutes.

Quantity		Ingredient
U.S.	**Metric**	
¼ oz	5 g	Fresh yeast
6 fl oz	180 ml	Water, lukewarm [*max 90°F (32°C)*]
20 oz	600 g	Bread flour
14 fl oz	420 ml	Water
¼ oz	5 g	Fresh yeast
½ oz	15 g	Salt
1 fl oz	30 ml	Olive oil
1 bunch	1 bunch	Rosemary
As needed	As needed	Sea salt

Learning Outcomes

Making a cobbler
Making a canned fruit
    filling

Equipment

Knives:
N/A

Tools:
Mixing bowls, wooden
spatula or spoon, 1 quart
baking dish

Pans:
Heavy-bottomed saucepan

Serving/Yield

One 3 pound/1.5 kilogram
fruit cobbler, 8–10 servings

The fruit cobbler was a dessert born out of necessity in a difficult time and place. The roots of the cobbler can be traced back to the American "Old West." The people of the American frontier used the cobbler as a simple hearty dessert that was extremely versatile, utilizing any type of fruit available to them. The name *cobbler* originally stems from people in the shoe repair trade, whose ability to assemble shoes spawned the term *cobbling* (throwing something together clumsily). The fruit cobbler gained its name from this term, and refers to the haphazard way the dessert is assembled. The cobbler is a true American favorite and is known by many other names (including crisps, crumbles, brown bettys, slumps, grunts, and buckles), depending on the area of the country. Served à la mode or on its own, this dessert is, without a doubt, comfort food at its finest.

FRUIT COBBLER

Method

Preheat the oven to 375°F (190°C).

1. Butter a 1 qt baking dish.
2. Sift (**tamiser**) the flour. Using your fingertips, incorporate the butter into the flour until it resembles a coarse meal.
3. Sift the sugar, salt, and the baking powder and then mix into the butter and flour. Make a well in the center and add the heavy cream. Gradually incorporate the dry ingredients until a dough forms. Set aside.

Make the Filling

1. Place all of the ingredients into a heavy-bottomed saucepan and mix well. Place over medium heat and bring to a low boil. Cook until the mixture thickens and the liquid becomes clear. Remove from the heat and allow to cool slightly.
2. Pour the filling into the prepared baking dish. Crumble the dough evenly over the top covering evenly. Dot with butter.
3. Bake until the dough is nicely colored and the fruit begins to bubble, approximately 25 to 35 minutes.

Quantity		Ingredient
U.S.	**Metric**	
5 oz	150 g	Butter
14 oz	400 g	Cake flour
6 oz	180 g	Sugar, granulated
⅓ oz	10 g	Salt
½ oz	15 g	Baking powder
5 fl oz	150 ml	Heavy cream
		Filling
10 oz	300 g	Canned fruit
3 fl oz	90 ml	Drained juice
1 fl oz	30 ml	Water
1 oz	30 g	Cornstarch
¾ fl oz	25 ml	Lemon juice
3 oz	90 g	Sugar
¼ oz	5 g	Salt
½ oz	15 g	Butter

Learning Outcomes

Making fudge

Equipment

Knives:
N/A

Tools:
Wooden spatula, candy thermometer

Pans:
8 x 8 in. (20 x 20 cm) cake pan, heavy-bottomed saucepan

Serving/Yield

1½ pound/680 gram portion of fudge

This ultra-sweet confection is thought to have been created by accident in America in the late 1900s. The polite expletive "Oh fudge!" pre-dates the candy and it is thought to have been the cry of a modest candy maker who ruined a batch of caramels and unwittingly created a delicious snack. From its unusual origins, fudge became a popular fixture of enterprising students at American women's colleges. The first written mention of the candy as "fudge" is found in a letter by Vassar College student Emelyn Battersby Hartridge, in which she described how a classmate's cousin had made 40 cents a pound selling fudge in Baltimore, Maryland. She decided to make her own fudge and sold it at her school's senior auction. The candy was a big hit and soon women from other colleges all over America were reproducing the recipe.

FUDGE

Method

1. Prepare an 8 X 8 in. (20 X 20 cm) pan by lining it with foil.
2. Place sugar, chocolate cut in small pieces, corn syrup, and cream in a heavy-bottomed saucepan. Stir until the chocolate has melted and mixture is combined. Place a candy thermometer in the mixture and cook to 238°F (115°C) without stirring. Once it reaches 238°F (115°C), remove from the heat.
3. Add the butter, salt, and vanilla, and allow to rest without stirring until the mixture cools to 110°F (43°C). Then beat with a wooden spoon until the mixture loses its shine and stiffens. Immediately transfer to the prepared pan and spread evenly.
4. Set aside to cool completely.
5. Once cooled, remove from the pan and cut into small squares.
6. Store in an airtight container.

Quantity		Ingredient
U.S.	*Metric*	
13 ¼ oz	400 g	Sugar, granulated
2 oz	60 g	Unsweetened chocolate
1 fl oz	30 ml	Corn syrup
5 ¼ fl oz	160 ml	Cream
1 oz	30 g	Butter
Dash	1 g	Salt
¼ fl oz	5 ml	Vanilla, extract

Learning Outcomes

Creaming method
Cutting shapes

Equipment

Knives:
N/A

Tools:
Mixing bowls, sieve, rolling
pin, cookie/biscuit cutters,
wire rack, spatula

Pans:
Baking sheet

Serving/Yield

4½ pounds/2 kilograms
of finished dough

HISTORY

Crusaders returning from the Middle East were the first to introduce Europe to gingerbread. European monks are generally credited for the proliferation and popularity of gingerbread, and often baked the much-loved spiced cookies during festivals and holy days. The name *gingerbread* is not actually derived from any etymological correlation to the word *bread*. These cookies are named for the preserved ginger that forms the underlying flavor that defines them. The Latin word for ginger is *zingebar* and it is from this root that the old French word *gingebras* originated. Over time, this evolved into the contemporary *gingerbread*. Gingerbread was often a staple food of European festivals that came to be known as gingerbread festivals. It was at these festivals where the tradition of selling wooden cutting instruments to create festive gingerbread shapes began. The most famous of these shapes are those used to build the intricate and ornate gingerbread houses, and making these houses has become a common Christmas tradition. Gingerbread houses first began to appear in 19th-century Germany after the publication of a Grimm fairytale about two children named Hansel and Gretel who are abandoned in the woods by their wicked stepmother. They wander around until they discover a house made of gingerbread that is decorated with candy. The Germans took their gingerbread very seriously and, for a long time, only a special gingerbread guild was allowed to produce any for sale. Due to this group's dedication, Germany soon emerged as the producer of the finest gingerbread (which they refer to as *lebkuchen*) in the world. The German tradition of making excellent gingerbread continues to this day, and the city of Nuremberg (the center of German gingerbread making) still has the reputation of being the best in the world.

GINGERBREAD

Method

Preheat the oven to 325°F (165°C).

1. Sift (*tamiser*) together the flour, baking soda, cinnamon, ginger, clove, and salt.
2. Cream (*crémer*) together the butter and brown sugar. Add the molasses and mix until smooth. Add the water to the butter mixture and stir it in well. At this point in the recipe, the mixture should resemble cottage cheese.
3. Add the sifted dry ingredients and mix in until a homogenous dough forms. Wrap the dough in plastic and allow to rest in a cool place for about 20 minutes.
4. On a lightly floured surface, roll the dough out (*abaisser*) to a thickness of about ⅛ in. (5 mm), using more flour as needed to prevent the dough from sticking.
5. Cut out the desired shapes and place them onto a heavy baking sheet, leaving about 1 in. (2.5 cm) apart. Bake until the cookies become fragrant and the edges begin to brown. Transfer to a wire rack to cool.

Quantity		Ingredient
U.S.	Metric	
37 oz	1050 g	Flour
⅓ oz	10 g	Baking soda
⅓ oz	10 g	Cinnamon
⅔ oz	20 g	Ginger
Dash	Dash	Clove
¼ oz	5 g	Salt
8 oz	250 g	Butter
8 oz	250 g	Brown sugar
8 fl oz	240 ml	Molasses
8 fl oz	240 ml	Water, cold

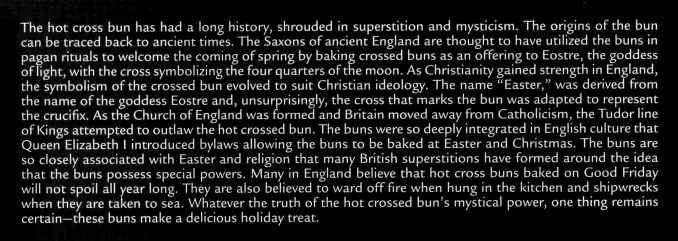

Learning Outcomes

Making a yeast dough
Piping
Shaping dough

Equipment

Knives:
N/A

Tools:
Mixing bowls, sieve, whisk,
pastry brush, corne or
dough cutter

Pans:
Baking sheet, saucepan

Serving/Yield

16 buns

The hot cross bun has had a long history, shrouded in superstition and mysticism. The origins of the bun can be traced back to ancient times. The Saxons of ancient England are thought to have utilized the buns in pagan rituals to welcome the coming of spring by baking crossed buns as an offering to Eostre, the goddess of light, with the cross symbolizing the four quarters of the moon. As Christianity gained strength in England, the symbolism of the crossed bun evolved to suit Christian ideology. The name "Easter," was derived from the name of the goddess Eostre and, unsurprisingly, the cross that marks the bun was adapted to represent the crucifix. As the Church of England was formed and Britain moved away from Catholicism, the Tudor line of Kings attempted to outlaw the hot crossed bun. The buns were so deeply integrated in English culture that Queen Elizabeth I introduced bylaws allowing the buns to be baked at Easter and Christmas. The buns are so closely associated with Easter and religion that many British superstitions have formed around the idea that the buns possess special powers. Many in England believe that hot cross buns baked on Good Friday will not spoil all year long. They are also believed to ward off fire when hung in the kitchen and shipwrecks when they are taken to sea. Whatever the truth of the hot crossed bun's mystical power, one thing remains certain—these buns make a delicious holiday treat.

HOT CROSS BUNS

Method

Make the Dough

1. Sift the flour, salt and sugar (*tamiser*) and make a well in the center (*fontaine*).
2. Heat the milk to 100°F (37°C) and stir in the yeast. Pour these ingredients into the well, then add the eggs and mix until a dough forms.
3. Knead lightly in the bowl until smooth.
4. Add the softened butter a little at a time, add the candied peel and currants.
5. Set the dough aside to rise until it has doubled in volume. Once it has risen, punch down the dough, divide it into 16 pieces, and then shape it into rounds. Arrange the rounds in a baking pan and set them aside to rise until doubled.

Crossing Mixture

1. Sift (*tamiser*) the flour into a bowl and whisk in enough water to make a firm paste.
2. Place in a paper cornet.

Bun Wash (Simple Syrup)

1. Bring the sugar and water to a boil, then remove from the heat and add 1 to 2 drops of bun spice.

Preheat the oven to 400°F (200°C).

Assembly

1. Once the buns have risen, pipe (*coucher*) a cross on the top of each with the crossing mixture.
2. Bake until golden brown about 20 to 25 minutes. Transfer to a wire rack and, while still hot, brush with the simple syrup. If desired, sprinkle with nibbed sugar. Allow to cool.

Quantity		Ingredient
U.S.	**Metric**	
8 oz	250 g	Flour
1 oz	30 g	Sugar, granulated
1 pinch	1 pinch	Salt
4 fl oz	120 ml	Milk
½ oz	15 g	Yeast
1 pc	1 pc	Egg
2 oz	60 g	Butter, softened (en pommade)
1¾ oz	50 g	Mixed candied peel
1¾ oz	50 g	Currants
5 oz	150 g	Flour
As needed	As needed	Water
4 fl oz	120 ml	Water
3 ¼ oz	100 g	Sugar
As needed	As needed	Bun spice*
As needed	As needed	Nibbed sugar (optional)

*Bun spice can be found in shops in the UK. In its absence, you can add a little cinnamon and nutmeg to infuse with the syrup.

Learning Outcomes

Making pie dough
Cutting method

Equipment

Knives:
N/A

Tools:
Corne, sieve

Pans:
N/A

Serving/Yield

4 single crusts or 2 double crusts

The cooking method of baking pastry-wrapped ingredients that we now call *pies* dates back thousands of years. There exists evidence of pie preparations by the ancient Egyptians, and the first written pie recipe is found in the Roman cooking text *Apicus* from the 1st century AD. Pie crust has traditionally served several less-evident functions than do the pie crusts of today. One of the main early functions of pie dough was the preservation of food. By baking meat in a pie crust, early voyagers were able to seal meat and lock the juices in a lightweight packaging. The dough is also thought to have often been used only for protecting the ingredients within the pie during the baking process. Early ovens could not be relied upon to cook something evenly without burning it. Pie dough allowed the filling to be protected and evenly cooked even if the exterior crust was being burned. In fact, there are some who speculate that pie crusts were often not eaten at all, and that they were often reused to bake the fillings of different pies over and over because of the expense of flour.

PIE DOUGH

Method

1. Sift (**tamiser**) together the flour, sugar, and salt.
2. Cut the butter and shortening into small pieces and then combine with the flour.
3. Using a plastic scraper (**corne**), cut the butter and shortening into the flour. Add the ice cold water to the mixture, and mix by hand until a uniform dough forms. Flatten the dough and tightly wrap it in plastic until needed.

Quantity		Ingredient
U.S.	Metric	
1 ½ lb	750 g	Pastry flour
¼ oz	10 g	Salt
1 oz	30 g	Sugar, granulated
8 oz	250 g	Butter
8 oz	250 g	Shortening
6 fl oz	180 ml	Ice cold water

Learning Outcomes

Making a double crusted pie
Crimping dough (*chiqueter*)
Making a filling using fresh
fruit

Equipment

Knives:
Paring knife (*couteau d'office*) or scissors (*ciseaux*)

Tools:
Mixing bowls, rolling pin, wire rack

Pans:
9 in. (23 cm) pie tin

Serving/Yield

1¼ pounds/750 grams
of pie filling

The pie has existed in various forms since antiquity. Over the centuries, the fillings for pies have run the gamut of almost every type of fruit, meat, and seafood known to man. Historically, most pies have been savory preparations. While modern pies have rich and delicious pastry crusts, traditionally the filling was considered the most important element in baking pies. Due to the inconsistency of ovens in the past, crusts were often simply utilized to protect the filling from being burned. The modern sweetened fruit pie, which is eaten as a dessert, really only became popular in the 19th century. It is interesting to note that while everyone has heard the expression "as American as apple pie," the apple pie actually originated in England and was brought to America by the pilgrims.

OLD FASHIONED PIE FILLING

Method

Preheat the oven to 400°F (200°C).

1. Prepare a mealy pie dough for a double crust (see Pie Dough recipe on pages 332–333).

2. Divide the dough in half and roll it out into a large circle approximately 2 ½ in. to 3 in. (7.5 cm) wider than the pie tin. Roll the dough onto the rolling pin and then gently unroll over the pie tin, making sure it is centered. Lift the dough while turning the tin to make sure there are no air bubbles. Using a small knife or scissors, trim the excess dough leaving about 1 in. (2.5 cm) of dough hanging over the edge. Brush the edge with water.

3. For apples: Place the trimmed apples in a large bowl. Add the lemon juice, sugar, cornstarch, salt, and spices. Toss the mixture well and then transfer it to the dough-lined pie tin. For cherries: Carefully remove the stems and pits from the cherries and place them in a sieve. Rinse under running water and then gently pat them dry with a paper towel. Set aside. In a clean mixing bowl, mix together the cornstarch, sugar, and the fruit juice. (If you choose to add spice, you would add it now). Add the cherries to the mixture, toss gently untilt they are well coated and transfer the fruit to the dough-lined pie tin.

4. Roll out (*abaisser*) the second piece of dough to the same dimensions as the first. Roll the dough onto the rolling pin and gently lay it over the fruit, making sure the dough is centered. Using a paring knife or a pair of scissors, trim off the excess dough to be even with the edges of the bottom crust.

5. Lightly pinch the dough together, then crimp the edges by pushing the dough between your thumb and index finger. Make 4 to 5 small cuts, evenly spaced, to allow steam to escape during cooking. Bake until the crust is golden brown, approximately 45 minutes. If the dough is coloring too quickly, reduce the oven heat by 25°F (5°C).

6. Remove from the oven and allow to cool on a wire rack.

Quantity		Ingredient
U.S.	Metric	
500 g	1 lb	Hard fruit, peeled, pitted and sliced
¼ oz	5 mL	Lemon juice (or juice of hard fruit being used)
3 ¼ oz	100 g	Sugar, granulated
¾ oz	24 g	Cornstarch
Dash	Dash	Salt (only if using apples)
Dash	Dash	Spices
As needed	As needed	Butter

Learning Outcomes

Making a crumb crust
Baking in a bain-marie

Equipment

Knives:
N/A

Tools:
Mixing bowls, whisk,
rubber spatula, aluminum
foil

Pans:
10 in. (25 cm) springform
pan, deep roasting pan,
wire rack

Serving/Yield

One 10 in. (25 cm) cake

While cakes infused with cheese have existed since the time of the ancient Greeks, the New York style cheesecake is a fairly recent creation. The invention of the New York cheesecake is generally attributed to Arnold Reuben, creator of the Reuben sandwich and the owner of the famous New York institution, Reuben's Deli (now closed). Reuben created the cake in the early 1900s and, over the decades, the Jewish delis of New York began refining the recipe, competing to create the most perfect version. This creation was made possible by two technical innovations of the time: the creation of American cream cheese and the graham cracker. American cream cheese was invented by dairy farmer William Lawrence in upstate New York in 1872. The graham cracker was created by a New Jersey reverend named Sylvester Graham in 1829. The Reverend created the cracker with the belief that bland foods would help to curb people's "unhealthy carnal desires." The New York cheesecake is defined by the richness and creamy simplicity of its central ingredients. The cake forsakes the accoutrement of other cakes for the pure decadence of thick cream cheese, which is contrasted by the simple flavor of the graham cracker base.

NEW YORK STYLE CHEESECAKE

Method

Preheat the oven to 350°F (170°C).

1. Butter the sides of a 10 in. (25 cm) springform pan.

2. Mix the graham cracker crumbs with the sugar and melted butter. Press the cracker mixture into the bottom of the prepared springform pan to form the cake's base.

3. Bake the cracker base for 10 to 12 minutes. Remove it from the oven and allow it to cool on a wire rack. Once cooled, wrap the outside of the pan with heavy duty aluminum foil.

4. Place the sour cream in a bowl. Begin adding the cream cheese to the sour cream in small increments, carefully combining (*crémer*) them together until smooth. Stir the cornstarch into the sugar and gradually add the sugar mixture to the cream cheese mixture. Add the lemon juice and vanilla. Then add the eggs one at a time mixing after each addition.

5. Pour the cream cheese mixture into the prepared pan. Set the springform pan in a deep roasting pan. Place the cake in the oven and pour boiling water into the roasting pan until it reaches halfway up the sides of the cake pan (bain-marie).

6. Bake for 45 minutes, then reduce the heat of the oven to 325°F (160°C) and bake for an additional 30 minutes. The cake should be set but still soft in the center.

7. Open the oven door slightly and leave the cake to bake for about 1 hour.

8. Remove from the oven and place the cake on a wire rack to cool completely. Chill thoroughly before serving (preferably overnight).

Quantity		Ingredient
U.S.	**Metric**	
10 oz	300 g	Graham cracker crumbs
2 oz	60 g	Sugar, granulated
3 fl oz	90 ml	Butter, melted
2 lbs	1 kg	Cream cheese
1 oz	30 g	Cornstarch
12 ¼ oz	370 g	Sugar
5 ¼ oz	160 g	Sour cream
1 fl oz	30 ml	Lemon juice
1 fl oz	30 ml	Vanilla, extract
4 pcs	4 pcs	Eggs

Learning Outcomes

Using gelatin

Equipment

Knives:
Paring knife *(couteau d'office)*

Tools:
Six × 4 oz (120 ml) molds, chinois, mixing bowls

Pans:
Saucepan

Serving/Yield

Six 4 ounce/120 ml portions

The name *panna cotta* is Italian for "cooked cream," which is apropos because the dish is little more than cream cooked with gelatin and whatever flavoring you desire. This preparation's delectable simplicity is part of the reason why it remains one of the most popular desserts in the world. With panna cotta, the cream base acts as a blank canvas for chefs to express themselves as creatively as they wish. The flavor possibilities are as boundless as the imagination of the chef creating it.

PANNA COTTA

Method

1. Soften the gelatin in a bowl of cold water.
2. Heat the cream, sugar, vanilla, orange zest, and rum until the mixture just comes to a boil. Remove from the heat. Squeeze out any excess water from the gelatin and add to the hot liquid. Stir well until the gelatin is dissolved, then strain through a fine strainer (*chinois*).
3. Divide the mixture into 4 oz (120 ml) molds or dishes and transfer to the refrigerator to chill until set.
4. To unmold the panna cotta, loosen around the edges with the tip of a small knife, then dip the molds into hot water for 10 seconds. Turn the molds over onto a chilled plate and give them a firm shake, allowing the contents to come loose. Carefully lift off the mold.

Quantity		Ingredient
U.S.	**Metric**	
6 sheets	6 sheets	Gelatin
19 fl oz	600 ml	Heavy cream (or half milk)
4 oz	120 g	Powdered sugar
½ pc	½ pc	Vanilla bean
1 pc	1 pc	Orange zest
½ oz	15 ml	Rum

Learning Outcomes

Creaming method

Equipment

Knives:
N/A

Tools:
Mixing bowls, wooden spatula, sieve, spoon, fork

Pans:
Baking sheets, wire rack

Serving/Yield

36 cookies weighing
18 grams each

HISTORY

The history of peanut butter cookies, just like the history of peanut butter, can be traced back to one man—the great African American hero George Washington Carver. When the boll weevil wiped out the American cotton industry in the early 1900s, Carver encouraged poverty-stricken farmers to diversify their crops by planting peanuts as well as cotton. In conjunction with this advice, in 1916 he produced a pamphlet entitled, *How to Grow the Peanut and 105 Ways of Preparing it for Human Consumption*. In this document he details three separate recipes for peanut-based cookies. The actual use of peanut butter in the preparation of cookies would not occur until the 1930s when the large-scale commercial development and production of peanut butter began. The first written recipe that called for the use of peanut butter was the Pillsbury Corporation's 1933 edition of *Balanced Recipes*. Interestingly enough, this is also the first recipe that calls for the peanut butter dough balls to be pushed down with the tines of a fork, giving the cookie its distinctive crisscross pattern. This practice is still considered an essential step in baking these cookies, even though no one knows for certain why. There is speculation that because of the extreme density of the dough, the cookie needs to be mashed into the crisscross pattern so the dough will bake evenly.

PEANUT BUTTER COOKIES

Method

Preheat the oven to 375°F (190°C).

1. Sift (*tamiser*) together the flour, baking powder, and salt.
2. Cream together (*crémer*) the butter, sugar, and light brown sugar. Add the peanut butter and mix until smooth. Mix in the egg and vanilla, then add the dry ingredients.
3. Scoop up the dough by the spoonful and roll it into balls. Place the dough balls onto a baking sheet, leaving them about 2 in. (5 cm) apart to expand.
4. Create the crisscross pattern using the tines of a fork, dipping the tines in water occasionally to keep the dough from sticking.
5. Bake the cookies until the edges just begin to brown. Remove them from the oven and gently transfer to a wire rack to cool.

Quantity		Ingredient
U.S.	**Metric**	
6 ¾ oz	200 g	Flour
⅓ oz	10 g	Baking powder
Pinch	Pinch	Salt
4 oz	120 g	Butter
4 oz	120 g	Sugar, granulated
3 oz	90 g	Light brown sugar
2 ¾ oz	80 g	Chunky peanut butter
1 pc	1 pc	Egg
1 tsp	1 tsp	Vanilla
1 oz	30 g	Dark chocolate, optional

Learning Outcomes

Making a clear custard
Making and using a pie
dough

Equipment

Knives:
Paring knife *(couteau
d'office)*

Tools:
Rolling pin, mixing bowls,
whisk

Pans:
9 in. (23 cm) pie tin

Serving/Yield

6–8 servings

The pecan is one of the only major nut species native to North America. The Native Americans of the southern United States and Mexico have been consuming the pecan for centuries. When the French settled in the area of New Orleans in the 17th century, the natives were the first to introduce Europeans to this tasty nut. The settlers didn't take long to begin incorporating the nuts into their cooking and were soon adding the pecan to their pie preparations. The pecan pie is thought to have been created from the adaptation of existing sugar pie recipes of the time. The layer of roasted pecans on top adds a delicious balance to the sweetness of the sugar filling. While pecan pie has always been a favorite dessert in the southern United States (due to the European settlers being introduced to the pecan by the Native Americans), the pie has also long been intimately associated with the holiday of Thanksgiving in North America. The people of America and Canada are all too aware of this association, and most have had the experience of being so stuffed with turkey they feel like they are about to burst, but always finding room for a delicious slice of pecan pie.

PECAN PIE

Method

1. Make a pie dough (see page 332).

Preheat the oven to 350°F (175°C).

2. Line a 9 in. (23 cm) pie tin with mealy pie dough and crimp the edges.

3. Beat the eggs until combined. Add the brown sugar, corn syrup, salt, and vanilla and mix together thoroughly. Whisk in the melted butter.

4. Pour the mixture into the lined pie tin. Arrange the pecan halves on top.

5. Bake until a paring knife inserted in the center comes out clean and the pie's filling only jiggles slightly when the pan is lightly shaken, approximately 35 to 40 minutes.

6. Remove the pie from the oven and allow to cool on a wire rack.

Quantity		Ingredient
U.S.	Metric	
1 recipe	1 recipe	Pie dough (see page 332)
4 pcs	4 pcs	Eggs
6 ½ oz	195 g	Brown sugar
3 fl oz	90 ml	Corn syrup
¼ oz	5 g	Salt
¼ fl oz	5 ml	Vanilla
1 fl oz	30 ml	Melted butter
10 oz	300 g	Pecan halves

Learning Outcomes

Making a flat bread

Equipment

Knives:
N/A

Tools:
Mixing bowls, rolling pin,
kitchen towel

Pans:
Heavy baking sheet

Serving/Yield

6–8 pitas

Originating in the Middle East, pita bread is quite possibly the earliest form of bread known to man. This versatile, flat, slightly leavened bread has been a staple of Middle Eastern and Mediterranean cooking for centuries. The tendency of the bread to become hollow upon baking and its flatness have made it a perfect edible dish or plate for eating meat, which has been a major reason for its incredible longevity. The Arabic word for pita bread is *khubz adi*, which means "ordinary bread." The name *pita* stems from the Greek word for flat bread *plakous*, which evolved to mean a thicker bread or cake, while the word *pitta* came to describe the thin form of flat bread we know today. It is interesting to note that the Greek word *pitta* was adapted by the people of Northern Italy to describe a flat bread preparation of their own: *pizza*. The Greek word came to be westernized into the name *pita*. Whether it is being used for dipping hummus or wrapping souvlaki and shawarma, the oldest bread on earth still remains one of its most popular.

PITA BREAD

Method

1. In a mixing bowl, dissolve the yeast into the water. Stir in the olive oil and salt.
2. Sift (*tamiser*) the flour. Add the whole wheat flour and then the bread flour. Work the mixture until a dough forms. Turn the dough out onto a work surface and knead until smooth and no longer sticky.
3. Place the dough in a lightly oiled bowl and cover with a towel. Set aside in a warm area to proof until doubled in size, approximately 90 minutes. Punch the dough down and shape it into balls. Cover the dough balls with a towel and leave them to rest for an additional 20 to 30 minutes.
4. While the dough is resting, place a heavy baking sheet in the oven and preheat the oven to 450°F (230°C).
5. Roll the dough out (*abaisser*) to a thickness of ¼ in. to ⅛ in. (3–4 mm). If still too elastic, cover and allow to rest for a final 10 minutes.
6. Once rolled out to the required thickness, open the oven and quickly place the rolled dough on the heated baking sheet. Bake for 3 to 4 minutes. Remove the pitas and set aside to cool.

Quantity		Ingredient
U.S.	Metric	
8 fl oz	250 ml	Water
1 oz	30 g	Yeast
¼ fl oz	5 ml	Olive oil
¼ oz	5 g	Salt
1 ½ oz	45 g	Whole wheat flour
5 oz	150 g	Bread flour

Learning Outcomes

Cooking rice in milk
Tempering eggs
Making a custard

Equipment

Knives:
Paring knife *(couteau d'office)*

Tools:
Mixing bowls, whisk, wooden spatula

Pans:
Ovenproof dish, saucepan

Serving/Yield

6–8 servings

Rice pudding is a simple preparation made from a mixture of rice, milk or cream, and whatever desired flavorings you would like to add. Rice pudding is one of the most widespread dishes on earth—almost every country on the planet enjoys some variation of it. Its origins are believed to stem from the Middle East, which has been creating rice-based dishes since ancient times. In particular, a dessert called *firni* closely resembled modern rice puddings. This ancient preparation is a sweet, milk-based dessert that incorporates rice/rice flour, nuts, spices, and fruit and was traditionally served cold. The dish was thought to have originated in the Middle East or Persia and was introduced to India by the Mughals in their conquest of Northern India in the 16th century (where it remains a traditional dessert to this day). Due to the ease of the preparation, the widespread availability of the central ingredients, and the plethora of potential flavorings, this dish has successfully spread to every corner of the world, and remains an international favorite even today.

RICE PUDDING

Method

Preheat the oven to 350°F (175°C).

1. Lightly coat an ovenproof dish with butter.
2. Using a paring knife, split the vanilla bean in half lengthwise and scrape out the seeds. Wash the rice thoroughly to remove the starch, then add the rice, milk, cinnamon, salt, and vanilla seeds to a medium saucepan. Simmer the mixture over medium heat for approximately 30 to 40 minutes, or until the rice is tender.
3. Combine the sugar, cream, and egg yolks and temper the combination with a little of the hot milk from the rice.
4. Off the heat, stir in the egg mixture and mix well. Transfer the mixture to the ovenproof dish.
5. Bake for approximately 20 minutes, until the top becomes golden brown.

Note

Rice pudding may also be baked in individual ovenproof serving dishes.

Quantity		Ingredient
U.S.	Metric	
1 pc	1 pc	Vanilla bean
8 oz	250 g	Rice
Pinch	Pinch	Salt
1 ½ quarts	1 ½ liters	Milk
Pinch	Pinch	Cinnamon
8 oz	250 g	Sugar, granulated
5 fl oz	150 ml	Cream
3 fl oz	90 ml	Egg yolks

Learning Outcomes

Making a ganache
Making a Sacher sponge
cake
Making a meringue

Equipment

Knives:
N/A

Tools:
Mixing bowls, wooden and
rubber spatula, whisk, sieve,
cornet, wire rack

Pans:
9 inch mold (*moule à
manqué de 9 in*), saucepan

The Sacher torte is one of the most beloved cakes in all of Austria. It is so well loved that it is said to be the only cake to have ever been the subject of a court case. The Sacher torte was created in 1832, commissioned by the great diplomat Klemens Wenzel von Metternich. The story goes that Prince Metternich was hosting a dinner party and so he commissioned his head chef to prepare a new dessert for his guests. When the head chef took ill, the task befell his 16-year-old apprentice, Franz Sacher. As if this didn't place enough pressure on the young Sacher, the bullheaded Metternich reportedly left Sacher to his work saying "Let there be no shame on me tonight!" Demonstrating true grace under pressure, Sacher created the Sacher torte, which was a big hit with the prince's guests. Franz Sacher went on to become one of the great culinary artists of Europe, plying his craft all over the continent before eventually resettling in Vienna. Sacher's son, Eduard, followed in his father's footsteps, becoming a great chef in his own right. Eduard worked for Vienna's famed Café Demel and went on to open the Sacher Hotel, continuing to make his father's torte at both establishments. Both began selling the cake under the title "the original Sacher torte," which led to a heated battle and eventually a court case. After 7 long years in court, the Sacher Hotel prevailed and claimed the right to sell the only "original Sutcher torte" (despite some connoisseurs claiming the Demel torte to be truer to the original).

SACHER TORTE

Method

Make the Ganache

1. Chop the dark chocolate into small pieces and place them in a bowl.
2. Bring the cream to a boil.
3. Once the cream comes to a boil, immediately pour it over the chocolate. Mix the combination gently with a wooden spatula and then allow it to cool.

Preheat the oven 340°F (170°C).

Make the Biscuit Sacher

1. Butter and flour a 9" mold *moule a manqué* (**chemiser**).
2. Sift (**tamiser**) the flour and almond powder. Melt the dark chocolate with the butter to 105°F (40°C). Add the egg yolks to the melted chocolate and whisk them in well. Then add the sifted dry ingredients.
3. Beat the egg whites until they are foamy and then whisk in 1 ¼ oz (40 g) of the sugar. Beat the whites to soft peaks (**monter les blancs**). Gradually whisk in remaining sugar and beat until the whites become firm and glossy. Fold the meringue into the chocolate mixture.
4. Transfer to the prepared mold and bake for about 25 minutes. Allow the biscuit to cool in the pan before unmolding.

Prepare the Syrup

1. Bring the water and sugar to a boil, stirring until the sugar is completely dissolved. Remove from heat and allow to cool, then add the kirsch.
2. Trim the top of the biscuit to flatten (if needed). Turn it over and cut the biscuit in 2.
3. Remove the top layer of the biscuit and set it aside. Wet the cut side with the syrup and then spread a ½ in. (1 cm) layer of apricot jam. Replace the top layer and wet the surface. Place it in the refrigerator to chill for about 1 hour.
4. Once the cake is well chilled, mask the sides and top with the ganache. Place it back in the refrigerator to set for about 10 minutes. Mask the cake with a second layer of ganache and place it back in the refrigerator. In the meantime, place the remaining ganache over low heat to melt (do not heat over 85°F/30°C).
5. Place the cake on a wire rack, coat it with the ganache, and then smooth it out with a spatula.
6. Put the cake back in the refrigerator until set. Transfer the remaining ganache to a cornet, keeping it warm.
7. Finish the cake by piping the word *Sacher* with the remaining ganache.

Quantity		Ingredient
U.S.	**Metric**	*Ganache*
5 oz	150 g	Dark chocolate
5 fl oz	150 ml	Cream
		Sacher Sponge (Biscuit Sacher)
1 ¼ oz	40 g	Flour
½ oz	20 g	Almond powder
8 oz	250 g	Dark chocolate
1 oz	30 g	Butter
3 pcs	3 pcs	Egg yolks
7 ½ oz	225 g	Egg whites
4 oz	120 g	Sugar, granulated
5 fl oz	150 ml	Water
3 ¼ oz	100 g	Sugar, granulated
½ oz	15 ml	Kirsch
6 ¾ oz	200 g	Apricot jam

Learning Outcomes

Sabler method

Equipment

Knives:
N/A

Tools:
Parchment paper, sieve,
mixing bowls, pastry brush,
wooden spatula

Pans:
Baking sheet

Serving/Yield

6–8 pieces

What is generally assumed to be native to the tables of the English at breakfast or afternoon tea, the scone is, in fact, of Scottish origin. Although there is some debate among etymologists, the naming of these small, triangular quick breads is likely from the town of Scone, in the Scottish council area of Perth and Kinross. The scone is likely a refined version of the somewhat hardier bread called *bannock*, which tends to be cooked with bottom heat in a cast-iron pan as opposed to scones, which are almost exclusively baked in an oven. Because of its versatility in terms of nutrition and preparation, North American Native peoples adopted bannock from early Scottish explorers, particularly in northern Canada; subsequently and for the same reasons, it is also appreciated by the Cubs-and-Scouts set. If bannock is at home around a campfire, by contrast, scones are a little uppity, preferring instead a white table cloth and tea poured from a china pot.

SCONES

Method

Preheat the oven to 400°F (200°C).

1. Line a baking sheet with parchment paper.
2. Sift (*tamiser*) the flour, baking powder, and salt. Then add the sugar and mix thoroughly.
3. Rub the butter into the flour (*sabler*) and stir in the raisins (if using).
4. Whisk the milk and egg together, add this to the sifted ingredients, and mix until a dough forms.
5. Chill the dough for 20 minutes.
6. Place the dough on a lightly floured surface and roll in a circle approximately 1 in. (2.5 cm) thick. Cut the dough into wedges and arrange them on the lined baking sheet.
7. Beat together the egg, egg yolk, and salt. Brush the mixture onto the top of each scone.
8. Bake for 15 to 18 minutes or until the scones are golden and firm.

Quantity		Ingredient
U.S.	Metric	
7 ½ oz	225 g	Strong flour
¼ oz	5 g	Baking powder
½ oz	3 g	Salt
1 ½ oz	40 g	Sugar, granulated
1 ¾ oz	55 g	Butter, chilled
1 ½ oz	40 g	Raisins (optional)
1 pc	1 pc	Egg, beaten
2 ½ fl oz	75 ml	Milk
1pc	1 pc	Egg
1pc	1 pc	Egg yolk
Pinch	Pinch	Salt
Serve with clotted cream and strawberry or raspberry jam		

Learning Outcomes

Making a nut crust

Equipment

Knives:
Palette knife *(spatule)*,
paring knife
(couteau d'office)

Tools:
Mixing bowls, wooden
spatula, rolling pin, pastry
brush, wire rack

Pans:
8.5 in. (22 cm) tart mold
with removable bottom

Serving/Yield

One 8 ½ in. (22 cm) tart

HISTORY

Johan Konrad Vogl, a Bavarian confectioner drawn to the town of Linze, Austria for the love of a local woman, is said to have created the tart that would put the town of Linze on the map internationally (at least among European foodies of the mid-1800s). The story implies that the tart itself was created with the passion of a confectioner in love. While this idea certainly does justice to this sweet, regional delicacy, the story conflicts with the fact that very similar recipes for the preparation can be found predating Mr. Vogl's arrival in Linze. Still, we shouldn't always, as the saying goes, "let the facts get in the way of a good story."

TARTE LINZER

Method

Preheat the oven to 350°F (180°C).

1. Butter an 8.5 in. (22 cm) tart mold.
2. Sift (*tamiser*) together the flour, almond powder, baking powder, and cinnamon.
3. Cream (*crémer*) together the butter and sugar. Add the egg and mix well, then add the milk.
4. Mix in the sifted dry ingredients until a stiff dough forms. If the dough remains too soft, chill until it becomes firm enough to roll.
5. Lightly dust the surface of the dough with flour, then roll it out (*abaisser*) to a thickness of about ⅛ in. (½ cm). Carefully roll onto the rolling pin and unroll over the buttered mold. Gently lift the edges, manipulating the dough into the corners of the mold. Trim the edges with the back of a paring knife.
6. Beat the raspberry jam until it forms a smooth consistency. Spread over the dough-lined tart mold. Roll out the remaining dough (*abaisser*) and cut it into 1 in. (2 cm) thick strips. Arrange over the top, crisscrossing the strips. Press down at the edges.
7. Lightly brush the dough with the egg wash then place in the oven, baking until the dough is golden brown, approximately 30 to 35 minutes.
8. Remove from the oven and allow to cool on a wire rack before unmolding. Dust with powdered sugar before serving.

Quantity		Ingredient
U.S.	**Metric**	
10 oz	300 g	Cake flour
5 oz	150 g	Almond powder
¼ oz	5 g	Baking powder
½ oz	10 g	Ground cinnamon
6 ¾ oz	200 g	Butter
5 oz	150 g	Sugar, granulated
1 pc	1 pc	Egg
1 fl oz	30 ml	Milk
10 oz	300 g	Raspberry jam (with seeds)
1 pc	1 pc	Egg
For dusting	For dusting	Powdered sugar

Learning Outcomes

Making ladyfinger sponge
(*biscuit cuillère*)
Making a pastry cream
(*crème pâtissière*)
Making a Chantilly cream
(*crème Chantilly*)
Making a diplomat cream
(*crème diplomat*)

Equipment

Knives:
Serrated knife *(couteau-scie)*

Tools:
Large glass serving bowl,
mixing bowls, whisk,
strainer, rubber spatula,
piping bag, various tips,
wire rack

Pans:
Saucepan

Serving/Yield

8–12 servings

The name of the English trifle is derived from the old French word *trufe*, which means "of little importance"; however, this quintessential British dessert has been anything but unimportant as a mainstay of British cuisine for centuries. The first known recipe for trifle appears in T. Dawson's cookbook, *The Good Hyswife's Jewell*, in 1596. The trifle (also known as *foole* in early recipes) had humble beginnings. In its earliest form, it consisted of little more than spiced cream and sugar. As time wore on, the trifle evolved from a simple cream mixture to a creative method of disposing of leftovers. Without the ability to refrigerate food, leftovers needed to be used before they spoiled. This meant that old cakes, biscuits, fruits, and cream were thrown together as a practical and tasty way to get rid of old food. From its modest start, the trifle has evolved into a luxuriously rich dessert incorporating alcohol-soaked ladyfingers, custard, fresh fruit, and jam to the existing base of cream and sugar. Today, the trifle remains a beloved British favorite and a deliciously decadent indulgence.

TRIFLE

Method

Preheat the oven to 380°F (195°C).

1. Line a baking sheet with parchment paper.

Make Ladyfingers (Biscuit Cuillère)

1. Separate the eggs and sift (*tamiser*) the flour.
2. Whisk the egg yolks with half of the sugar until it becomes light in color and a ribbon forms when the whisk is lifted from the bowl. Mount the egg whites (*monter les blancs*), then meringue with the remaining sugar. Fold the egg whites into the egg yolks, but before it is completely incorporated, fold in the flour.
3. Transfer the mixture to a piping bag and pipe out long finger shapes onto the prepared baking sheet. Bake until dry to the touch, about 8 to 10 minutes. Transfer the ladyfingers to a wire rack to cool.

Make the Pastry Cream (Crème Pâtissière)

1. Pour the milk into a medium saucepan and bring to a boil over medium-high heat. Add about one-quarter of the sugar to the milk and stir it in to dissolve it. Meanwhile, place the egg yolks in a small mixing bowl and add the remaining sugar.
2. Whisk the sugar into the eggs until it completely dissolves and the yolks lighten in color (*blanchir*). Add the flour and the custard powder to the yolks and stir until well combined. When the milk begins to come to a boil, remove it from the stove and pour one-third of it into the egg yolks. Stir well to temper the yolks, then whisk the tempered mixture into the remaining hot milk. Place back onto the heat and cook until the crème pâtissière begins to bubble.
3. Continue whisking (being sure to press the whisk around the corners of the pan) and allow to cook for about 1 minute in order to cook the starch. The crème pâtissière will become very thick.
4. Spread onto a platter lined with plastic, cover, and allow to cool. Place in the refrigerator to chill.

Prepare the Fruit

1. Rinse the fruit thoroughly, then hull the strawberries and slice them evenly. Set aside.

Make a Crème Chantilly

1. Whisk the cream to soft peaks with the powdered sugar. Set aside.

Quantity		Ingredient
U.S.	Metric	Ladyfinger Sponge (Biscuit Cuillère)
4 pcs	4 pcs	Eggs
4 ¼ oz	125 g	Flour
4 ¼ oz	125 g	Sugar, granulated
7 oz	200 g	Raspberry jam
To taste	To taste	Sherry
		Pastry Cream (Crème Pâtissière)
1 pint	500 ml	Milk
2 ½ oz	75 g	Sugar, granulated
5 ½ oz	165 ml	Cream
1 ¼ oz	35 g	Custard powder or flour
1 lb	500 g	Strawberries
1 lb	500 g	Blackberries
1 lb	500 g	Raspberries
1 lb	500 g	Blueberries
		Chantilly Cream (Crème Chantilly)
1 pint	500 ml	Cream
3 ¼ oz	100 g	Powdered sugar
½ fl oz	10 ml	Vanilla
As needed	As needed	Sliced almonds, toasted

*Crème Diplomat is created by combining the crème pâtissière and the crème Chantilly as directed in the method.

Method

2. Place the cooled crème pâtissière into a mixing bowl and whisk until smooth. Gently fold in half of the crème Chantilly to create a crème diplomat. Put some of the cream in the bottom of a large, glass serving bowl. Arrange a layer of ladyfingers (**biscuit cuillère**), then sprinkle with some of the fruit, and cover with some crème diplomat (see note in ingredients list). Repeat the process, finishing with the cream. Transfer the remaining half portion of crème Chantilly into a pastry bag fitted with a large star tip.
3. Pipe the cream decoratively to cover. Chill before serving.

CONVERSION CHART

A Note about Conversions

For cooking and baking, the metric system is probably the easiest to manage and an electronic scale can become your most valued tool in the kitchen! When making conversions, we took the liberty to sometimes round off the measurements as long as the proportions in the recipe were still respected.

Volume

U.S.	METRIC
¼ fl oz	5 ml
½ fl oz	15 ml
¾ fl oz	25 ml
1 fl oz	30 ml
2 fl oz	60 ml
3 fl oz	90 ml
4 fl oz	120 ml
5 fl oz	150 ml
6 fl oz	180 ml
7 fl oz	210 ml
8 fl oz	240 ml
9 fl oz	270 ml
10 fl oz	300 ml
11 fl oz	330 ml
12 fl oz	360 ml
13 fl oz	390 ml
14 fl oz	420 ml
15 fl oz	450 ml
1 pint (16 fl oz)	500 ml
1 quart (2 pints)	1 L (1000 ml)
2 quarts	2 L (2000 ml)
3 quarts	3 L (3000 ml)
1 gallon (4 quarts)	4 L (4000 ml)

Weight

U.S.	METRIC
¼ oz	5 g
½ oz	15 g
¾ oz	20 g
1 oz	30 g
2 oz	60 g
3 oz	90 g
4 oz	120 g
5 oz	150 g
6 oz	180 g
7 oz	200 g
½ lb (8 oz)	250 g
9 oz	270 g
10 oz	300 g
11 oz	330 g
12 oz	360 g
13 oz	390 g
14 oz	420 g
15 oz	450 g
1 lb (16 oz)	500 g
1 ½ lb	750 g
2 lb	1 kg

Common Household Equivalents

U.S.	METRIC
¼ tsp	1 ml
½ tsp	3 ml
¾ tsp	4 ml
1 tsp	5 ml
1 tbsp	15 ml
¼ cup	60 ml
½ cup	120 ml
¾ cup	180 ml
1 cup	250 ml
¼ lb	120 g
½ lb	230 g
1 lb	450 g
1 pint	500 ml
1 quart	1 L
1 gallon	4 L

U.S. Measure Equivalents

3 tsp	1 tbsp	½ fl oz
2 tbsp	⅛ cup	1 fl oz
4 tbsp	¼ cup	2 fl oz
5 tbsp + 1 tsp	⅓ cup	2 ⅔ fl oz
8 tbsp	½ cup	4 fl oz
10 tbsp +2 tsp	⅔ cup	5 ⅓ fl oz
12 tbsp	¾ cup	6 fl oz
14 tbsp	⅞ cup	7 fl oz
16 tbsp	1 cup	8 fl oz
2 cups	1 pint	16 fl oz
2 pints	1 quart	32 fl oz
4 quarts	1 gallon	128 fl oz

INDEX